The BBC television adaptation of

THE
ALAN CLARK
DIARIES

with John Hurt as Alan Clark
and Jenny Agutter as Jane Clark
is taken from

Diaries: In Power 1983–1992

and

The Last Diaries 1992–1999

'The best diarists, from Pepys and Boswell to "Chips" Channon and Harold Nicolson, have been the souls of indiscretion. But none so indiscreet as Mr Clark. If he is made the scapegoat for the Matrix Churchill affair, he may be written down politically as Baroness Thatcher's little loose cannon. But literature and the great British game of gossip will judge him for his diary. For its Pooterish self-assessment, for Mr Toad's enthusiasm for new things, for Byron's caddishness, for its deadly candour, it is one of the great works in the genre' *The Times*

'Frank and vivid diaries . . . Mr Clark performs the invaluable service of cheering us all up and giving us something to talk about' *The Times*

'Unputdownable' David Mellor, *Mail on Sunday*

'Diaries are the raw material of history and these are elegantly and pungently written' Sir Charles Powell, *The Times*

'Absorbing . . . staggeringly, recklessly candid . . . tells the truth as he saw it without fear or favour'
Anthony Howard, *Sunday Times*

'A wonderful book . . . these diaries combine the naive candour of an Adrian Mole with the imagination of a devil and an angel'
Matthew Parris, *Sunday Telegraph*

'The best political book for at least a decade. It is unlikely that Thatcher, when her autobiography is published, will provide such an entertaining and incisive account of the personalities, scandals and conflicts of her years in office' *Scotsman*

'The sheer fun of politics shines through . . . this wonderful book' Robert Rhodes James, *Guardian*

Alan Clark, MP for Plymouth (Sutton) 1974–1992 and Kensington and Chelsea, 1997–1999, was Minister of Trade, 1986–1989, and Minister of State, Ministry of Defence, 1989–1992. He made his reputation as a historian with *The Donkeys: A History of the BEF in 1915*, followed by *The Fall of Crete, Barbarossa: the Russian–German Conflict, 1941–1945* and *Aces High: The War in the Air Over the Western Front 1914–1918*. He also published three novels. In 1973 he edited the private diaries of Viscount Lee of Fareham, *A Good Innings*. After quitting the House of Commons in 1992 he published the first volume of his *Diaries*, the following year. His political history, *The Tories: The Conservatives and the Nation State 1922–1997* was published in 1998. Alan Clark was married with two sons. He lived until his death in 1999 at Saltwood Castle, Kent. The second volume of his *Diaries*, *Into Politics*, was published posthumously in 2000, and the third volume, *The Last Diaries: In and Out of the Wilderness*, was published in 2002.

By Alan Clark

Bargains at Special Prices: A novel

The Donkeys: A History of the BEF in 1915

Summer Season: A novel

The Fall of Crete

Barbarossa: The Russian-German
Conflict, 1941–1945

The Lion Heart: A tale of the war in Vietnam

Aces High: the War in the Air
over the Western Front 1914–1918

A Good Innings: the private papers
of Viscount Lee of Fareham (edited)

Suicide of the Empires:
The Eastern Front, 1914–1918

Diaries: In Power, 1983–1992

The Tories: Conservatives and the
Nation State, 1922–1997

Diaries: Into Politics, 1972–1982

Back Fire: A Passion for Cars and Motoring

The Last Diaries: In and Out
of the Wilderness

DIARIES

In Power
1983–1992

ALAN CLARK

PHOENIX

A PHOENIX PAPERBACK

Originally titled *Diaries*

First published in Great Britain in 1993 by
Weidenfeld & Nicolson
This paperback edition published in 2004
by Phoenix,
an imprint of Orion Books Ltd,
Orion House, 5 Upper St Martin's Lane,
London, WC2H 9EA.

Reissued 2001 as *Diaries: In Power 1983–1992*

A CIP catalogue record for this book
is available from the British Library.

ISBN 0 75381 859 0

Typeset by Selwood Systems, Midsomer Norton
Printed in Great Britain by
Clays Ltd, St Ives plc

For my beloved Jane,
around whose cool and affectionate personality
there raged this maelstrom of egocentricity
and self-indulgence

CONTENTS

ILLUSTRATIONS

A section of photographs from the author's collection
appears between pages 202 and 203

PREFACE

Diaries are so intensely personal – to publish them is a baring, if not a flaunting, of the ego. And for the author also to write a preface could be thought excessive.

Let me explain. These are not 'Memoirs'. They are not written to throw light on events in the past, or retrospectively to justify the actions of the author. They are *exactly* as they were recorded on the day; sometimes even the hour, or the minute, of a particular episode or sensation.

I wrote, in longhand, in a variety of locations; principally at Saltwood, or in my room at the House of Commons, or at my desk in the Department(s). Also in trains, embassies, hotels abroad, at the Cabinet table in Number 10 and at international conferences. When I had completed an entry I closed the notebook and seldom turned to that page again.

During the whole of this period, nearly eight years, I was a Minister in three successive Tory administrations. Politics – Party, Governmental and Constituency – dominated my life and energies. But on re-reading the entries I am struck by how small a proportion – less than half – is actually devoted to the various themes that dominated political life over the period.

So, in order to help those who want only to read selectively, I have allotted an abbreviated title to practically every entry and these can be found listed, with their separate dates, at the start of each 'Chapter' (each year in the period constituting a chapter).

Expurgation, from considerations of taste or cruelty, I have tried to keep to a minimum. My friends know me, and know that I love them, and that my private explosions of irritation or bad temper are of no import. And as for taste, it, too, is subjective. There are passages that will offend some, just as there are excerpts that I myself found embarrassing to read when I returned to them.

Much of course has been excised. But of what remains nothing has been altered since the day it was written. Is this conceit – or laziness? A bit of both, I suppose. But I found that when I attempted to alter, or moderate, or explain, the structure and rhythm of the whole entry would be disturbed.

There remain certain passages that vex me considerably. Mainly they refer to friends and colleagues with whom I have worked – or who have worked for me with loyalty and dedication: for example, Dave, my competent driver for many years; Rose, my sweet diary secretary at DTI who coped with 'harassment' with dignity and decorum; Bruce Anderson, one of my closest confidants; Tom King, Secretary of State above me in two departments, whom I still regard with affection in spite of the way in which we treated each other in the heat of our political careers. And there are many others to whom references coloured by the irritation of the moment are ill-suited.

There are also passages that, to some readers, will be unintelligible. Family joke-words, Eton slang, arcane references to events in the past, crude expletives, all these are present but I have done my best to illuminate the unfamiliar in a glossary that covers events, locations, individuals and so forth.

Sometimes lacking in charity; often trivial; occasionally lewd; cloyingly sentimental, repetitious, whingeing and imperfectly formed. For some readers the entries may seem to be all of these things.

But they are real diaries.

AC

GLOSSARY

FAMILY

Jane
James – AC's eldest son (aka 'Boy', 'Jamie')
Sarah – James' first wife
Sally – James' second wife
Andrew – AC's younger son (aka 'Tip', 'Lilian')
Colette – AC's sister (aka 'Celly')
Colin – AC's brother (aka 'Col')
Ming – Colin's third wife
Christopher – AC's nephew (son of Colin and Ming)
Lord Clark (aka Bonny papa) – AC's father
B'Mama (aka Bonny mama) – AC's mother
Nolwen, Comtesse de Janzé – AC's stepmother
Aunt Di – one of Jane's aunts

STAFF AND ESTATE

Eddie – groundsman at Saltwood
William – butler at Saltwood
Linley – Lord Clark's butler at the Garden House
Nanny (aka 'Greenwood') – nanny to James and Andrew, lived in a
    grace and favour cottage on the Saltwood Estate
'Newy' – governess to AC and Colette
Miss Newman – Newy's sister, occasionally substituted for her and
    strongly disliked by the children
Juliet Frossard – AC's secretary in Wiltshire
Anna Koumar – the Clarks' housekeeper in Wiltshire
Tom – Jack Russell terrier
Max – a tame jackdaw at Saltwood
Eva – Jane's Rottweiler

OFFICE

Joan – AC's driver at DE
Dave – AC's driver at DTI
Pat – AC's driver at MoD
Jenny Easterbrook – Head of AC's Private Office at DE
Judith Rutherford – her successor
Matthew Cocks, Marjorie and Glyn Williams – successive Heads of
    AC's Private Office at DTI
Steve (Stephen) – Assistant Private Secretary at DTI
Julian Scopes – Head of AC's Private Office at MoD
Doug Widener – Number Two in AC's Private Office at DTI
Simon Webb – Head of Tom King's Private Office
Jane Binstead – Number Two in Tom King's Private Office

CARS

SS 100 – owned by AC since his undergraduate days
The Rolls-Royce Silver Ghost – the nicest of all to drive on a fine
    day if you are not in a hurry
The Porsche (aka the Little Silver) – used most often by AC when alone
The Citroën (aka the Chapron) – the *decapotable* belonging to Jane
    and used only for holidays
The 2CV – another Citroën, used when in de-escalation mode
The 'Bustard' – a very old $4\frac{1}{2}$ litre Bentley
The Loco – an old chain-drive racing car of 1908
The 'Wee One' – an old Land-Rover, MOT failure, used at Eriboll
The Mehari – a little plastic truck with an air-cooled engine and a
    very light footprint used for clearing grass clippings and prunings
    from the gardens because it does not mark the lawn. A kind of
    mobile wheelbarrow.
The Argocat – performs the same function at Eriboll, but will also
    go through peat bogs, and swim
The Hayter and the Osprey and the Atco – mowers designed to
    tackle the Saltwood lawns at their various stages of growth

HOUSES AND LOCATIONS

SALTWOOD

Various rooms: the Great Library; the Tower Office; the Green Room (the Clarks' informal sitting room in the old staff wing); the Muniment Room

The Bailey (inner and outer) – the two courtyards (see also lawns)

The Machines – an area of a distant field where agricultural machinery is parked

Chittenden Stone – an old milestone reputedly dating back to the Pilgrims' Way from Saltwood to Canterbury

The Seeds – a large arable field at Saltwood Farm

Courtneys (aka the Secret Garden) – an enclosed lawn in the inner Bailey

Gossie Bank – a steep climb at the far end of Saltwood Farm

Quince, the grandest cottage on the Saltwood Estate occupied by Nanny (qv) until her death

Garden House – a large bungalow built by Lord Clark in 1971 when he moved out of the castle

Sandling – the railway station for Saltwood

Grange Farm – owned by the Simmons, next door neighbours

The 'Black Route' – a walk along the sixty foot high wall of the ruined chapel in the Inner Bailey

ERIBOLL

The Creaggan Road – the road that connects Loch Eriboll to Loch Hope by way of the Creaggan Ridge, some seven miles in length and climbing from sea level to 600 feet at the ridge

The Lodge – principal house on the estate

Shore Cottage – Jane's house at Eriboll, where Jane and AC always stay

Foulain – a shepherd's cottage at the foot of the Loch

Strathbeg, a remote croft at the head of the Polla Valley

Arnaboll and Cashel Dhu, crofts on the Loch Hope side of the estate

Ardneackie ('Anson's') – the peninsula that juts out into Loch Eriboll

ZERMATT

Chalet Caroline – the Clarks' house in the village

The Kiosk – built by the Clarks in 1985, adjoining the chalet

Trift – an inn at an early stage in the ascent to the Rothornhutte

Othmars – an inn on the Blauherd

MISCELLANEOUS

The Mews – composite name for various vintage car dealers'
establishments in Queen's Gate

Upper Terrace – Lord Clark's house in Hampstead until 1951

Albany – Chambers shared at various times by AC, Lord Clark and
Andrew

Seend (aka Broomhayes) – the Clarks' house in Wiltshire, which they
now visit seldom, but retained by them after the sale of Seend
Manor when they moved to Saltwood in 1971

Bratton – Town Farm, Bratton-Clovelly. The Clarks' first house,
thirty-five minutes north of Plymouth

SLANG

There are a number of family sayings and shorthand expressions
dotted about in the text. Displayed as a glossary I recognise that
they seem both pretentious and slightly mad, but for the curious I
annotate below.

ACHAB – (lit.) 'anything can happen at backgammon', a saying
originally from 'the Room' at Brooks's where games can swing
at a late stage on an unpredictable run of the dice, used often as a
consolation in times of depression.

Cutting peat/Burning heather – activities in Scotland used as a
general cover for the theme of escaping to the Highlands

Thompson – defecation

Satisly – arousing satisfaction, inducing complacency

Sadismoidly – virtually the same as sadistically, though less *transitive*
in meaning; the suffix -moid, or -moidly is often attached to
adjectives

Dutch – blustering confident though tainted with insecurity (variant
of Dutch Courage, though without inference of alcohol)

Men's tea – elevenses in the kitchen at Saltwood where all employees
assemble (if they wish)

The bike rule – introduced after James had a serious accident on a
motorbike at the age of fifteen. Children out at night had always
to check in no matter how late they returned (guaranteed to stop
parents sleeping until this happened).

Straight to the Lords – another consolation phrase (see ACHAB)

Lala – self-regardingly overdressed or noisy (females only)

Ego – particularly assertive or insensitive (of personality or behaviour)

Tinky – diminutive, insignificant

Artists Materials – sometimes declaimed as an excuse for poor
  performance

Rest the eyeballs – sleep

Two second rule – a parable recounted in a graveyard illustrating
  finality: 'You can't put the clock back – not even by two seconds.'

Softies – casual clothes

Greywater – diaorrhea

Oopsy-la – see Lala

M. Goisot – white Burgundy (the proprietor of the small vineyard at
  St Brie from which the Clarks import their house wine)

Nonnoish – buffer-like

EMT – early morning tea

ABBREVIATIONS

NAMES

AC – Alan Clark
CP – Charles Powell
DH – Douglas Hurd
DY – David (Lord) Young
GJ – Tristan Garel-Jones
IG – Ian Gow
JM – John Major
LB – Leon Brittan
MA – Michael Alison
MH – Michael Heseltine
NL – Norman Lamont
NT – Norman Tebbit
PM – Peter Morrison
QM – The Queen Mother
RA – Robert Atkins
TK – Tom King

ACRONYMS

AAC – Army Air Corps
AF – Armed Forces
ATP – Aid and Trade Provision
BAC – British Aircraft Corporation
BAe – British Aerospace
BMATT – British Military Advice and Training Team
CAP – Common Agricultural Policy
CCO – Conservative Central Office
CFE – Conventional Forces Europe
CFS – Chief of Fleet Support

COMEX – Commodities Europe (in Chicago)
COREPER – Council of Permanent Representatives
CSA – Chief Scientific Adviser
CDS – Chief of the Defence Staff
DE – Department of Employment
DOAEH – Defence Operational Analysis Establishment
DOE – Department of the Environment
DTI – Department of Trade and Industry
ECGD – Export Guarantee Department
EFA – European Fighter Aircraft
EFTA – European Free Trade Association
EMT – Early Morning Tea
EOC – Equal Opportunities Commission
EXCO – Executive Council (Hong Kong)
FCO – Foreign and Commonwealth Office
FO – Foreign Office
GMBATU – General, Municipal, Boilermakers and Allied Trades
    Union
G-PALS – Global Protection Against Limited Strike
IEPG – European Programme Group
ISS – Institute of Strategic Studies
LegCO – Legislative Council (Hong Kong)
MEP – Member of European Parliament
MFA – Multi Fibre Agreement
MGO – Master-General of Ordnance
MOD – Ministry of Defence
MSC – Manpower Services Commission
NEDC – National Economic Development Council
OBN – Order of the Brown Nose (passim *Private Eye*)
ODA – Overseas Development Agency
OD(E) – Overseas Defence Committee of the Cabinet
OECD – Organisation for Economic Co-operation and Development
PC – Privy Councillor
PES – Public Expenditure Survey
PO – Private Office
PSA – Property Services Agency
PUSS – Parliamentary Under-Secretary of State (the lowest Ministerial
    rank)
RCB – Regular Commission Board
RFC – Royal Flying Corps

ROE – Rules of Engagement
RUSI – Royal United Services Institute
SWP – Socialist Workers' Party
UKREP – United Kingdom Representation (at European
    Commission)
UNCTAD – United Nations Commission for Trade and Development

1983

1983

A fine evening at last, with delightful and abundant birdsong. It has been so wet that the ground squelches under foot and even the Mehari[1] marks the lawn. The greenery is lush, bursting on every side; so many vistas of tone across the arboretum. We visited the young trees this afternoon and were pleased by a copper beech that Jane had planted down in the spinney to carry the eye along from the Park. On the way back I had a confrontation with the 'country bumpkin' man, an inveterate trespasser. I cursed him, and he crumpled disarmingly.

Andrew[2] is back from Sandhurst, and looking wonderful. But my poor father lies adying in the Hythe nursing home where, unhappily, he receives visitors. Together we went to see him, and found him weak and quavery. He went in for colonic lavage, to 'clear up' his diverticulitis (which he hasn't got, of course; but the fool of a doctor can't see, or won't accept that Nolwen[3] is poisoning him).

Then he broke a hip trying to get out of the impossibly high hospital bed; then an operation to cure this led to (how?) a blocked urinary tract. Now he's on a catheter as well as heavily in plaster, and mildly doped. Before the operation he said to me, 'I am perfectly clear, and I say this with all deliberation, that I will not be alive in a week's time.'

I am sad, though not as sad as I used to be, that I never really made contact with him. And, as I think about it, I suppose I'm sorry that I reacted away from the world of 'Art', because that shut off a whole primary subject that we could discuss together. The world of 'Civilisation'. I must have been very crude and rough in my teens and early twenties (still am, some would say).

I am interested in Clare, the au pair whom Nolwen has just installed at Garden House.[4] I strolled over this evening, deliberately entered by the back door and chatted her up. She's not pretty, but is sexual. Dairymaid. Reminded me of Portmeirion.

---

[1] The little Citroën truck used for clearing the lawns at Saltwood.
[2] AC's younger son, serving in the Life Guards.
[3] AC's stepmother, Nolwen, Comtesse de Janze, 1925–90, married Lord Clark in 1977. AC and she did not enjoy good relations.
[4] The Dower House on the Saltwood estate, built by Lord Clark in 1972, and lived in by him until his death.

Tomorrow we are off to Bratton[1] for a three-week Election campaign and my journal (such as it is) – school meetings, canvassing, 'Wotya going to do for me then, guv?', walkabout, 'I say again . . .' etc., etc. – will be recorded in the day diary. I intend to cut as many corners as possible. At least we'll save money, staying at Bratton.

But before closing I should record my last speech, in the last adjournment of the old House, knocking poor dear Tam[2] around as he ploughed on with his batty arguments about the *Belgrano*. So what does it matter where it was when it was hit? We could have sunk it if it'd been tied up on the quayside in a neutral port and everyone would still have been delighted. Tam is too innocent to see this.

Halfway through Tristan[3] came sidling up, sat down on the bench and offered me an even £100 that I would be in the next Government. He always knows everything, but I took the bet all the same.

I think I will be too – but as what?

Charing Cross train   *Friday, 20 May*

The Election campaign is less than halfway through, but I am returning, somewhat reluctantly and uncertainly, on account of my father's imminent (or so we are told) death.

Last night, as Jane and I approached the Hoe Conservative Club, following a successful Adoption meeting at which I spoke from the heart about the Falklands and got a standing ovation, we were accosted. Several drunk middle-aged buffers were congregated on the steps of the club, a faded Edwardian building in the grand part of the city. In the twilight – it must have been about nine o'clock – a man in 'beadle's' regalia peered at me. 'I know you', he said, breathing pungent whisky fumes.

It turned out he was the Town Crier of London, *really* was,

---

[1] Town Farm, Bratton Clovelly. The Clarks' cottage in Devon, twenty-five miles from Plymouth. AC was first elected for Plymouth Sutton, February 1974, and was about to fight his fourth Election campaign.

[2] Tam Dalyell, MP for West Lothian since 1962, was now to contest Linlithgow.

[3] Tristan Garel-Jones, MP for Watford since 1979. A close friend of AC, he had been an assistant Whip in this Parliament. His name crops up frequently in these diaries.

although at first I thought he was mobbing.[1] We had a light-hearted conversation. Then, unexpectedly, he said, 'I'm sorry to have to tell you that the police have been round. There is an urgent message for you to telephone Hythe in Kent.'

How good of him. None of the others had thought to let me know. Well-meaning and muddled, they groped their way through to an inner office (the 'Steward' had long since gone and no one could find the light switches) and showed me a telephone. I suffered a momentary *frisson* during the ringing tone in case it was something to do with the boys, and got through to Linley[2] who was calming, though shifty.

I could just have made the sleeper that night but decided against. This allowed me to attend the 'Mayor-Making', probably the most grindingly boring of all the obligatory constituency fixtures with its self-satisfied, repetitious speeches, hard chairs and defiantly bogus applause. But the MP has to be *seen* there.

At lunchtime I rang the nursing home and spoke to the floor sister. I didn't like it. She was evasive. On being pressed she admitted that there were certain 'irreversible' signs. Like what? Well, reduction, or disappearance, of a pulse at the extremities, ankle, etc. ('The King's life is drawing peacefully to a close', all that. But that announcement was signed by Dawson[3] after he had poisoned George V, wasn't it, so he really knew.)

I went straight to the station and took the 125 to Paddington, taxiing across London to Charing Cross. Eddie[4] met me at Sandling, and I dropped him at the bottom of the drive and drove directly to the nursing home.

Linley was in the car park. 'He's not too good.' (If my father were going to survive he'd have said 'his Lordship'.)

My father's door was open (a bad sign). He was sitting up, breathing rapidly but shallowly, with his eyes closed. Nolwen was bending over him, mare-eyed; Catholic peasant at a deathbed. Guillaume[5] (what the hell was *he* doing there?) stood looking out of the window.

---

[1] Etonian parlance for 'making fun'.
[2] Len Linley, Lord Clark's butler at the Garden House.
[3] Lord Dawson of Penn, physician to King George V, and generally reported to have 'eased' the monarch's passing in its closing stages.
[4] Edwin Wilson, head gardener at Saltwood.
[5] Guillaume de Rougemont, nephew of the Comtesse de Janze.

Nolwen immediately detached herself, came up to me and started talking about arrangements for the funeral! After a bit this got too much for my father and he became agitated, groaning and coughing. Nolwen was completely incapable of dealing with this. I strode over to the bed and said, 'Papa, it's Al.'

'Ah, Al. That's good, very good.' He seemed greatly relieved.

'Will you all please leave,' I said loudly. They shuffled out. Then I got hold of his wrist, very cold and clammy it was, and said, 'Papa, I think you're going to die very soon. I've come back to tell you how much I love you, and to thank you for all you did for me, and to say goodbye.' He mumbled, but his breathing calmed right down. Quite remarkable and fulfilling. I held on to his wrist for a good while, then left, kissing him on the brow.

I should have stayed longer, and I should have made him open his eyes. But I'm so glad I made it. I went back to Saltwood where Nanny gave me a thin cheese salad and the following morning Nolwen phoned to say that he had died at one in the morning.

Bratton   *Sunday, 5 June*

It looks as if we are heading for a substantial victory. A new Conservative Government. Will I be in it? We have spent the day lying on the front lawn, newspapers scattered around, just as we used to do twenty or more years ago, though now fully clothed and *white*-footed. I look at pictures of southern seas and bathing beauties. I have an awful feeling that this is my very last 'free' Sunday.

I just can't make up my mind if I want a job or not. Fool, Clark, of course you do. The House won't be much fun with nigh on 400 estate agents, merchant bankers and briefless barristers all OBN-ing. Do I provide the opposition, with a few chums? We are having a private lunch at Brooks's on 15th for the 'Shadow Cabinet'. Should be pleasing. Then I want to go to the Chalet[1] and walk out on to the verandah and touch the silver birch leaves and smell the clarity and ozone of the Alps.

---

[1] The Chalet Caroline, AC's house in Zermatt, which his family had built in 1959.

I'm madly in love with Frances Holland.[1] I suspect she's not as thin and gawky as she seems. Her hair is always lovely and shiny. Perhaps I can distract her at the count on Thursday and kiss her in one of those big janitors' cupboards off the Lower Guildhall.

The General Election on June 9:
Conservative: 397; Labour: 209; Alliance: 23.

Saltwood   *Monday, 13 June*

It was Ian Gow[2] who telephoned. I had been getting more and more irritable all day as the 'junior' appointments were leaking out on to the TV screens, and had taken refuge on the big Atco. I was practically on the last stripe when I saw Jane coming across the lawn with a grin on her face. But when she said it was Ian I thought he must be ringing to console me. Surely it's the Chief Whip who gives you the news? And even then a slight sinking feeling at his words, 'The Prime Minister wants you to join the Government.' – 'Go on.' 'It's not what you wanted.' But still a certain delight when he actually enunciated the title, 'Parliamentary Under-Secretary of State at the Department of Employment'.

I had to ring Norman Tebbit.[3] (I don't really get on with Tebbit, he always seems slightly suspicious of me. I don't net into his style of humour.) 'Hur, hur, you've drawn the short straw,' then a lot of balls about 'the rations are good . . .' but to come in the following morning at nine a.m.!

Almost immediately afterwards Jenny Easterbrook (of whom, I don't doubt, much, much more) rang and said that she was my personal private secretary and what time would I like my car?

No point in hanging about. I dressed up, grabbed a briefcase,

---

[1] Frances Holland was AC's twenty-two-year-old Labour opponent in the 1983 campaign. They had established a *rapport* doing a hospital radio show together.
[2] Ian Gow, MP for Eastbourne since February 1974. He had served Mrs Thatcher as her PPS since May 1979. AC's chief friend in the Commons.
[3] Norman Tebbit, MP for Chingford since 1974, had been Secretary of State for Employment since 1981. Created Life Peer, 1992.

straight to Sandling. In London I collected the coven[1] and off we went to Brooks's for dinner. At intervals Joei said, 'Gosh, Al, are you really a·Minister, zowee.' Valerie was less forthcoming. Ali sulked and sneered. Endless well-wishers telephoned. I went in and out of the dining room like someone with prostate trouble. The only amusing call was from Morrison[2] and Goodlad[3] who were dining opposite at Whites. Peter said, 'Look, Alan, your secretary Jenny Easterbrook is very pretty. Whatever you do, don't lay a finger on her.'

Goodlad grabbed the phone, 'Especially in the lift.'

'Drunken youths,' I told them.

Driving away, we went past the Ritz and Joei said, 'Gosh, is that the Ritz? I wish we could go in there.'

'Why?'

'To go to bed, of course.'

I was thoughtful.

I have always been culpably weak in such matters.

And when I got home I thought to myself – a new life, a new leaf.

Department of Employment   *Wednesday, 15 June*

Jenny Easterbrook has a very pale skin and large violet eyes. Her blonde hair is *gamine* short, her sexuality tightly controlled. She makes plain her feelings on several counts (without expressing them): one, that I am an uncouth chauvinist lout; two, that it is a complete mystery why I have been made a Minister; three, that my tenure in this post is likely to be a matter of weeks rather than months.

I did, though, get a reaction when I asked, in all innocence, if she would take dictation. She had, after all, described herself to me only yesterday as 'a secretary'. And I wanted to clear my head by writing my own summary memo. 'Can't you do shorthand?'

'I'm an official, not a typist.'

Faster than I can digest them great wadges of documentation are

---

[1] Three girls related to each other by blood whom AC had known for many years.
[2] The Hon Peter Morrison, MP for Chester since 1974. Currently Minister of State at Department of Employment.
[3] Alastair Goodlad, MP for Northwich, 1974–83, when he became MP for Eddisbury.

whumped into my 'In' tray. The subject matter is turgid: a mass of 'schemes' whose purpose, plainly, is not so much to bring relief to those out of work as to devise excuses for removing them from the Register. Among my other responsibilities are 'statistics', so it will be me who has to tell the House each month what is the 'jobless' total.

The Enterprise Allowance Scheme, the Job Release Scheme, the Community Scheme. Convoluted and obscure even at their inception, they have since been so picked over and 'modified' by civil servants as to be incomprehensible. I ought to welcome these devices, and must try and master their intricacies. But my head is bursting. I understand Nabokov's analogy of a traveller in a foreign city, whose language he does not speak, attempting in the middle of a power strike, in the late evening, to find his hotel.

Department of Employment   *Thursday, 16 June*

This morning I woke up with a a jolt at 4.10 a.m., – the first anxiety-waking since the mid 1970s when Hoare's were holding the deeds of Saltwood and I used to worry about repaying the overdraft. Interestingly, my anxiety translated itself into a financial dream. I had asked the Manager of the UBS in Brig the state of my account and he told me that I was SwFrs. 250,000 overdrawn – but of course it is quite all right, Mr Clark, we have the security of the Chalet. In fact I'm not overdrawn at all in Brig. But the anxiety syndrome had surfaced in its old form – although in the days when I was short of money I never used to *dream* about it. I lay awake for some hour and a half, thinking how in the hell am I going to cope with this; how long is it going to take me to comprehend, to dominate this completely new field of expertise.

I made tea at about six a.m., got to the office at seven thirty a.m., unlocked the Red Box and started reading. Normally I am a slow reader, but in the last forty-eight hours I must have read more than in the previous two months.

Albany   *Friday, 17 June*

Today I hosted the 'Shadow Cabinet Lunch', in the Oval Room at Brooks's.

During the campaign, irritatedly contemplating the general dreariness of the Government, being it seems composed mainly of subservient toads or grumpy ex-Heathite heavies, I sent out a number of invitations.

Everyone accepted. We were young, and crisp (excepting possibly dear Julian Critchley[1] – but he is such a wit as always to embellish any gathering). Chris Patten[2] and I had, indeed, just put our foot on the first rung, and we hailed each other as being 'complementary' in terms of balance. Conversation waxed jollyish – but only *ish*.

I followed Ed Streator's[3] practice of, at a certain point in the meal, inviting each guest in turn to deliver a little soliloquy. The theme was, What the Government Should be Doing with Its Huge New Mandate, etc.

Some were cagey, some, notably Nick Budgen,[4] a little on the whingey side. Robert Cranborne[5] was laid back and funny. But it was curious – perhaps due to shyness or reserve – how few, if any, of the speakers saw the broad canvas, still less drew on it.

I fear that we all still suffer from a lack of confidence. Very deep-seated it is, running back as far, perhaps, as before the war and those Admiralty memoranda saying we couldn't even take on the Italian Fleet in the Mediterranean. So when we win something we can barely believe our eyes. There is no follow-through.

Entertaining is part of the fun of politics, and in the Conservative Party it used to happen every weekend, while three days a week Margesson[6] kept a table at the Mirabelle. Now we are all too busy – and too poor.

---

[1] Julian Critchley, MP for Aldershot since 1970.

[2] Chris Patten, MP for Bath since 1974. Parliamentary Under-Secretary, Northern Ireland Office.

[3] Ed Streator, American diplomat. Currently Minister at the US Embassy in London.

[4] Nick Budgen, MP for Wolverhampton South-West since 1974. An Assistant Government Whip, 1981–2.

[5] Robert Cranborne, MP for Dorset South since 1979. Heir to the Marquess of Salisbury.

[6] David Margesson (1st Viscount). Legendary Tory Chief Whip from 1931; appointed Secretary of State for War by Churchill in December 1940, but made the scapegoat after the fall of Singapore in 1942.

Saltwood   *Sunday, 19 June*

Ever since I was elected, no, adopted for the Sutton Division there
has appeared annually, or more often, in the minutes of whichever
executive council meeting I have been unable to attend, devoted to
the topic of fund-raising and social events, the flat resolution (passed
unanimously), 'Alan Clark to invite a Personality'. Invariably it annoys
me. I find it presumptuous and insulting as well as being unclear. And
so far – to their irritation – I have always been able to dodge it. But
this last weekend they had a Euro Party, to raise money for the
'EuroConstituency' (a function always enthusiastically attended, as it
is known that I am filled with distaste for all things 'Euro') and I had
resolved, in celebration of our famous victory, to produce a 'surprise'
personality.

I am ill at ease with people in show business. I prefer the company
of journalists, or other politicians, or fellow Old Etonians, or classic
car dealers, or dons. But Jane and I agreed that there was one person
who was sympathetic, and whom it would be fun to have down –
Reggie.[1]

It was soon apparent, though, that he had suffered a *coup de*
something-or-other.[2] He said nothing in the car, nothing in the train,
nothing in the Mayflower Post – whither I took him to show his
rooms and ply him with drink before we went over to the Guildhall.

In some gloom Jane and I went off to change. 'A man of few
words,' I said.

'*Few*? He's *totally* dumb.'

But once the evening got under way Reggie performed pro-
fessionally. He grinned his way through the lionising, made a 'funny'
speech ending with a joke (was it blue? I didn't get it, anyway) about
Anna Ford and 'Alan Clark's hammer'. Yet the moment we were out
of the building, he reverted. Hardly said another word. Strange. I
hope he's all right.

---

[1] Reggie Bosanquet, an old friend, who was newscaster at ITN for many years.
[2] At that time (and quite unknown to the Clarks) Bosanquet was tragically suffering
from cancer of the liver from which he was to die later in the year.

Department of Employment   *Monday, 20 June*

At 8.56 a.m. I heard Jenny's phone ring in the outer office. 'Yes, he's here,' I heard her say (so Yah Boo to whoever is asking, I thought). It was Donald Derx.[1]

Jenny padded in with that special sly gait when she thinks she has caught me out with something.

'Have you read the brief on the revised conditions for the Job Splitting Scheme?'

'Yes.' (Lie.)

'Good,' she said (meaning, good I have caught you out), 'because Donald Derx would like to come round and discuss it with you.'

'When does he want to come?'

'Well, in about five minutes.'

'All right,' I said gritly. 'Have him round in five minutes.'

I calculated that I could just about read it well enough diagonally to be able to bat the ball back at least, in about five minutes. But some eighty seconds later the door opened, and Jenny showed in Donald Derx. He must have left his office immediately after he had put the phone down, as it takes roughly one minute to get from his office to mine.

He talked quite interestingly, and sagely, about certain changes that had to be made. I had *just* absorbed enough, using my Stabilo Boss illuminator, to be able to keep a discussion going, periodically taking a sly glance at the briefs which lay open in front of me.

The whole thing was a complete ambush. First, he wanted to see what time I came into my office, second, he wanted to see the extent to which I was reading the contents of the boxes. Jenny knows perfectly well that the earliest train I can get from Saltwood is the 7.19 a.m. This means that on a Monday I cannot get to the office before about 8.48 a.m. (as opposed to my usual time of eight o'clock). At best, i.e., if it had been the very first document I read on opening the box, I would have had seven minutes, maximum, in which to read it. In fact, of course, it had been hidden about a quarter of the way down the box. But I am already wise to this trick and don't take things out in the order in which they are arranged. I fillet them first, and extract

---

[1] Donald Derx, Deputy Secretary at the Department of Employment and senior civil servant under the Permanent Secretary, Michael Quinlan, who moved to the Ministry of Defence, 1988.

those little photocopied flimsies marked 'PUSS to see' and Jenny's initials, which are the really tricky items.

Department of Employment   *Tuesday, 21 June*

I was lunching with Jerry Wiggin[1] in the House and he told me the horror story of his sacking.

The phone rang at his home on Sunday night.

'Jerry, hello, it's Ian here...'

'Oh yes, hello.'

'Jerry, the Prime Minister would like to see you at Downing Street tomorrow.'

Jerry's spirits soared, but before he could even say Yes, Ian went on, 'I'm afraid it is not very good news...' and his spirits plummeted cruelly as Ian went on, '... so would you mind coming to the back door.'

Oh, what a chilling, ghastly experience. I am very good at detecting from people's voices whether what they have to say is good or bad and I don't think I would have been misled by Ian's presumably sepulchral tone as he invited Jerry's attendance. What I do think I would have said, however, is, 'Stuff your fucking door, I am not going to bother. She can just write to me.'

And yet, as poor Jerry admitted, although he had meant to be dignified, when he actually got into the room, he plucked and pleaded and blubbed.

What on earth did he expect – to go in and change her mind, to get her to go back to her desk and cross somebody else's name out? When I told this tale to another Minister he wisely and shrewdly observed that in the end we are all sacked and it's always awful. It is as inevitable as death following life. If you are elevated there comes a day when you are demoted. Even Prime Ministers.

---

[1] Jerry Wiggin, MP for Weston-Super-Mare since 1969. Parliamentary Under-Secretary at Ministry of Defence, 1981–3.

Department of Employment   *Thursday, 23 June*

It's not yet eight o'clock and already I've been in my office half an
hour. I like to get here early, before anyone else arrives, then I can
scowl at them through the communicating doorway as they take their
places around the outer office. I am still so ignorant of the basic
material that this is one of the few ways I can start to assert an
ascendancy.

It is (naturally and heartbreakingly) a glorious summer morning,
and I have drawn back to their maximum extent the sliding windows,
thus buggering or – I trust – partially buggering the air conditioning
system. There is a tiny *balcon*, a gutter really, with a very low parapet,
below knee height. Certain death on the Victoria Street pavement
eight floors below. Sometimes I get a wild urge to relieve my bladder
over it, splattingly on the ant-like crowds. Would this get one the
sack? Probably not. It would *have* to be hushed up. Trivial, but at the
same time bizarre. Certainly it would tax the powers of Mr Bernard
Ingham.[1] I might do it on my last day.

Yesterday evening I outstayed Jenny (a pang of jealousy, mild, but
for the first time, when I heard her take a telephone call, presumably
from an intimate). As soon as she'd gone I left and went round to the
Farmers' Club, where the '92[2] were having a dinner. Dreadful food,
grey beef and gravy, roast potatoes (on a hot June night) hard as Mills
bombs.

Proceedings formless, totally out of control, as Paddy Wall[3] is
useless. Is he gaga or just frightfully deaf? Doesn't like me for some
reason, although I've never done him any harm, and so will never call
me to speak. In fact this is one of those evenings when the prudent
man *doesn't* speak as most of the discussion was about whether we
should back Edward Du Cann[4] or Cranley Onslow[5] for chairmanship
of the 1922 Committee. Whoever we back gets it. But I am in two

---

[1] Bernard Ingham, Chief Press Secretary at Number 10.
[2] The '92 Group was a 'secret' society of right-wing Tory MPs who banded together
to work as a block vote in committee elections, and to influence policy.
[3] Sir Patrick Wall, MP for Beverley since 1983 after twenty-nine years representing
Haltemprice, Hull.
[4] Edward Du Cann, MP for Taunton since 1956. He had been Chairman of the
1922 Committee since 1972.
[5] Cranley Onslow, MP for Woking since 1964. Succeeded Du Cann as Chairman of
the 1922 the following year.

minds. Edward, I suppose, is on the way down now (less than ten years ago he was seriously, and I mean seriously – I wrote it all up at length at the time – being pushed for the Leadership). Cranley has inner reserves. Dropped from the Government once, then taken off the back benches to be Minister of State at the Foreign Office. Grand wife. Probably a better choice.

After the ten o'clock vote it was still light and I walked across Green Park. In Brooks's Jerdein and Miller were playing head on. So what? I watched for a few minutes only, then ambled down Jermyn Street. Two new 500 SLs. So what? I'm off shiny cars. I'm off just about everything. The material at DE is so turgid, so repetitious, so irrelevant to anything that real government should be about, that it requires a huge effort of intellect to comprehend it. By the end of the day my brain is completely *désseché*.

The only thing I am learning is how the Civil Service works. Perhaps this'll be useful one day.

Department of Employment   *Friday, 24 June*

Jenny continues to bait me with her indifferent stare, and flat northern vowels. Why is our relationship so difficult? If only we were lovers.

This morning she was agitated about Sir Robert Armstrong, when could she put him in the diary, etc. I was offhand. She had said something about this yesterday, that he 'wanted to see me'. I assumed that it was some kind of social call, new junior Minister, make him feel at ease, show him the ropes. I wasn't bothered.

'I don't think so.'

'He's a friend of my sister. They're both Trustees of Covent Garden. She's probably told him to be nice to me.'

'I don't think so.'

'Oh well, do as you like, put him in then.'

'Mid-day.'

'But what about Donald Derx?'

'Sir Robert is head of the Civil Service. Derx is a Dep Sec.'

---

[1] Sir Robert Armstrong, GCB, CVO, Secretary of the Cabinet since 1967.

Joan[1] drove me round to the Cabinet Office. He kept me waiting in an ante-room. When he came out, didn't invite me into his office. Rudeish. A certain amount of rather wary small talk, and I could feel our mutual dislike rising. He made tepid boasts about working for Ted, writing his speeches. (That's all the unfortunate Ted needed, I thought.)

'Who do you admire most in the Commons?'

'Dennis Skinner.'[2]

A longish pause.

Then, like a conjuror, two files appeared in his hand, one red, the other orange.

'There are certain matters that the Prime Minister has asked me to raise with you . . . '

'Really? Go ahead.'

'You have been spoken of with approval . . .' he paused, and I got ready to preen myself. Then he opened the red file. ' . . . by the National Front.'

'Not at my solicitation.'

'If any of them should at any time try and make contact with you, I must ask that you inform my office immediately.'

Better not make an issue of this, I thought. 'Of course. It's most unlikely, but of course.'

He put down the red file on the table between us then, seeing my hand move, pushed it out of reach.

'There are also certain matters of personal conduct . . . '

I glared at him. We were on the orange file now.

' . . . which could quite possibly leave you open to blackmail.'

Shit!!

'No, no. Perfectly all right. They've all married into grand Scottish families by now.'

To do him justice, a very, very faint smile – what novelists call *wintry* – crossed his features. 'How's Celly?' he asked, and a few seconds later saw me out.

'How did that go?' asked Jenny when I got back to the office.

I suppose it was my imagination, but her eyes seemed slightly slit, malevolently gleeful.

'Perfectly all right. He's a dreary old thing, isn't he?'

---

[1] AC's driver.
[2] MP for Bolsover since 1970.

She flounced out and back into her own room.

I thought about it for a little while. They *must* have been bugging my phone. There was no other explanation. And for ages.

In the evening, I told the whole story to Christopher.[1] He said he found it encouraging. 'It shows how well we are governed.'

Saltwood   *Sunday, 26 June*

Took the day off. We went to the Bentley Rally in Kensington Gardens, then to lunch with Selmes. He's looking ghastly – presumably got AIDS. He's got this new house, definitely downmarket from Lindsey[2] and it's being done up in what one might term Aggressor-Deviant mode. Mad great black painted walls; a pink Francis Bacon with a youth's demi (only) detumescent penis blotchily prominent.

'We're going to have a white spiral staircase here, this is going to be the *fun* room, I'm taking out the dividing wall the whole way along here . . .' etc., etc. But it remains a rather dud Edwardian building, isolated Pont Street Dutch.

The previous owner, a German, had replaced all the window panes on the street side with black one-way-vision glass, like a cocaine addict's limousine. And why do 'active' buggers create these giant, terrifying great rococo master bedrooms in which (to me, at least) it would appear impossible to sleep, never mind perform the sex act, satisfactorily? Ian McCallum[3] – come to think of it he actually *died* of AIDS only a short while ago – had one in his house in Bath; and of course the creepiest of all is Peter Pitt Millward's bedroom at Gloria.[4]

We ate a delicious picnic in the garden, with far too much to drink. If it's Chassagne Monrachet, I always overdo it. After his fifth glass of Dom Perignon Christopher scintillated. He can still be

---

[1] Christopher Selmes, a friend of many years who had made a fortune in the City at the age of twenty-seven, but lost most of it during the 1974–5 crash.

[2] Lindsey House on the Embankment, next door to Paul and Ingrid Channon, had just been sold for £1,250,000.

[3] Ian McCallum, Curator of the American Museum at Bath.

[4] Paco da Gloria, the seventeenth-century palacio in northern Portugal, which was bequeathed to AC's brother Colin by Peter Pitt Millward.

divinely, hurtfully, witty. But his skin is scabeous, white and flaky. Poor fellow.

We travelled back by train, and by the time we arrived at Sandling I was acid and bad-tempered. But after some tea and a stroll in the arboretum, so dark and lush, I felt better.

Not for the first time I let my thoughts ramble around the many different ways that one could 'improve' the place – all, needless to say, involving vast expenditure and thus impossible. The great unexploited resource is the old lake, drained by the breach which the Parliamentarians opened in the dam in 1648 and now a lush meadow, rich in mushrooms. To close this up, contain the stream, produce a beautiful reflecting surface carrying water lilies, where one could drift in a punt and think great thoughts, with a weir and a series of waterfalls cascading through the arboretum – *Grandes Eaux* – that would be spectacular. But to what end? A beautiful private sanctuary, or a 'Stately Home' with the public trampling and soiling and scattering crisp packets?

Anyway, I can't contemplate such a scheme until I recover my liberty. I told Jane, I'm imprisoned for eighteen months, then moved to another prison – perhaps an 'open' one – or discharged. What I can't allow is for them to keep me at DE for the whole four years just so as to be 'out of the way'.

Albany   *Tuesday, 28 June*

Today is the sixty-ninth anniversary of the assassination of the Archduke Franz Ferdinand at Sarajevo, the date from which the world changed. At the time no one realised what it meant, though I often think of that prize-winning spoof headline in the *New York Daily News* in 1920: 'Archduke found alive, World War a Mistake'. Surely the two best repositories of black humour are the Bronx and the Household Division.

I am a privileged prisoner. I sit in my little cell room off the top, white, ministerial corridor, listlessly opening a *mountain* of constituency mail, 'taken into solitary confinement for his own protection'. My mental process is already torpid with *ennui*. I wake up, get up, earlier and earlier. There is about an hour, from 5.45 to 6.45, when the mind is relaxed, its muscles deknotted by sleep. Then, once the clock hands are past seven, the pressure is on, the light tension headache starts behind the eyes.

Last night I drank with Franko[1] in the Ritz. He is so clever, his wit and insight so engaging. And he is a scholar. I feel on my mettle. But he is a pessimist *au fond*. After a bit we both got depressed. Various lovelies, brown and rich, drifted about in their silk diaphanous dresses. We were gloomy voyeurs. The aura of power is an aphrodisiac, and all that. But I felt eunuch-like. It's all too bloody pasteurised. I'd like to revert to the old Ischian Al,[2] and get it raw.

Department of Employment   *Thursday, 30 June*

I still like to go to Prime Minister's Questions. I sit on the little cross bench below the bar on the Labour side, which allows me to hear a lot of what is said on their benches and also gives a good diagonal enfilade of our side.

Poor Bob Dunn,[3] one of the five back-bench promotions, made the most frightful hash of his Question Time, fumbling, stumbling and sitting down halfway through the answers until a Labour Member cruelly suggested (Bob is a junior Education Minister) that he may consider taking a course in articulacy. The Speaker, meaning kindly, attempted to defend him, but this only made matters worse. I dread my own Questions, set for 19 July; it must be absolutely terrifying. Once or twice in the last couple of weeks I have sidled into the Chamber in the mornings and held the Despatch Box and looked round. A very odd feeling.

Tony Kershaw[4] asked the Prime Minister the very question that I had in mind and would have tried to get in with had I been in my usual place – something to the effect of how she had forced the

---

[1] Frank Johnson, political correspondent and commentator. At this time writing the parliamentary sketch for *The Times*.

[2] AC often averts to his bachelor holidays in Ischia, where he would stay with John Pollock and Constance Mappin at Forio.

[3] Robert Dunn, MP for Dartford since 1979. He had just been appointed junior Education Minister.

[4] Sir Anthony Kershaw, MP for Stroud since 1955.

resignation of the SDP Leader, of the Labour Party Leader, how the successor to the Labour Leader had already lost his voice, and the Leader of the Liberal Party had retired to the country with a nervous breakdown. She was delighted and led it on by saying, '... and I am happy to tell my Honourable Friend that personally I have never felt better'. For some reason this made me uneasy.

Plymouth train   *Friday, 1 July*

An absolutely glorious day; not a cloud, save the hanging vapour trails of aircraft in the Heathrow 'stack', gradually broadening into woofly white Christmas decorations. *Invariably* does it seem on such days that I am committed not to be heading south to Saltwood and sweet Jane and the gardens, but West, to the Constituency where, I am complacently told, no fewer than twenty-two people are booked for surgery. I won't even get a cup of tea there, and if there are too many life stories I won't even manage the 6.25, which is the last train that allows me to make the connection to Saltwood.

I have a stuffed box, mainly dreary PO cases[1] which will prevent me getting at this month's *Motor Sport* or, even better, resting the eyeballs. And when Joan meets me at Paddington (assuming I make it back to Paddington) there will be another box, possibly two, on the back seat.

And yet, I am enormously fortunate. I am not *compelled* to do any of these things, to endure any of these discomforts. And the boys are so lovely and strong and handsome. There was a fearful helicopter accident at Bristows yesterday.[2] No survivors. Always, unspoken in the background, Death lurks, carrying his scythe and lantern.

---

[1] Private Office cases arise where an MP refers the problem of an individual constituent directly to a Minister for investigation.

[2] AC's elder son, James, was working as a helicopter captain, flying AeroSpatiale Super Pumas on the North Sea oil rigs for Bristow Aviation.

Department of Employment   *Tuesday, 5 July*

Norman Tebbit is truly formidable. He radiates menace, but without being overtly aggressive. He seldom smiles, but goes straight to the heart of a subject, never gets diverted into detail, always sees the political implications.

I have just come from a meeting on 'Special Employment Measures' (these tacky schemes to get people off the Register). My own mind is a maelstrom of nit-picking detail, eligibility rules, small print of a kind that civil servants relish – not least because they can browbeat Ministers as a team, with one bespectacled *Guardian* reader in sole charge of each 'Scheme' and thus in complete command of its detailed provisions. The unfortunate Minister blunders about like a bull on sawdust with the picadors galloping round him sticking in their horrid barbed *banderillas* (if that's what they are).

'But no, Minister, ha-ha, in that case the eligibility entitlement would have lapsed . . . '

'Ah, yes, Minister, but there is no provision under the Order for . . . '

'Mmm, Minister, it would have to be discretionary and that could only be exercised in exceptional circumstances . . . '

This particular tautologous cliché always irritates me. 'I beg to enclose the enclosed enclosure,' I said.

The officials looked startled. Is the Minister going soft in the head?

But the moment Norman came in he took complete control. Admittedly, the Secretary of State is always right. Rule Number One of Whitehall. Even if he's as thick as a plank officials must rally round, and 'help' him. Norman's own position is particularly strong, as he is known to be a special favourite of the Lady, of whom they are all completely terrified. And with good reason. The wretched Donald Derx apparently became impatient with her thought processes some time ago – early in the '79 Parliament before the old *nostra* had been undermined, and these changes confirmed by the electorate; and at their first meeting was emboldened to be 'cutting' in response. She marked his card on the spot, and he is going to take early retirement, having 'had it conveyed to him' that he will never make Permanent Secretary.

So they arse-lick, massively, with Norman. Which he accepts, expressionlessly, but without letting it deflect him. At one point he turned to me. 'Well, what do you think, Alan?' I was tongue-tied. I couldn't speak the way he did, crudely but shrewdly; nor could I express myself in Whitehall, convoluted phrases, double negative conditionals. I was useless. Will I ever get any better? I've only been here three weeks, I suppose, although it feels like a lifetime. The trouble is, it's *so* boring, the material. I simply can't 'master' it. If only I was at the Foreign Office, or the MoD. Still, better get fit in the prison yard first.

Jenny is fussing about some Order I've got to put through the House on equal pay. Endless briefings she's arranging. What's the point? It's after hours, everyone will have gone home, all I have to do is stand at the Box and read a Civil Service briefing.

But I *am* a bit twitchy about 'First for Questions', now coming over the horizon. A couple of times I've been into the empty Chamber, and stood at the box on the Government side, tried to get the feel of the geography. It doesn't help. I get butterflies in my stomach.

Department of Employment   *Wednesday, 6 July*

I sat drinking late last night, after the vote (Roman hot it was at eleven p.m.), with Jonathan Aitken in the garden of his house in Lord North Street.[1] I remember thinking these houses were a bit poky, blackly crumbling, when I used to go to Sybil's 'ordinaries'.[2] I now see, of course, that they are the choicest thing you can have if you are a Tory MP. Number 8 is bigger than the others; was Brendan Bracken's in the Thirties, and he built on a long drawing room at the back. Furniture not bad, but pictures ridiculous, art dealers' junk. Not even shiny decorative Mallet pieces, but smudgy gilt on cheap frames.

Jonathan was very complimentary about my prospects. He said it was no disadvantage getting in late; said I could go 'quite remarkably high'. I knew what he meant, and dissimulated delightedly. But everything depended on one's performance at the Despatch Box. I told him about my exchanges with Sir Robert Armstrong. He was

---

[1] Jonathan Aitken, MP for Thanet East since 1974, had at the Election become the Member for Thanet South.

[2] An 'ordinary' was a party given by Lady Colefax, who, unlike Lady Cunard, another political hostess of the period, was not well off. She discreetly billed her guests a few days after the event.

sensible and wise and funny. We both agreed on how well Ian Gow was doing. His maiden speech demolishing Kaufman[1] was a classic. Ian is shaping up as a true heavyweight.

All this cheered me up, and I needed it, because that evening I had been to Joei's party, and felt old and passé. *Very* handsome young men everywhere. Joei lounged and struck attitudes; she's going through a phase when she thinks she's Nancy Cunard. Ali, though friendly, was for some reason tearful. Everyone beautifully turned out; but an unsettled atmosphere, a mood of urgency suggesting dependence on narcotics rather than on alcohol. I left early, and with no regrets. Public life now absorbs all my energies. I can't socialise. Politicians who try to do both can't be much good at either.

In the sleeper to Paddington   *Friday, 15 July*

What a day! On the go without let-up from the early hours. Jenny had put in place a murderous schedule, quite deliberately, and came along (v. rare) to make sure there was no malingering.

It came about like this. When my appointment was reported in the *Herald*[2] I foolishly and fecklessly answered 'Yes' to the question (semi-spastic, like all the *Herald*'s questions), 'Now you'll be able to do something about Plymouth's unemployed, won't you. Will you be calling in on the Unemployment offices in the city? Da, da, etc.' Result, banner headlines on the Friday after: ALAN CLARK TO VISIT CITY UB OFFICES. Further result, according to the local DE office (why is there such a thing? Waste of money and personnel) who faxed through copies of the paper to Jenny, that all the staff were keyed up for my visit and disappointed when I didn't show up – 'Typical'.

Jenny snorted and stomped around saying 'visits' had to be organised in advance, was I going there as an MP or as a Minister, anyway I couldn't go there as an MP if I *was* a Minister, Ministers couldn't make impromptu visits, had to be accompanied at all times, the local office must be informed, we'd have to bring a press officer 'in case there were questions . . . ', *ad infinitum*.

---

[1] Gerald Kaufman now MP for Manchester, Gorton, after representing Manchester Ardwick from 1970; Shadow Home Secretary.

[2] *Western Evening Herald*, Plymouth newspaper.

Bleakly I heard her out. 'All right, then, lay it on.'

So there we were in the breakfast train to Exeter, the beautiful Wiltshire countryside rolling past, the fields parched and yellowing but the hedgerows and deciduous trees still heavy with foliage. Drought in a temperate climate induces pleasing, unexpected colours and vistas.

I am always nostalgic for Wiltshire, a delicious pain, where we lived so happily when the boys were tiny, and every day seemed free and golden. There is something about the train's wheel note, something in the subconscious anyway, that I always wake up, whatever I'm doing or reading when the train goes past the Lavingtons.[1] There is a lovely rambling farm there, where Jane went to a 'contents' sale; I should have bought the whole thing, lock-stock-and, moved into it and lived happily ever after. But in fact, at the time, I was restless. I wanted to get into politics, and the years were going by. I could see my friends just beginning to get old, and starting to repeat themselves. I couldn't get through a dinner party just listening to Michael Briggs asking me if I remembered what Alistair Londonderry did on the way back from Porto Ercole in the summer of 1966, or whatever.

Damnably, although I have a mountain of briefing on our visit(s), Jenny has not packed in the box(es) the folder on First for Questions, now ominously close at 2.30 on the afternoon of Tuesday of next week. Is this deliberate? Yes and no. She wants me to concentrate on it over the weekend. But that leaves hideously little time to clarify the errors and omissions in the crib. Never mind. Perhaps there'll be a *huge* IRA bomb in New Palace Yard and the whole thing will be cancelled. That's how I get to sleep at night, anyway.

All too soon Exeter came up. And there was a local big cheese, who'd come down from Bristol, to drive us about. Angela Croft, the press officer, is attractive. Smart summer suit, pretty legs. Jenny is Victorian, no, *sanatorium* pale, in her silk frock. I ought to be full of testosterone as I stride along the platform with these two cerebral cuties clip-tripping beside me. Quite the opposite. They've got me in a tungsten steel jock-strap. Within, there is nothing better than a champagne cork.

The big cheese had a new (red) Volvo. Thankfully, I made to slump in the back. But no, wouldn't you rather sit in front as it was

---

[1] From the stretch of line between West Lavington and Market Lavington could be seen the giant elms on the second escarpment where the Clarks inhabited the manor house, 1964–72.

'easier to point things out'. After about twenty minutes we arrived at our first destination, a settlement for Unfortunates.

First, a 'conference'; introduced to good-natured and worthy staff, heard their presentations. Then a Working Lunch. (As I don't take lunch, and made as much clear to my Private Office when I got to the Dept, they now get round this simply by tagging on the prefix 'working'). Small talk, rather dying away by the time we had coffee. Then a tour; the theme is 'Rehabilitation' and the inmate's tasks are simple. Conversation is far from easy.

It was a relief to get to the UBOs. Some pretty operatives. One, who I know actually was called Sharon because I asked her, let me look into her computer screen. I moved closer, she moved closer, I moved closer, etc. Jenny scowled. No one else seemed to notice.

Then the Job Centres. Another conference, another tour. Here the buzz theme was 'the Disabled'. But why? It's the *able* I want to get back into work. If civil servants think their career prospects are centred round what they can do for the disabled, that is what they will focus on. But it all causes long-term dilution. Society will become an inverted pyramid with the whole load of pensions, benefits and hand-outs for minorities being carried by a few tough and house-proud workers. This is the kind of thing I went into politics to stop. And here I am going round saying yes, yes; well done, keep up the good work.

Gloom, frustration.

Finally, I got rid of Jenny and Angela. Surgery was almost a treat. Two hours, and at the end I had a mug (I *loathe* tea in a mug) of weak tea with powdered milk.

Two lunatics. Macrae, and little Mrs Thingummy with her thirty-nine murder attempts. Fourteen 'normal' cases. One must be polite. They are so sweet, most of them. They don't whinge, really. They're just bewildered, and put upon.

It must have been well over 80° all day, more than that in the poky little constituency office. Constantly, I perspired. In the gaps between interviews I thought of the gardens of Saltwood. How many perfect days like this am I going to jettison? Will I ever have anything to show for it? I can get very sentimental and long for darling little Jane who is left alone for so long, and always so game and jolly.

It wasn't until half past eight that I was free. But then I had a treat,

supper (quite by chance) in Si Lam's[1] with David Owen.[2] He's so engaging, such good company. Like me, he despises the Liberals. Like
me, he admires the Lady. What is to become of him? I said, 'You must
be Prime Minister' and later, 'You *will* be Prime Minister.' It's extraordinary how this extravagant compliment invariably gives pleasure,
however ludicrously improbable, to whomsoever it is addressed. But in
David's case it could happen. And we could do a lot worse.

Saltwood   *Sunday, 17 July*

By the pool, before breakfast. A warm breeze, a *Föhn* it is, blows yew
needles into the water and the filter is choked. The water is 82°, its
hottest ever, but dark yellowy green. When we returned from the
Election campaign the pool was still blue, but now the algae are out
of control. We have tried drenching it with chemicals, but this simply
has the effect of making the water translucent; not transparent. You
can't see the bottom. I go down with the mask, and the floor is
covered with dark algae slime.

Yesterday, to much apprehension, we staged a musical evening for the
Historic Houses Association. In fact, and to our surprise, it was
quite delightful. Martin Muncaster recited and gave readings. The
Dolmetsch twins played most pleasingly. Many excerpts which I didn't
know, a contemporary pastiche. Moving and painful was the exchange
of letters between Henry VIII and Ann Boleyn. His first avowing his
love and torment; hers in dignity and solitude, three years later, before
the scaffold. Oh, how the human predicament endures.

Saltwood was absolutely glorious, unique, the roses incredible.
One of the loveliest places in the whole world. This coming week is
my test and crisis. First for Questions on Tuesday; an Order to 'lay'
before the Standing Committee and, after ten p.m., before the whole
House. I wax and wane between confidence and inspiration; and

---

[1] Chinese restaurant in North Hill, Plymouth, where AC could often take late supper
before catching the sleeper back to London.
[2] David Owen, Leader of the Social Democrat Party. MP for the neighbouring
constituency of Plymouth Devonport since 1974 (as Labour until 1981, then
SDP). From 1966–74 he represented AC's Plymouth Sutton seat.

sheer terror and fatigue. I can only thank God that I have this lovely place to fall back on; and, please, to spare the boys.

Saltwood   *Friday, 22 July*

Fool, Clark. Fool, fool, fool. This week I went up a stubby ladder; then down a very long snake.

Questions were fine. The first one (my very first Question on the floor of the House of Commons; how many more will I answer before I am done?) came from Cyril Smith.[1] Naturally,. the crib didn't cover it, but Norman told me the gist of an answer out of the corner of his mouth as I rose to my feet. Cyril whumphed back in his seat with a sulky expression. Canavan[2] tried to give a bit of trouble but was maladroit, and I scored. Others were barely noticeable. To my great delight I read sideways in the Whip's book (it was Hamilton[3]), 'Clark dealt v. well with Canavan. He has a nice slow delivery which holds the attention of the House.' Could one ask for more? Afterwards Nigel Forman,[4] a good judge of most things, said, 'It's nice to hear a genuine toff's accent at the Box occasionally.' Many other compliments were paid.

Alas! An odious over-confidence burgeoned. Anyone can do this. Child's play. My friends encouraged me. In the dining room Tristan said, 'We're selling tickets for Al's performance tomorrow...' I resolved not to disappoint them. Looking back now, I realise I was amazingly, suicidally, over-confident.

I was booked to dine with Christopher, for a *wine-tasting*. I left the Department unusually early because I wanted to go to the Braque exhibition at the Tate. Tony Newton[5] (whom I like) was wandering round, and said something about it was nice to see Ministers broadening their minds even though they would be 'performing' in a few

---

[1] Cyril Smith, MP for Rochdale since 1972.
[2] Denis Canavan, recently elected as MP for Falkirk West, having represented West Stirlingshire from 1974.
[3] Archie Hamilton, MP for Epsom and Ewell since 1978, junior Whip. Later PPS to the Prime Minister and Minister of State, Ministry of Defence.
[4] Nigel Forman, MP for Carshalton since 1976.
[5] Tony Newton, MP for Braintree since 1974, later Secretary of State for Social Security and Leader of the House of Commons.

hours' time. Airily, I told him that I wouldn't be back in the House until ten; I was going on to a dinner.

That fucking text! I'd barely looked at it. Norman had sent for me at tea time, said good luck and all that, and 'just stick to the text'. In fairness, and presciently, he had also said, 'Don't try any jokes.' Situation not helped by the fact that officials had twice called in their original version and 'incorporated certain changes, Minister'. So I didn't really start to mark it up until I was in the back of the car going from the Tate to Christopher's house (not far). It seemed frightfully long. So long, indeed, that I would have to excise certain passages.

But which? And yet this didn't really seem very important as we 'tasted' first a bottle of '61 Palmer, then 'for comparison' a bottle of '75 Palmer then, switching back to '61, a really delicious Pichon Longueville. Geoffrey Roberts was the only other guest. By 9.40 I was muzzy. Joan had already been waiting ten minutes. I was meeting officials 'behind the Chair' before the ten o'clock vote. The text was still virtually unmarked and unexcised.

A huge Havana was produced, and I puffed it deeply while struggling with my speech under the tiny little reading light in the back of the Princess.

There were the officials, all anxious but deferential. I exhaled smoke at them. Grand seigneur. I couldn't talk, I had to pee. In the lav, that nice clean one off the Aye lobby, was Barry Jones[1], my 'shadow'.

'This shouldn't present any problems.'

'None whatever. They all want to get to bed.'

'That goes for me too.'

Nice chap. Good relations.

The Chamber was unusually full for an after-ten event. When I was called there was a ragged, undeferential cheer from the benches behind. But an awful lot of Labour people seemed to be in as well. Including, it seemed, every female in their parliamentary strength. I recognised many of the *tricoteuses* who kept us up night after night in the summer of 1976 filibustering (successfully) the committee stage of Bill Benyon's Bill to reduce the maximum age at which babies can legally be murdered from six months to three.

As I started, the sheer odiousness of the text sank in. The purpose

[1] Barry Jones, MP for Alyn and Deeside since the Election (Flint East, 1970–83).

of the Order, to make it more likely (I would put it no stronger than that) that women should be paid the same rate for the same task, as men, was unchallengeable. In my view, in most instances, women deserve not less but *more* than the loutish, leering, cigaretting males who control most organisations at most levels. But give a civil servant a good case and he'll wreck it with clichés, bad punctuation, double negatives and convoluted apology. Stir into this a directive from the European Community, some contrived legal precedent and a few caveats from the European Court of Justice and you have a text which is impossible to read – never mind read *out*.

I found myself dwelling on, implicitly, it could be said, sneering at, the more cumbrous and unintelligible passages. Elaine Kellet-Bowman,[1] who has a very squeaky voice, squeaked, kept squeaking, at me, 'Speed up.'

Some of the House got the point, enjoyed what I was doing, but I sensed also a certain restlessness starting to run round the Chamber. I did speed up. I gabbled. Helter-skelter I galloped through the text. Sometimes I turned over two pages at once, sometimes three. What did it matter? There was no shape to it. No linkage from one proposition to another. The very antithesis of an Aristotelian pattern.

Up bobbed a teeny little fellow, Janner[2] by name, a Labour lawyer who always wears a pink carnation in his buttonhole. He asked me what the last paragraph 'meant'.

How the hell did I know what it meant? I smoothed away. He started bobbing up and down as, it seemed, did about fifteen people on the other side, plus I couldn't see how many on my own, to my side and behind me. This had the makings of a disaster. Never mind. 'Heads down, bully, and shove.'[3]

Then, the inevitable. The one sure-fire way of breaking through a speaker who won't give way. 'Point of Order, Mr Deputy Speaker.' I sat down. A new Labour member whom I had never seen before, called Clare Short,[4] dark-haired and serious with a lovely Brummie accent, said something about she'd read that you couldn't accuse a fellow member of being drunk, but she really believed I was incapable.

---

[1] Elaine Kellet-Bowman, MP for Lancaster since 1974.
[2] Greville Janner, MP for Leicester since 1970.
[3] A slogan from the Field Game (played in the winter term at Eton).
[4] Clare Short, MP for Birmingham Ladywood since the Election.

'It is disrespectful to the House and to the office that he holds that he should come here in this condition.'

Screams, yells, shouts of 'Withdraw', counter-shouts. General uproar. On and on went the Points of Order. I sat, smiling weakly, my lips as dry as sandpaper. The Chamber began to fill up, and there were at least fifteen people standing at the bar of the House. (It is a golden rule: Points of Order on the annunciator screen for more than two minutes means a good row, so put your head round the door and enjoy it.)

On the whole, I'm pretty relaxed about rows and flare-ups. As far as Ministers go, provided they avoid taking money or money's worth from anyone except the Fees Office, even the most turbulent row will die down and soon be forgotten. But this had an ominous feel to it. On and on went the shouting. 'ORDER,' kept bellowing dear old Ernie Armstrong, the Deputy Speaker.[1] The House was alight. Soon, wearing an uneasy half-smile, definitely *not* catching my eye, appeared the figure of the Leader of the House, John Biffen,[2] to sit in his appointed place.

Now this was a bad sign. The Leader only attends business after ten o'clock when there is a *major row.* And a truly terrible threat began to seep through to me. Perhaps we were going to 'lose the business'. This is not the same as being defeated on a vote. It simply means that the whole thing has to be brought back before the House at a later date. The entire Government legislative schedule is put out of kilter – and the Whips loathe it. Indeed, as far as the Whips go, no other misdemeanour compares. I could see anxious conferrals starting up with the Chair, and behind.

Bob Wareing[3] asked if it would be in order for an honourable or right honourable Member to address the House if he were drunk. Ernie said that this was a hypothetical question, 'and now we must get on with the debate'.

Passions were (temporarily) spent and I rose to my feet. But the atmosphere was different. I had lost confidence and in its special extra-sensory way the House knew that something 'wasn't quite right'. My supporters were silent. And others on our side were emboldened to

[1] Ernie Armstrong, MP for NW Durham since 1964, Deputy Speaker since 1981.
[2] John Biffen, MP for Shropshire North since the Election (Oswestry, 1961–83), Leader of the House since 1982.
[3] Bob Wareing, MP for Liverpool, West Derby since the Election.

be portentous and, by implication, reproachful. I forced my way through to the end, another fifteen minutes or so, feeling like Lucky Jim at the award ceremony, before coming to the magic signing-off phrase, 'I commend these regulations to the House.'

Now if there's one vice in which the House really likes to indulge, it is being sanctimonious. Each speaker took his cue from the last: so sad, such an opportunity cast away, the great traditions of the Department, Walter Monckton, Ernest Bevin, Macleod (how the fuck did he come into it?), Harold Macmillan, Stockton, breadth of understanding, unpardonable levity, offensive to both sides of the argument (what argument?), after-dinner speech. And, of course, incomparably menacing, that the House should have a full opportunity to debate the issue, send for more papers, data should be placed in the Library.

I assumed gravitas. Dear Peter Morrison was sitting beside me, his face pouring sweat. Periodically I said to him, 'We must *not* lose the business.' 'I think it'll be all right. I've had a word with Ernest.'

I held my breath. It was coming up to midnight and, thank God, it had been agreed that I was not expected to 'reply' to the debate. This in fact was a trap which Labour had laid, hoping that the Speaker would then rule that the matter should be heard another day. Sure enough, with only a few minutes left, Nigel Spearing,[1] one of their best barrack-room lawyers, rose and cited Standing Order No. 3 (1) (b), which gives the Speaker a discretion to decide that the matter be adjourned. Very splendidly, Ernie said that he 'had had this provision in mind throughout the Debate'.

One more brief kerfuffle, and the Division was called. Nobody spoke to me much in the Aye lobby, although little garden gnome Peter Rost[2] sidled up and said, 'After a performance like that I almost considered voting against.'

Poxy little runt, what's he ever done?

In the car Joan asked, 'What was all that row about, Minister?' (Knowing full well, I don't doubt.)

'They were saying I was drunk. But I wasn't, was I?'

'No, Minister, of course you weren't. I've never seen you drunk.'

That's that, then.

---

[1] Nigel Spearing, MP for Newham South since 1974.
[2] Peter Rost, MP for Erewash since the Election (Derbyshire South-East, 1970–83).

Department of Employment   *Thursday, 28 July*

The House rises today, in effect. But we don't get our holiday until September. Other Ministers will take theirs in August, and come back fresh. It'll be, 'Where's Alan?' and when my office say 'On holiday', it'll be, 'Clark's still on holiday'. *Les absents ont toujours tort.* Jenny is taking hers (thank God) in mid-August, but is busy filling up the rest of the month with dreadful draining visits to boring and inaccessible locations.

In the dining room conversation was mainly on this topic. Our table was joined by little Douglas Hogg, now a junior Whip.[1] I can't decide whether he is likeable or not. (But I should say that many do not have this difficulty.) I don't mind people being rude, provided that they are not uncouth with it. But he is colossally self-satisfied – or is it a chip? I suspect he has a tearful side. It is said that in the days of their courtship he used to follow the object of his desire and her paramour at a distance, and stalk them, peeping from shop doorways, like a bad secret agent.

'Well,' I said, 'how are you keeping all the new boys in order?'

Without a second's hesitation he got my middle stump. 'By offering them your job.'

Department of Employment   *Wednesday, 3 August*

I went to the NEDC meeting in the morning representing the Department. Norman had sent his apologies. Lawson[2] chaired it, podgy and jowelly, and there is a suspicious henna tinge to his hair. Is he tinting, or rinsing? But he is an effective chairman.

We sat at a round table on the top floor of the CBI building and many notables were in attendance. Five members of the Cabinet; Keith Joseph,[3] with a permanently bored, but slightly agonised, expression on his face combining, I-have-seen-it-all, and are-we-all-mad? Cecil Parkinson – if ever anybody deserved the over-worked

---

[1] Douglas Hogg, Tory MP for Grantham since 1979. Elder son of Lord Hailsham and married to Sarah, daughter of former Tory Minister, John Boyd-Carpenter.

[2] Nigel Lawson, MP for Blaby since 1974. Chancellor of the Exchequer.

[3] Keith Joseph, MP for Leeds North East since 1956. Education Secretary since 1981.

expression 'amazingly youthful', it is Cecil.[1] He is not impressive reading from a prepared brief, but is very good when spontaneous. I was sitting next to him and watched him keenly, as he is of course my choice to succeed the Lady.

Peter Walker[2] was there in a country suit and spoke turgidly but with 'oh-what-a-good-boy-am-I' overtones. 'A very impressive contribution,' I muttered to Cecil. He is a real Neddy star, he agreed discreetly.

On the other side Ian Gow was sending me irreverent notes, 'What are we all doing here, what's the point, who are all these ridiculous highly paid people sitting at the back of the room', etc. Robin Leigh-Pemberton[3] was unexpectedly good, crisp and clear. Terence (or Terry, as he likes to be called) Beckett[4] was not quite as bad as I expected, suffering, though, from a heavy tobacco cough.

Moss Evans was almost completely silent, a distinguished drawn face, immaculately dressed like a Mafia godfather, twice as formidable as any of the other TU heavies who were there.[5] Terry Duffy[6] was just a dear old thing; Frank Chapple a professional rough diamond.[7]

I was nervous about having to contribute, but in fact the Chancellor *rushed* the Agenda item − absurdly, but menacingly, entitled 'Where are the Jobs Coming From' − on which there was a Departmental responsibility. I assume because he wanted to choke off monologues from the TUC end of the table. The whole thing was a complete waste of time. No conclusions, no recommendations, no action taken or suggested. Job creation scheme for civil servants, and way of embarrassing Ministers.

Joan drove me round immediately to the Trustees' meeting[8] at Christie's but the traffic was so bad that I had to bail out at the bottom of St James's Street, ran up the little arcade past the entrance to Rhodes and Co., the money lenders where I remember unhappily borrowing

---

[1] Cecil Parkinson, MP from 1970; for Hertsmere since the June Election, and before that South Hertfordshire and Enfield. Currently Trade and Industry Secretary.

[2] Peter Walker, MP for Worcester since 1971. Appointed Energy Minister after the Election following four years at Agriculture.

[3] Robin Leigh-Pemberton, newly appointed Governor of Bank of England. Friend of AC since they were at Eton.

[4] Terence Beckett, Director General, CBI since 1980.

[5] Moss Evans, Transport and General Workers Union.

[6] Terry Duffy, Amalgamated Union of Engineering Workers.

[7] Frank Chapple, Electrical, Electronic, Telecommunications and Plumbing Union, and the current chairman of the TUC.

[8] Of Lord Clark's settlement.

£500 in 1947. Now I was on my way to discuss carving up ten million. But nothing else seems to have altered much.

Department of Employment   *Thursday, 4 August*

Last night I dined with Ian. I asked him if he was happy and he said he was not. To my horror he told me that he had not seen the Prime Minister since 14 June, which was the day that Michael Alison[1] took over. How ruthless women can be − far worse than men. Ian was completely in love with the Prime Minister and utterly devoted to her. He must have seen more of her in the last four years than anybody else except Denis, and possibly more even than him. He was enormously influential, too. And yet now the court has sealed over the vacuum created by his departure and I doubt if he will ever recover an equivalent position. Ian said that he would gladly stop being a Minister at any moment and that he would gladly 'go back'. But you can never go back. It is the Two-second Rule. I said that he would be in the Cabinet in the next reshuffle and resume his old intimacy. But I am not so sure, and nor is he.

We both agreed that Michael Alison, although a pleasant and saintly man, could not possibly provide the Lady with the same alternating course of stimulus and relaxation. Of course MA sits in on Cabinet meetings, as a Privy Councillor, which Ian never did. But Ian told me how he used to wait in his little office at the bottom of the stairs at Number 10 and emerge to catch doubtful members of the Cabinet as they were coming in before an important meeting, haul them into his room and explain to them that a particular decision was something to which the Prime Minister attached crucial import-ance. I can visualise the dedication, the *intensity* − with which he used to do this. It is something which Michael, with his diffident manner, simply could not manage.

Ian told me that even the present Cabinet could only guarantee her a majority of two when the chips were really down − 'and

---

[1] Michael Alison, MP for Selby since the Election (Barkston Ash, 1964–83) was appointed Parliamentary Private Secretary to the Prime Minister in the new Government and Ian Gow was tranferred to the DoE, where he became Housing Minister.

supposing Geoffrey[1] is away?' Is that margin of one constituted by
Willie?[2] I didn't ask, although his name has returned to the forefront
with this ludicrous assurance that he is ' . . . standing by at his farm in
Cumbria' in case the Lady goes blind and the ship of state becomes
rudderless.[3]

It should have been a celebratory dinner, as last time we had
dined the future was uncertain. Now we are both Ministers with a
Government majority of 140 and no Opposition of any kind in sight.
But there was a certain melancholy too. How often is it better to
travel than to arrive.

Department of Employment   *Monday, 15 August*

An absolutely perfect morning of late summer, temperature already
66° and a light dew with mist in the valley. I walked the dogs at seven
a.m. up past the dump and over the Seeds, and groaned aloud at the
sheer *crucifixion* of having to go to London and visit the Brixton
Remploy Office – of all places.

Ministers' Sundays are blighted by the prospect of Monday's
workload. By the evening I find myself short-tempered and grimacing.
Even the very minimum of correspondence and attention to pressing
estate matters has been neglected. Saturday morning is wrecked by
the box. Sunday morning is eyestrain headache as one trawls one's
way through the ten or twelve thousand words of political commentary
in the tabs and the broads. Yesterday afternoon I broke the lanyard on
the Osprey on the twenty-seventh muck-sweat and cursing attempt
to get it pull-started. I had to mow the whole Bailey lawn with the
faithful (but tiny) Hayter as at this time of year the Atco won't cut the
plantains. Up and down I went, sweating and muttering, each length
a strip no wider than twelve inches.

More depressing, because more relevant to today, and indeed to

---

[1] Sir Geoffrey Howe, MP for Surrey East since 1974 (Reigate, 1970–4; Bebington,
1964–6). Foreign Secretary since 1983.
[2] William Whitelaw, MP for Penrith since 1955. Home Secretary, 1979–83. Following the Election, created 1st Viscount and appointed Lord President of the
Council and Leader of the Lords.
[3] Mrs Thatcher was having an operation on her eye.

the whole Whitehall purgatory, I had spent some time in the muniment room. In a desk I had come across some of my father's old engagement diaries of the Forties and Fifties. Endless 'meetings' fill the day. Civil servants drift in and out. Lunches. Virtually indistinguishable from my own. What's the point? Nothing to show for it at all. He will be remembered only for his writings and his contribution to scholarship. His public life was a complete waste of time.

Department of Employment   *Thursday, 1 September*

I was working late at my desk, and Jenny had gone home, when the phone rang. It was Norman Tebbit. He invited me round for a 'chat'.

Norman talked interestingly. He knows where in the Party his strengths lie, and he knows, too, which of the grandees want to do him down. St John-Stevas,[1] of course; but then he's not a proper grandee, just popishly disapproving. And Willie. Sometimes Willie harrumphs menacingly about Norman, but is too shrewd not to recognise his qualities. There are others, who sneer and talk behind their hands to the pink press, but they are of little moment.

I fear Norman does have a chip, but it doesn't show – not all the time at least – and anyhow who could blame him?

We talked for a very long time. So long that the light started to fade, and as dusk entered the room so his style became more confessional.

What he really wants to do – curious how many serious politicians covet the post – is to be Chairman of the Party. Not just yet, I feel, but to keep it in his sights.

Now there was disconcerting news.

'She wants to appoint a Parly Sec.'

'*What?*' (I did not say 'who?', judging that if he wanted to identify the person he would have named him.)

'She thinks we need someone young, to counter the Steel-Owen image.'

I said the image didn't matter. In the first two years after the

---

[1] Norman St John-Stevas, MP for Chelmsford since 1964. Leader of the Commons, 1979–81.

Election the need was for organisational, not presentational skills.

Norman is of the same mind. But we agreed, the Lady does often want to 'bring forward' the very young. Reacting, I suppose, against Willie, Peter Thorneycroft,[1] Humphrey Atkins[2] – all these oldies who have been leaning on her since February 1975.

'It's a matter of having someone young and fresh to go on television the whole time and answer Owen and Steel.'

'At this stage it doesn't matter a damn. You must talk her out of it.'

He didn't answer, rose from his chair and switched on the light. I realised we had been talking for an hour or more, and went back to my own office.[3]

Saltwood   *Thursday, 8 September*

I am at my desk in the tower office, absolutely drowning in estate papers. Filing piles and Immediate piles and Pending piles are stacked haphazard on top of each other. I try to differentiate by stacking them criss-cross, like bricks, but I caught some that were sticking out with my sleeve and the whole Pisa-like tower collapsed, cascading the private and personal papers all over the floor.

So what? I haven't picked them up. I just walk on them. I will soon have plenty of time for the estate.

I am convinced that I have been allocated the black spot. To be dismissed at the earliest opportunity. Norman Tebbit doesn't address a word to me, of either welcome or farewell at the start, or finish, of meetings. Peter [Morrison] is more distant, it seems. This bloody Equal Ops Order still hangs round my neck. Albatross. Mill-stone.

---

[1] Peter Thorneycroft (Life Peer, created 1967). A former MP and Minister in the Macmillan and Douglas-Home Governments: Chancellor of the Exchequer, 1957–8; Chairman of the Conservative Party, 1975–81.

[2] Humphrey Atkins, MP for Spelthorne since 1970 (Merton and Morden 1955–70). Northern Ireland Secretary, 1979–81; Lord Privy Seal, 1981–2, when he returned to back benches.

[3] Three days later John Selwyn Gummer, MP for Suffolk Coastal since the Election (Lewisham West, 1970–4; Eye, 1979–83) and AC's co-Parliamentary Secretary in the Department of Employment, was appointed as Chairman of the Conservative Party.

Ill-wishers cite my performance as an excuse to object to the whole thing, get it 're-opened'. Tricky meeting coming up with Lady Platt (who is not an ill-wisher, but, unlike me, does understand the small print).[1]

Adrian Moorey[2] has a permanent sneer on his face. Is he being privately briefed by Ingham that I am for the chop? Often he comes into the outer office and talks in low tones with Jenny; he doesn't come on in here.

Even so, anything can happen. Norman had to 'go to the bathroom' twice during a meeting yesterday. Cecil looked *awful* on television, with sores showing on both upper and lower lips. The Lady's eye operation may go wrong.

Jenny came back from her holiday with a very very slight gold tan. Looks stunning in her oatmeal suit. At least now she allows me eye contact. I said, 'I don't expect I'll be here much longer.'

'Oh? We'll miss you.' Her stare is very direct, though limpid.

Department of Employment   *Friday, 9 September*

A lot of pointless activity in the Department, as officials start to drift back from their holidays. (We haven't had ours yet. Will we even get one, sometimes I ask myself?) Because the House isn't sitting Private Offices are having quite a little challenge to manage fulfilment of their Number One precept – *Ministers' diaries must be kept filled*. What they really like are full-scale meetings, preferably with so many in attendance that they have to be held in the small conference room. A far more economic solution would be just one intelligent civil servant guiding the Minister through the paper in his own office.

We had one of the PES[3] preliminaries today. First time I've done one of these, and I was totally out of my depth. I'm responsible for all these spastic, money-consuming Employment 'measures', so the idea

---

[1] Baroness Platt of Writtle (Life Peer). Recently appointed Chairman of the Equal Opportunities Commission.

[2] Adrian Moorey, press officer in the Department of Employment, then moved to Trade and Industry.

[3] PES: Public Expenditure Survey.

was that I should sparkle knowledgeably as a prelim to putting in higher 'bids'. I heard them out in sulky silence. Was finally goaded by Fred Bayliss, the Under Secretary, who appears to be our resident Chief Accountant. He mumbled along, ' . . . looks as if there is going to be a shortfall as our overall provision is £408 million and at present we are going to be pushed to get expenditure over £335–360 million'.

That's not a fucking 'shortfall' I thought, or at least not my idea of one. It slowly sank in that he was rambling round for suggested ways of getting last-minute expenditure authorised so as to 'approach more closely our provision'. 'Look, Fred, Ministers in this Department are members of a Government which is dedicated to – whose *raison d'être*, you could say, is – the reduction of public expenditure. Surely it's a matter for congratulation?'

Ah no, don't you see – 'It's important to get as close as possible to last year's provision in order to have a firm base from which to argue for increases this year . . . '

This was crazy. Nightmare. Kafka.

Like other officials above the rank of Principal he won't call me 'Minister'; they try and avoid calling me anything.

Is it like this with all Parly Secs, or just me? Icily I asked in what other Departments of State 'is this kind of budgetary practice prevalent'?

'All of them,' they shouted triumphantly.

General laughter, of a *tee-hee* kind.

Afterwards Jenny said, 'It's not really a good idea to get the wrong side of Fred.'

'Yeah?' I was quite pleased with myself.

Saltwood   *Saturday, 10 September*

We are host to a company of actors, who are making a children's film for television. *Tripods* is the title of the story. What a jarring name. Arthur Ransome, and (above all) Beatrix Potter knew what children really like. And adults, come to that. Myself, I am always ready to while away half an hour or so reading the tale of Squirrel Nutkin or Johnny Townmouse, and feel calmer as a result. These days authors write not so much to please the children as to earn the esteem of their own peers or, more importantly, librarians in trendy boroughs.

The team have been here for ages, it seems. But I like it. We charge a whopping location fee, and the gaiety, the costumes, the whirl of activity is all fun, and invigorates the place. They have put up a huge marquee in the car-park field where *delicious* meals (particularly breakfast) are served, and this pleases Eddie and William who have standing invitations to partake. Jane and I also stuff ourselves there, when the moods takes us.

The plot, insofar as one can follow it at all, is muddled. The story 'hops' from the eighteenth century to the late 2000s and back again. But the heroine is a pretty little thing called Charlotte Long,[1] who I know would feel exactly like Ali; same hair, colouring, bone structure. She has a really sweet nature, not at all show-business or ego. And sometimes our eyes meet across the tent, and she smiles shyly. Now come to think of it, she must be the grand, *great* grand-daughter of Walter Long[2], who was leader of the landed interest in (sic) the Conservative Party during Ll G's premiership, and was always getting in Arthur Lee's hair when he was Minister of Food in 1917[3].

Charlotte's (fictional) father, the (needless to say) 'Count' has a grey beard and wears satin breeches most of the time. He, and many others of the cast, have fallen in love with the place – which in the script has become the 'Château Ricordeau'. Charlotte wanders dreamily along the battlements to pastiche Brideshead music, murmuring about 'the loveliest place in the whole world'.

But the one I would really like to be is the Duc de Sarlat, so young and handsome and villainous, and eager to challenge a duel, with sabres.

---

[1] Tragically, Charlotte Long was killed only a few weeks later in a road accident on the M4.
[2] Walter Long, 1st Viscount Long of Wraxall, 1854–1924. Succeeded by his grandson, who in turn was succeeded by his uncle, whose son, Richard (the 4th Viscount), was appointed a Government Whip in the Lords in 1979. Charlotte was his daughter.
[3] Arthur Lee, MP for Fareham, 1900–18, when he was created 1st Baron Lee of Fareham. He had been Personal Military Secretary to Lloyd George, July–December 1916. He was made 1st Viscount in 1922.

Saltwood   *Friday, 23 September*

I sit at the long table in the Great Library. The last entry of the year from this seat, because tomorrow we load up the Decapotable and set off on our holiday. We won't really be back here until after the Party Conference. By then the light will have gone, the place become too chilly for a *reflectif*. The deep autumn will be on us – mud and gumboots and log fires and early teas with brown toast and crab-apple jelly.

Yesterday was forecast as the last one of this lovely Indian summer and at lunchtime I went down to Hythe beach, being pleased to find it deserted. High tide and clear sunlight, with an onshore breeze that slapped the waves into friendly gusts of vertical spray. I lay on the breakwater, and thought of times past – the golden summer of 1955 when I was running Anne, Marye and Liz, all of them living within half a mile of each other. Another occasion, later on, when I had jogged the whole distance from the Imperial and back, and threw off my tracksuit, plunging naked into the November sea.

My total fitness held up for so long, with only tiny degradations, until *Parliament* took over. It's the late nights that are shredding it. I always hated late nights, and avoided them if ever I could, until well into my forties. And this allowed me to bank a lot of energy. My lymphatic system is still very low mileage.

I took off my clothes and swam for a long time. The murky salt-tasting water was a delicious contrast to the metallic chlorine tang of the swimming pool.

Zermatt   *Monday, 3 October*

We've been here a week, but I have neglected my diary. Glorious weather, navy-blue skies but Alpine cold in the early evening and on waking up. I feel rested and randy, and reassured by my performance in the hills.

On Wednesday we went to the Schönbühlhütte, a hell of a climb, where three years ago (was it?) I saw a wild cat just at the point where

---

[1] Jane's open Citroën DS which the Clarks habitually use for their summer holiday.

the rock track peters out and you have to rope up. Only a very few tourists. The season is over and many of the inns in the village are already closed. We took six and a half hours and by the time we got to the cable-car station at Furri the last one had left and they were closing for the night. Weary and footsore we stumbled down the hillside, the lights of Zermatt seeming to take an eternity to come within reach.

Yesterday we went across the Gornergletscher to the Monte Rosa-hutte. God, glaciers are frightening. A white maze, lifeless and implac-able, so that the sight of a crushed plastic cup or, better, a fox's wispy business is reassuring beyond measure. The *patrouille* must have packed up some weeks back, because the skew poles and bright red and white tape that give early warning of the crevasses were in many places neglected or broken. Sinister and bluey-green, and *deadly* quiet (because at this season they remain frozen all day and there are no drips) these channels are interwoven for hundreds of yards, forcing detour after detour.

We must have been zig-zagging for more than an hour before we reached the moraine on the far side. I have never climbed Monte Rosa, always wanted to since, at Eton, reading Whymper's own account of the first climb which he accomplished, there and back *in a day*, alone and wearing little different than one would stalking hind in Argyll in October 1862.

Outside the hut a mound of fur moved sluggishly. 'Oh dear,' Jane said. 'It's a poor marmot who is too ill and decrepit to hibernate. He's stuck, and will die of cold.' Far from it. He was huge, massive, thrust and barged at us as we ate our sandwiches, rummaged in the rucksack, insisted on a 'tip' before we left. The 'Gondola Man',[1] we agreed.

Jane's stamina is incredible, and she is more supple than me. On the way back we both raced up the side of the Rotenboden cliff, getting to the mountain railway station in forty-three minutes from the edge of the ice, and catching the train by a whisker. It was standing only. I was bathed in sweat and my pulse rate must still have been over 120. But I looked complacently at the other passengers. The gap between athletes and spectators.

---

[1] Gondola man: a family saying denoting the man who always turns up out of nowhere just as you've found a gondola and demands 500 lire for standing beside it, like the commissionaire outside a hotel holding open the door of a taxi.

Zermatt   *Tuesday, 4 October*

Our last day. We watched Sulag's men start opening the ground for the Kiosk foundations,[1] then climbed up to the Winkelmatten chapel, where I always find it easy to pray.

I was low at having so soon to return to the Department, its drudgery, sterile and repetitious. But as my head cleared I realised how absurd, and ungrateful it was to complain. What does it matter, the stuffed boxes and the unwashed 7.19 a.m. train from Sandling? Tip is back safely from the Yemen, and through RCB.[2] Jamie has got to nearly 2000 hours flying the oil rigs, and soon to be pulled out. What good fortune attends us. Yesterday Fons[3] was chatting, up by the Guides' Wall. He said to Jane, 'You haven't changed at all, not one little bit in twenty years,' and walked off shaking his head. We each lit a candle. I did Boy's, as he is a wee bit out of kilter at the moment, and Jane did Andrew's, which was easier.

I have had a Fernandez type haircut,[4] and am looking forward to Conference next week at Blackpool. My first as a Minister, to swagger and ponce.

Department of Employment   *Monday, 10 October*

In the first days back after a vigorous holiday one is always full of zest. Spitefully, although other Ministers were meant to be covering my routine stuff, Jenny has kept a lot of it back and so there were bursting boxes, sitting like red tombstones on my desk. But I *ripped* through them, shouting queries and instructions through the open door. I've got much more confidence with the Civil Service now. Most of them are rather second-rate, with teeny vision scales. They're really quite

---

[1] The Clarks had got permission from the Commune to build a new chalet at the bottom of their garden, which would harbour a 'kiosk' for the Sunnegga railway station. Sulag was the building contractor.

[2] Andrew had passed the exams for the Regular Commissions Board.

[3] Alfons Franzen, the guide who gave basic skiing tuition to the family, and looked after the Chalet Caroline for many years.

[4] A hairdresser in St Tropez favoured by AC on account of his gift for endowing a 'boyish' appearance to his customers.

glad to submit to a forceful personality, provided he knows what he wants.

Some of my colleagues are in trouble, and this always makes me calm. Poor Cecil Parkinson looks like being in what Edwardians called *hot water*, as the girl is making paternity claims.[1] But he can ride that, surely? Perhaps not. It could be that the constituencies turn nasty. They mirror, resolutely, the unhealthy combination of prurience and hypocrisy to which editors competitively pander. And Conference, where they all cluck and whisper, starts assembling today.

Then there's little Peter Rees.[2] For some reason all the commentators think he's going to be sacked. Malcolm Rutherford (*Financial Times*) today: ' . . . the most likely to become a casualty'. (No mention of me anywhere in all this, I'm glad to note.) In addition Nick Scott[3] is making a balls-up at the Northern Ireland Office, and Julian Critchley[4] has suddenly written (anonymously, thus also incurring the stigma of cowardice) an offensive piece about the Lady, referring to her as 'the great she-elephant', and in other terms of disrespect.

Albany   *Thursday, 13 October*

We drove down from Blackpool this morning, as my father's memorial service is to be held in the church of St James's in Piccadilly in the afternoon.

Poor old Cecil had a bad time. The Lady is determined to save him, but Sara Keays is equally obsessed about getting her pound of flesh. The delegates are divided, and it is not easy to tell in what proportion. Those who support Cecil are vocal of course, and give little interviews

---

[1] Sara Keays had had a long-term relationship with Cecil Parkinson whose secretary she had been 1971–9. She was now pregnant with his child.

[2] Peter Rees, MP for Dover since 1970. Minister for Trade, 1981–3, when he was moved to the Treasury as Chief Secretary.

[3] Nicholas Scott, MP for Chelsea since 1974. He survived a further four years at the Northern Ireland Office.

[4] Julian Critchley was beginning to make a reputation as a writer.

to the camera. But I have a nasty feeling that there is a silent majority who are disapproving, and shocked.

Cecil himself is handsome and fresh-faced. Seems at times almost to be the injured party. But what an ordeal! His wife, his mistress and his boss, all throwing scenes, sometimes all within the same hour.

Apparently little Gummer, who is demonstratively *churchy* and (unlike the Lady) moralistic, is making a lot of trouble.

My father's memorial service was strange. A motley collection of strays. Poetic justice, as he himself never went to anybody's.

Yehudi Menuhin played the violin, and I read the lesson in a very clear and sardonic voice, trying to convey that they were all a shower, Nolwen in particular. If you die in old age, of course, you get a completely different kind of attendance than if you are taken by the Gods.

Myself, I don't want one. Better just to disappear, like Zapata.

Plymouth train   *Thursday, 20 October*

In order to make time for a solid raft of engagements in the Constituency I crammed everything in yesterday. A really draining day.

Started at nine a.m. with Wronski (dim German Senator). Wasn't a bad egg in one of the Bond films called Wronski? Boring. Stilted. I feel ashamed, when receiving visitors from abroad, of my poky little room. There are a few things, I suppose, that might make them prick up their eyes if they are 'connoisseurs', but they never are. And the rest of the stuff − cheap desk, stained carpet − says, unmistakably, junior Minister (very).[1]

Then straight through to the Home Office for the Race Relations Advisory Council. Leon Brittan[2] really *too* drawly, sneery-drawly almost. Why? Even Etonians don't drawl that much. But he does know his stuff. No stumbling around his notes, whispering to officials, puzzled pauses. I felt rather sorry for the Blacks, who declaimed their

---

[1] AC embellished his office with an Impressionist Victor Passmore, a painting by Graham Bell and two Roman porphry urns as paperweights on his desk.

[2] Leon Brittan, MP for Richmond, Yorks, since the Election (Cleveland and Whitby, 1974–83). Home Secretary. Previously Chief Secretary to the Treasury.

woes. But it is in the blood for thousands of years, atavistic. As was said (in another context) – you might as well try and limit sexual intercourse by decree.

My own brief was excellent. But I still had to improvise, and be prompted by David Hodgkins.[1] D.H. does not have a high opinion of me, nor does he conceal it. He won't call me Minister, leans forward and says 'Excuse me' quite loudly. Bloody ridiculous and impertinent.

I walked back slowly, past that pub in Caxton Street where they have tables out on the pavement. My footsteps did *not* want to turn into the Dept. What fun to cut and run – just disappear.

As I got out of the lift Les, Jenny's new Number Two, replacing Kate, was waiting in the corridor, holding the brief for the next meeting. (I selected Les at the interview stage because he was nice and keen and smartly turned out, though only just out of a Comprehensive. But at the moment he is over-conscientious, something of a fusspot.) Straight in to a roomful of officials to talk about the Enterprise Allowance Scheme. David Hodgkins was already there, 'sat in' at the back, not at the table, superciliously. The whole encounter quite formless, without beginning, middle, or end.

I had hoped to pop across to the House, have baked beans and a nap in my office over there, with the phone pulled out. But the new S of S, Tom King[2] wanted me to sit in on his 'introductory'. He's going on TV tonight, and is clearly meant to be Mr Nice, after Tebbit's Mr Nasty. All I could get was eight minutes in the leather chair with my eyes closed.

First, he was going to meet some Union leaders. This was a bad augury. I thought we'd got rid of all that 'consultation' balls? There was much talk, comfortably in their old ways I thought, by civil servants, of 'Solomon Binding'. 'Bugger Solomon.' I said, 'It's "Binding" we want.' To Michael Quinlan I quipped, 'Solomon Gomorrah.' He laughed uneasily, and inaudibly.

The assembled Barons were led by Bill Keys, who is rumoured to have bone cancer, and looked terrible. Len Murray, fidgety, sat beside him. Ken Gill, clearly the most formidable, on Keys' left. The rest of

---

[1] David Hodgkins, an Under-Secretary at the Department of Employment.
[2] Tom King, MP for Bridgwater since 1970. Following the resignation of Cecil Parkinson, Norman Tebbit was transferred to the DTI, and Tom King took his place as Secretary of State for Employment.

the company were under a vow of silence, stirring occasionally or, in the case of Clive Jenkins, tittering.[1]

Tom King was amiable, very different from the bleak and sardonic NT. I passed a note to Jim Galbraith:[2] 'The Czarina is dead'. I didn't put 'Carlyle', which I would have done for anyone else except Quinlan, as it might have offended him. He laughed, but not in a manner that made me think he understood.

Afterwards, we repaired to Tom's room. 'Well, that went quite well.' Plainly he sees himself as a great arbitrator. But there's nothing to arbitrate *about*.

Suddenly Len Murray appeared in the doorway, breathless and furtive. Was there a basis for an intimate contact team, two on either side, to propose agenda, sort out loose points, etc? He pretended he was anxious not to be caught in there. But it looked to me like a put-up job. They were on the run. Now they want to put in place fresh 'machinery'. Yes, yes, yes, he was told, and sent on his way.

We went down to the press conference. 'Industrial' correspondents are a scruffy lot. There wasn't a member of the Lobby to be seen. Tom was amiable but not, in my view, assertive enough.

Finally back in my office for a meeting with dear Angela Croft, with her very dark, almost gipsy dark, long hair, who was worrying about the EOC Press release and Lady Platt's misgivings. I was tired, and the subject was *de minimis*. I am so weak, I am easily distracted by pretty legs and I don't expect I made much sense.

Now I am in this train with the lovely West Country fields going by, and I would rather be in the Bustard[3] thundering on 'B' roads and stopping too often for ale.

Tomorrow two boxes will meet my train at Paddington and, because it is Friday, Jenny will have arranged to keep me in the office until very late.

---

[1] Bill Keys (Society of Graphical and Allied Trades), Len Murray (TUC General Secretary since 1973), Ken Gill (Amalgamated Union of Engineering Workers), Clive Jenkins (Association of Scientific, Technical and Managerial Staff).

[2] Jim Galbraith. Under-Secretary, Department of Employment Industrial Relations Division.

[3] Family name for an old Bentley sometimes used in the summer months (also referred to in other entries as 'the $4\frac{1}{2}$').

Department of Employment   *Thursday, 27 October*

I am in low water. A lot of little things are going wrong, and are irritating me.

First, I have got 'Willie's Eye'.[1] It makes me look awful. I was at a Number 10 reception with Jane last night, and the Lady said I looked 'tired'. Blast! I have to read so much, there's no reason why it shouldn't last for months.

Then, again, Max is missing.[2] He's been gone for days, nearly two weeks. I know the 'daws all go off and scavenge the harvest fields', he's done it before. But he should easily be back by now. Max carries a lot of my good luck with him.

I'm apprehensive as my role in this sodding Committee Stage[3] approaches. I can handle it. But the sheer work*load* on top of all the other drudgery will be unbearable.

November is always a bad month for me. On Wednesday night I was playing backgammon late at Brooks's and Bartosik started to annoy me. I leaned across the table and thumped him. I must say he took it in the most gentlemanly way, even though bleeding quite badly. But Maurice Lancaster was outraged, has reported me to the Committee.

People are gloating.

Saltwood   *Saturday, 5 November*

Ghastly night. The young people are staying, guaranteed (bless them) to give bad nights. The old bike rule is still in place – rightly – which means one gets only fitful slumber until they have checked in.[4]

At dinner James had rung, soft-spoken, to say he would be 'about (sic) midnight'. At one-ish the dogs started barking and our bedroom

---

[1] A rheumy condition (named after William Whitelaw) that afflicts the whites and the iris of politicians' eyes.

[2] Max was a tame jackdaw, who had been reared by the Clarks after falling from his nest as a chick, and returned to the wild. He came very regularly to the window for tit-bits, and did in fact live to a very great age.

[3] AC was lead Minister in the Committee Stage of the Trade Union Bill.

[4] From the days when James and Andrew rode motor-bikes (James nearly lost his leg in an accident). Always check in on your return.

door opened. Andrew. Looking beautiful, though with hair too long for a subaltern, even in the Cavalry. We chatted for a while. Just after two thirty James turned up – totally bland and matter of fact – said goodnight affectionately.

I had some difficulty falling asleep and woke with a start, convinced that lights had been left on. Stumbled out on to the landing, followed a trail of blazing light bulbs to – the Green Room, where James was calmly reading a book. It must have been nearly four o'clock. What can one do? I woke with the sparrows cheeping, but was still blearily in pyjamas when Matcham[1] arrived with the weekend box.

The box took nearly three hours, then Col turned up for a walk. The only way out of this sort of hell-sequence is to torture the body. I left him at the bottom of Gossie[2] and turned in a record time of 2.50, helped by the hard ground.

Then one of The Four Worst Things happened – I LOST TOM.[3] We flayed around on Gossie for about an hour, returned to the Castle – no sign; tried the farm – no sign; went back to Gossie with Jane. She is so observant, and I am always terrified that he might get caught in one of Felce's horrible fox snares – but no sign. At last, with the light failing, Anne phoned to say he had turned up and she had him in the kitchen at the farm.[4]

Whole day gone, nothing since a boiled egg at eight thirty. Ravenously, I stuffed on carbohydrates, sloshed down Indian tea.

Now I'm sitting in the tower office, contemplating a miserable and congested week. First for Questions on Tuesday, Second Reading of the TU Bill, Plymouth on Thursday, then *back* to Plymouth on Saturday for the wreath-laying at Remembrance, so no weekend at all. Another bad night in prospect, as the boys are going out to a firework party.

It all makes me feel so old. Reading last year's entries I realise how much I have aged just these last twelve months. I remember how quickly my father went off – although in his case there was no, as it were, environmental, reason. I saw Gunther Sachs on TV last night –

---

[1] The postman.
[2] A steep cliff of downland at Saltwood.
[3] The family Jack Russell terrier.
[4] Felce and Anne: a local farmer and his mother.

totally unrecognisable from his old clips when he was courting Bardot. Men are OK from thirty to forty-five; if they're careful they can stay about the same. After that it's an increasing struggle because of jowl and neck lines, even if the waist can be restrained. And the bruising of repeated sexual rejection starts to show in the eyes.

Hotel Amigo, Brussels   *Tuesday, 22 November*

I'm here for some kind of Employment sub-committee of the Council of Ministers. Grandish hotel in the old part of the town, block booked by UKREP.[1] Jenny is with me, but I don't even know the number of her room. I share the facilities with other, nameless Europeans. Most of them, it seems, and doubtless for historic reasons, appear to be from the EFTA countries. Breakfast in sepulchral gloom, tiny pats of recycled butter in solid foil nodules.

Last night dreary sub-social dinner with a junior(ish) FCO official and his bright little Scottish wife who 'kept the meal going' à la Heddle.[2] When we got back here there was a convivial hubbub in the foyer, laughter from the bar.

'Come and have a drink,' I said to Jenny.

'Why?'

'Oh, all right, don't then.'

Earlier she had been made cross. At the airport there was one of those machines that measure your pulse through your handgrip. 'Go on, try it.' She scored 81. 'Watch this.' (I have always had a very slow pulse.) The band was graded – normal range, high normal, some hypertension, see your doctor, etc. I held on, far beyond the prescribed time. Obstinately, the needle wouldn't budge from the far green quadrant, under 55, the category – ATHLETE.

'Pah!' she said.

A succession of meetings, but no possibility whatever of getting anything changed – not at my level anyway. Everything is fixed by officials in advance. Ministers shaking hands are just window dressing. But I can see that the French are loathsome, the Germans amiable – and serious.

---

[1] The permanent UK delegation at the EC in Brussels.
[2] Neighbours of the Clarks in Kent. Practitioners of the 'extended meal' theory.

Department of Employment   *Tuesday, 29 November*

Stale air, bad diet. I have barely got the energy even to do yoga.

Anton Dolin is dead.[1] Another link with the carefree days of my flowering youth. Monte Carlo, the Beausoleil. If only one could return.

Dolin was the clipped, *un*-camp sort of homosexual. He outlasted – just – John Gilpin,[2] his golden tart and great love, who died some weeks ago after his own brief marriage to a Grimaldi bad egg. I am always sad when I think of my days with the Festival Ballet. Pam was such a dear girl, she is one of the very few I feel guilt about, along with that sweet child at the Gulf Breeze.[3] Because, in their own ways, most women are as lecherous and predatory as men, they just do it differently. It's the Thurber Sex War.

Later

Just back from a meeting with S of S, to discuss possible Government amendments to the Employment Bill at which I (a) dropped off, and (b) made one of those remarks which shows one understands nothing. Can't be good, as I am handling it 'upstairs'[4] starting next week.

I feel weary. My dilemma is, if I stay on I waste the substance; if I return to the estates can I even rebuild any longer? And even if I do, what's it in aid of?

---

[1] Anton Dolin, dancer and choreographer, who began with Diaghilev in 1923. Organised the Festival Ballet, 1950. Knighted, 1981.

[2] John Gilpin, dancer. Originally with Ballet Rambert. Festival Ballet, 1950–60.

[3] AC worked a bell-hop at the Gulf Breeze Hotel, outside Sarasota, in 1950.

[4] In Standing Committee.

Department of Employment   *Thursday, 8 December*

I have only just found time to write up my ghastly experiences last Tuesday.

Jenny had been going on and on about the day I started in Committee, etc., was I fully prepared, did I want further briefing, etc.

'No no, I'll be quite all right, all I have to do is read out notes which officials pass me, yes, yes.'

But, actually, I was a little uneasy because I remember that the last time she had fussed like this was with very good reason – before the Equal Ops order.

'You've never *dunn* anything in Committee have you?'

'Of course not, how could I have?'

'Have you ever attended a Committee?'

'Not really.'

'Have you ever read a Hansard of Committee proceedings?'

'No, have you?'

'Yes.'

'OK then, what happens, what's it like?'

'Batty. Komm-pletely batty.'

In a way this cheered me up. But it was a bloody nuisance because it was going to take the whole morning from ten o'clock until one, and I had to start answering Questions in the Chamber at two thirty. Also the sapping up time had been curtailed by Peter Morrison calling a Ministers' meeting for 'nine-ish'. Les rang them twice, but they were still 'getting ready'. When finally I got in they were all sitting round, room full of cigarette smoke (i.e. Morrison must have smoked at least one) and *coffee cups empty*. Nobody said anything.

Afterwards I made a row with Barnaby[1] and that pasty round-shouldered maiden whom I discovered is called Di. 'Why wasn't I told in time? I'm not a dilettante. I get here before all the other Ministers.'

Naturally my colleagues, delighted, just thought I'd come in late.

Labour has a very tough team. Little John Smith, rotund, bespectacled, Edinburgh lawyer. Been around for ages. Their Whip is John Evans, AEU, tough, thick. Two from the far Left; a nasty young one called Fatchett, and a nasty (the *nastiest*) old one – Mikardo. And two

---

[1] Head of the Secretary of State's Private Office.

bright boys called Brown and Blair. Also two chunks of old heavy metal, Frank Haynes and Mick Martin.[1]

I was on my own. Our team are under express instructions not to open their mouths. Tom King never comes in, although, crampingly, he had appeared in that morning to 'see me started'. Little Gummer isn't allowed to do anything affecting 'contributions' as he's Party Chairman. (I don't follow this rule.) And of course it's nothing to do with Peter at all and he isn't even a member of the Committee.

Smith finished winding up, and I rose.

I had made some rough notes, intention being to be smooth, conciliatory, just 'get the Bill through'.

Huh! I got into difficulties immediately. They were bobbing up all over the place, asking impossible, spastic, questions of detail – most of them, as far as I could make out, to do with the fucking *Rule Book*. (I should have realised that this is a complete minefield. That's all the Unions are really bothered by, lazy sods. Work-to-Rule, all that.)

The cribs were scrabblingly written out by officials, seated in an anxious row, at right angles to us, beside the 'Chair' (in this case that very splendid fellow John Wells, the MP for Maidstone). TK passed them up to me, thick and fast, with a resigned expression on his face. I couldn't read many, because they had been written out so urgently. Anyway, if you don't understand the question, how can you understand the answer? But when I could read something I recognised passages from the original brief that I had found so muddling or, in Jenny's phrase 'batty', that I had avoided them. Gah!

'We've got a right one 'ere,' Mikardo kept saying in his special plummy *artisan's* voice.

Gummer and TK whispered unhappily to each other, 'He's not up to it, what are we going to do?' – all that.

For two pins I'd have bolted from the room, driven down to Jane and the hens, never left the walls again.

---

[1] John Smith (MP for Lanarkshire North since 1970), John Evans (MP for St Helens since the 1983 Election), Derek Fatchett (MP for Leeds Central since the 1983 Election), Ian Mikardo (MP since 1945, currently for Tower Hamlets), Gordon Brown (MP for Dunfermline East since the 1983 Election), Tony Blair (MP for Sedgefield since the 1983 Election), Frank Haynes (MP for Ashfield since 1979) and Mick Martin (MP for Glasgow, Springburn since 1979).

Department of Employment   *Wednesday, 14 December*

Things were slowly improving in Committee. I am managing to impose acceptance of my own style, getting (both sides) to laugh occasionally. It is a totally different ambience, and requires an adapted technique, to the floor of the Chamber.

For a start (good) there are never any press there, so gaffes and cock-ups go unreported. The Official Report is printed late, and by the time it's out nobody bothers. But there is a kind of *tenu* to the whole thing, and if one ignores this one offends the Committee's corporate *amour propre*. There's always the risk, too, of an adverse report by the Whips, although in the main they're not concerned with 'performance', only with getting the business through smoothly. As for the esteem of colleagues, they're busy doing their constituency correspondence, and it needs a pretty monumental disturbance to attract their attention.

But (bad) there is this infuriating convention that Members can get up and down as often as they want. Unlike the Chamber, where you don't *have* to give way, in a Committee there has to be a very good reason – repetitious filibustering being really the only one which is acceptable – to refuse.

This afternoon I got completely tied up, with full brain seizure. Batty subclause (6) full of lawyers' gibberish. '*Nothing* which is done . . . shall affect *anything* . . . , etc.' I looked round early on for Leigh[1] to help me. He wasn't there! Total panic. An unknown civil servant standing in for him supplied illegible and inadequate notes.

I can't stand much more of this. And yet I've got to do the whole of Part III (Financial Contributions), on my own, because little Gummer is barred, and TK is too 'busy' (i.e. idle) to show up.

This morning I woke at three a.m. and couldn't get back to sleep. Someone (I can't recall who) had mentioned John Davies.[2] Wasn't his brain tumour caused *entirely* by overwork? I am vulnerable. This *insupportable* load of absorption which presses. The other side now

---

[1] Leigh Lewis, a Principal at the Department of Employment, who greatly assisted AC with the Bill.

[2] John Davies had been Director-General, Confederation of British Industry, before becoming an MP in 1970. He served under both Heath (in government) and Thatcher (in opposition). He died in 1979.

realise that any amendment can catch me out, have spotted me as the weak link in the array.

Thank God there are the Christmas hols coming up before it gets too frightful. But there are so many chores to do. I must stop now, to go over before the House 'Shop' shuts and buy ten tons of whisky, port, sherry and disgusting cigarettes for my own claimants. Outgoings, outgoings, all the time outgoings.

Later

I looked in on Jonathan Aitken's party. Didn't stay long. Too crowded. Tessa Kennedy[1] was there, totally unchanged in twenty-five years, i.e. good-looking, but clipped and guttural.

A Dudley woman said, 'Whatever you do, don't sell pictures.'[2] Thanks.

Somewhat disconsolate, I strolled back to the House and ran into Cecil on the Green. We had a long talk. I said it was a disaster, the whole thing. He would have been Prime Minister. Yes, he admitted, all this he knew privately. He was the Lady's own choice, she had been grooming him, introducing him to the Royals – especially the Prince of Wales. He was going to the Foreign Office, would have really sorted it out, shifted it from 'diplomacy' to trade promotion. The switch could then have happened when the time was ripe, certainly no later than her tenth anniversary.

Was he, could he come back? Yes. Yes, if she wants me.

But he had to pine in the wilderness for some little time. Colleagues were determined to keep him out. Of course they are, I thought. 'Oh no, surely not. Who?'

Wakeham[3] was being unbelievable. The biggest leaker known to man, 'he'd even brief journalists *in the street* on the way back from Cabinet.' Cecil could never trust Gummer. Sanctimonious little creep. And Cecil suspected that Willie was against him also.

---

[1] Mrs Kennedy had for a short while been married to Dominic Elwes, an old friend of AC and Jane Clark.

[2] AC was at that time engaged in deep family consultations as to which pictures in Lord Clark's collection should be sold to pay estate duty.

[3] John Wakeham, MP for Colchester South and Maldon since the Election (Maldon 1974–83). Chief Whip.

'Plus all the mediocrities,' I said, 'like Fowler,[1] who are scared you'll show them up. But Tebbit?'

Even Norman, he wasn't so sure. (Nor am I, because with Cecil out of the way Norman *has* to be the candidate of the Right). 'He phoned me, said we were three; now we're down to two.'

Cecil said that the Prime Minister was much tougher than anyone realised. She was getting stroppy letters from Colonel Keays, all kinds of threat, never turned a hair. But once she decided to chop him, that was it.

Cecil said he could never see the child. But what, I asked, if it was a son? He didn't reply. You would have to embrace it. You would have to go down on your knees to Ann, and ask for permission.

He drew the conversation to a close and we parted.

What a waste. He is a good man, Cecil. Underrated just because he is handsome. But he has come the whole way on his own. And once he had actually *got* there, no longer had to dissimulate, I think he would have been importantly good.

Saltwood   *Friday, 16 December*

I had a meeting with Ian. He tells me that he is working his way back in with the Prime Minister. She can't do without him, and he goes round to Number 10 very late, when all her engagements are over, sometimes even when she gets back from an official dinner, and they go upstairs to the flat and drink whisky.

She has no one to confide in. Not to confide in *personally* that is, although I think she is probably pretty candid on policy matters with Willie.

Alison is useless. Saintly, but useless. You need someone with guile, patience, an easy fluent manner of concealing the truth but drawing it out from others in that job. It is extraordinary how from time to time one does get people who have been through Brigade Squad, taken their commission and served, seen all human depravity as only one can at Eton and in the Household, and yet go all naive

---

[1] Norman Fowler, MP for Sutton Coldfield since 1974 (Nottingham South 1970–4). Secretary of State for Social Services. (AC had a low opinion of Fowler (see 1 February 1991).)

and Godwatch. The Runcible[1] is another – and he actually saw action.

Apparently (but some allowance must be made for Ian's jealousy and also for his own impossibly high standards of attendance) Alison is also a wee bit neglectful of his timing, comes in around nine a.m. and tends to disappear in the evenings, only emerging for the ten o'clock vote. Does he attend the Party Committees? Apparently not regularly, except the '22.

How to correct this? Not simply by a change of incumbent. She needed something stronger, more permanent. Something on the lines of a Prime Minister's Department, with a Lord Privy Seal (or some such) sitting at Cabinet, and a couple of PPSs, the senior of whom would be a Minister of State. That's, Ian strongly implied, where I (whoopee) came into it.

The more I think this over, the more delicious it seems. Escape on magic wings, attached Mercury-like to my golden feet, from the hatefulness of Caxton House, the fire-and-water of Stage III of the Employment Bill, and to land with one bound into the very centrum, the vortex, of Power. And working closely with my oldest friend, someone who knows all my strengths (and weaknesses), who thinks alike on almost every issue.

He is seeing the Lady over Christmas at Chequers and will explore the idea further.

Saltwood   *Friday, 23 December*

Evening of the first day of the Christmas hols.

I don't seem to have done anything except get rid of a lot of cash filling all the cars with petrol. And cash is so scarce over Christmas. Again and again one goes down to the bank to draw, always the last cheque until the New Year.

At tea time I wanted pliers. I could not find pliers. Nowhere in this whole fucking place, with its seventeen outhouses, garages, sheds, eighteen vehicles. After stealing tool kits from every car I've sold on over the last twenty-five years – could I find pliers?

---

[1] Robert Runcie, Archbishop of Canterbury since 1980. Served in the Scots Guards in World War II and was awarded the MC.

I was screaming frail. I ransacked the china room, where I kept my most precious things. My new red vintage tool locker was empty, except for a lot of useless stuff for an Austin Heavy Twenty. Why? I am surrounded by unreliables.

I've done practically no shopping. How could I? When? Yet tomorrow is Christmas Eve.

As for the Dept, I never want to go through its doors again. Total shit-heap, bored blue. Strained and befuddled by all the paper work. Fuck them.

Fortunately, I'm dining with Ian on Wednesday next. I hope he gives me a boost.

Letter to Ian Gow   *Saltwood Castle*
                                                                        Hythe

                                                             December 27th, 1983

My Dear Ian

As always, a lovely evening. I can't tell you how much it lightens the cares, and the frustrations of our calling to be able to discuss everything so freely, and in such good humour and mutual accord.

I don't usually refer to the substance of what we talk about – but I must urge you to get the Prime Minister's dept promulgated as soon as possible, with yourself at its head and sitting at (preferably in) Cabinet. There is a long haul ahead, and these things are better done at moments of tranquillity rather than when the need urgently presses.

Complementary to this, I couldn't make out whether you were sounding me on taking MA's post. Of course I would jump at it, all the more so for having first experienced the privilege of a spell in Government. But who am I to say what I will, or will not do? To paraphrase a more sinister admonition:

La Signora comanda, il piccino va ..e fa!

Both these changes shall take place as soon as possible – certainly before the House reassembles on 16 Jan.

                                                        Yours affectionately,
                                                                        Alan

Saltwood   *Saturday, 31 December*

New Year's Eve. I *always* go to bed early on New Year's Eve, and
sleep the better for thinking of all those silly sods compulsorily 'seeing
it in', drinking and driving.

Christmas was jolly. Jane and James had their ritual row, but got it
over quite early on. Col was here, and there was much discussion of
my father's estate, the snail's pace at which settlement with the
Revenue proceeds, 'Mr Thom' as a Double Agent.[1]

At present he (Thom) is fussing about the Maillol bust of Renoir,
why are there conflicting valuations, where is it, wouldn't it be better
if the bank held it for 'safe-keeping', etc.

'It's broken.'

'Uh?'

'Smashed.'

'The Revenue will want to see the pieces.'

'I've thrown them away.'

No, Col suggested, show Thom a broken bit of flower-pot; the
Revenue won't know the difference. Pleasing.

Last night I drank a lot of Sauvignon and had a strange dream.
The Table Office had refused one of my Questions because 'by the
time this comes up, you won't be an MP'. I realised that I had been
concentrating on the 'new possibility' (Folkestone?) and had 'missed
the nomination' for Plymouth.[2] I was crying as I explained to Jane (in
a hotel bedroom, was it Blackpool?) that I was now *out*. But twice I
woke, and realised that it wasn't true, and was delighted. What does
this portend? At dinner on Wednesday there was no doubt that Ian
was sounding me on the possibility of taking Alison's place. But I got
the impression that the 'large solution' had grown less likely.

---

[1] Mr B.D. Thom, Manager of the Clydesdale Bank Trustee Department. Lord Clark's
estate occupied the family attention for much of 1983–4.

[2] The previous year AC had been actually considering offering himself to the
Folkestone Association to take the place of the retiring MP, Albert Costain.

1984

1984

Two boxes arrived this morning, stuffed with PO cases and what officials call 'reading'. First thing, always, on top of all the folders are the grey sheets of diary pages. My heart sank as I looked at the stuffed days, the names of dreary and supercilious civil servants who will (never singly) be attending. I've got three months of this ahead of me, without a break.

At dinner the other night Peter [Morrison], who is a workaholic (not so difficult if you're an unhappy bachelor living on whisky) showed Ian and me, with great pride, his diary card for the day following. Every single minute, from 8.45 a.m. onwards, was filled with 'engagements'.

'Look,' he said. 'How's that for a diary?'

Ian, unexpectedly and greatly to his credit, said, 'If my Private Office produced a schedule like that I'd sack the whole lot, immediately.'

After Peter had gone, Ian and I returned to the subject, which is occupying a lot of my thinking time at present, of how to reconstruct the Prime Minister's Office. He *must* push the Lady a bit on this. Her natural caution will cause her to delay otherwise, and the opportunity will recede. I must write to him on the weekend with my considered thoughts.[1] How delicious if I can bring this off!

Back in the House, the Club, but immensely strengthened by experience as a Minister, and yet commanding attention wherever I am seen – tea, smoking or committee room.

Letter to Ian Gow   *Saltwood Castle*

                                                              January 15th, 1984

Dear Ian

I write with regard to the matters we have been discussing. I believe them to be urgent and I want to commit some thoughts to paper before our heads go back into the sand of our Departments (there are three boxes in the house this weekend!).

---

[1] Text of letter 15 Jan below.

I start with the premise that the Prime Minister is *everything*: what
diminishes or threatens her diminishes or threatens the country – just
as the country is itself enhanced by whatever does so for her authority
and freedom.

She must have a department of her own. Small – as it were a floor
of the Cabinet Office. The Paymaster General does not exist at the
moment: he should be re-born, and much departmental paper 'copied'
to him. (If necessary, some additional responsibility should be attached
to him for presentational reasons.)

It is an awkward thing to say, other than to those one can trust,
but policies are neither determined or evolved on a simple assessment
of National, or even Party, interest. Personal motives – ambition,
mischief making, a view to possible obligations and opportunities in
the future, sometimes raw vindictiveness – all come into it. The Prime
Minister needs someone who can provide early warning, counsel *and
conduct lightning*.

One must never forget that the mob is always ready and its leaders
are in the Senate. I so well recall those early very anxious days of the
Falklands crisis when you could not attend a Party committee without
one or other of the predictable front-men making their coded statements, whose real purpose was to prepare the way for a coup if events
should lead to humiliation or disaster. To this day, I remember vividly
the Chairman of the Select Committee on Defence [Timothy Kitson]
hanging about the Tea Room Corridor, telling anyone he could
waylay that *Hermes* had propeller shaft trouble; that *Invincible* had sailed
without her electronics, etc, etc.

The question of the PPS is complementary to this. When you
held that job, your knowledge of the Parliamentary Party was such
that you could predict the reaction of practically every Member to
any given aspect of policy. The collation of Intelligence both through
social contact, committees, and Prime Minister's Questions was more
subtle than the Whips' Office and its reflexes faster. But now there
are over a hundred new Members, the first glow of their new status
has worn off. They want recognition (in every sense) and are a prey
to blandishments from many different quarters.

I cite an example of how these two requirements might interact
in the next 12 to 18 months. Michael[1] will have to cut defence

---

[1] Michael Heseltine, MP for Henley since 1974 (Tavistock 1966–74). Defence
Secretary since the 1983 Election.

spending by at least £2bn in the lifetime of the Parliament (as you know, I think it could be done by as much as £4bn quite safely). If he chooses to go to the stake on this and we have not made pre-emptive arrangements, he will greatly enlarge his own franchise. He picks up the Wet ticket at will. All of a sudden he will be able to bid for the Union Jack buffs also.

We can't tell what the future holds and it would be less than prudent not to do what one can to forearm against surprise.

Alan

House of Commons   *Wednesday, 18 January*

The office have found a new way of keeping me utterly exhausted. My time, already deeply curtailed by the demands of the Standing Committee, is being copiously allocated to an endless series of 'Fit for Work' presentations.

Like all Whitehall-speak, the term does not mean what first it would appear to. It is an 'Award' given, as far as I can see, to the (many) firms who 'imaginatively' overfill their statutory quota of disabled employees.

Joan drives me, accompanied by at least two officials, at breakneck speed to addresses in 'the Home Counties', or I take InterCity trains.

One mustn't be ungracious. It's a day off for many of the staff, who gather to peep and peer; there is a bad buffet, and someone who hopes that it may result at some future date in their 'recognition'. Etched with fatigue, compounded by boredom, I make the presentation, and off I go. Minimum three working hours poorer. Back at the Department in the late afternoon I read and sign till supper, then the ordeal of the Standing Committee until after midnight.

I must get out of this. I had a word with Ronnie Butt[1] about machinery-of-Govt difficulties, tried to coax him toward suggesting a 'Prime Minister's Office'. I think he took the bait. Of course I've

---

[1] Ronald Butt, political columnist on *The Times*.

got no control of the *form* in which he might put this in his article –
even supposing he does – but the importance of 'constructive leaking'
is to condition minds.

Plymouth-Paddington train   *Wednesday, 25 January*

On the way back from another of these sodding Award ceremonies.

Yesterday was one of *incredible* pressure; head-clutching. Standing
Committee all morning, and boss-eyed with fatigue as we were kept
up until well after midnight on Monday. (This for no reason at all,
pure Whips' incompetence; although just as likely it's deliberate, like
a sadistic battalion CO periodically – when the weather is bad –
ordering a compulsory five-mile run.)

I *loathe* Committee. I still get rattled even though, technically, I
know the stuff. Yet little Gummer sails along by GABBLING. He
gabbles away, and *they* don't understand *him*. While I speak slowly,
and try and give rational answers, applying my mind to questions
which are repetitious, badly constructed and ill-intentioned. It's like
bad 'discussion-therapy' in a loony-bin.

Things were going quite well this morning until I had a slight
skid, revealing that I didn't know what GMBATU[1] stood for. Dennis
Skinner (you've got to hand it to him, he's so quick on the ball) raised
it at Questions on the floor, later. I affected blandness.

In the meantime, Ronnie Butt has run his article, almost going
too far, running the whole concept of a Paymaster General, etc. Refers
to the concept coming 'from impeccably loyal sources'. This might
alarm IG. 'Al not reliable, not fully secure, better think again.' This
close, one can't tell.

Saltwood   *Saturday, 18 February*

The daylight is already getting longer.

This evening I shut up the hens, meandered around the Outer

---

[1] GMBATU: General, Municipal, Boilermakers and Allied Trades Union.

Bailey and down to the Cloisters. I sat for some little while in the 2CV, which we use so seldom now, and my mind wandered back to when we bought it in Lyons in 1964. We whirred merrily down to the Bastide,[1] and on to St Tropez, Fernandez and Cannes.

Jane flew off to see her mother in Spain. I had the hots for the red-haired telephone girl, but was so nervous for Jane's safe arrival in Malaga that I was incapable. Nostalgic evocations.

Yesterday I travelled down by train, and a plump young lady came into my compartment at Waterloo. She was not wearing a bra, and her delightful globes bounced prominently, but happily, under a rope-knitted jersey, as the new coach/old chassis train joggled its way over the many points and junctions.

I gave her a huge grin, couldn't help it. After a bit I moved over and sat beside her. She was adorable. Am I crazy? Death wish? Above us in the luggage rack the Red Box gleamed like a beacon. She works as a shop assistant in Folkestone.

Department of Employment   *Thursday, 29 March*

I was in Peter Morrison's room early. Out of the blue he told me that my suggestions for reforming the Lady's Private Office would in all probability be put into effect over Easter. But who was going to be put in charge? None other, or so he claimed, than David Young.[2]

This is appalling. I hardly know the man. But from what I've seen he's simply a rather grand H.R. Owen, the big Rolls-Royce dealers' salesman. I got to know the type well when I was working as a runner in Warren Street just after the war. Very much *not* one of the 'Club'.

Worse was to come. Peter told me that he was going to have a Red Box, Minister of State rank, and '*operate from the Lords*'. It is virtually signed up, as Peter has to find a replacement as head of MSC. The co-ordinating structure at Number 10 will be promulgated during the Easter recess. I said I was not too keen on the idea. The Party

---

[1] Home near Apt of Hiram Winterbotham, a friend of AC since his school days.
[2] David Young, property developer, director of the Centre for Policy Studies, 1979–82. Currently Chairman of the Manpower Services Commission and a Special Adviser to the Prime Minister.

never likes outsiders getting high ministerial rank without going through the mill.

This threatens to be the end of an era in more senses than one. It finally writes off Ian's chances of getting back to the epicentre of power, as well as any role for me in that scheme of things. I left early for lunch and tipped him off using one of the lobby phones. As I would have expected Ian was businesslike, showed no emotion. But he must have felt shattered. He said, as the appointment was so imminent there was nothing that could be done to alter it. That's right, I told him.

But I determine to have one try. There is only one journalist influential enough to make an effective scene about this if he minded to do so, and that is Peter Riddell of the *FT*.[1] He is well informed about all three Parties and writes with great insight.

But he might approve. Supposing he likes DY? I contemplated leaking the story to him, and made an assignment to speak to him in the Lords' corridor. Then I got cold feet; too easily traced.

Almost immediately afterwards a brilliant idea, my old friend and standby for many a dirty trick, Jonathan Aitken. I told him the problem. He was very understanding, got the point at once, and promised that he would attend to it immediately.

House of Commons   *Friday, 30 March*

The fish has taken! A critical account, on the *front page* of the *FT*, setting out the Prime Minister's intentions, her decision to appoint David Young, the rank intended for him, etc., plus a beautifully restrained piece of comment about 'reservations' in the Party concerning DY's 'controversial past' in property development, etc.

It is very late, but might just do the trick,[2] partly because it is a leak of the intention, partly because it is couched in such distinguished, though disapproving language.

---

[1] Peter Riddell, Political Editor of the *Financial Times*.
[2] David Young's appointment was, in fact, deferred until the autumn. As subsequent diary entries show, AC's initial assessment of his qualities was entirely at fault and the two did become personal friends as well as allies in politics.

Department of Employment   *Tuesday, 3 April*

Last night, at last, the closing stages of the TU Bill, Report, on the floor of the House.

I had been nervous all day as we are resisting the Labour new Clause 4, on 'Political Objects', their *chef d'oeuvre*, and I expected trouble. But when it came, it was easy. The Whips wanted my speech foreshortened (for some obscure business reason of their own) and this gave me the excuse to avoid 'giving way'.

Even so, plenty of people tried to intervene, and the House almost got restive. I am still more constrained than I ought to be by the exposed *feel* of standing at the Box, being verbally jostled. I prefer to extemporise, but was forced into reading from the brief more than I like.

For TK's speech the PM came in. She sat next to me (first time ever) and, like Chips and 'Neville', I radiated protective feelings – and, indeed, feelings of another kind(s). She has very small feet and attractive – not bony – ankles in the 1940 style. (Julian Amery[1] will nod his head sagely, and say in a gruff voice, 'There's blood there, you know, no doubt about it, there's blood.'[2] And I see what he means.)

The Prime Minister's foot twisted and turned *the entire time* although her eyes were closed, and her head nodded at intervals. The back of her hair is perfect, almost identical to previous days. It can't be a full wig, as the front is clearly her own. But I suspect it is a 'chignon'.

We engaged in desultory conversation, though without warmth on her side. At one point she rummaged in her bag and purse.

'Can I get you anything?'

'No,' she said, in tones of surprise. 'No.'

At the vote I walked with her into the lobby, and told her I was dining on Sunday with Jeane Kirkpatrick.[3] 'Oh are you? Where? She's coming to see me that evening.'

---

[1] Julian Amery, MP for Brighton Pavilion since 1969 (Preston, 1950–66). Married to Catherine, daughter of Harold Macmillan. Served in the governments of Macmillan, Douglas-Home and Heath.

[2] 'Blood'/Breeding. The upper classes at one point (before the cause became hopeless) tried to appropriate Mrs Thatcher by spreading the rumour that her mother had dallied with Christopher Cust, a notorious *coureur* on the northern Great House circuit, or more bizarrely, with the 10th Duke of Grafton.

[3] Jeane Kirkpatrick, academic, senior member of the State Department and US Ambassador to United Nations under Reagan.

She's on the ball about everything, in spite of all her worries – the miners, the 'machinery of Govt', Carol (a sad, distant piece in today's papers), Mark (must be a source of anxiety).

Yet she is *not* forthcoming to me. Distantly abandoned me in the lobby on entering, and started talking to Dykes,[1] of all people. She used to be so friendly when we were in Opposition. Does she disapprove of my 'laid-back' style (today's *Telegraph*)? Or are people making trouble?

Alison never escorts her the way Ian used to. Ian did it so beautifully, just so that she never seemed alone, abandoned that is, but always accessible. She still needs him and, let us hope, me.

House of Commons   *Monday, 9 April*

I drove up on Sunday evening in the SS 100. Should have been great fun, but the wrong side of Swanley the clutch went and I had to go the whole way through South London clutchless, which meant switching off the engine at red lights then doing Le Mans button starts in bottom gear when they changed to green. Tiring. And 'hairy'.

Joan picked me up at New Palace Yd, took me to Ed Streator's for the Kirkpatrick dinner.

I was curious to meet this Anglophobe harridan. She, and a tall, albino official at the State Department called Enders (whom Willie used to call 'the White Rabbit') were adamantly, subversively pro-Galtieri during the Falklands crisis. Even up to the end she was urging Reagan to put pressure on the Prime Minister to allow the Argentine army to leave the Islands 'bearing arms' (thus allowing a kind of 'heroically these men fought the whole British Navy to a standstill' propaganda myth to arise), which might just, I suppose, have saved the General's bacon domestically. The line is, she's so clever, she's an academic really, all that shit. But where was she? At intervals Ed would withdraw, then return looking uneasy. 'She's so tired. She's desperately tired, you know ... '

Finally she appeared, a mixture between Irene Worth and Eleanor Roosevelt. Immediately began 'putting it away'. Halfway through the

---

[1] Hugh Dykes, stockbroker. MP for Harrow East since 1970.

meal, as is Ed's custom, general conversation ceased and the honoured guest delivered a monologue, invited (reluctantly) questions.

Odious, totally stalinist, humourless. Trotted out the Party line, consequential sentences, no rationale at all. Shades of 'Miss Newman',[1] loathsome.

Department of Employment   *Tuesday, 10 April*

I was in vile mood this morning, even on arrival. I had done a lot of washing-up, drying, wiping, etc., at Albany, and I always find this enervating. I do it so badly and so slowly. For someone as great and gifted as me it is the *most* uneconomic possible use of time.

Then, triumphantly 'marked up', a page of Mediascan[2] was pushed under my nose. *Impending sackings* (!!). Named were Arthur Cockfield,[3] David Mitchell,[4] Bob Dunn, John Butcher[5] and myself. Flushed and shocked I became.

Either way it's a bore

(a) that anyone should believe that I am a candidate

(b) it becomes self-feeding (journalists draw from each other)

(c) a plant from Ingham and Downing St

As long ago as 6 February I wrote in my Day Diary, on the space for 23 April (when we come back from the Easter break) 'Am I free today?' But now that I am actually faced with the prospect of being dropped as – allegedly – no good, I don't like it. All the gabblers are of course immune. As always, AS ALWAYS, Heseltine and that podgy life-insurance-risk Kenneth Clarke[6] are approvingly tipped. Appar-

---

[1] Miss Elizabeth Newman, the Clarks' governess during the school holidays.

[2] Mediascan: photocopied digest of all references to the Department and its personnel in the day's press.

[3] Arthur Cockfield (Life Peer, 1978). Businessman (Boots), made Chairman of the Price Commission (1973–7). Brought into Government in 1979. Trade Secretary, 1982–3, currently Chancellor of the Duchy of Lancaster.

[4] David Mitchell, MP for Hampshire North-West since 1983 (Basingstoke, 1964–83). Currently Parliamentary Under-Secretary of State at Ministry of Transport.

[5] John Butcher, MP for Coventry South-West since 1979. Currently Parliamentary Under-Secretary at Trade.

[6] Kenneth Clarke, MP for Rushcliffe since 1970. Currently Minister of State, Department of Health and Social Security.

ently (this is what makes me think there is a bit of Ingham in it) the changes will not take place at Easter, but during the Whitsun break. Or (much worse) in September, after a summer of travail and misery.

I am going on *Question Time* in a couple of days. Might gallop.

Albany   *Wednesday, 11 April*

Today has been vilely full. Went early to Leicester after a late, late vote and impossible to drowse in the train as officials were watching me beadily in case (their excuse) anything in the brief 'needed explaining'. I dropped off, as good as, several times during monologues at the various offices. Heavy-lidded, I must have looked.

There was a demo by the unemployed. Uglyish mood, they created to 'rock the car' (the one thing of which civil servants are absolutely terrified). Police useless, as always, like Hindus defending a trainload of Muslims. One puzzled constable, a 'trainee' and a pi-faced young WPC.

'I must speak to them.'

'No, no, Minister, please don't try. Minister, you must not get out of the car. Please, Minister.'

Wretched people, they were angry, but taken aback by my actually dismounting to listen. Some SWP yobs tried to get a chant going, but the others really wanted to air their grievances. One man, quite articulate, looked dreadfully thin and ill. He had a nice brindle greyhound on a leash, but it looked miserable too.

Gravely I listened. At intervals I asked *them* questions. I told them that if there was no 'demand' no one could afford to pay them to make things. They quietened down. But that's a glib point really. It's foul, such a waste.

Uncomfortable, I thought what Soames[1] and I can spend between us on a single meal at Wiltons.

---

[1] Nicholas Soames, MP for Crawley since 1983.

Later
House of Commons

I had intended to stay alcohol-free in the run-up to *Question Time* tomorrow evening. But my old friend[1] asked me along to his rooms for white wine.

I partook of very little indeed, and our talk rambled. His room has been redecorated, *un*successfully. Bathroom Pugin instead of the lovely heavy old red paper and curtains. (What happened to them, I wonder?)

He told me he was thinking of retiring (he's sixty). He'd sat in that chair for the last twenty-nine years, and was still slim and 'active', though hair thin wisps, and whitey-grey.

I had thought of bringing Soames round and looked for him in the smoking room but – fortunately, as it turned out – without success. The generations would not have mixed.

Yet I still think of myself as multi-generational. Today I saw several pretty blondes, all clones with lovely grey eyes and clear freckly skin – the BBC girl, the one on Nottingham station, the new waitress in the dining room – they could all tell I was 'interested', but smiled nonetheless.

It seems only a few years ago, say three, that the Todd Buick[2] was rumbling over the cobbles in Merton Street. Yet there are other things that seem distant by an eternity.

Albany, 7.40 a.m.   *Friday, 13 April*

A spot of turbulence.

Yesterday afternoon the car was waiting for me in New Palace Yard, to put me on the train for Bristol and *Question Time.* I just thought I'd pop up to the Chamber and listen to the Navy Missile

---

[1] A term used by AC to describe any single individual in his own close circle. In this case Euan Graham, a Clerk in the Judicial Office of the House of Lords.

[2] The Buick 'Roadmaster' owned by an American friend of AC, Burt Todd, who was up at Oxford at the same time. AC, and several others would borrow it for 'courting'.

announcement, which came up on the annunciator as I was leaving the Members' cloakroom.

The moment I saw it was being done by Geoffrey Pattie[1] I knew we (the British kit) had lost.[2] If it had been good news with a bit of Union Jack PR potential, Heseltine would have taken it. Geoffrey is good at the box. Knows his stuff and pretty unflappable. But it was bad news. One more domestic industrial capability diminished, still further reliance on the US inventory. I ran downstairs without waiting for the Opposition response and just caught the train.

Robin was *en retraite* for some reason and his place was filled by Sue Lawley.[3]

Although (perhaps because) I get on well with Barbara and Liz[4] we did not 'hit it off'. The worst possible basis for a relationship – she, an 'attractive woman', spotted at once that I have lecherous tendencies, but did not actually fancy her. She thought to put me in my place in her introduction by saying, '*He* went into politics because he thought it would make him more attractive.'

Ugh! She was paraphrasing some crack I'd made ages ago round Malcolm Muggeridge's dissertation on the aphrodisiac effect of money, 'Power is money in pasteurised form.' Embarrassment.

About halfway through came the question (must have been planted as the news only broke after the audience had started assembling) on the lines of 'does the Panel think it right that we should always be preferring American weapon systems to British ones'.

I didn't nibble at the bait. I swallowed, and most of the line, the float, the rod, the fisherman's waders, the lot. Sod it, I knew as much about this subject as anyone, a bad decision had been made – say so.

I expounded on the unwisdom of becoming more and more dependent on the Americans, the shrinkage of our own industrial capacity and (most recklessly and mischievously in answer to a supplementary) that 'it takes a very strong Secretary of State to resist

---

[1] Geoffrey Pattie, MP for Chertsey and Walton since 1974. Currently Minister for Defence Procurement.

[2] The Ministry of Defence had decided to purchase the American surface to surface anti-submarine missile 'Harpoon' in preference to 'Sea Eagle' which had been tendered by British Aerospace.

[3] Sir Robin Day, renowned interviewer and chairman of BBC TV's *Question Time*. Sue Lawley was currently a presenter of BBC TV's *Nine O'Clock News*.

[4] Barbara Maxwell and Liz Elton, BBC production team for *Question Time*.

recommendations from civil servants even though these are often quite narrowly founded'.

Sue Lawley, still bitchlike, said, 'Well, since the Minister isn't prepared to defend his own Government, is there anyone in the room who is?'

Afterwards, in the hospitality lounge, there was a slight kind of mouths-agape atmosphere. Barbara said something on the 'Gosh, that was a pretty racy answer' lines. But I thought little more of it on the return journey, being more apprehensive of the dear old boy charged with driving me back down the M4 in a hot, silent Granada. Terrible lurching swerves as, all too often, he 'nodded off'.

My first warning was from Tip who, night owl that he is, was hanging around the porter's lodge when I got back. He'd seen the programme. He's such a good mimic. But I became uneasy. 'Surely my answer on Sea Eagle was all right, wasn't it?'

He thought for a bit, then all he could manage was, 'Tricky subject, Officer.'

Oh dear.

Woken at seven thirty by the *Standard*, who read me the PA tape: 'Junior Minister disowns Govt. decision . . .' and plenty more. I just had the wits, through my sleep, to refer them to the DE Press Office. Poor dear Angela, what will she make of all this?

But FUCK, all the same.

Later
House of Commons

I got to the Dept as soon as I could. I was Dutch, blasé.

'Perfect timing,' I shouted to all and sundry. 'Sacked for Easter.'

Peter Morrison was waiting in my office (a bad sign). Mediascan was critical. 'The accident-prone Mr Clark . . .' In the *Telegraph* George Jones, who always articulates the mainstream (sic) Party viewpoint (i.e. talks to Mates,[1] the Whips, and a couple of people on the '22 Executive) refers to 'another gaffe by Mr Clark'.

---

[1] Michael Mates, MP for East Hampshire since 1983 (Petersfield, 1974–83).

Dear Peter said gravely, 'You don't really want to be sacked, do you?' and advised writing to the Chief, which I did immediately.

Then, 'The Secretary of State wants to see you, Minister.'

TK was shaken, or pretended to be. Said the Chief Whip had been on to him at midnight. Of course, he's an old sidekick of Heseltine's, isn't he? I bet H. was 'on' to him as well. 'We'll do our best to hold the line . . .' said rather in tones of I-don't-think-I-can-stand-much-more.

What the hell? I was almost elated. At least I would be dismissed for something that related to my own subject, a hero in my own eyes.

On the bench I ran into George Young.[1] He was very supportive, said I was quite right anyway.

By the time I got back to the Dept, the atmosphere had entirely changed. Angela reported on the Number 10 briefing: ' . . . sees no reason why he should resign'. The latest PA tape is now headlined, 'No rebuke for Minister'.

Bernard's formula is bare-faced. He's simply issued a statement saying, 'What Mr Clark meant to say was . . .' and then something (*utterly* different from what in fact I said and is recorded on the video) about 'need to look carefully at all the options and give preference to British products wherever possible'.

Dear good kind sweet Lady.

Department of Employment   *Tuesday, 24 April*

The Easter recess is still on, but my 'In' tray groans and creaks. In New Palace Yard I ran into John Biffen. He told me that Heseltine had been determined that I should be sacked for 'undermining' him. Only he (Biffen) and Norman Tebbit had come out in support.

'And where it counts, of course,' he said, laughing.

---

[1] George Young (6th Bt). MP for Ealing since 1974. Parliamentary Under-Secretary at Environment since 1981.

House of Commons   *Wednesday, 25 April*

A glorious spring evening after a cloudless day. Starlings chatter in New Palace Yard as they jostle for their night-time perches. But in here the air is fetid. I am infinitely depressed. The passage of time, the prospect of another beautiful summer lost. I seem, rather pointlessly but quite pronouncedly, to have acquired a number of my father's mannerisms. This, too, is lowering.

This morning we had a meeting in the conference room; I've already forgotten what it was about, some MSC[1] balls. Somebody drew the attention of Peter, who is having a war with David Sheppard, to a quotation in this week's *Private Eye*. 'I remember dancing with him in 1952, and thought him rather gorgeous.'

'We were all "rather gorgeous" in 1952,' I said gloomily.

'I was eight,' he said.

'In your sailor suit,' I suggested.

I've been going such a long time. Yet sometimes it seems like yesterday. That year I was living in Netherton Grove, behind the incinerator stack of St Stephen's Hospital, which I was only to visit once, some twenty-five years later, to call on Joei, palely in bed after a suicide attempt. Tanya frequented the house, together with James Cameron, Anthony de Hoghton, both now dead. James 'rolled' by Rough Trade in Blackheath; Anthony from drink and 'abuse' in Dublin.

Now I am crouching in terror at the prospect of a rowdy wind-up this evening on TU Bill Third Reading. It's too much. The House is only back one day and I am already trembling. I'm *bound* to be sacked in September. But I can't let the Lady down by quitting before then.

---

[1] Manpower Services Commission, for which Peter Morrison was responsible, were putting in place a scheme that in one of its locations involved the Diocese of Liverpool, where the Rt Rev David Sheppard, former England cricketer, is Bishop.

House of Commons   *Thursday, 26 April*

One backbencher who is a great success is Nicholas Soames. In the old days I used to see him roaring in the Clermont, often with annoyingly pretty girls. I thought he was just a great chinless slob. Then he began to look for a seat. One Christmas Eve I saw him at Floris buying masses of presents. Afterwards, complaining to Jane, I was put in my place when she said, 'Don't be beastly. So few of the upper classes go into politics these days, you've all got to stick together.'

In fact, since getting in here he has been a great embellishment to the place. He is always in the Chamber and very often comes to lunch in the Members' dining room, just to keep in touch, even on days when the business is dreary. He has an endless fund of funny (genuinely funny) stories and his energy is inexhaustible.

Last night we had a very late vote at 3.15 a.m. and Jill Knight[1] went through the lobby in her fur coat in order to be first in the taxi queue.

As they were waiting for the Whips to open the lobby doors I saw Nick put his arm on her shoulder and bellow, 'Now then, you're not going to wander about on your own are you?' She flinched, but did not acknowledge.

A joke made purely for his own enjoyment, as we were all dead beat, and no one who could have appreciated it was within earshot.

Brussels Airport   *Thursday, 10 May*

Flying back to Gatwick after another Eurosession.

Forty-four years ago, to the hour, the Heinkels were returning from Rotterdam and Eben Emael, the great Belgian fortress on the Albert Canal, had fallen to the *Fallschirmjäger*. It was the opening day of the German attack in the West. The first Dorniers were flying tentatively down the Channel, as we were now, to probe the English air defence.

Now it's all conferences, and interpreter-speak and protocol and 'in the interests of achieving a harmonious solution' (preamble to

---

[1] Jill Knight, MP for Edgbaston since 1966.

statement conceding whatever it is you didn't want to give away).
The Germans are correct and courteous, almost apologetic. Don't
any of them think, 'Hey, just a minute. We had all this completely at
our feet once. What the shit went wrong?'

This time I enjoyed the conference. Got the hang of things more.
It's such an advantage to speak French impeccably, and really no one
on our side does. Even the officials, whose grammar and syntax are
OK, speak stiltedly, with Language-School accents. Robert Cotal,
who is 'close' to Pierre Bérégovoy, who is 'close' to Mitterrand said
what a pleasure it was to converse with me.

I understand how one could easily become Euro-addicted. Everything done for one, so smooth and painless. Girls everywhere, cute
little receptionists who chatter away to each other in *flamand*.

These visits make me realise how good I'd be at the Foreign
Office. I startled an FCO official (all FCO personnel start with an
ingrained suspicion and contempt for Ministers – I was going to say
'in other Departments', but of course it's true of their own as well)
by interrupting a couple of Belgians who were talking to each other
about a contentious passage in the communique, '*Mais les nuances sont
très importantes.*' He was both awe-struck, and cross.

Now I'm going back, Cinderella-like, to the drudgery of the DE.
More or less solid boredom, yet with always the possibility of an anti-
personnel mine. Peter is an ally now, he leans on me more and
more. Little Gummer barely puts in an appearance, even at Ministers'
meetings. He's always late, and when he does turn up just 'sits in'
without opening his mouth. He fidgets, though, like someone with
a lot on his mind. By now it must be getting back to him how very
badly everybody thinks he's doing the job of Party Chairman. S of S
is unpredictable, save that if there is something disagreeable to do,
he'll dodge it, if he possibly can, and stuff me with it instead.

Saltwood   *Saturday, 12 May*

Yesterday, we went to Johnny Spencer's sixtieth birthday ball at
Althorp.

Just after leaving the motorway at Thame I noticed a dark red
DBS V8 Aston Martin on the slip road with the bonnet open, a man

unhappily bending over it. I told Jane to pull in and walked back. A DBS V8 in trouble is always good for a gloat.

'Anything I can do to help?' He said something about a banging noise. I made him start the engine and, indeed, there was an absolutely *horrendous* noise which could only come from a broken camshaft, or, at best, a timing chain. 'You mustn't drive this. Let me give you a lift.' He mumbled, got into the back of the Rolls.

There was something curiously sibilant and familiar about him. He was bending over the back seats collecting some hand luggage before locking and leaving the car, and as he turned round I couldn't resist pointing out to him that he looked very like 'an actor called Rowan Atkinson'.

Sure enough it *was* he. We drove him for some considerable distance, first to a phone box, and then to a friend's tea shop in Thame. I told him how much we enjoyed 'The Podule Sequence', a sketch in one of the *Not The Nine O'clock News* series. But actors don't appreciate being paid compliments on anything that is past, they live entirely for the present. He didn't sparkle, was rather disappointing and *chétif*.

We were staying with Nick Bonsor.[1] A nice rambling house, mainly Jacobean, in red brick with a reasonable, slightly undulating home farm surrounding it. Pot-holed drive, bent, but not totally derelict, iron railings. He walked us round outside (before changing and bar); garden a bit of a mess and very few flowers in the house.

Nick pointed out a tumbledown black-and-white 'Tudor' shed that he claimed to have sold to America for a vast sum.

Dinner guests not especially memorable, except for a cheeky chappie in 'sharp' clothes with a Eurasian wife whom nobody knew (presumably parked on the Bonsors by Raine[2]). Apparently he was mega-rich and owned some shipping line. After a few drinks his accent 'went' completely and he communicated solely by nudge-and-wink.

Francis Dashwood[3] turned up and announced at dinner that he was worth £10 million. People often say they have 'got', or are 'worth', whatever it may be, but usually arrive at the figure by counting their assets and not subtracting from the total their liabilities. Whether

---

[1] Sir Nicholas Bonsor (4th Bt), MP for Upminster since 1983 (Nantwich, 1979–83).
[2] Raine: Countess Spencer. Previously married to Gerald Legge, Earl of Dartmouth.
[3] Sir Francis Dashwood (11th Bt), owner of West Wycombe Park.

he was doing this or not I don't know. In any case, it isn't much. Over the port there was much talk from him, Nick and myself about the impending collapse in the value of agricultural land. This aroused the indignation of some of the young farmers present. Jane was pleased by the behaviour of the second Lady Dashwood, of Mediterranean origin, who asked her how old her sons were, and on being told snapped acidly, 'step-sons then'.

At about ten p.m. the great cortège, led by a minion of Nick's driving a Volvo station wagon, departed. (Nick had promised Raine that we would arrive by nine-thirty p.m. and it was a forty-minute drive.) The order was Volvo wagon (Bonsor), Rolls Shadow (us), Rolls Spirit (the cheeky chappie), Range Rover (young farmers) and Mercedes 500 SEC (Dashwoods).

Fortunately the minion in the Volvo drove extremely slowly otherwise we would never have managed the cross country journey. I was already tight, so Jane took the wheel. Althorp itself was beautifully floodlit and looked perfect in scale, almost tiny. The arrangements for parking the cars – *endless* fleets of Shadows – were very efficient.

When we went into the Hall a magnificent sight presented itself: Barbara Cartland[1] wearing an electric pink chiffon dress, with false eyelashes, as thick as those black caterpillars that give you a rash if you handle them, was draped on the central staircase with her dress arranged like a caricature of the celebrated Cecil Beaton photograph of the Countess of Jersey, at Osterly. She and Mervyn Stockwood[2] were making stylised conversation, he complete with gaiters, waistcoat, much purple showing here and there, and various pendant charms and crucifixes.

All very gay and glittering. Even at dinner Jane ranked no more than equal third on the carat count, although she was wearing both the leaf diamonds and Aunt Di's necklace. Some of the more mature ladies at the ball itself could hardly move, so encrustulated were they. The Princess of Wales, on the other hand, looked absolutely radiantly beautiful and was wearing not one single piece of jewellery.

All the minor royals were there, but very few politicians. Besides us I only spotted George Thomas,[3] Norman St John-Stevas, the

---

[1] Barbara Cartland, romantic novelist and Raine's mother.
[2] The Rt Rev Mervyn Stockwood, retired as Bishop of Southwark, 1980.
[3] George Thomas, created Viscount Tonypandy, 1983, on retirement as Speaker. MP for Cardiff West, 1945–83.

Heseltines and little Norman Lamont.[1] NL is a social mystery, a complete *je-suis-partout*. Why? He is quite amusing, but I don't see the full cachet. Various other fashionable figures made their appearance, Rupert Lowenstein, *totally* unchanged and as he used to be when we all pennilessly frequented the Green Room in 1952. Having, as Oscar Wilde said of Max Beerbohm, been granted the gift of perpetual old age he now found that all his contemporaries had overtaken him, looked older than he, and was ebullient. A smattering, too, of fashionable dons, Tony Quinton, Isaiah and, grotesquely pedantic, Professor Asa Briggs.[2]

Jane and I detached ourselves from the throng and cased the pictures. Everything has been restored and the effect is pretty spiffing although, sadly, gold leaf has not been used where it should on the frames. I see that even if all the restorers in the world had been working simultaneously, they could not have done a proper job in that time on the eighteenth-century paintings. So many of these look rather hastily *scrubbed* and thin. As for the furniture, every single piece has been covered with new leather, or new veneers, or inlays, etc., etc., so that although there are some magnificent pieces, the overall effect is slightly that of the Schloss at Pontresina.[3]

Soon we had to leave, as I was due to make a speech to the Industrial Law Society's one-day conference at ten a.m. the following morning and they could have got the wrong impression if I had addressed them in a dinner jacket. I drank nothing at the ball so could drive the whole way. At two thirty a.m. the North Circular Road is deserted and sodium-lit yellow.

---

[1] Norman Lamont, MP for Kingston-on-Thames since 1972. Currently Minister of State, Trade and Industry.

[2] Anthony Quinton (Life Peer, 1982). Philosopher. Currently President, Trinity College, Oxford. Sir Isaiah Berlin, Fellow of All Souls College, Oxford. The first President of Wolfson College and latterly President of the British Academy. Asa Briggs (Life Peer, 1976). Historian; Vice-Chancellor, University of Sussex, 1967–76. Currently provost, Worcester College, Oxford.

[3] A beautifully furnished hotel reserved for grand German tourists.

House of Commons   *Wednesday, 23 May*

This morning the House is still sitting after a hideous night of divisions and ill-temper on the GLC Paving Bill. Ian Gow and I had arranged to dine and Morrison was to join us for coffee, but due to the way the divisions fell Peter caught up with us rather sooner than I would have liked.

IG was holding forth about Gummer's inadequacies, how everybody was complaining about him, even at Central Office. I suppose Selwyn G. will survive because those on whom the Lady smiles can do so indefinitely. But there is unanimity about his poor performance, coming from CCO staff, leading Lobby correspondents, officials in the Department here, who feel neglected, many backbenchers, and even the Executive of the 1922 Committee. They, apparently, have told the Prime Minister that in the interests of propriety he should resign from one or other of his positions.[1] At present he is being paid by the taxpayer to do both jobs though he never comes into the DE any longer.

Ian also told me that even so loyal and devoted a person as Peter Hordern[2] had been upset by the Lady's behaviour in snapping and sneering at him when the '22 Executive went to see her and gave her their views on the problems of the day. This is silly of her. She's storing up trouble.

As always I was impressed by Ian's wisdom and feel for politics. How lucky I am to be his friend. Certainly I owe my position in Government to him. His is a real talent, because he is also so effective on the floor of the House. But he has his enemies and now that he is somewhat distanced from the Lady I fear that they will try and make trouble for him.

We got back to the Commons about eleven p.m. and repaired to Morrison's room where *very* substantial quantities of drink were dispensed. I cannot bear drinking alcohol after nine p.m. as I get so terribly disoriented, so I *conceal* slurped, raising the glass to my lips, but not actually swallowing anything. Whisky, brandy, port and champagne were all open and being poured. Different visitors came and

---

[1] John Selwyn Gummer continued to double as Chairman of the Party and Minister of State at the Department of Employment.
[2] Peter Hordern, MP for Horsham since 1964.

went. At one point Stradling Thomas came in.[1] He is, I think, overrated. As a former Deputy Chief Whip he must know a lot of secrets (including a good many of mine, I suppose), but is rather dull company and makes the kind of jokes at which I find it impossible to laugh. Francis Maude was there – much the best of the PPSs, sensible and quiet, but with a good mind and sense of humour.[2] As the night wore on others came and went. Michael Spicer, Cecil's former acolyte, still somewhat bemused from his many disappointments.[3] He was made a Party Vice-Chairman at an early age and then seemed to go nowhere, although heavily tipped to be both IG's successor in the Lady's Private Office and to get a junior ministry under Cecil's whim.

About halfway through the night at one of the divisions I spotted Soames and thought to get him down and invite him to sparkle. But it was not a great success. He bellowed away assertively but didn't quite catch the mood, which was ruminative, melancholy almost. He kept asking me who I thought should be sacked from the Government. This is a question to which you cannot give an answer unless you are speaking exclusively with other members of that Government. I dodged it a few times but he persisted. Is Andrew Rowe a member of the Government? I asked in the end, rather feebly.[4]

House of Commons   *Wednesday, 6 June*

This evening I dined with Charlie Douglas-Home.[5] *Very* ascetic. Cold salad, and a bought-out 'sweet' with a bottle of Perrier water to slake one's thirst. At intervals sub-editors brought in copy, which Charlie approved, or, in some cases, altered. The great paper was 'going to

---

[1] John Stradling Thomas, MP for Monmouth since 1970. Currently Minister of State, Welsh Office.

[2] Francis Maude, MP for Warwickshire North since 1983. Currently PPS to the Minister of State, Employment. His father, a former journalist and MP, was Paymaster-General, 1979–81, and created a Life Peer in 1983.

[3] Michael Spicer, MP for South Worcestershire since 1974. Currently Conservative Party Deputy Chairman.

[4] Andrew Rowe, MP for Mid-Kent since 1983. Always a *bête noire* of AC from their days as backbenchers.

[5] Charles Douglas-Home, nephew of former Prime Minister. Editor of *The Times*. Died of cancer in 1985.

bed' round us. If you are Editor you can never get away for an evening. It's worse than a herd of dairy cows.

Charlie is very lame and gets about on two walking sticks with heavy-duty rubber grommetts at their tips. He seems to have been lame for at least ten years.

I remember him calling on us at the châlet and he was in plaster for something or other then, sat in a deckchair which collapsed and he broke (another) bone in his wrist. This evening he told me he had been 'getting better', but a stool which he was using to mount a horse at the weekend had collapsed (again) and this had caused him a setback.

I have known Charlie for a very long time. He was teeny when we were children. My mother (with characteristic, but I now see hurtful, *insouciance*) used audibly to refer to him as a 'dwarf'. I remember one summer evening we, and his brother Robin, whom I preferred and who was brilliant on the accordion and later committed suicide, were having a bicycle race. I was in the lead and ran into a strand of barbed wire which had been stretched across the road, tearing the skin on my inner forearm, which caused blood and tears. I still carry the vestiges of the scar.

In 1960 he was sent out by Max Beaverbrook to interview me in Zermatt, just before *The Donkeys*[1] was published. As a reporter he was (then) completely useless. We parted, but I had second thoughts and, stopping the car, dictated the whole article for him from a pay-phone in Martigny.

Charlie is well informed and thinks intelligently. He is a committed Conservative and a great supporter of the Lady, although he said she now drinks too much. He described an establishment dinner at Dorneywood.[2] She sat on the sofa with him and drank three Cointreaux and told him she would not bring Cecil back into the Government.

Charlie says the Prime Minister is extremely worried about the succession and that is why she intends to stay on for longer than she would have preferred. He says she is completely alone, no one to comfort her at all except Denis, and if anything happened to him she would pull out immediately.

I mumbled something about Ian. He said yes, but now she had

---

[1] *The Donkeys, A History of the BEF in 1915*, a book by AC, 1961.
[2] Dorneywood, the official residence of Lord Whitelaw.

discarded him. She never went backwards. No one was ever retrieved. We agreed that Cecil had ruled himself out now – not so much by the act of infidelity, but by the hesitations, blunderings and general aura of nerve-loss which had surrounded the episode. But who the hell was it to be? Between Tebbit and Heseltine – and of course one had to opt for Tebbit, although that was awkward and risky. Both aroused misgivings in the Party. But head to head H would probably shave it.

The subject of the Prime Minister's Inner Cabinet came up and I told Charlie of how I put the brakes on David Young.[1] That really took his breath away. He agreed it had been absolutely lethal, even though his own preference would have been for David Young to get the job.

He talked interestingly and constructively about defence. He has always been a maritimist and reminded me that he had written a paper about the ISS as long ago as 1968. I congratulated him on his leaders, which had been personally critical of Heseltine and of the [Defence] White Paper in general. He said that the answer was to put me there as Minister of State with a dry stick of an S of S, who would simply do what he was told and defend the more radical changes deadpan at the Box. Our first choice was Patrick Jenkin, but apparently he is already demoralised and wants to get out in the next couple of years, claim a peerage and pick up some compensation directorships.[2]

(How awful to be worried about one's pension! – That crumpled-faced man in the advertisements.)

Charlie finally came up with the best choice, namely, Peter Rees. Hard, beady, very good with figures and impervious to criticism from within the Party. We talked round the subject for a very long time.

When he saw me out I noticed that the ridges around the back of his jacket collar were absolutely filled with dandruff. Charlie is in bad shape. I hope he lasts out.

---

[1] See entry for 29 March 1984.
[2] Patrick Jenkin, MP for Wanstead and Woodford since 1964. Currently Environment Secretary. Created Life Peer in 1987. Became Chairman of Friends' Provident Life Office, 1988.

Department of Employment   *Monday, 11 June*

Today I have been a Minister for exactly a year. Very clearly I remember Ian Gow's voice on the telephone, *just* as I was getting into a condition of total hysteria, frustration and chagrin on that hot June Monday when the 'second rankers' were being chosen.

The first two months were hideous – drowning in paper, relentlessly bullied by Jenny with her very clear blue eyes and flat northern vowels. Then, in mid-winter, the nightmare of the Trade Union Bill. Deep breathing in the little white office before going down to face the lions. Unprecedented pressures.

But now that is behind me and I am on easier terms with my officials.

The workload is really quite slight. It has been useful and instructive getting to know how Whitehall works, and I suspect that the lessons are more deeply learned when one is in a Department and coping with a subject which is uncongenial.

But I have been here long enough and I want to move on, or (equally probable) out.

I was booked to be in Plymouth today canvassing for the Euro Elections, but in fact spent the morning at Saltwood doing standard odd jobs on the estate, moving timber off-cuts. I said to Jane, 'Downhill all the way now, only one more Question Time and then the Recess and (from some indeterminate date in September) back to Saltwood for keeps' – 'Count and Conservationist'.

Today's schedule was completely upset as a large twelve-volt battery which I had been carrying about in the Chevrolet had fallen over and spilled at some point – presumably when I lent it to Andrew at the weekend and he 'threw it (the car) about'. The whole of the boot was filled with dilute sulphuric acid, which hissed and fizzed ominously and ate through carpet, rubber and paint at nightmarish speed. Everything had to come out, hoses were played on the offending liquid and bags of bicarbonate of soda spread abundantly.

Tonight I am dining with Charles Moore.[1] A sort of cult figure with the Young Fogies. Simon Hoggart[2] told me that he canvassed them as to who they wanted to lead the Tory Party. Unanimous vote

---

[1] Charles Moore, Editor of *The Spectator*.
[2] Simon Hoggart, former political correspondent on *The Guardian*; currently feature writer on *The Observer* and a political columnist for *Punch*.

was, The late Sir Hugh Fraser;[1] when told that that was not allowed, a majority vote for 'Dr Alan Clark'.

Lygrove House, Badminton   *Thursday, 14 June*

On the lawn at Christopher Selmes' new house. We've got here before him, having come from Plymouth and a tour (curtailed from ennui) of the Euro Election Committee rooms.

It is Carolingian, grey Gloucestershire stone and tiles, with the highly polished floorboards and pleasing smells of the Thirties/Forties, before 'fitted carpets' came along.

I took very much to the housekeeper, a Mrs Jenkins in her sixties, who 'came with' the house. Clearly a Treasure, although perhaps a weensy bit too genteel. Heaven knows what she will make of Christopher's guests – particularly if some of them 'scream'. After a bit, surely, she will be made uneasy by the fact that there are no young ladies?

Mrs Jenkins had been instructed to ply us with champagne, which of course we didn't want at all. A face was made when I asked for 'Indian' tea, but eventually an enormous silver pot of Darjeeling appeared, very very pale at first, but darkening up nicely with the fourth cup.

There's nothing quite like a manicured Gloucestershire lawn in high summer, with dark dark trees on the boundary, and rooks cawing. One feels a long way from the sea and, almost, from the century. It is one of the few *ambiances* where I can get carried back to the summer of 1914, or worse, the year following when the telegrams started to arrive thick and fast, pedalled up the drives of the Great Houses by sly sideways-looking postmen, and Kipling lost his only son at Loos.

---

[1] Sir Hugh Fraser, MP (died 1984) and first husband of Lady Antonia Pinter.

Albany, 6.30 a.m.   *Tuesday, 24 July*

I have slept badly.

Today I must take two groups of Government Amendments through the Standing Committee. The second session is to go through the night, i.e. until breakfast. In between there is an important Cabinet Committee (at five p.m., just when I would be eating a toasted bun in the Members' tea room and putting my feet up) at which I have to defend Tom's wet approach to deregulating small firms.

At the very point that I should sparkle, cynically but creatively, my mind will be clogged by all these hellish gobbledygook amendments.

Taking Questions next week will be almost a relief. The more I see of Government close up like this, and how difficult, cloying, time-consuming and skiddy (road surface) it is, the less I like it.

I really am *sick* of DE. I could only stay on if I were to be promoted to Minister of State and really *do* something – like winding up the whole MSC.

This would upset Peter of course, which I don't want to do. He has so many good points. He really understands the Party, a most valuable gift.

I'd think such an endowment was genetic, coming from old Lord M,[1] but look at Charlie.[2] Wet defeatist, utterly useless.

The MSC is a completely Socialist concept. Nanny State, with just a hint of Orwell. But when Peter goes to Sheffield[3] they treat him like the great Panjandrum, and he falls for it.

Saltwood   *Sunday, 29 July*

Tipped for the sack in the *D. Tel* today (by, inevitably, George Jones).

This is always out-putting. Two days ago Euan[4] rang up, concealing

---

[1] Lord Margadale. As Captain John Morrison (created Baron 1964) MP for Salisbury 1942–64. Father of Peter Morrison (third son) (see 10 Jan. 1984 and passim).

[2] Charles Morrison, second son of Lord Margadale. MP for Devizes since 1964.

[3] Headquarters of the Manpower Services Commission, for which Peter Morrison had ministerial responsibility.

[4] Euan Graham.

(but only just) his satisfaction at having heard from Perry Worsthorne[1] that I was going to 'go'.

Now I come to think of it, Perry is himself something to do with the *Telegraph*, isn't he?

Presumably my name was the unanimous choice at some spastic 'Editorial Conference'.

I sometimes think the only reason I want to stay on is to prove all those wankers wrong. Not that journalists ever notice – still less admit – when they've made a mistake.

They complain about this trait in politicians, but in fact they're far worse. Like share tipsters on the financial pages, they should be compelled to publish an annual audit.

Department of Employment   *Friday, 31 August*

I called in at Seend this morning, on my way back from the West Country, and said a prayer in the church – must be one of the few remaining where the vicar obligingly leaves the door open.

It's too frustrating, I can now only get this sense of peace, and of communication – something of the confessional, I suppose – in empty churches. There, in the silence, through which I can hear the whisperings of gossip and desire, the intoned devotions of two, three centuries, I feel tranquil. Strangely, I should think I have prayed here more often since we left, than in all the time that we lived in the village.

I was glad to see that the Guide, which I wrote, at Archie Kidd's insistence, with dear old 'Mr Wiltshire' (yes, I have to keep reminding myself, the sage of Wiltshire was actually *called* 'Wiltshire') is still on offer in the racks.[2]

But no proper Bible, or King James' Prayer Book. I am completely certain that this degradation of the ancient form and language is a calculated act, a deliberate subversion by a hard core whose secret purpose is to distort the beliefs and practices of the Church of England.

---

[1] Peregrine Worsthorne, columnist and associate editor of the *Sunday Telegraph*.
[2] AC had been persuaded to write a guide to Seend parish church.

Every time – usually by accident – that I attend a service where 'Series III' is used, and suffer that special jarring pain when (most often in the Responses) a commonplace illiteracy, straight out of a local authority circular, supplants the beautiful, numinous phrases on which I was brought up and from which I drew comfort for thirty-five years, my heart sinks. All too well do I understand the rage of the *Inquisitadores*. I would gladly burn them, those trendy clerics, at the stake. What fun to hear them pinkly squealing. Or perhaps, as the faggots kindled, they would 'come out', and call on the Devil to succour them.

The 'Secret Garden'[1] is now totally overgrown and the glasshouses lush and tropical with unpicked grapes and fireweed. The big green double gates still batteredly leaning, done up with baling twine, just as we left them when, two years ago, we called by to load the Range Rover with apples. The whole flavour of the place a little more remote, now twelve years or more away, and through a glass darkly. I climbed over the wall from the churchyard, trying not to put too much weight on the rickety corrugated iron roof of the Gravedigger's hut. A beautiful orange dogfox, as big as a setter, ran out of the potting shed and slithered away into the undergrowth, like Sredni Vashtar. A good sanctuary, the hounds will never find him there. The key for the Marley store was still under its usual stone and I let myself in, prowled about for a little while, collected some Bentley bits, yet still got to Chippenham in time to catch the 10.08 to Paddington and the Boxes.

Last night I stayed at Lygrove. Atmosphere very subdued, conversation (in contrast to our last visit when it had been squawky), flat. At intervals Christopher had long telephone conversations with a man called Suter. They would start slowly and calmly, rise in pitch and go accusatory and loud. The only other topic was some new drug which is being 'tried out' in New York. AZ-something-or-other. It was working a dream, and would soon be readily available.

You can't get AIDS from bedlinen, can you? But plates and cutlery, I'm not so sure. I was trying to drink from the glasses like a fish, without actually letting my lips go round the rim. I'm not going there again for a bit.

---

[1] A piece of land, an old walled garden in the village, which the Clarks retained after selling the Manor House.

Saltwood   *Saturday, 9 September*

Got back late and tired this evening from Beaulieu. I've been meaning for ages to go to the annual Autojumble,[1] and thought shrewdly to book a stall and go as a trader. This would allow me to get rid of a lot of junk and also an advance snoop-up of what other dealers were offering on the evening before the public were let in. (Actually, there's no such thing as 'public' in the classic car business. Every single person involved fancies himself as a 'business man', i.e. all-purpose liar, cheat and conartist).

Dear Edward,[2] however, is incredibly beady. I always remember how, ages ago, he 'caught' Jane and me within seconds of our putting our noses into the walled garden, when we were just being spontaneous nosey-parkers, and insisted we came in for tea. Very sympathetically, and in the time-honoured role of stately home proprietor, he had been peeping from behind the curtains in his first floor flat, *counting the visitors*. How well I know that. It's a kind of sample polling technique. A given number at a particular locality at a given time will allow one to predict, fairly accurately, what the daily total is going to be.

Anyway, seeing our name on the list of applicants for a stall he had very nobly and generously insisted we stay the night before with him.

Naturally we were late leaving, as it took ages to collect all the stuff, which we ended by throwing, literally, into the back of the old Chevrolet, finally lumbering off with a trestle table sticking out of the boot.

Edward, as always, was kind and mischievously amusing, though *distrait* at all times. He lives in a flat in Palace House, a prisoner in his own surroundings. Very few of his (so-called) employees recognise him, or even get his name right. The youthful guard at the museum end where – mistakenly – we drew up, quackle-quackled into his portable phone, 'Mr Clark here to take tea with Mister (sic) Montagu...' This went uncorrected by 'Control', who clearly didn't, himself, know any better. And when Edward went to get us our

---

[1] A 'car boot sale' devoted entirely to motoring items.

[2] Lord Montagu of Beaulieu (3rd Baron) founded the Montagu Motor Museum in 1952 and created the Beaulieu Museum Trust in 1970 to administer the new National Motor Museum. Also President of Historic Houses Association.

tickets he stood meekly in the queue at the guichet. No one seemed to bother much.

I quite see why he prefers the Beach House, where we were all to meet up for dinner, and sleep. The pressures at Palace House must, during the summer 'Season', be intolerable. Edward had given us keys and later on, as we let ourselves out of his personal door, we saw three very obvious burglars, one of them a half-caste, trampling over the private lawn, laughing and sneering. The sort of thing that, at Salt-wood, would have made me dash back indoors and fetch the 12-bore. But who to tell? What to do? Edward was doing his rounds; the 'guards' (if you could find one) were gormless and pasty.

Bleakly isolated amid dunes and scrub heath of the Solent shore, Beach House is a big wooden bungalow, with transom windows and thin walls through which you can hear the other occupants conversing (and, indeed, farting).

These modern (modern*ist*, I should say) houses are nearly always a failure. As we approached Jane said something about the Sainsburys[1] and, sure enough, it turned out that Hugh Casson had had a hand in this too.[2] I am doubtful if he ever brought anything off. Garden House really the best of the bunch.

A jolly children's party was in progress. The only other people at dinner were unexciting. The man had an Italian name and said he 'used to be' a barrister, now apparently something to do with concessions to sell Hamburgers – so there's a 'service' industry for you. But he gave me a bad night by saying you could go to prison for having an Anstalt.[3] But not if you declare it, surely? Yes, yes, *when* you declare it. All v. odd. But disconcerting. Like Hemingway, I am getting more and more paranoiac about 'The Revenue' as I grow older. Now that I don't owe the banks anything, the tax inspectors have taken their place.

We all parted after an early breakfast. The Autojumble was *totally* exhausting and, inevitably, I spent more than I 'took'. Many people ignored our offerings, set out on the trestle table, but tried to buy the Chevrolet itself. A Dutchman gave us some trouble. I was offering an

---

[1]John and Anya Sainsbury had commissioned a modern house near Lympne, some few miles from Saltwood, which they inhabited in the early 1960s.

[2]Hugh Casson, architect; currently advisor to Commons Services Committee and President of the Royal Academy.

[3]A Swiss bank personal trust.

old, slightly travel-stained badge of the Royal Netherlands AC; the price was £30. He didn't want to pay cash, but to swap it for a *new*, but identical badge. Presumably a post-war fake. Sorry, man, I said (repeatedly). This wasn't the answer he wanted. He hung about, muttering, rephrasing his request. Semi-threatened us with EC Regs. Dr Strabismus.

We left early, making an hour better time by going all the way back to the M25, round it, and out on the M20. At intervals the great V8 motor 'hunted', seemed on the verge of 'missing'. Perhaps, after all, I should have taken an offer. But I hate to sell faithful machinery. It's as bad as parting with horses. That's why Saltwood is completely cluttered up with wrecks and dead hulks.

Zermatt   *Saturday, 15 September*

I was determined to get away, out of reach, before the reshuffle got started. We were a day late because Nanny had to be moved to Quince[1] first. I would *not* pay a gang of piggy-eyed, nicotine-smelling removal men £300 or thereabouts simply to carry her furniture across Castle road from one cottage to another, and so did the whole thing personally, most ably and heroically assisted by Eddie. Now she can cluck away and polish things in her new nest while we are absent.

We had two wonderful days crossing France in the Citroën, meandering, almost, on the Routes Departmentales, crossing, transversely, the principal Lemming routes and watching satisly the belting straining jockeying holiday traffic and the massive dicing juggernauts. We kept the hood down for almost the entire journey. And for the first time we circled to the south of Lake Geneva, staying the night at Evian, and not linking up with familiar roads until we reached Aigle.

I fantasised, deluding myself that I might be going to go 'sideways' into Ray Whitney's job.[2] If I am going to have any future in politics I've got to get to the Foreign Office or MoD. Now that I know how to deal with officials, how the machine works, the time is ripe. I quite see how it is better to learn these tricks in a disagreeable dept, where

---

[1] A cottage on the Saltwood estate, preferred by staff as it is 'modern' (built in 1953).
[2] Ray Whitney, MP for Wycombe since 1978, had been sacked from his post as Parliamentary Under Secretary at the Foreign Office.

you have to 'keep a proper lookout'[1] at all times. But that's over now. I've served my apprenticeship, taken a Bill through its Committee stage. I'm fully fledged. I didn't say anything to Jane, fearing disappointment, but secretly hoping for wonderful news.

But it was Renton who was chosen. Renton. I was very dejected at first. Then cheered up a little, as I don't see that this necessarily rules me out in future. He was Geoffrey's PPS, had a cursory acquaintance with the FCO, was now due for a job.[2]

I am sitting at the desk in my study in the Chalet and the French windows are open on to the balcony. Fifty feet away the Wiesti foams and tumbles past, swollen by the melting glaciers. The Matterhorn is in full view, and the whole house carries that delicious aroma of high summer, pine needles and sweet geranium.

How distant, how very very distant and odious is the arid little left-right-left turn by the green fire escape sign, as I get out of the lift on the sixth floor. The messengers scuttling round with their sheaves of turgid paperwork. The unbelievable tedium of the subjects – Financial Management Initiative, Ombudsman cases (I no longer look even at the conclusions of these), anything-to-do-with-the-Disabled, the 'Measures'. This isn't politics, it's compulsory obsessional disorder.

The fact remains that there have been three vacancies now, at PUSS level, in Defence and Foreign Affairs, since I became a Minister. And I have missed out each time. Am I doomed to hang on at DE, suffering periodic humiliations, until summarily dismissed in September of next year?

I think hard of pre-empting, ' . . . at his own request', getting free to argue for Toryism *à l'outrance*, to scorn the obligations of Party discipline (so often nothing more than the convenience of the Whips' Office) and become a true Maverick. Bang would go the 'K', of course, and any chance under the ACHAB rule. But one would gain a year. And I am uneasy that my reputation in the Commons may start to fade if I have to go through another year's drudgery. It really is impossible to dazzle at the box on the Job-splitting Scheme.

One's status is embellished by 'at his own request', diminished by being sacked.

---

[1] A family phrase. (Barristers' standard 'pleading' in statements of claim in motoring litigation.)

[2] Tim Renton, MP for Mid-Sussex since 1974. PPS to John Biffen, then Geoffrey Howe, both as Chancellor of the Exchequer and as Foreign Secretary.

Zermatt   *Sunday, 16 September*

This evening I *tortured* the body by going flat out up Othmars. Took thirty-seven minutes from the doorstep, and on the downhill jog back my knees felt like water.

The bath was cold – why? The baths are never cold here – and this put me in a filthy temper.

In fading light I set off for the Winkelmatten chapel, which always calms me. I found it locked. This is unheard of. In thirty-five years that chapel has always been open for climbers before they set out for the Hornlihutte, or to give thanks for their safe return. There are never less than twenty candles burning.

Now it is surrounded by scaffolding. I peeped though the keyhole, and the interior has been stripped. The pews, altar, effigies, all have gone. Only a barely intelligible notice in German pinned to the door, advising of *Revisionen*.

First I was cross, then gloomy. Perhaps it's an omen. I returned by the back route, and saw that the dear little chestnut-wood Chalet where that Belgian cutie (how shameful to have forgotten her name) had digs in the winter of '56 – '*pourquoi que tu me prends . . .* ', all that – had been demolished and there was just a great hole in the ground in preparation for some monstrous concrete garni.

It had been one of the prettiest private chalets in the town, with a charming garden of shrubs. Quite soon the 'Caroline' (and of course the Brunmatte[1]) will be the only real private houses in the Inner Zone. That's why I am taking such pains – and expense – to make the Kariad[2] really pleasing. Two fingers to the poxy *garnis*.

Anyway, it's all too much, and we've decided to head for home on the day after tomorrow.

---

[1] The name of a beautiful Zermatt chalet belonging to the Gentinetta family.
[2] The name of the 'kiosk' chalet which the Clarks were constructing.

Saltwood   *Thursday, 20 September*

A gloomy blustery day. Low dark clouds. Saltwood is sleepy, almost as if we had been away a month instead of a week. Getting ready for its hibernation.

This afternoon, as I strolled round, I thought the one thing I am really loathing is the prospect of being back at the bloody House of C, being yerr'd at the Box by a lot of spiteful drunks, on subjects that bore and muddle me. I'd gladly chuck the whole thing in and become a Count[1] if it were not for the satisfaction this would give to others.

The nicest thing in the waiting postbag was a lovely letter from Julian Amery.

I'm amazed you survived the Reshuffle. You stick out like a red poppy in the hayfield of mediocrities surrounding you. It is very offensive to them to be original, intelligent, courageous and rich.

What a marvellous compliment, from someone who has been in public life for almost forty years. Julian has known, closely known, Tito, Winston, Anthony [Eden] and Uncle Harold [Macmillan]. The *real* times. He's entirely right. What we could do, he and I. He so nearly made Foreign Secretary when Carrington[2] legged it in '82. Loss of nerve by the Lady. She wasn't sure she was going to survive, took the Whips' advice, chose Pym[3] – with whom she quarrelled incessantly thereafter.

Or was it? Perhaps she recognised something he and I won't accept. The climate has changed.

Saltwood   *Friday, 12 October*

'At any moment I could be killed by an assassin or a lunatic.' I often quote the Führer's reflective aside to Rauschning (and indeed he

---

[1] Alternative family slang for retiring. Cf. 'Burning heather'.
[2] Lord Carrington, served every Conservative Prime Minister since appointed as Parliamentary Secretary, Ministry of Agriculture in Churchill's 1951 government. Foreign Secretary, 1979–82. Resigned following the Argentinian occupation of the Falkland Islands in April 1982.
[3] Francis Pym, MP for Cambridgeshire South-east since 1983 (Cambridgeshire, 1961–83). Foreign Secretary, 1982–3. Now returned to back benches.

himself is recorded as repeating it to Goebbels and, by Halder, to Keitel). In my case, though, I am thinking more about Estate Duty and my luckless descendants – than of Posterity.

But today a vivid illustration, followed in the late evening by a curious, almost spooky episode of imagery *foretelling*.

Yesterday at Brighton (Party Conference) the DE debate was first off in the afternoon. TK bumbustioso'd, did a pretty smudgy job of introducing his 'team'; although pleasingly I got what, for a junior Minister, was quite a good cheer from the floor (due, I assume, to the coverage in Monday's *Mail*[1]). This disconcerted TK, who faltered momentarily.

I had a few meetings and oddments to attend to after the 'Debate', and Jane went off to go round an Art Nouveau exhibition with Charles Moore before we met up for tea. Later, the American Ambassador was having a small party (but wives, oddly, were excluded).

Tea at the Metropole is always fun. So much traffic of 'notables', so much peeping, prying and listening to do. The egos flare and fade and flare again like a stubble fire. The journalists dodge about excitedly, fearful of missing something. I prefer it to the hotel lobby later on, when everyone has 'had a few' and is slower (though louder). But when we had finished, and were standing on the steps wondering whether to take a walk along the front, it being such a beautiful afternoon of late autumn, a pleasing escapist impulse came to us both simultaneously: 'Bugger the American Ambassador. Let's just go home.'

We sometimes get these urges. Notably during Elections, when we have been sent off on our own with a lot of canvass cards.

I cancelled the room, settled the account. We hopped straight into the car and were comfortably back here for supper.

But that evening an unsettling experience. The last episode of *Tripods*. Little Charlotte wandered around Saltwood, everything so beautiful and timeless. Then she was 'claimed' by the Tripods – remote, sinister, not of this world. She ascended, higher and higher (on that great lamp-engineers' lift, which made such a mess of the

---

[1] AC had been instrumental in closing off a particular kind of fraudulent claim by foreign students at benefit offices.

moat when they were shooting). Sadly she waved, and called her
farewells. On its own the scene was curiously, unexpectedly moving.
Now, with the knowledge that she had, at that time, been less than
three weeks away from death, sliced in half on the M4 by some callous
brute in a 30-ton artic, it was unbearable.

More was to come. Before breakfast, when I returned with the
dogs, Jane told me that there had been a huge bomb at Brighton, the
hotel had been all but demolished. They had 'got' Tebbit, Wakeham,
Tony Berry,[1] various dignitaries. Amazing TV coverage. The whole
façade of the hotel blown away. Keith Joseph (indestructible), wandering about in a burgundy-coloured dressing gown, bleating. The
scene was one of total confusion, people scurrying hither and thither,
barely a police 'officer' to be seen.

Mrs T had been saved by good fortune (von Stauffenberg's
briefcase!) as she was in the bathroom. Had she been in the bedroom
she would be dead.

But what a coup for the Paddys. The whole thing has a smell of
the Tet Offensive.[2] If they had just had the wit to press their advantage,
a couple of chaps with guns in the crowd, they could have got the
whole Government as they blearily emerged – and the assassins could
in all probability have made their getaway unpunished.

Saltwood   *Tuesday, 7 November*

I am somewhat underemployed at the moment.

My day-to-day work is hateful, and boring. But I have now
mastered it. It no longer holds any terrors for me. Indeed I am faster
and clearer than many of the officials who come in to 'explain' it.

Before Questions I used always to repair to the drinks cabinet in
my office in the Commons and down a teeny slug of neat vodka. No
lunch, keep the stomach empty and then, in the very last seconds
before going into the Chamber for Prayers – *Skol.*

---

[1] Anthony Berry, MP for Southgate since 1964. Younger son of Lord Kemsley, who
had owned the *Sunday Times*, and nephew of the proprietors of the *Daily* (and
Sunday) *Telegraph*.
[2] Tet Offensive: as part of the general offensive in South Vietnam in 1970, the
VietCong also made a brief foray into the US Embassy.

I no longer need it. I had another good session last time, knocked everyone around including poor old Eric Heffer.[1] I used to be frightened of him but not any longer. He is suddenly ageing, quite fast. Afterwards John Stokes,[2] no mean judge, went out of his way to congratulate me, and the following day Godfrey Barker[3] gave me half his column, full of praise.

So what should I be doing? Slowly, too tentatively, I am working up a paper for the Lady. On the subject of defence, yes; but a strategic overview, a twenty-year projection. Does anyone else do this? Not as radically as I, that's for sure. And it needs to be done under a whole range of subject headings: overseas trade; industrial policy; diplomacy in the late Nineties, with whom we should be aligned, our relations with the new Pacific powers.

The FCO are sometimes said to be working on 'secret' long-term papers of this kind. But no one ever sees them. Mainly devoted, I would guess, to argument for expanding the Corps Diplomatique and the number of congenial 'postings'. I am not sure, even so, how kindly the Lady will take to my reflections, which is probably why I only turn to them intermittently. Dear creature, she is somewhat *blinkered*. (But hastily I add, as is obligatory among believers when her faults are identified, 'this of course can also be a source of strength'.)

It's a gamble. Either she'll think 'he's wasted in that hole' or 'he's crazy. For God's sake keep him where he is, indefinitely.'

Saltwood   *Saturday, 10 November*

Tristan Garel-Jones asked himself down. Odd, you could say, for a Whip to take five hours off to see someone with whom he could converse for as long as he liked the following Monday.

He is candid. At least he *seems very* candid. Slagged off most of the '22 Executive. Said there was 'absolutely no point' in discussing the Under The Bus Syndrome (then devoted some fifty minutes to doing so). 'If it happens, at any time, we – i.e. the Whips – will cope.'

[1] Eric Heffer, MP for Liverpool Walton since 1964. He died from cancer in 1991.
[2] John Stokes, MP for Halesowen and Stourbridge since 1974 (Oldbury and Halesowen, 1970–4).
[3] Godfrey Barker, parliamentary sketch writer in the *Daily Telegraph*.

Tristan said she would now lead us into the next Election; then we'd have to choose someone 'from your generation'. This pleased me (presumably intended to).

He agreed that Ken Clarke was a 'butter ball' (my phrase), said that Chris Patten said the same about him. Good. We gave Tristan a lot of sticky cakes, and William served tea from the Fabergé teapot, and off he went.

Department of Employment   *Thursday, 20 December*

Yesterday I attended a meeting of the Lambeth Inner City Partnership. 'Red' Ted Knight, and others.

Closed room, so no press, no posturing. Knight quite impressive. The negotiations (if that be the term) were simply about *money*.

Unspoken (because hollow) were threats by either side to 'expose' the other. Our parsimony, their profligacy.

But they are really getting in deep.

Buying votes, of course, can be very expensive. Even more costly is having to appease all the total weirdoes who clutter up the middle ranks, all of them jockeying against, and bitter about, their confrères.

Who's going to settle all these debts in the end? Not the ratepayers; it just isn't there. It will finish by falling, somehow, on the DoE, who are apprehensive.

At lunchtime we had the departmental carol service. Everyone on best behaviour, a kind of mass office party in reverse. In the choir I recognised certain pasty maidens and maddish, steel-rim bespectacled males whom I have encountered at various marginal meetings during the year. TK read the lesson, oh-so-firmly.

Boring. Tedious.

Tomorrow the holiday starts. But we only get a week. Sadistically, the Dept will be open – 'Private Offices only', on 28th.

A very quiet Christmas. Poor Daisy[1] came, bringing a few cases of '61 (not, emphatically not, as a gift). He's gone to pieces really. About six months ago he wanted to 'handle my investments', but without telling me what he was buying and selling. To use my money, in other words, to prime his own dodgy little deals.

OK in 1972, not any longer. I have, in John Mendelson's pleasing phrase, 'seen the movie'.[2] Get lost, I said.

Then, partly to placate him, I asked him to get some claret. He's always going to the sales, makes out he's an expert. What did he do? Go out and buy a lot of '61s. He knows I'm up to here in '61s, all bought – yes, on his advice – fifteen years ago. Now they're far too expensive. 'You're averaging,' he said. Bah.

James and Sarah turned up, full of the pleasures and plans for Eriboll. As a Christmas present I'd bought a Dodge Command Car – nominally for getting stalkers to the Hill, but actually as a big toy – and we played with it.

On Friday the Gows came over to dine and stay the night. The evening never really took off, in spite of copious, and heavily permutated, wines. Nearly boring, with both of them thanking us repeatedly in supplicant, almost tearful voices. I've noticed this tendency in Ian is becoming a little more pronounced. He *parodies* himself, 'toys with' his audience even though he knows they are getting impatient.

Also, he is never at his (conspiratorial) best when he has Jane with him, even though he is devoted to her.

---

[1] A nickname for Christopher Selmes.
[2] John Mendelson, at that time chief financial guru to Dean Whitter, the New York broking house.

1985

1985

I am not suffering quite the same degree of apprehension as I did this
time last year, with the Employment Bill and, in particular, the dreaded
Part III solo role overhanging. But the sheer dreariness and drudgery
of the Department; the cold and miserable squalor of Albany, still (I
assume) with its full sink of dirty china; the prospect of long, pointless
and disagreeable night votes – all this is lowering. With something of
a shock I realised that I will, this June, have been in the same Dept,
and at the same rank, for two years. Guy Sajer.[1] And I have a nasty
feeling that there won't be a reshuffle until September.

An article in *The Times* today by Selina Scott. She says that in two
years at Breakfast TV she aged ten. I have done exactly the same in
Parliament – a ratio of five to one. At this time of the year I find
myself pining for white sand and lapping waters. But that, too, must
be a sign of growing old. Because formerly I would want to get to
the slopes, and ski divinely.

House of Commons   *Friday, 15 February*

Ponting, amid much turbulence, has been acquitted.[2] There are accu-
sations of 'lying' and insult. A set-piece Debate (inevitably it will be
disappointing) is imminent, probably for Monday.

You can find people – some of them quite influential and canny
people like Peter Morrison and G-J – who are saying that John
Stanley[3] will have to resign.

Of course he *won't*. No one these days resigns for anything.
(Perhaps, still, for direct proof of a huge bribe from a civil contractor?)
But as I would greatly like his job, I am being extremely circumspect
in my comments. 'No more than I myself would have done in the
same circs.'

---

[1] Sajer, author of *The Forgotten Soldier*, a book to which AC often turned, served on
the Russian front for three years without relief.
[2] Clive Ponting, a civil servant in the Ministry of Defence, revealed details of the
sinking of the *Belgrano* during the Falklands War. He was tried for breaching the
Official Secrets Act and found Not Guilty by the jury.
[3] John Stanley, MP for Tonbridge and Malling since 1974. Minister for the Armed
Forces since 1983, where he remained until 1987.

This *could* be the moment, though. For although I would have loved to have gone to MoD immediately, if I do get there in the end I will be far stronger, because I have accumulated so much 'Whitehall' experience to back up my expert knowledge, hunches and prejudices. If John is sacked I must be among those with a claim to succeed him.

In the dining room last night John Wakeham shouted across from the Chief Whip's table to me that he had a special message – that I was 'loved'. And Tristan has a tale (one never quite knows with Tristan's tales, his motives are never singular) that Willie was defending me vigorously.[1]

Little Alfred Sherman[2] came to see me yesterday, at the Department, at his own request. He said that he 'wanted to discuss the Thatcherite Succession'.

Alfred said that he could 'steer me into it' using my wealth (!), that he had 'made' Keith, and then Margaret, and that he could do the same for me.

I could hardly not have been flattered, but I said little. He offered to write my speeches – but I don't like that. And anyway, time has moved on; we want not more, but less, of his medicine.

I can't decide whether Alfred would be a help or a hindrance. And anyway, have I got the oomph?

I'm not a 'hungry fighter', being too fond of my Baldwinesque leisure and hobbies.

Also, like many who have had an unhappy childhood, I am frightened of being laughed at.

Perhaps that is why I like making people laugh *with* me.

Saltwood   *Saturday, 16 February*

Before leaving London for the weekend I took time off to go to the Westminster Hospital to see my old, almost old*est* friend, John Pollock – 'Gianni' – who is dying there. He lay in 'Erskine' ward; a

---

[1] AC was getting a bad press at this time because a senior civil servant had leaked his private (but 'politically incorrect') comment about Bongo-Bongo land.

[2] Sir Alfred Sherman, journalist on the *Daily Telegraph* since 1965. He co-founded the Centre for Policy Studies in 1974 and was its Director of Studies until 1984.

miserable room, full of geriatrics, terminals and no-hopers, but where the staff were pleasant and obliging.

Gianni was frail, thin and bearded, with a sinister purple cross on his upper breast-bone where the radium gun had to be pointed.

'I've got this lump,' he said. 'Can you see this lump?' – and indeed I could.

Was it attached to the bronchial tubes? Why on earth couldn't they operate?

Gianni needed funds, presumably for cigarettes and 'miniatures'. I gave him all the cash I had in my pockets, some twenty-eight pounds in notes.

'What about the silver?' he asked. 'Aren't you carrying any silver?'

He stuffed the notes into his pyjama jacket, and the change into a box of 'Cook's Matches' on his bedside table.

Apparently the other patients, no matter how ill, crawl over and steal from those who are asleep.

I used always to visit Gianni, and his elderly patronne, Constance Mappin, on the shores of the Mediterranean during long vacation, and at other times.

Sometimes Constance was broke ('waiting for War Loan') and one evening, when 'the tables were unkind' – she was a raging gambler – I bought from her the turquoise and diamond ring which Jane still wears on occasion.

I have vivid, almost entirely pleasurable memories of Cannes, and Grasse, and Ischia. Of Don Cesare, and 'Phillipo', and Pat Hecht – one of the wildest and most exciting girls I have ever met.

Jane and I stayed with them at Positano on our honeymoon. Christina[1] turned up, and a farcical triangular sub-plot developed with Milo Cripps's[2] boy friend ('Barry') falling for her, and tears shed all round.

It all seems a very long way from Westminster. Save for one minuscule and trivial linkage – Pat had her hair cut even shorter than Jenny Easterbrook.

---

[1] Christina was living in AC's house at Rye when he became engaged to Jane.
[2] Now the 4th Baron Parmoor.

Department of Employment   *Wednesday, 24 April*

I went on a ministerial visit to Wrexham. A pretty, peaceful town, with the sun shining. How fortunate are the contented bourgeoisie in such places – or are they too racked by pressures and frustrations? They certainly didn't look it.

On the way up I saw Robert Atkins[1] in an adjoining carriage and went and had a talk with him. He told me that David Young had spoken to him for half an hour, asking RA what he should say to the Prime Minister who was always asking him for advice about personalities. I winced, as Atkins and I dislike each other quite candidly. But he is a great show-off, besides having a keen political sense of a below-stairs kind. It is not hard to extract intelligence from him.

Poor Michael Jopling[2] is going to be sacked, and Peter Rees.[3] RA also thought Quintin[4] would go, although he recognised that there was a shortage of candidates for law offices. I told him how Paddy Mayhew[5] was desperate to get back into the main stream, but RA said that although this was known, Paddy was being considered as a possible Lord Chancellor (which of course he could not refuse, even though he might not wish it). We agreed that Adam Butler[6] was to go and RA said that John Stanley would also be moved, though not, of course, dismissed, and that this would mean two vacancies of Minister of State at Defence. He paid lip service, though not very convincingly, that I should have one of these. It is notorious that I do not get on with Michael Heseltine but RA said that there was some talk of Peter Walker going there as a reward for his performance at

---

[1] Robert Atkins, MP for South Ribble since 1983 (Preston North, 1979–83). PPS to Lord Young when he was created a Life Peer in 1984 and joined the Government as Minister without Portfolio.

[2] Michael Jopling, a farmer. MP for Westmorland and Lonsdale since 1964. Minister of Agriculture since 1983. In fact he survived until 1987.

[3] Peter Rees, Chief Secretary to the Treasury since 1983.

[4] Quintin Hogg, Lord Hailsham of St Marylebone. A Minister in the Eden, Macmillan, Douglas-Home and Heath Cabinets. Now aged seventy-seven and serving his second term as Lord Chancellor (his first, 1970–4). He did not finally retire until 1987.

[5] Sir Patrick Mayhew, MP for Tunbridge Wells since 1974. Solicitor-General since 1983.

[6] Adam Butler, MP for Bosworth since 1970. The son of R. A. Butler. Minister of State, Defence Procurement, since 1984.

Energy. It might just happen, as Defence is a poison chalice until the books have been balanced, and the Lady might at present rate embarrassing Peter Walker as a higher priority than humiliating Heseltine. But the question would still remain, what then to do with MH?

All this, and more, was little more than the general semi-informed small talk that one gets when gossiping with colleagues in the lower reaches of government about changes in the autumn. It was reassuring to hear that the Lady cannot stand Kenneth Clarke, and it is for that reason that he has been so long excluded from the Cabinet, which apparently (but not in my estimation), his merits demand.

RA did then produce a stick of dynamite. He told me that it was being actively considered that the whole Department of Employment be abolished! The payment of benefit would be delegated to the DHSS. The issue of work permits to the Home Office. Health and Safety matters to the DTI. Training and special measures to a new training division that would go into a revamped Department of Education. 'Science' would be shunted from Education to DTI. I could see only too well where this idea came from (although I had only been here a week to form the same opinion).

RA said that Tom King was a prat: 'a nice chap, but a prat'. This is not entirely fair as Tom King has got a shrewd Willie-ish side, but his balls are very weak. He always loses in Cabinet and will not hold out for anything. This, and his testy manner with officials, has eroded his support in Whitehall and the long, cumbersome and never finished sentences, of which my parodies are notorious across the Civil Service, have irritated many colleagues.

Anyhow, I did not waste any time on my return in repeating this communication to Tom personally. He took it very badly. He has felt somewhat threatened of late – indeed, since David Young's appointment was hailed with only the most perfunctory disclaimer by Bernard Ingham as 'Minister for Jobs' – and there have been many similar incidents that have led TK to believe that David Young was encroaching on him. He huffed and he puffed and got more and more agitated. Indeed, he exhibited under stress those same slightly uncoordinated and disparate reactions – lateral thinking, etc., that he so often shows in discussion. He said that David Young was not a member of the club, never fought an Election, always wheedling away, the only person who had time to make this sort of trouble, and so on. I tried to calm him by suggesting that presentationally it would be impossible to abolish the one Department identified in the public eye as being responsible for the country's principal social and economic problem, and he got well *lancé* into this theme, delivering a series of unfinished, and ungrammatical, monologues. His condition deteriorated further when I revealed that the machinery of government aspect had also been looked at, with Michael Quinlan going across to Defence and Robert Armstrong getting his cards a little ahead of time, and Clive Whitmore going across to be Cabinet Secretary.[1]

We ended with TK undertaking to go to the Chief Whip and 'tweak his nose', also to Willie. Willie is not the man he was, as in the old days he would certainly have resisted this. But John Wakeham – I am not so sure.

Duke of Cornwall Hotel, Plymouth   *Thursday, 9 May*

Wasting time, and substance. Yesterday I was in the Midlands, job centres and benefit offices. I tried to be polite as well as grave. I'm good at that. People expect something different and then they're pleased.

After the vote I boarded the sleeper, uncomfortable and smelly. Walked, a lovely clear morning, from North Road station, but no breakfast served here until 7.30. Then I will walk again, saying 'brush'[2] and hoping to be widely seen and reported, from the hotel to the constituency office for my 'surgery'. There will be either twelve mendicants or three – it's impossible to predict. Let us hope three, as I have to take the 10.25 train *back* to London for an afternoon's work at the Dept. Then tomorrow back again, this time getting off the train at Exeter, motoring to Bratton where I will field a lot of phone calls from people complaining, or trying to make my flesh creep (usually both) about the SDP landslide which – by all accounts – is already

---

[1] Michael Quinlan, CB, Permanent Secretary, Department of Employment; Sir Clive Whitmore, KCB, CVO, Permanent Under-Secretary, Ministry of Defence, since 1983. This last was the only prediction that was not, in fact, fulfilled: Sir Robin Butler succeeding Armstrong (and Armstrong did in fact survive until the Civil Service retirement age of sixty).

[2] The Clarks believed that when constantly (but inaudibly) saying 'Brush' the features compose themselves in an expression of benign concern.

under way.[1] The next day, Saturday, it's the Dunstone Ward annual supper (Dunstone always choose a Saturday because Nan Howard[2] knows I prefer Fridays, so as to allow me to get back to Saltwood for the weekend) and more, this time 'live', complaints.

'The sheer hell of being an MP.'[3]

Some wanker called 'Caserly' (that just has to be a false name, probably someone on the editorial staff) has written an open letter in the *Herald*,[4] saying how arrogant and 'out of touch' (yeah) I am, will lose my seat, SDP Wave of the Future, usual balls.

Financially everything is still a mess. For the first time I am beginning to think that *I* may die before my father's estate is settled, and that Jane and the boys will have to cope with two sets of death duties simultaneously. I sometimes wonder whose side Thom is on. He rolls his 'R's with relish when, as he always does, calling them 'The Revenue'. This week he told me that they would be 'looking for' another £150,000.

In the meantime I have half agreed to sell the mask to Jerdein for $450,000, which is a whopping price really,[5] but after we had packed it up its *eye* looked reproachfully at me from where it was lying on the kitchen floor in Albany and I decided there and then to 'withdraw' it. There is so much ju-ju in that object. God knows what strange rituals it must have commanded, in steamy incense-ridden pagan temples. Blood, fertility and revenge, it carries the aura of all of these, and it is not seemly that it should be just bartered around for money in dealers' 'galleries'.

I am apprehensive, too, that once it went I might desperately want or need its return; some misfortune might be visited on me. I took it straight back to Saltwood and hung it in the strongroom where its mother-of-pearl eyes catch the light as the door opens. I am mindful, too, of that account in Ruth's diary of how Arthur[6] badgered and

---

[1] The Local Government Elections of 1985 marked the high point of SDP favour with the electorate.
[2] Mrs D. O'N Howard, Chairman of the Ward.
[3] The title of a review of a TV series about an MP entitled *The Nearly Man*.
[4] The *Western Evening Herald*, Plymouth newspaper.
[5] The Torres Strait tortoiseshell mask which belonged to Picasso. Charles Jerdein, an art dealer and friend of AC.
[6] Viscount Lee of Fareham, politician and collector. AC edited his papers, *A Good Innings*, published by John Murray, 1968. The diaries of Lady Lee (Ruth) are an integral part of the volume.

badgered an impoverished collector to sell him a little Giorgione. The man kept refusing, said he feared that once parted with it he might die. Arthur bullied and blustered, said such thoughts were 'unchristian', that he must meet his maker 'with conscience clear', pushed and nagged. Eventually the man sold. Less than two months later he was dead.

Then, yesterday, came interesting news. The client on whose behalf Jerdein was bidding, a rich Frenchman, had just had his daughter kidnapped and was in a dreadful state. Very powerful ju-jus can operate at long range. We know that.

Bratton   *Saturday, 11 May*

It's so lovely here. Slow and peaceful, buds everywhere and bright greeny-yellow leaves bursting. Jane is so pretty, her hair always gets tawny streaks in the springtime. But my balls ache, and my lower back is stiff and creaky. I have been doing the weights, but not much, surely? I will *not* give in to middle, still less old, age. Maurice[1] always said that that was what did for poor old Ian Fleming, insisting on carrying Annie's bags up and down the stairs, even when gasping.[2] But he was on forty a day and I've never smoked one cigarette in my entire life.

Now tonight we have the Dunstone supper, in the Elburton Red Triangle Hut, with everyone along to gloat and discomfit. Some stupid prick has done a 'projection' in one of the heavies showing that the SDP will have a massive overall majority in the House of Commons, we'll be down to thirty-two seats (or is it eighteen?). There is talk of mass desertions.

In fact *any* fixture after *any* year's local elections is always tricky. The councillors and canvassers are flushed with their own efforts; eager to relay stories of how 'on the doorstep' people have been complaining that they 'never see' the MP. Much talk along the lines

---

[1] Sir Maurice Bowra, Warden of Wadham College, Oxford, from 1938 to 1979.
[2] Ian Fleming, creator of James Bond, married Ann Charteris as her third husband. Her first, Lord O'Neill, was killed in action in 1944; she married Lord Rothermere in 1945. They divorced 1952 when she married Fleming, who died in 1964 aged 56.

that 'you're going to lose the seat unless you do something...' If I say
'Like what?' I never get any further than 'go walkabout in the
Broadway on Saturday mornings' (and of course I ought to be doing
that now, this minute, instead of lolling on the lawn at Bratton with
milky coffee and fruitcake) or 'get more coverage in the press, Alan'
(by which they mean, not what they call 'the London papers', but the
bloody *Herald*). Janet Fookes,[1] whose vast arse is seldom undisplayed
in the *Herald*, did in fact suffer an almost identical swing in her part
of the city. But if I gently point this out it is unheard.

People have been ringing, how am I going to reply ('*respond* is the
word', I say through gritted teeth) to Caserly's letter. They're so
fucking stupid down here they've only got to read something in the
Herald and they think it's true. Buttocks.

Jane cheered me up. Told how Eileen Smith had come up to her
after her talk,[2] and said 'How *do* you do it?', i.e., put up with the life
of being married to an MP.

Saltwood   *Sunday, 23 June*

A pleasing tale. Something of the Charley's Aunt donnée. William
has always loved uniforms and panoply. For the last two years he has
been 'due' a ticket to the Birthday Parade (or 'Trooping the Colour',
as he calls it). Once again Lilian,[3] silly little fool, had left it too late.
Or had he? At the last moment, and most covertly, he snatched or
snitched one off the desk in the empty Adjutants' office at Knightsbridge. Didn't look at it too closely, stuffed it in his pocket.

I say 'ticket'. It was a beautiful embossed invitation, on stiff card.

William was delighted. Went up very splendidly in *full butler's
regalia*, looking the picture of saturnine (though diminutive) elegance.
Showed his ticket to a 'Greeter'.

'Aha, Excellency, how kind of you to come. Lovely. Good.'

---

[1] Miss (later Dame) Janet Fookes, MP for the Drake Division of Plymouth.
[2] Jane Clark had given a talk on 'The Stately Homes Business' to the Conservative
Women's Association.
[3] 'Lilian': a family nickname for Andrew of ancient nursery standing, used when he
is being unsatisfactory.

William, who is nobody's fool, drew on his long years of experience in 'service'. Kept mum, grunted only.

'I hope you'll be comfortable here. Seats can get a bit hard after a
while, ha-ha. But I can offer you a cushion.' (*I never get a bloody
cushion*, I told him.) 'I do hope you enjoy the Parade . . . '

Better and better it got. After the Anthem the Greeter reappeared.
'This way Excellency, Excellencies . . . '

In company with other bemedalled and exotic-uniformed dignitaries William was gently shepherded across the gravel and through
the wall gate into the garden at Number 10!

At one point Mrs T. made a brief appearance and dreamily
mingled. The tiny pearl-handled assassin's pistol (could have) nestled
in William's breast pocket.

I don't expect the Prime Minister was concentrating very much
in the company of these Corps Diplomatique medium-fry. But she
would surely have sharpened up if she'd been told that among them
was Al's butler from Saltwood.

Bratton   *Thursday, 8 August*

Yesterday I did something for the last time.

When you do something for the first time, you always know.
Gosh, I haven't done this before. That's what it's like, is it – nice,
nasty, try it again sometime, or whatever.

But when you do something for the *last* time, you very seldom
know. Until, months or years later you realise – 'That was the very
last time . . . Never again.'

This is a phenomenon that induces melancholy. It is so closely
interleaved with the passage of time, the onset of infirmity. Death at
one's shoulder in the market square of Samarra.

Constituency rubbish all day yesterday, and I should have left for
Saltwood this morning. But at breakfast I saw in the *Western Morning
News* that Mrs Barnard, the fearsome matriarch of Penhalt High
Farm, had died, and the property was for sale. Something made me
drive over, if only to look at the beach hut which I had coveted so
long and so hard all the time we were living down here, when the
boys were tiny.

Out on the Bude road, through Stratton, where a lovely and very young blonde used to stand at the crossroads in the summertime and wave. Past Widemouth sands where once Tip was almost swept away, and had to be revived, soaked, in the back of the car. And where when alone and driving the blue jeep I picked up the girl from Bray shop, and her Ma. Then over Millhook and down to Crackington Haven, and the beach hut still stood, intact.

It was in the early Sixties that we used to come here most often. And I remember one of the Barnard sons – strange and inbred they seemed at our one and only meeting in that charcoal-smelling kitchen with its long black range – baiting me by recounting how special seasoned planking from (?) the *Mauretania* had been used to build the hut.

Even in those days the paint had blistered and peeled, and the Atlantic gales were lashing the bare wood for five months in the year. But still it stood, the walls almost stripped, but without warp or rot. Several panes of glass had been broken, and the door was off its hinges. Someone had written 'Fuck Thatcher' with an aerosol spray, and there was the detritus and excrement of 'Travellers', as they style themselves. The stream was brackish, and the whole area seemed smaller and more cramped, as do often the sites of golden memories, when revisited.

I ground back up that very steep hill, with the 1 in 4 hairpin, which so often I descended, having to use bottom gear, in the [Citroën] ID 19 'Brake', loaded with children and picnic things. And for some reason, I can't tell why, my mind strayed to the possibility of 'starting again'.

I suppose it could still be done. But not while Jane is alive. I could not, would never wound her, the best human being in the entire world. And if she was taken from me I would be so shattered I couldn't do anything. All these thoughts were turning in my mind as I passed by the entrance to Penhalt High Farm and, out of curiosity, I turned in, walked some way along the track, then returned and got the car, undoing the baling twine on the gate.

It was completely deserted, not a soul. No livestock, no cat. Even the blue tits and house sparrows were in the fields.

They are handsome things, these walled Devon farmyards of the eighteenth century, with their low granite buildings, and the milking stalls floored and divided by Cyclopean fragments of slate. And there was a curious aura that hung over Penhalt, as it slept in the afternoon sun, with the seed grass everywhere overgrowing, knee-high.

I prowled about, scrambled over a wall into the little garden on the south side, terribly neglected but with two fig trees against the wall of the farmhouse, and some nice shrubs surviving. Intensely hot and still, a marvellous place for a pool.

Across the fields I could see one of those four-steepled Devon church towers, lying so perfectly in the trees in the hamlet of Trevinnick, and I entered the mind of others, the ghosts of former times, who must have looked upon this same view and, like me, felt wistful. Had someone, surely they must have done, served in the DCLI,[1] and looked on this for the last time on home leave from Flanders?

I was suspended; on but not of, this earth. I had detached myself from time, could move in any direction. Curious, but not in any way frightening, almost as if I had died not once but very many times.

I cannot tell how long my trance, or reverie, endured. But I became aware of a deep, heavy roaring sound, mingled with the fluttering noise of airscrews on coarse pitch. And very low, 200 feet at the most, a single Lancaster flew directly over the house, and on across towards Exmoor, being soon lost to sight.

Afterwards, of course, on the journey home, I did my best to rationalise a supernatural experience. It is true that I often transpose the loss of young lives in the World War I no-man's-land, and the repetitive sorties by Bomber Command. And there is only one Lancaster left. And the 'Battle of Britain Flight' is stationed a very long way from Penhalt. And they are precluded from flying below 1000 feet, except at displays.

But the twenty-fifth anniversary comes up in a few weeks' time. He must have been practising.

Saltwood   *Tuesday, 13 August*

I am so *bored* by my work. It spreads right across and affects everything so that I am beginning to feel stale, and déjà vu, with all aspects of public life.

At the Cavalry Club last week Ian and I had our ritual summer 'round-up' lunch. But even that was not the same. We gossiped. But

---

[1] Duke of Cornwall's Light Infantry.

Ian's contributions did not have that electric quality which used to run through them in the days when he had come straight from the Lady's presence. He is peevish, and fussed about Ireland.

I said, don't. Ireland is a ghastly subject. Intractable. Insoluble. For centuries it has blighted English domestic politics, wrecked the careers of good men.

Ian said the pressure to concede everything to Dublin (and thus expose the decent Loyalists in Ulster to the full force of IRA terrorism) is coming from the Foreign Office, who are themselves reacting to pressure from Washington. One must never forget that the Irish vote in America is bigger than it is in Eire. We agreed that the Foreign Office now exists solely to buy off foreign disapproval by dipping into the till marked British Interests.

There will be a reshuffle next month. 'Quite a big one.' Norman Tebbit will be made Chairman; Peter Rees and Patrick Jenkin will be 'dropped'.

On the subject of the juniors Ian was more cagey, although said that Macfarlane[1] had been a disappointment.

'If you want a change, you should tell the Chief Whip.'

'Oh, come on, Ian, everyone knows what I want.'

Once I am back here, sawing and working on the land, Whitehall and its drudgery seem remote. Only when I read something really interesting, like that article by Laurence Freedman on nuclear targeting, do I pine for what could, dare I say, 'ought' to be.

Danair, Inverness – Heathrow   *Tuesday, 3 September*

I return to London suddenly and in grumpy form.

Jane, quite rightly, said you must return *at once* as the new Ministers will be all over the place, preening themselves and bagging portfolios. You will be left with all the ullage. But what now? The holiday is buggered and I doubt if we will ever get to the Citroën for the escape.

---

[1] Neil Macfarlane, MP for Sutton and Cheam since 1974. Sports Minister (Department of the Environment) since 1981.

Am I really to be stuck for another year in that ghastly hellhole?[1]

So this morning I rose at four a.m. and took James's Saab, thrashed my way to Dalcross in blinding rain, great splashing puddles that wrench at the steering, and swirling mists. It is not possible really to exceed forty mph in many places between Eriboll and Lairg, all of fifty-two miles.

But after 'The Wee Scottish Soldier'[2] I drove at 110–115 mph wherever I could, hating every minute of it.

I keep dropping off to sleep as I write this.

Yesterday, after the junior appointments had all been announced, we set off on a walk along the shoreline, southerly towards the Viking dock and 'Grassy Knoll'.[3] Periodically I declaimed, in a rage, about the march of the greys. Practically every reshuffle there has ever been has made me angry – almost worse now I am in Government than when I was on the back benches, critical and expectant. On and on we walked, stopping at intervals to collect driftwood, which we placed in little cairns for collection by the Wee One.[4] We took supper very late, it being still light at eleven o'clock, and I cannot have had much more than three hours' sleep.

Albany   *Later*

I went straight from Heathrow to the Dept. Officials are genuinely glad I am still there – which is nice, though of little value. Peter Morrison rang from his new office at the DTI, too well-mannered to gloat[5] (not that he has much to gloat about, considering that for most of the spring and summer he was expecting to be made Chief Whip) and we went to the Ritz for lunch.

---

[1] The postings in the autumn reshuffle were finally announced. AC was chiefly affected by Tom King's appointment to the Northern Ireland Office and the arrival of David Young as Secretary of State at the Department.

[2] The war memorial at Bonar Bridge.

[3] Grassy Knoll: a promontory thus described on the Admiralty charts of Loch Eriboll.

[4] A forty-year-old Land Rover which had failed its MOT and is used for local work on the estate.

[5] Peter Morrison had been moved 'sideways' from the Department of Employment to become Minister of State for Industry.

Peter was full of how, already, he was sorting out his civil servants. They were trying to put upon him 'a female' as head of his Private Office. 'I couldn't possibly have that.'

'Really? I've had nothing but women in charge of mine. I find it rather congenial.'

'Yes, but you see, she couldn't carry my guns.'

I grumbled away disconsolately. Peter tried to cheer me up by saying that there was 'bound' to be a 'really big' shuffle next Easter. Whatever for? I thought.

But of course Peter himself wants to get closer to the Cabinet soon. He is much younger than me, could indeed be my son, but I would guess our shelf life is about the same. After lunch, very sleepy and *désoeuvré*, I sat at my desk, riffled a few dreary PO cases.

Punctually (first difference from Tom) David Young had me in at the appointed time. He is pleasant, charming almost, and fresh (as distinct from stale). He talks at twice the speed of Tom King, but listens too, cracks jokes, is full of bright ideas. I quite see why the Lady fancies him. He is utterly different from the rest of the Cabinet – yet without being caddish.

I dined at the Beefsteak with Bruce Anderson.[1] We were the only people in the room, except for Anthony Lejeune, who looked exceedingly ill.[2]

Eriboll   *Wednesday, 4 September*

I caught the 8.50 flight, and sat next to a quite pretty blonde in a white jacket. Her husband, or consort, was miniature, bearded, scruffy – but had an upper-class voice. Who the hell was he? Normally one knows every one of any consequence on that aircraft.

I headed north, at a leisurely pace, and after Altnaharra took the Loch Hope road instead of going through Tongue. It was the first sunny day for two weeks, and there were climbers' cars parked in the layby where the start of the Hope ascent is marked. To my shame I have never climbed Hope, and suddenly, irresistibly, I thought, why not?

---

[1] Bruce Anderson, political columnist on the *Sunday Telegraph*.
[2] Anthony Lejeune, author, reviewer of crime fiction for the *Daily Telegraph*.

There were some heavy shoes in the car, and in one of the door pockets I found a thermal belt. But I was suited, waistcoated, tie, collar stiffeners – Whymper.

A white TR 6 had parked close by, and a man was putting on a lot of gear; bright nylon windcheater, hood, gloves, special backpack. I set off immediately, nonchalant at his stare of disapproval. I was carrying nothing, not even a thumbstick. I didn't have so much as a Mars Bar in my pocket.

The ascent became a duel. He must have left a minute or so later, and made two attempts to close the distance. But on each occasion I anticipated, knowing from experience on the Trift, and other frequented climbs, that there are few things so disheartening as to make a special effort and find your quarry, mysteriously, is still at the same distance. After about an hour I sensed he was content to pace me, but I still took care whenever I was in dead ground, to accelerate to my utmost, or even to run.

The last thirty minutes to the summit are steep and debilitating, a track through scree, easy to lose in the cloud which, from about 3800 feet, was persistent. I reached the second marker cairn – there was a double summit – in under two hours, without stopping once, and was pleased with myself. For the time being it quite compensated for Whitehall and its disappointments.

But this evening I am exhausted and must have been poor company at dinner. When I recounted to Jane how relaxed and congenial David Young was she said of course – but he doesn't have to fill his mind with constituency detritus the whole time, suffer his weekends being ruined by mendicants, stay up until gone midnight voting on spastic and unnecessary measures.

Too right. The democratic overhead.

As I brood on all this, I find myself becoming crosser. I've had it. Chris Patten has been made a Minister of State; OK, he's brilliant. But so has Renton, and he isn't.[1] I can read the signs. At some point in this coming term I must seek out the Chief Whip, or possibly G–J. I want 'out' at Christmas.

---

[1] Christopher Patten had become Minister of State at Education and Science; Tim Renton, Minister of State, Foreign Office.

House of Commons   *Tuesday, 26 November*

Today my old friend made his resignation speech.[1] The House was full. And by the time I arrived my usual place behind the Prime Minister had been taken and I sat at the far end, between Carol Mather[2] and Peter Bottomley.[3] Kinnock was on his feet and, as it moved on to economic subjects, was making a hash of things and had 'lost the House'.[4] There was a general murmuration.

'When is Ian speaking?' I said to Carol.

He grunted non-committally. He is a Whip of the old school and they do not like resignations.

Last week a cruel piece by Peter Riddell in the *Financial Times* had treated Ian's resignation dismissively, for 'his career is already in decline', etc., etc., and other unwelcome truths.

Thinking it was a Whips' Office plant, I had complained to Garel-Jones, who affected horror and dismay. I remain suspicious. I believe that it was a pre-emptive plant fed to Riddell on the day of Gow's resignation in case he gave trouble. In fact, and as could have been readily predicted by anyone who knows him, he gave no trouble. But the piece was used nonetheless.

Ian was dejected and flat in tone. He spoke from the second row from the back, which is *not* a commanding position, because you fall between two banks of microphones, and this technical handicap aggravated the loss of confidence and authority in his voice. Everything that Ian said about Ulster was painfully true and although, perhaps, he over-quoted from humble correspondents in the Province it was moving and, among nationalists like myself at least, induced unease and guilt.

But the personal passage at the end was, frankly, embarrassing. He described how disagreeable resignation was; how he spoke from the bottom of his heart − 'and it is a very big heart' − (oh dear). Ian went on to say the Prime Minister might welcome the resignation of some of her colleagues more than others and he did not know (sic) into

---

[1] Ian Gow had resigned from the Government in protest at the Anglo-Irish agreement (see also entry for 13 August 1985).

[2] Carol Mather, MP for Esher since 1970; a Whip since 1975.

[3] Peter Bottomley, MP for Eltham since 1983 (Woolwich West, 1975–83). Parliamentary Under-Secretary, Employment, since 1984.

[4] Neil Kinnock, MP for Islwyn and Leader of the Opposition since 1983 (Bedwellty, 1970–83).

which category he fell. How he had enjoyed – exulted in? revelled in? – working for the Lady for four years; her great and indeed paragonesque virtues, 'the finest chief, the most resolute Leader, the kindest friend that any Member of this House could hope to serve'.

Cruel and sardonic, Peter Bottomley turned to me and said in the middle of this eulogy, 'Give him a job.'

Will he ever get a job again? I doubt it. One more example of Beaverbrook's dictum that politicians are irreparably flawed by going up to Heaven in their early forties and coming back to earth shortly thereafter. Originally said of Curzon, I can think of no one to whom it doesn't apply, with the possible exception of David Owen. But even he, although purged by passage through fire and water, may never in fact have a 'job' again.

It is this *absolute* unpredictability that makes politics so irresistible. Who in 1982, when he was rightly described as the most powerful man in the Government, could have predicted that IG would be the first of her Ministers to resign?

I think it is probably true that she was getting irritated with him in his closing months as her Secretary. Like many men who find their love unrequited, he was becoming more and more subservient and attentive. The stooping, obsequious family retainer, speaking very often in a special high-pitched tone that was almost tearful (my father, too, I have seen practising this technique).

I saw Nicholas Soames standing at the bar and afterwards he told me that during the embarrassing passage the Lady closed her eyes and went quite rigid in expression.

Much later, in the smoking room, Soames and Budgen plied me with Black Velvet and spoke indiscreetly about Ian's speech. I say indiscreetly because Ian himself was sitting only one table away with Cecil and a couple of backbenchers. On the way out Ian paused at our table and I said something gauche about not a dry eye in the House. Worryingly, he took this badly and stomped off. Poor monk![1] My only true friend in the Government. Who can I talk to now? Peter Morrison is in another Department, and too preoccupied these days. Garel-Jones is fun but unreliable, and Celtic in his motivations.

These ironic cycles and visitations of Nemesis (not that poor Ian

---

[1] Ian Gow was sometimes known as The Monk (as, indeed, but for different reasons, was Keith Joseph).

ever showed hubris in the slightest degree) occur quite frequently but
do not, regrettably, usually punish the most appropriate targets. IG
loathed Bottomley, whom he thought, not incorrectly, to be a closet
Liberal. Out of mischief I had sent IG a cutting from Bottomley's
local paper in which he said that he was, 'basically a good Liberal',
and that his views 'enormously overlapped' with those of John Cart-
wright, his SDP neighbour. I thought no more of it until I heard later
through Private Office channels that Bottomley had been carpeted by
the Chairman and this made me feel uneasy.

The previous day the Chairman [of the Party] had given a pep
talk to junior Ministers, telling us to be 'more political', to get around
the country making speeches and generally fluff up the Associations.

I do not mind (much) fluffing up other Associations, and it usually
goes quite well. Although I grudge them the time, particularly at
weekends. But my own is irreparably lost. I find most of them boring,
petty, malign, clumsily conspiratorial, and parochial to a degree that
cannot be surpassed in any part of the United Kingdom. Once
contempt and irritation passes a certain level, I am not good at
concealing my feelings and I fear that it has been widely felt. My
tactical energies are devoted simply to the narrow goal of beating
them to the draw with the announcement of my 'standing down'.

Letter to Ian Gow   *House of Commons*
                                                          27 November

Ian
When we spoke briefly in the smoking room last night after your
speech I fear that I may have seemed a little frivolous.

Alas, it is in the nature of my (– is 'background' the right word?)
upbringing to affect casualness in the face of great and unwelcome
events. You will understand this.

Yes, I was embarrassed as were others in the House by the personal
note that you struck at the end.

But this embarrassment was founded not in the unease with which
one attends on the ritualised and the synthetic, but in that deeper

unhappiness of the soul which is restrained from its natural inclination to spring up and acclaim and say,

'Yes you are right. Speak your message, speak it again. We are with you.'

Affectionately

Alan

Department of Employment   *Thursday, 28 November*

I suffer from some unease as I contemplate my time in Government, and in Parliament, drawing to a close. Because you are only a shadow, a wraith, a phantasm once you have announced your intention to 'stand down'.

I still do love the clubbable side. The swinging studded Pugin doors which exclude those unentitled; the abundance of facilities; the deeply comfortable leather chairs at the 'Silent' end of the library where one can have a sleep as deep and as refreshing as under the eaves of the Chalet Caroline. There is constant access to snacks, 'nips' and gossip. There are excellent and attentive library staff who will do all your work for you.

But all this is fully enjoyable only in winter time.

In summer and late spring it becomes oppressive and fetid. I get sudden, intermittent – like powerful twinges of pain – realisations of how *old* I am becoming. I spring in my step, look at girls, like laughs and fresh ideas. But when I was talking about this with Jane during one of those interminable telephone calls that we make most evenings, we agreed, what is my life expectancy? Fifteen years? If I spend two-thirds of that in London, or in the Constituency (actually it's more) what have I got left? Effectively – five.

At what stage does one's reserve of years change from being inexhaustible – of no concern or consequence – into a rapidly diminishing triangle of sand at the neck of the glass, which is scru-tinised obsessively?

Yesterday, at lunch time, I drove the SS 100 still, forty years on, getting that wonderful evocative thrill as I settle into the driving seat and look down the long louvred bonnet.

At the Princes Gate traffic lights out of Hyde Park I drew up beside a black BMW, driven by a blonde, registered ANY 1. I looked sideways and saw browner, thinner in the face, but still with 'something', Andy Colquhoun.

As the lights went amber the faithful SS, always unbeatable for the first fifty feet of a standing start, yelped the racing diamond tread of its 18-inch wheels, and was off – the BM was nowhere. She pursued me, *screeching* the revs to ignition cut-out, but locked brakes and overshot the right turn to the Albert Hall.

Had Andy recognised me? Or have I changed too much? Some disturbing photos have come up recently from the Press Office, showing a heavy jowel, but loose neck folds.

Department of Employment   *Tuesday, 17 December*

If I look back on the last three weeks I can see nothing of any moment whatsoever that has happened to me, save that I suffered, absorbed and phlegmily surmounted a filthy cold in the head.

I have made various 'visits', mainly it seems to workshops for the disabled, to please officials and to give the illusion of activity. But all that has happened is that I am that much older and iller, and I have been kept from the company of my loved ones. I have done nothing for my country, and I would guess that (for example) there are more people out of work today than there were a month ago.

Today we had the DE carol service. As always, ego and 'rights' to an unbelievable degree. I only can properly enjoy carol services if I am having an illicit affair with someone in the congregation. Why is this? Perhaps because they are essentially pagan, not Christian, celebrations.

Next, thoroughly disillusioned with everything, and in foul mood, I traipsed around the precincts of the Palace of Westminster looking for Alison in order to seek his advice on how I should convey to the PM that I wanted 'out'. He was nowhere to be seen. His office was sterile-tidy, deserted. I switched objectives and searched for Tristan. But he had flown. Off, already, to Spain. The House is emptying fast. It echoes, and workmen have appeared, smelling of nicotine and perspiration, and muttering to themselves.

I am frustrated, but soon I too will be in my beloved county of Sutherland, where I can torture the body, and replenish the spirit.

Eriboll   *Sunday, 29 December*

Unbroken clear skies all day, with the air quite still, and six to seven inches of snow lying. We went up the Creaggan Road to the summit, to be joined by James and the labs in the Argocat. Incredible light, with variations the whole time. The slopes of Cranstackie were rose pink from the low, low sun; but there was a great slate-coloured ridge of cloud out to sea, merging with the blues and blacks of the loch mouth. On coming down we picked up the dogs and took the road to Stra'beg, walking as far as the hirsel fence line that gives a view of the mountain hut at the top of the valley.

Got back here, thoroughly exhausted, happy and hungry after four and a half hours on the hill.

My physique is improving. As I cut logs in the little woodshed I began to think that all this talk of retiring is balls. Stay on as Minister, and do the job. ACHAB, etc. Yet this view alternates with a kind of somnolent contentment. While I love to be out of doors all day long, I do start to feel tired and escapist if I have to consider any decision relating to Saltwood, the office, the Constituency, construction plans in Zermatt, husbandry at Broomhayes, or any one of a hundred things that I carry at the back of my mind.

It is not only Whitehall that is so far away. Everything going on in the world seems remote and unimportant. We have no television, hear no wireless save the shipping forecasts. We get one newspaper, the *Aberdeen Press and Journal*, which is resolute in its parochialism, and most soothing as a result.

I have to talk to the office occasionally, although I try to do it as little as possible. Judith[1] is telling me that the Westland row, which was smouldering when we broke up, is now ablaze. 'People are saying Mr Heseltine is going to resign.'[2]

---

[1] Judith Rutherford has taken charge of AC's Private Office in the Department following the promotion of Jenny Easterbrook.

[2] The future of Westland Helicopters, which was under-capitalised, was the subject of two conflicting recommendations by the Ministry of Defence (under Michael Heseltine) and the Department of Trade and Industry (under Leon Brittan). Heseltine wanted 'a European solution' with joint venture arrangements with the European helicopter manufacturers. The DTI's preference was for an injection of capital from the US manufacturer Sikorksy, with whom Westland had often worked in the past.

I don't believe it. It's just the press stirring. Anyhow, no one resigns when the House is not sitting.

But Michael has always had this slightly scatty side. It is the only even half-endearing trait that he possesses. He is the man who pushed further out the definition of *folie de grandeur* than it has ever been hitherto.

Anyway, so what? If he does – good riddance.

1986

1986

I was on the phone gossiping to Peter Morrison at his office in the DTI when Judith tiptoed in and put a piece of paper under my nose. 'Michael Heseltine has resigned.'

I whooped, and gave him the news, but at that very moment his own Private Office had done the same. I looked demi-stupid because until that point I had been saying how I didn't see how he could, it was not in his character, he was too ambitious.

Peter said, 'Well, this could mean some interesting changes,' and we both hung up in order to take more soundings.

Shortly afterwards the Sec of State rang. Would I come along for a chat?

David recounted to me the scene. Michael appears to have done it semi-spastically, *not* the *grand geste.* When he slammed his brief shut and walked out a lot of people just thought that he'd been a bit rude, and then gone out to the loo. But the photographers were all waiting in Downing Street, so he must have tipped them off in advance. Now he was holding a 'press conference' in the big lecture hall at the MoD. What was his authority for doing that, pray? I asked. He should be emptying his desk.

David referred *veiledly* to 'accompanying changes'. Said, reassuringly, 'I know what you want.'

Secretly cheered by this, I did not like to break the spell by telling Jane when we spoke on the telephone. Perhaps this was a mistake.

Sensing 'developments' I cancelled a visit to Plymouth and came down here. At Men's Tea the Downing Street switchboard rang. 'Mr Alan Clark? The Chief Whip wants you.'

John Wakeham came on. Some pleasantries about being snowed up, and then, 'The PM's contemplating a few changes and I wanted to ask if you'd like to be asked (heart leaps) to dur-dur-dur, move *sideways* (sic with a vengeance, heart sinks) and help Nick Ridley at Transport?'[1]

---

[1] Nicholas Ridley, MP for Cirencester and Tewkesbury since 1959. Secretary of State for Transport since 1983.

I had taken the call under the stairs, and bought time by saying that I was getting it transferred to the office. Foolishly, I think, I didn't tell Jane all, only that the Chief Whip was on the phone, but my heart was pounding. I had to refuse.

'John, I don't want to seem to be difficult about this, but I have been a Parly Sec for over two and a half years. For the last eight months I have really been doing a Min of State's work as I have had to cover for Gummer since he was made Party Chairman. To be perfectly honest, I was a bit miffed at not getting Peter Morrison's rank last September when I took over all his duties.'

'Mmm. What would you like me to say to the Prime Minister?'

I put down smoke about the Channel 'Fixed Link',[1] how it was a Department of Transport responsibility but I owned a lot of the land at the mouth of the tunnel (if there was a tunnel). Could look awkward if I was a Minister in that Department. John affected to understand. He said he 'did not rule out' the possibility of an upward move later. Said the Lady had a high opinion of me 'in spite of all I tell her' (joke).

Saltwood   *Friday, 24 January*

And still the 'events' accumulate (though not yet any announcement about Lynda Chalker's job, now vacant a fortnight).[2] This week it has been all leaks and statements and counter-leaks, and fevered rumour.

On Wednesday the pressure mounted all day long for the Prime Minister to make a statement on the Purloined Letter,[3] accompanied by – source? – tales that LB[4] 'wouldn't go quietly'.

The story became current that she was tied until, in her statement, she could announce that she had accepted LB's resignation. The unhappy fall guy.

But the House might not like that. Too obvious. In the evening I

---

[1] As Eurotunnel was known at the time.
[2] Lynda Chalker, MP for Wallasey since 1974. Minister of State, Transport, since the 1983 Election, she had just been appointed Minister of State, Foreign Office.
[3] A letter from the Attorney General to Michael Heseltine rebuking him for breaking the ministerial convention, which had been leaked to the press (as it subsequently turned out) by the Press Office at the Department of Trade and Industry.
[4] LB: Leon Brittan had been Trade and Industry Secretary since 1985.

called on John Biffen in his office behind the Speaker's Chair. I said that it was better to defuse, or rather preempt, the row by her coming to the House and making the statement *now*, i.e., after the ten p.m. vote. Some of her tormentors would possibly be away and, in any case, this would allow her to outwit the morning press and to reduce the time available for them to organise. John completely agreed. He was cagey, but I formed the impression that he had already recommended this very course.

However, the vote came and passed, and no sign.

We all drifted home eventually, but late and after much chattering in the smoking room and the corridors.

This morning the lobby was ablaze. Reporters everywhere, and the atmosphere of a bazaar (as in the East, rather than the Constituency). Marcus Kimball[1] had turned up and was standing about – always a sign that something is afoot. He told of dining with Willie the previous evening, and that there had been much talk of 'too many jewboys in the Cabinet'. It appeared that the Prime Minister had decided against a statement last night and had opted for the 'Resolute Defence' (as opposed to the 'Muzio Gambit'[2]) and would be making a statement at the usual time this afternoon.

I wandered along to the dining room and lunched with Julian Amery and Robert Jackson,[3] whom I like for his dry, donnish sense of humour. I say 'with' but there was much jocularity at our end of the room, and shouting across from one table to another. Julian had a good bottle of Burgundy in a basket, and let me have a couple of glasses. He told various tales, and pronounced judgment as an experienced statesman.

Then, unexpectedly, the Chief Whip came over and sat with us. He showed me a copy of the statement. I read a few paragraphs, started a *faux-rire*. I couldn't help it. 'I'm sorry, John. I simply can't keep a straight face.' The paper passed from hand to hand. Others agreed, but were too polite to say so.

How *can* she say these things without faltering?

But she did. Kept her nerve beautifully.

I was sitting close by, and could see her riffling her notes, and

---

[1] Marcus Kimball, MP for Gainsborough, 1956–83. Created Life Peer, 1985.
[2] Muzio Gambit: a reckless and now little-used opening gambit in chess.
[3] Robert Jackson, MP for Wantage since 1983, had been MEP for Upper Thames, 1980–4. At Oxford he was President of the Union and Prize Fellow of All Souls.

turning the pages of the speech. Her hand did not shake *at all*. It was almost as if the House, half horrified, half dumb with admiration, was cowed.

A few rats came out of the woodwork – mainly from the *Salon des Refusés* – Fletcher,[1] Wiggin, a couple of others. Serene and haughty, at its end she swept from the Chamber, and a little later came to a meeting of the '22. The mood was wholly supportive of her, and the Scapegoat was duly tarred.

This morning came the news. Leon Brittan has resigned.

But is that the end of it? Clearly it is intended to be; but I'm not so sure.

Saltwood   *Sunday, 26 January*

A lovely still day, clear and crisp. As I set off with the dogs before breakfast, Bob went past with a trailer of loose straw for the shippon – the pleasures of husbandry and the land. I walked over to the Machines, then round the Lake, along the valley and up to Chittenden Stone.

At intervals I stole glances at *The Observer*. We are not out of the wood, and the Lady is still terribly beleaguered. There is to be an emergency debate on Monday.

Is this the end of an era? Uneasily, I feel it may be. Perhaps they're actually going to get her, the same way the weevils got de Gaulle. Will I, alarmingly soon, be back with the books and the Heritage – but without the *cachet*?

Last night IG rang, full of gloom and portent. I discounted him, but that was before I had seen this morning's press. Ian's trouble, though, is that he is, *au fond*, a man of honour. Personally, I don't give a blow. Lie if necessary.

I have just put the phone down from Peter Morrison. Not much news, though he, too, is not optimistic. Peter said that F. Pym might vote against, with 'bad consequences' in the Lobby. Is the Conservative Party going through one of its recurrent bouts of epilepsy?

---

[1] Alex Fletcher, MP for Edinburgh Central since 1983 (Edinburgh North, 1973–83). Successively Parliamentary Under-Secretary to the Scottish Office and Trade and Industry. Returned to back benches in 1985.

House of Commons   *Monday, 27 January*

Every seat in the House had been booked with a prayer card, and they were all up the gangways.

For a few seconds Kinnock had her cornered, and you could see fear in those blue eyes. But then he had an attack of wind, gave her time to recover.

A brilliant performance, shameless and brave. We are out of the wood.

Saltwood   *Friday, 31 January*

The last day of an absolutely incredible month.

Last evening Jane met me at Sandling. I could see she was excited. 'Do you want the good news or the bad?'

'Always the bad first.'

'You've got to go back up to London.'

I groaned.

'The PM wants to see you at Number 10 tomorrow morning at nine thirty.'

Wow! I rang Judith immediately. She had received a terse message from Wicks.[1] He wouldn't enlarge. But it was Trade, Paul Channon's old job.[2] David Young had confirmed it 'in the lift', talking to one of his own staff, and the news was all over the building.

Jane and I talked incessantly. We had a complete *nuit grise* with me turning on and off the light to make notes in my little green wallet. I rose before five, and paced about, my mind ranging.

Why on earth didn't I get an earlier train, the milk train, indeed? As it was, timing was tight. The 'usual' train was (inevitably) late, and instead of a leisurely grooming and preening at Albany I had to dress in a scrabble, plopped some toothpaste on my suit, spilt the aftershave, was my parting straight? etc.

---

[1] Nigel Wicks. Since returning in 1985 from Washington as Economic Minister at the British Embassy had been Principal Private Secretary to the Prime Minister.

[2] Paul Channon, who succeeded his father, Sir Henry ('Chips'), as MP for Southend in 1959, had been promoted to Secretary of State following Leon Brittan's resignation.

I just got to Number 10 in time. Well, not really, as I was *on* time
and I should have been a deferential eight minutes early. No one
seemed to know who I was or why I was there. I hung around in the
little waiting room, repressing the urge to put my head round the
door and see what now happened in Ian's old study, where he used
to lie in wait and pull in Cabinet Ministers before a meeting and tell
them 'what the Prime Minister was hoping to achieve'.

After a bit Wicks appeared.

'Right.'

'Eh?'

I followed him up the stairs.

'She's got a cold,' he said.

A man of few words. Five, to be precise.

But there was no sign of a cold at all. The Prime Minister looked
wonderful, was effusive, genuinely friendly. Unusually, she saw me
alone, not in the Cabinet Room, but the little 'parlour'. She told me
how important the job was. I was to be Minister for Trade, *not* just a
Min of S. It was the second most important Minister outside the
Cabinet after the Financial Secretary – 'but don't shout that around'.

'Negotiation is the key. And I need someone with a *presence*,
charm, someone *different* . . . and of course with a brilliant brain.' (No,
really).

She said someone (I wonder who[1]) had said that I would be
unacceptable to, e.g., the Nigerians because of (conveyed but not said)
my remarks about Bongo-Bongo land. 'But of course you will be,
perfectly acceptable, won't you?'

Then she praised me for my work in the Department, said I was
the only person she could rely on there (uh?), how few of us there
were. At the end, when she spoke of her determination to go on, and
her blue eyes flashed, I got a full dose of personality compulsion,
something of the *Führer Kontakt*.

An agreeable vignette occurred when 'Professor' Brian Griffiths,
a courtier, came in.[2] After some small talk he said, 'No Minister for
Trade has been appointed.'

The Prime Minister indicated me, and his demeanour altered
quite markedly.

---

[1] On his own subsequent (that evening) admission, it was Douglas Hurd.

[2] Brian Griffiths, banking and economics academic, had been Head of the Prime
Minister's Policy Unit since 1985.

I returned to the Dept. Hugged the girls, and began to pack up my papers.

Department of Trade and Industry   *Monday, 3 February*

I am in my lovely new spacious office. I have rearranged the furniture so that my desk is up the far end, with a 'conference' table three windows down towards the Private Office door – and this I insist is always kept open, being the best way of asserting discipline.

It means that visitors have to cover a good distance as they approach me. Mussolini-like. And is particularly welcome in the case of the diary secretary, who is called Rose. Rose (primly she signs her notes, of which there already have been a good number, 'Rosemary') has hips, and a bust, which are almost too noticeable in someone of only (say) 5 foot $4\frac{1}{2}$ inches. She looks very coolly and directly at me when she speaks. And when she comes into the room she holds her head up and does not shuffle or stoop.

The principal Secretary, Matthew Cocks, is very good news. High IQ, pleasant sense of humour, unshockable.

I had a good press – the *FT* was particularly complimentary – and this has cheered the outer office. But I lost no time in circulating my last 'Protectionist' article from the *Daily Telegraph*, and certain Hansard extracts from way back. Matthew told me that there are still believers in the various Desks, but of course they have to stay quiet at the present time, because the vogue has altered.

We'll see about that, I said. Matthew has an engaging way of biting his lip when suppressing a giggle.

Later

I went and had a chat with Paul Channon. He is quick, and funny. His rapid style of speech may make him seem more nervous than actually he is. At one time in the past he was very cross with me, did indeed upbraid me in the library, for saying unpleasant things about Chips, his snobbish, *arriviste*, but intensely observant father.

Paul has been in the Department for ages. And for long periods – the various interregna, particularly when Norman Tebbit was recovering from his wounds – acted virtually as Secretary of State. It is quite proper that he should have been promoted.

Paul was lively and amusing about my (until last week his) job. 'It's very much an independent command.'

And his predecessors. 'I have seen three Secretaries of State sitting in this very chair, sobbing.'

Both Leon and Cecil had, in their different ways, piccolo nervous crises.

Paul also told me, as indeed have many others already, that every Minister for Trade ends up in the Cabinet.

My head is swollen.

At the Council of Ministers,   *Tuesday, 18 February*
Luxembourg

I came out last night, dined and stayed the night at the Embassy. Just before leaving Peter caught me on the DTI Ministers' landing, and warned me against HE's wife. Apparently she likes to provoke (argument, as distinct from advance). 'She will be wearing a tartan skirt.'

It is a heavy, handsome building; warm and comfortable with masses of Wilton everywhere. Big wash basins, everything well lit, makes Saltwood really *absurdly* tatty. And a huge decanter of whisky in my room (but not things I actually *need*, like shampoo or Redoxon).

Yes, the Ambassador's wife was wearing a tartan skirt. A big woman, a kind of up- (but not much up)market constituency ward chairman. She 'enlivened' the meal by making a series of ludicrous and – even by my sceptical standards – highly eccentric remarks about the Community, NATO, foreign policy, and so on. Cowlike, really.

'Yes, yes,' I agreed. 'Absolutely. Go on. More!'

We developed our themes while, at the far end of the table, the Ambassador smiled benignly, though with just a touch of unease.

This morning I reported early to the Council Chamber, and was soon closeted in the UKREP suite with officials. They were twitchy, but curious. Totally Europhile. Sole objective, as far as I could see, being to 'expedite business' – i.e., not make a fuss about anything, however monstrous. Or at least, you *could* make a fuss, but only a 'show' fuss in order to get kudos from, soon after, surrendering 'in the interests of making progress'.

I took against one in particular. This female, after I had spent over an hour getting my speech notes beefed up by a few degrees, literally snatched them away five minutes before I was due to perform, and substituted a pencilled text of her own.

Earlier I had noticed her scribbling away manically, like those demented women in Lincolns Inn Hall during Bar finals. All my points had been 'toned down' out of sight. In had come or, I should say, *back* had come, great slabs of Eurospeak – total gibberish to anyone not part of the cult.

'What's all this?'

'It's the new "Line to Take"!'

'How do you mean, "New"?'

'There's just been' (plainly a lie as she wouldn't look at me) 'a telegram from Number 10.'

I was cornered. The little Portuguese (for the whole of my time as Minister for Trade I am going to find myself, at every international conference where the participating countries are identified in French – *Royaume Uni* – sitting next to a little Portuguese) was coming to his peroration.

Not, really, that it makes the slightest difference to the conclusions of a meeting what Ministers say at it. Everything is decided, horse-traded off, by officials at COREPER, the Council of Permanent Representatives. The Ministers arrive on the scene at the last minute, hot, tired, ill, or drunk (sometimes all of these together), read out their piece, and depart.

Strange, really. Because the EC constitution is quite well drawn. The Council of Ministers is sovereign, and can/could boss COREPER around. But, as always in politics everywhere, democratic or autocratic, it's the chaps on the spot who call the shot.

The civil servants beaver away, massage and congratulate each other, while the politicians treat attendance as a chore.

Now what I should have done – what every Minister should have been doing is – after the 'Conference', to call the officials in, get fully briefed on the next subjects to come before COREPER, and instruct *them* on *their* 'Line to Take'. So that, in good time, the Minister would know what was happening, what had been conceded, what was still open to play for.

But no, I was bundled off – Phew, that's him out of the way for a bit – and took a bumpy little Fokker to Paris, to link up with an Air France flight to Heathrow and straight back to the Department for a bit of late pressure and a nice full 'In' tray.

At de Gaulle I forced Matthew to buy omelette and chips from the airport *frite*, which we consumed in the company of a cross black man and two incredible, showdykes.

Then the pleasing Airbus – always so much nicer than the baby Boeings – but spoiled by the Air France personnel, who are odious. Grumpy in deportment, lumpy in appearance. At the end of a flight the BA girls always line up at the door and say 'Thank you' (and they must get quite a quota of leers and sneers) and it *is* pleasant, although I myself am often guilty of snubbing them if my mood is foul, or preoccupied. The AF crew just scowl at you in silence.

Albany   *Sunday, 2 March*

I loathe London on Sunday evenings, but today Jane and I were lunching with Willie at Dorneywood.[1] She has gone on down to Saltwood while I stay here to blitz the boxes, and tomorrow make a dawn raid (which, as it will be a Monday, the office will not be expecting).

I am really *in the Government* now. A completely different status and experience from the days of 'Parly Sec' with the officials either patronising or incredulous; journalists and colleagues alike regarding it as a fluke, liable to end with a bump, at any moment. Now officials (and Ambassadors) are curious but, in their varying degrees, deferential. All the accoutrements – attitude of the Whips, of (with wide variations) ministerial colleagues, drivers, policemen, journalists – are enhanced. I have a huge airy office, and, at last, *interesting boxes*.

It is deliciously enjoyable, and I feel full of adrenalin most of the time, although conscious that I am draining the substance. My hair is, at last, thinning and beginning to show grey.

---

[1] Dorneywood, near Burnham in Buckinghamshire, the mansion left by Lord Courtauld-Thomson for the use of a senior Government Minister, at the discretion of the PM.

Dorneywood is a dreary red brick house in flat country much, and I would guess expensively, built over. Inside, though, the furniture is good. Pictures medium only, but some amusing ('amusing' means 'erotic' doesn't it, in an auctioneers' catalogue description, and they are only mildly that) murals by Rex Whistler. A lot of decent porcelain – mainly Wedgwood.

Lord Courtauld-Thomson looked down from the wall upon the lunch guests. I told Cecilia Whitelaw that his father had perished in the R 101 at Beauvais in 1932. (Or was I mistaken? Certainly a Secretary of State for Air at this time carried the same name.) Curiously, she didn't seem aware of this. And that his last radio message had been on the 'just-opened-our-fourth-bottle-of-Kummel' lines.

This made James Hanson, sitting on my right, splutter.[1] He and I got on well, letting our hair down rapidly and using 'fuck', 'arsehole' and 'shit' all too freely, although Cecilia gamely pretended not to hear. Poor Swinton, opposite, who used to be fat and objectionable is now diminished, having lost six stone (!) and is quiet-spoken and polite.[2]

After lunch the girls separated and Willie, pretty watery-eyed, boomed away about the Land-Rover balls-up.[3] Too extraordinary that no one told him about it until four days before the announcement. Yet I issued a warning minute to the whole of DE on 17 September last year. And I clearly remember thinking then that really I ought to slip a copy to Willie. I funked it as not having the rank or responsibility, and that he might think I was up to my sneaky ways.

But I always welcome confirmation of my infallible eye for what is or is not *political*.

Willie was very good about the need to *help* the PM see, in some situations, that there were other possibilities; excising her (erroneous) belief that if she threw her personal weight behind something it would

---

[1] James Hanson (Life Peer, 1983). Chairman of Hanson plc since 1965.
[2] Earl of Swinton (2nd Earl). Deputy Government Whip in the Lords.
[3] There was a tentative bid on the table for the former British Motor Corporation from Ford. AC had seen that one of the consequences would be that the ownership of Land-Rover would fall into US hands. When the bid became substantive this possibility gave rise to consternation among some members of the Cabinet.

always go through. Willie said that the PM's Private Office was greatly diminished by the loss of Robin Butler.[1]

Willie said that Nigel Wicks 'will be (sic) very good... is very good... BUT' – a marvellous Willyism. Everyone says Wicks is useless. The great man was also extremely funny, giving imitations of the juniors in the PM's outer Private Office. Little creeps and OBN-ers.

After Hanson had clattered off in his helicopter Willie took me on one side and said that I was *always* to contact him *immediately* if there was 'anything I wanted to talk about', which pleased me greatly. Also at the lunch was Woodrow Wyatt.[2] With the exception of Macmillan (and *he* does it on purpose) Woodrow is the only person I know who seems to be more ga-ga than he is. And the dreadful Henry Plumb,[3] who Jane said was just as flatulent and pleased with himself as always.

Department of Trade and Industry   *Thursday, 6 March*

Last night Tristan called me out of the lobby and said that the FCO were already making trouble. 'Uh?' A report had gone in saying that I was 'anti-European'.

It can only have been that fucking Ambassador in Luxembourg. I said that I was trying to humour his great plain wife, whom Peter had warned me (rightly) tried to shock the dinner guests. Tristan nodded gloomily. Once a report is in, it's in. That's why, if you're *really* ambitious, you have to be cagey.

Apparently the report has also gone to UKREP, who are worried about the way I am going to chair the Internal Market Council. Cunts. Of course I will be perfectly OK.

But this bloody Presidency does hang over me.[4]

---

[1] Robin Butler, after three years as Principal Private Secretary to the Prime Minister had moved in 1985 to the Treasury as Second Permanent Secretary, Public Expenditure.

[2] Sir Woodrow Wyatt, journalist and businessman (printing) and for twenty years a Labour MP. Now a Conservative and Chairman of the Horserace Totalisator Board. Elevated to the Lords as a Life Peer in 1987.

[3] Sir Henry Plumb, farmer (President of National Farmers Union, 1970–9); MEP, Cotswolds, since 1979. Elevated to the Lords as a Life Peer in 1987.

[4] The member states of the European Community rotate through the office of President every six months. During a country's Presidency each Minister chairs the Council at Brussels that accords most closely with their domestic responsibility.

At lunchtime today in came a couple of Euro-MPs who apparently cut ice, Ben Patterson[1] and Basil de Ferranti.[2] Patterson I remember from the Westminster Candidates circus in the old days. Like many who failed the Constituency Selection process he opted (after a spell in the CCO library) to join the 'Euro Parliament'.

Ferranti looked ghastly, pale yellow. And I could not remember whether it was him staying in Mark Birley's chalet at Verbier in 1966, and drinking 'Bull-Shots', or another, blackish sheep called Sebastian. Or whether, indeed, they are not the same person?

The two of them were totally consumed with it all, and knew the jargon backwards. Tiredly I listened, thinking what irrelevant balls.

Perhaps it showed, because from time to time I could see a mischievous half smile cross Matthew's features.

British Embassy, Brussels   *Monday, 10 March*

Comfortable here; pleasant, ex-Rothschild town house. A long, curiously narrow entrance hall, then a wide staircase with important pictures of a Salvator Rosa-ish kind hanging sombrely.

There is a little time before dinner and I prowl about my bedroom looking gloomily at the heavy mahogany furniture. I open the big, cupboard-shaped windows, and look at the clear spring sky and hear the birds sing to one another as they settle for the evening, 'going to bed'.

Today I talked to other Ministers – my counterparts – and got my way with officials.

But in the long mirrors I see myself jowelly and puffed. My shoulder muscles have almost gone.

How I pine for that long, long youth that I enjoyed! To leap and stride – with every new encounter a joy of *possibility*. The 'sluice of hearing and seeing'[3] that endured for so long.

Now, I suppose, in the timescale of my life, I am in the last week

---

[1] Ben Paterson, MEP, Kent West, since 1979.
[2] Tragically Basil de Ferranti was at the time (unknown to AC) suffering from liver cancer and subsequently died. His elder brother, Sebastian Basil de Ferranti, was former Chairman of Ferranti plc; a director of GEC plc since 1982.
[3] Louis MacNeice.

of a holiday – or however the analogy should be shaped – a Sunday afternoon. By Thursday, I will have to start 'packing'.

Boy has asked for a 'Mandat' to handle the Kiosk. I can hardly refuse. I go to Zermatt less and less now. But I have never been happier than I was at the Chalet. Although I came close to it when I used to call at the Guinness pub in West Lavington after walking the beagles on Salisbury Plain. Pure happiness. Everything was so perfect then, and I will always remember it, and thank God.

Palace Hotel, Helsinki   *Saturday, 27 September*

Got here today, pointlessly, unnecessarily early. Dave had driven me to Heathrow from Saltwood on a beautiful morning of late September through that wonderful rich countryside, polo at Cowdray Park, that rolls along both banks of the M25 on the Gatwick stretch. I didn't feel nostalgic or depressed; more kind of depersonalised. What *am* I doing? Why am I going out on the weekend?

These Nordic tours are a complete fuckface, redeemed only by the girls, so blonde blonde, so clean and, at first sight, so correct. Already a clear-skinned beauty has answered my call for room service.

But, as always, I am no more than a voyeur. Officials hover outside the door. Privileged prisoner.

The little Ambassador met me. All the usual stuff about they're very punctual, you must stay to the end, you know about the custom of speaking at meals, of course, it's rude to drink without raising your glass to someone at the table (I'm not going to touch the fucking stuff, I thought grimly) and of course if anyone catches your eye and raises their glass at you you must respond.

God knows what's going to happen tomorrow. A kind of 'getting to know you' day has been laid on, with fishing on the lakes, drinking schnapps and (I don't like the sound of this *at all*) a sauna. Doesn't everyone wander about sweating, but naked? I can't even urinate if someone else comes into the gents – which, I seem to remember, is *such* a bad sign that, if admitted, it could get you a discharge from the Army as being a moral danger to your brothers in arms.

Perhaps it's something to do with Eton?

But I don't in the least mind letting girls see my penis. I suppose it is because I fear – for quite extraneous physical reasons – becoming lightly, or indeed heavily, tumescent and attracting the attention of other men, either whose curiosity or disapproval being equally unwelcome.

It's incredibly cold. I went for a walk along the Quays, and over to a great Sally Line Baltic ferry, wearing every single article of clothing that I had brought with me – cardigan, muffler, David Owen mac, Citroën cap, gloves – and still got chilled ear canals, so that I lose my balance. This condition, I know from experience, can last a couple of hours or so, and people think you are tight.

Also Jane left the hotty out of my luggage, which could be a bore when I go to bed.

All the same, I like the Finns. They are serious, and straightforward. Like Germans, but without the sinister streak.

And there is not a Club Med to be seen anywhere. Still less a 'Heavy Suntan'.

I said to the Interior Minister, 'What is your immigration policy?'
'We don't have one.'
'Can anyone come into the country, then?'
'Sure. But there's just one thing . . . '
'What's that?'
'They have to look like us. Just like Finns.'
And he burst out laughing.

British Embassy, Belgrade   *Wednesday, 15 October*

They cram my diary so tight that even *forty seconds* is precious. And this makes me ill-tempered. So that I am rude to Embassy staff (though never to the minions, who are amiable and do their best), and to 'Businessmen', especially the cocky ones. Last night there was a great big red-faced one from Davy McKee,[1] calling all the shots, being deferred to. But my feeling is that he could go belly-up at any moment, and gave him short shrift.

We had a 'day off', although even here the schedule was drum taut. The 'Jugs' (a Thirties expression, I remember my parents using it, and think it came from Oliver Lyttelton) flew me to Sarajevo. A

---

[1] A publicly quoted (at that time) engineering company.

Lear – they are always fabulous on take-off, the Lears – flown by two
uniformed and identical dwarves with a young and dissolute-looking
navigator. We *just* got in through a gap in the early morning fog. The
approach was frightening, with a few Bosnian 'Munro's' peeping up
through a flat blanket of cotton wool.

Then, standard draining session with various local dignitaries
before a very fattening lunch.

But I began to enjoy myself, having insisted (and being thought
eccentric, even by my own Private Office, while the Embassy did
their best to put me off) that we foregather in the very hotel where
the Archduke Franz Ferdinand stayed his last night, and whence he
journeyed into the city. Not only that. But after lunch we ourselves
had to follow his *exact* route to the very point of his assassination.

It was quite short. We followed the tram lines, still there, having
been laid, I suppose, at the turn of the century. And soon I was
standing on the corner where Princip[1] had waited – totally unchanged
in scale and dimension; pave, granite kerbstones.

This was where the 'old coachman', gaga Czech chauffeur, had
taken a wrong turning (or did he do it on purpose? A line of enquiry
that has been insufficiently pursued) and gratingly engaged reverse
gear. For more than a few seconds the car must have been stationary.

And then the shots, at point blank range.

I could still smell it, just as one can in a haunted room. A colossal,
seismic charge of diabolic energy had been blown, released on that
very spot some seventy-two years ago, and drawn its awful price.

> Not in the hands of boys, but in their eyes
> Shall shine the holy glimmer of goodbyes.[2]

Nearby was the little Princip museum, showing the youth to be
exactly as I would expect. Tiresome, ego, mare-eyed, consumptive-
looking. Something between Seventies CND and Baader-Meinhof.

Afterwards I was taken to the old Muslim Quartier. And I smelt
here in the market for the first time that authentic Balkan tang –
incense and bad fat. Sausages always frying. The women are hideous.
Squat, moustachio'd and without shape.

---

[1] Gavrilo Princip, whose assassination in Sarajevo of Archduke Francis Ferdinand,
heir to Emperor Francis joseph of Austria, and his morganatic wife, Countess
Sophia Chotek, on 28 June 1914 precipitated the First World War.

[2] Wilfred Owen, 'Anthem for Doomed Youth'.

British Embassy, Budapest   *Friday, 17 October*

I was on the step yesterday, I can't think how. Knowing it was the last lap perhaps – because today we are clear, with a pleasant-sounding trip ahead of us to the great nature reserve at Lake Kiskunşág.

I was forced into round after round of meetings, straight from the aircraft. No time even to pee (always a favourite ploy of civil servants who, as is known, have fibre-glass bladders). But I sparkled, gabbled pressingly. Seven conclaves in succession and I was glad to see that by about five in the evening the interpreter took every opportunity to 'rest his eyes', and his head was nodding.

At dinner I sat next to the head of the National Bank, named Fekete. Very good company, a bankers' banker – stout, slow of speech, heavily Hungarian-accented, deeply pessimistic and cynical.

There is a certain vocabulary, a language that outside the profession only very rich people use: LIBOR, COMEX, the Long Bond curve. Ministers don't get any of that stuff in Treasury briefs. But Fekete and I were comfortable with each other. We went through the whole world scene considering 'possibilities'. In the end, concluding that Zurich, the good old Swiss Franc, was the only place. Perhaps a bit of Sandoz, or Brown Boveri.

Fekete told me a wry tale of when Kádár[1] had invited him to join the Government as Finance Minister.

'János, you ought to know that I played a part, as a boy, in the '56 uprising. There may be papers on file, photographs.'

'My dear fellow – what *does* that matter these days?'

'And also that my mother has Jewish blood . . . '

'Quite unimportant. Quite unimportant.'

Kádár paused for a little while, stroking his chin, then, 'What was that you were telling me about the '56?'

Earlier, at the reception, I had paid too much attention to one of the Hungarian ladies. Her skin was almost greasy, but beautiful nipples showed through her satin blouse. She curtsied and shimmied most pleasingly when we were introduced, and called me 'Minister' in exhalation – always erotic.

Now the car is coming to pick us up for a day in the care of

---

[1] János Kádár. As head of the Hungarian Socialist Workers' Party he suppressed the Hungarian Uprising of 1956 with the aid of Russian troops. Twice Prime Minister, he remained Party General Secretary until 1988.

Dr Bánkuri, the engaging and well-informed curator of the nature reserve, who has already pleased me by revealing his knowledge of Loch Eriboll and its importance as a staging point for northerly migrants. How delicious it will be to breathe fresh air for nearly all of the day.

Saltwood   *Saturday, 18 October*

Odiously, there were three boxes in the car at Heathrow. Several e.g.s of civil servants trying to backslide while I was away.

Here, poor Jane had a tummy upset; Andrew was being prosecuted for careless driving. Brodies have lost ground in the dispute with Anson's nephew over Ardneackie, and Bird & Bird have produced a hopelessly pessimistic opinion on our proposed action against Southern Water.

I look appalling in the mirror. So puffy and pink around the eyes – plainly pre-cancerous.

House of Commons   *Tuesday, 18 November*

I have been cross and snappy all day in the office.

A tedious Businessmen's lunch at the Stafford Hotel (I suppose I am too hard on them sometimes, poor dears. Is it diffidence, or just *thickness* that makes them so dreary as company? Their French and German counterparts are keen and quick and curious, and always stimulating to talk to. Perhaps it's just another variant of always preferring other MP's constituents to one's own.)

By the afternoon I was acid-feeling, and when I was kept waiting thirty-five minutes outside a BOTB meeting I thought, and said, fuck this, and just walked off. Officials were oggly, but impressed.

So I am over here, taking refuge. I did a quick trawl, to see if there was anyone sympathetic around, but it was a bad time of the afternoon. There are a multitude of telephones scattered around the Palace, in all the nooks and crannies adjoining the corridors. Every one of them, it seemed, had an MP crouched over it, pompously pontificating. It is the hour when one must catch the deadline for the local paper.

Most of them are buffers, or demi-buffers, or *buffers-aspirant*. They amount to nothing.

I couldn't go back to being a backbencher. It's so completely artificial. What democratic overheads we carry in our system of Government!

Also, I am soft-spoken and apprehensive about going on *Question Time* this week. In addition to my inability, in practically every instance, to answer a direct question from Robin Day on 'But what is the Govt's position on... ?' lines, I am on a hiding to nothing generally.

Whatever I do they'll get me. If I am grave and responsible, they'll say, 'Hasn't he gone off?' If I'm jaunty and reckless, it'll be, 'There he goes again, another gaffe.'

Interesting, that word 'gaffe'. Three-quarters of the journalists who use it don't, for a start, know what it means. It's monosyllabic, which is a help of course, to the Editor; and, to them, it signifies 'soundbite', or 'unpalatable truth'. A true gaffe is accidental. Mine never are. I like to shock, and I do it (though not as often as I could) deliberately.

Department of Trade and Industry   *Wednesday, 19 November*

Why is it that the coffee, quite discreetly served at Number 10, is so markedly better than the muck dished up, by defiant and oopsy-la trouts, at DE and DTI?

We were hanging around in the ante-room. The subject was to be Hong-Kong Transitional Arrangements, and the PM had circulated, through Charles Powell,[1] a scathing note about the 'flabby' suggestions that had come up from the Foreign Office.

Little Howe was padding about, lobbying. 'What we've really got to try and do is to prevent the PM discussing this whole thing *episodically*.'

She looked very *fatigué*. Her voice was flat-soft, but with a hint of impatience (further shades of B'mama).

Inevitably, her mastery of the brief is better than anyone else in

---

[1] Charles Powell, diplomat. Private Secretary to the Prime Minister since 1984.

the room, including the 'sponsoring' Department. She did let fall one aphorism – an aside, almost, but clearly from the heart.

'I've learned one thing in politics. You don't take a decision until you have to.'

Saltwood   *Friday, 26 December*

Boxing Day. We were over at the Garden House for drinks and a cold buffet. The Hubbards are staying with Celly, together with their daughter Katie, a real dish. Also in the house was Sam,[1] and Nanny came across from Quince. Col came down in his new(ish) Rolls, painted metallescent gold (or Jewish Racing Yellow, as apparently this colour is termed in the Mess at Knightsbridge). With him was Ming, and teensy weensy little Christopher.[2]

This practice of families coalescing (coagulating?) at Christmastide is OK, I suppose, but tempers can fray. The young people formed a separate group after a bit, and their laughs became loud. Then, through that big 'picture' window in the sitting room, we suddenly saw Col's Rolls, with Andrew at the wheel, James beside him wearing a silly grin, *slewing* on the lawn. The car got stuck in the big rose bed, burying itself deep, with spinning wheels.

The 'grown-ups' went for a walk, leaving the young to clear up. But when we returned their task had been discharged only imperfectly. They had drunk three-quarters of a bottle of akvavit (on top of everything else) which they had 'found' – a Christmas present from the Finnish Ambassador to me. How *do* they manage to take in so much alcohol? Both passed out in chairs in the Green Room when we got back here. But a few minutes ago, having 'come round', they were talking about going 'out', and not being back until around midnight. Oh dear.

I should be writing a résumé of the year, it is only a month off the anniversary of my appointment, but I too am muzzy and maudlin, from champagne followed by good burgundy.

---

[1] Sam, son of AC's sister Colette (Celly).
[2] Christopher, son of AC's brother Colin, by his third wife Helena (Ming).

I look back on a period of great and continuous pressure – travel, paperwork, schedules of a scale and complexity which I would never have regarded as tolerable if I had been warned in, say, 1971, when it was a great burden even to dress up and go over to Havant[1] for a 'function'. So many miles from those utterly carefree days when I used to take the beagles in the 2CV to Salisbury Plain, and drink a pint of Guinness in the pub at West Lavington before driving back along that flat road to Seend where Alex Moulton[2] used to test his big 'bikes, and past the Worton blondes, back to a supper of sweet Hungarian vegetables cooked by Anna Koumar. I still live off the physical capital accumulated during those middle years when my contemporaries were cooped up in fetid rooms, drinking at mid-day and going late to bed.

I am in better shape than all of them, still.

But what have I achieved, as Minister for Trade, this last year? Tightened up the MFA,[3] got a good mark for boosting the internal market. I've managed to get a few signals through to the Lady to show that I still exist.

A reasonable rapport there, although it can be dissipated in a trice.

A mildly amusing side-effect. I used to be so frightened of flying. Now, I no more notice it than I do taking the cable car to Trockener Steg[4] (come to think, I used to find that alarming until I got accustomed to it). Last year I made (including helicopters) 156 landings. Among them Brussels, Luxembourg, Paris, Bonn, Strasbourg, The Hague, Geneva, Rome, Lisbon, Budapest, Belgrade, Athens, Bahrain, Amman, Bagdhad, Singapore, Perth, Sidney, Melbourne, Canberra, Mackay (and grass strips), Auckland, Wellington, Pt Moresby, Tokyo, Hong Kong, Seoul, Oman, and Inverness.

Travel! When I was first appointed everyone said how lucky I was, being able to go to all these places. I suppose so, if you can't afford the ticket. But that's never been a problem for me. And, in any case, I haven't been a traveller – just a zombie in invisible hand-cuffs.

---

[1] In the early Seventies there was some possibility of AC being adopted as Conservative candidate for the safe seat of Havant and Waterloo.

[2] Alex Moulton, designer of the innovative Moulton bicycles, and rubber suspensions for the motor industry.

[3] The 'Multi-Fibre Arrangement', a form of treaty which protected the UK textile industry.

[4] A ski-station above Zermatt, served by a very long cable-car run.

1987

1987

The ground is dormant at present, with only a few snowdrops and early crocuses showing. For most of the day we were along the woodland walk, raking and pruning. The rake collects huge piles of dead grass, twigs and brambles, and we had several fires going.

Just after tea Peter M. rang with the news that poor Robin Cooke[1] had died. Robin was two years younger than me, and on occasion could look really quite youthful. He had been in the House for an eternity, having come in on a by-election in the first year of Macmillan's premiership. Robin overlapped even with Chips – who was himself by then bright red in the face and (as he candidly admits) feeling ghastly.

What was pleasing, and admirable, about Robin was his exceedingly blasé approach. He had a safe seat, but slowly ran the majority down from neglect, and by the Eighties his Association had got sick of him. His wife, Jenny, was bright and birdlike. And with his sardonic interrogatory style he could sometimes, on returning for the weekend, reduce her to tears. Jenny was née King and her father, a nasty old buffer who in former times had been a member of the Labour Party and a *headmaster* (it always shows), had changed sides and got elected for the safe seat of Dorset South.[2] When he retired (far too late; he was the same age as my father) it was intended that Robin should slip 'sideways', out of the clutches of the Bristol Conservatives, and start again.

But the plan went wrong – they always do – and Robert Cranborne was selected.[3] Probably better, all in all. But for Robin it was a sad blow. He had served notice on the Bristol Division, and could hardly retract. He was (ludicrous phrase, first amusingly, indeed indecently, deployed in my hearing by Archie Balfour) *between two stools*.

I am a great believer in the adage that deep disappointment can

---

[1] Sir Robert (Robin) Cooke represented Bristol West, 1957–79. At the time of his death he lived at Athelhampton near Dorchester.

[2] Evelyn King, Headmaster of Clayesmore School, 1935–50, doubling 1945–50 as Labour MP for Penryn and Falmouth. He resigned from the Labour Party the following year, joined the Conservatives and represented Dorset South, 1964–79.

[3] Robert, Viscount Cranborne, heir to the Marquess of Salisbury, succeeded Evelyn King as MP for Dorset South and would stand down at the General Election later in the year.

trigger a terminal illness. And I have no doubt that this was what happened with Robin. And worse was to come. Although he was a tremendous supporter of Mrs T. and part of her close Election team in 1983, she lost her nerve at the last moment. Robin, with all his special knowledge and feeling for the Palace of Westminster and his work for the Heritage, should have gone straight to the Lords. But he must needs console himself with a K which had, in any case, been his due for several years.

He was a great gardener, and personally used to cut the yew trees at Athelhampton every year, from tall and perilous-looking special ladders.

MPs die in batches. Just when one thinks that foul air, bad diet, unlimited alcohol and late nights ought surely to be exacting a higher toll, the Almighty springs a surprise. David Penhaligon was killed in a car smash over Christmastide.[1] And Number 10 have just been on the phone. Would I represent the Prime Minister at his memorial service in Truro Cathedral on *Saturday* (ugh) of this weekend.

What a bore. It's a long and tedious journey, that rail stretch after Plymouth. I won't even have time to dismount and make a splash on Plymouth Sound.

Still, always fun to represent the Prime Minister doing anything.

Truro-Paddington train   *Saturday, 10 January*

I have been talking with poor old Jeremy Thorpe.[2] He was sitting alone in the dining car, at one of the head-to-head double tables, being ostentatiously ignored by the Liberals who mill around, drab but noisy, and seem to have taken over the whole train. There is a hint of relief on this, the return journey, and drinks are being called for, and 'tossed off', as my mother used to say.

Jeremy has Parkinson's Disease, quite advanced, and looks gaunt, with staring eyes. He was pleased to have attention and, pathetically, tried to hold on to his right hand in order to prevent it trembling.

---

[1] David Penhaligon, Liberal MP for Truro since 1974.
[2] Jeremy Thorpe, MP for Devon North, 1959–79 and Leader of the Liberal Party, 1967–76.

I tried to get him to reminisce a little, tell a few Macmillan stories. But he did not find it easy to speak. The listener must concentrate hard. I reminded Jeremy of his peak moment of glory and, had he played his cards differently, of power, when the 'hung' results of the Election of February '74 were in, and Ted tried to do a deal, offering him the Home Office. Jeremy was barely intelligible, but his eyes were full of pain.

The Cathedral had been full to the aisles, with crowds outside in the streets and closed-circuit broadcasting. Personally I don't see what all the fuss was about. P. was an unmemorable figure really, with his (demi-bogus) West-Country vowels and *homespun* philosophy. But he personified, I suppose, a kind of soft-centre Cornish provincialism.

Come to think of it, he had something of a dud, down, down-market Jock Massareene,[1] who was at Saltwood yesterday and stood about uselessly while Jane caught and shrouded (a difficult and painful task) some peafowl that he needed, to replace casualties at Chilham.

Albany   *Tuesday, 27 January*

Sometimes there is just so much pressure at Saltwood that it is a relief to sink into the cushions, stale and dirty though they may be, of the Sandling train. For an hour and a half I am isolated, trundling along, and no one can get at me with a will-you, can-you, did-you, have-you, are-you, if-you, but-you? three bags full, query. But it's a kind of cop out, really, because I leave it all on Jane's lap, then ring in the evenings and bark at her.

I must be very near a nervous breakdown. The tower office [at Saltwood] is so bad that I dare not lift any stone there, for fear of what I may find underneath. And last night I dreamed – just before waking, always the most vivid kind – that I had hailed a taxi, then could not remember my intended destination.

This evening the Prime Minister came to the '92 dinner at the St

---

[1] John Clotworthy Talbot Foster Whyte-Melville Skeffington, Viscount Massareene and Ferrard, of Chilham Castle.

Stephen's Club. How déjà-vu it all seemed. Backbenchers bobbing up and down, trying to be goodboy. Same old subjects grinding round and round. Afterwards, I told Jane, I never want to be a backbencher again and will get out immediately I am sacked.

Even dear IG, next to whom I sat, was distrait and low. He basted me for not having chosen a PPS. Ian said, with much truth, that no one in any Government Department knows, or cares (except when it causes them trouble) about the House of Commons, and a PPS would keep me in touch.

Possibly. But I prefer to get my gossip over a bottle of wine with Budgen, or others.

Department of Trade and Industry   *Tuesday, 10 February*

Just back from Harold Macmillan's memorial service in the Abbey.[1] I am filled with melancholy.

The Grenadiers' Return was played, and I thought of the fife music, and of the decimated battalion marching back in from Hulluch on 26 September 1915, past the wounded laid out in rows on either side of the street, groaning from their injuries. And the young classical scholar, less than a year out of Eton, pale and shaken but heroic, nonetheless. When Macmillan enlisted Britain was at the very height of her power and dominion. The habitual bearing, stoicism, self-sacrifice, sense of 'fair play'; the whole *tenu* of the English upper class was in place and unquestioned, looked up to and copied everywhere. Now look at us – and them!

Julian Amery read the second lesson. His voice, which still can command the attention even of a crowded House (for the very reason, I think, because it is so genuinely cast in the tones of the olden days, without self-parody and unlike, for example, the embarrassing plumminess of Derek Walker-Smith) has lost a little of its timbre. I nostalgicised for government by the upper class; which is what I thought it would be – the whole thing really run by the OE mafia – when first I wanted to get in in 1964, and Julian and I had a long conversation at the Chalet and he said I was too old. I did just, *just*, I

---

[1] Harold Macmillan, 1st Earl of Stockton, had died aged ninety-two.

suppose overlap. But by the time that Ted had got rid of Alec he was determined to keep all the others out if he could.

And who is to blame him? Profumo exposed their essential rottenness.[1] The few who remain – Gilmour, Whitelaw, Carrington – are impossibly defeatist. With the exception, I think the *sole* exception, of Robert Cranborne the real toffs have opted out. A few garden openings like Charlie Shelburne,[2] otherwise they're just into tax avoidance and gossip columns. I looked up at the great circular window, to which I have raised my eyes at so many services, and thought, I must – *when* will I – write my great work, *Tories and the Nation State 1922–74.* Perhaps it is for this that I will be remembered? If I am spared.

Department of Trade and Industry   *Tuesday, 24 March*

Last night Heseltine, a bit flushed-looking, came up to me when we were going through the Aye lobby, and leered.

'Have I lost you your seat?'[3]

'Could be,' I shrugged. 'Could be.'

'Never mind. I'll write you a letter of apology.'

Odd. Unlike him. Many others would have found such behaviour disagreeable.

Saltwood   *Sunday, 5 April*

Had a bad, overhot night, which can often happen if one goes to bed too early. Two strange dreams, with which, I would guess, a soothsayer could have little difficulty. First, something muddled about the delib-

---

[1] In the closing phase of the 1959–63 Macmillan premiership, the War Minister, Jack Profumo, who was married to the actress Valerie Hobson, had become involved with a young lady who was also enjoying the attentions of the Soviet Military attaché.

[2] Charles Maurice Petty-Fitzmaurice, Earl of Shelburne, heir to the Marquess of Lansdowne, of Bowood House, Calne.

[3] Michael Heseltine had just announced his plans to 'privatise' the Royal Naval Dockyards in Plymouth.

erate infection of surgical instruments by 'sufferers'. Woke, muck-sweat, walked about. Stood at the open window.

Then, of finding a beautiful fountain pen, an old-style Parker, which wrote exquisitely. It was like a fabulous skiing sequence, when the moguls rise and fall in rhythm.

At mid-day the sun was high and we got the tortoises out of hibernation. I lay on my back on the freshly cut grass in Courtenays, looking at the sky, hearing the slow deliberate rustle as they emerged from their straw-lined boxes to a meal of tomato and sliced banana. Fortunate creatures. If humans could do this at will we, too, would live to be two hundred years old.

Department of Trade and Industry   *Tuesday, 14 April*

I am feeling sickish and tired. Is my lymphatic system packing up?

I have just returned (on foot) from a thoroughly unsatisfactory meeting with Tim Renton at the Foreign Office. Henry Keswick[1] had asked me to put in a word for British contractors, who are being edged out of various important deals in Hong Kong disgracefully, in some cases where the Crown is itself the customer.

Downstairs the desk had made a balls-up of the times, and I hung around, getting cross. Senior Ministers shouldn't be kept waiting, except in the comfort of special rooms set aside for the purpose. Was it always like this in the entrance hall, with ugly common people cackling and shouting and banging things? Probably yes.

On the first floor the rooms have very high ceilings. They must be double cubes. And the furniture is still good and heavy. Tim explained to me, effectively, that Hong Kong had 'gone'. UK influence in matters of this kind was nil. Autonomy, 'LegCo', 'ExCo', Chinese susceptibilities, all have 'to be taken very carefully into consideration'.

One more piece of wealth and real estate that has been allowed just to run through our fingers.

Through the anti-shatter lace curtains I watched some pigeons chasing each other along the balustrade.

---

[1] Henry Keswick, influential director of several Hong Kong businesses, not least Jardine, Matheson.

'It's not 1935,' I said, thinking of all these white-painted ships on the China Station which I used to memorise from the *Jane*'s of that year, the first in which I was given the book.

'No. Not even 1975.'

I lost interest in what he was saying.

Very little of the decor can have been changed in that room for many moons, and I wondered how many tricky subjects, gloomy 'meetings', unwelcome decisions had been played out there down the years.

I am blighted by the Foreign Office at present. Earlier today a creepy official, who is 'in charge' (heaven help us) of South America, came over to brief me ahead of my trip to Chile. All crap about Human Rights. Not one word about the UK interest; how we saw the balance, prospects, pitfalls, opportunities in the Hemisphere.

I'm Minister for Trade, for Christ's sake, what's the point of keeping an expensive mission in Santiago if they can't even tell me what to push? When I questioned him, he was evasive on all policy matters other than his own tenacious, *Guardian*esque obsession.

'Aha but,' soft-spokenly he gloated, 'Community policy is' we are but one in twelve, etc.

What *does* he mean? There is no exclusive 'Community Competence' in Foreign Affairs (yet!). I don't think that there is even a Foreign Affairs Commissioner, is there? This man is exactly the kind of mole who is working away, eighteen hours a day, to extinguish the British national identity.

I am depressed, and zestfree.

General Election, 11 June 1987:
Conservative, 375; Labour, 229; Alliance, 22.

Saltwood   *Wednesday, 17 June*

Tired and liverish with *reaction*. First day back at the House, and I was to rendez-vous with Soames in the smoking room for lunch.

Everyone very jolly – most had increased their majorities, although a few seemed to know I hadn't.[1] Jopling was in splendid form, grinning benevolently.[2] After being sacked, or 'dropped', that's really the only way – show your face in the smoking room at once – and mix it with the boys. (Whether I shall ever be able to do that is, I fear, extremely doubtful.) He'd always wanted Agriculture, and of course he was good with the farmers – the real ones anyway. But more and more the people who call the shots on the NFU are the nasty, computer-driven 'barons', who drench everything with nitrates and rip off the CAP. Thus, *mutatis mutandis*, Ministers don't spend their time any longer in tweed suits scratching pigs at county shows, but cooped up in the Charlemagne arguing with their 'counterparts' about the Green Pound. Hats off to him, though. Like most Chief Whips he knew who the shits were. Memorable remark about Heseltine: 'The trouble with Michael is that he had to buy all his furniture.' Snobby, but cutting. He and Gail (so pretty with her red hair and lovely skin) take their holidays in France, in leathers, on an old Honda. Now that *is* sporting.

As for myself – was I being unduly paranoiac in detecting a frisson of disapproval? Certainly Government colleagues – Renton, Baker, Mitchell, Patten J. – all in their different ways radiated 'distancing' and even John Wakeham, whose eye I had caught while we were listening to the Queen's Commission in the Lords, seemed to be saying, 'Phew, you really pushed it that time'.[3] That fat gossip Critchley said something about 'rocking the boat' – rich coming from him. Sometimes he affects the mantle of Bufton Tufton.

Soames was twitchy concerning his 'last chance', as the junior Whips' appointments were being made at that moment.[4] And the meal wasn't a great success as the top end of the dining room was full and we had to sit among the Labour tables.

Atkins joined us in sour mood.[5] He's just been made a junior Minister, at bottle-washer level, in my Department. He can't have expected anything more, surely?

Anyhow, he slagged away at anyone who was mentioned, radiating

---

[1] AC's majority fell from 11,000 in 1983 to 4000, owing to the threat of redundancies consequent on 'privatisation' of the dockyard (see entry for 24 March).

[2] Michael Jopling had been Minister of Agriculture for four years until the Election.

[3] A reference to an interview which AC gave during the Election campaign at which he had poured scorn on the Channel Tunnel project.

[4] In fact Nicholas Soames became PPS to the Environment Secretary.

[5] Robert Atkins had been made Parliamentary Under-Secretary at Trade and Industry.

bitterness and frustration, while Soames fidgeted. Alternately Nicholas shouted greetings at Labour Members, most of whom were pretty crestfallen, or swivelled round, trying at long range to join in the conviviality at the other end of the room.

This was the first occasion that I had witnessed the whole ceremony, processing through to the Lords, listening to all the opening speeches, everything. It's 'theatre', I suppose, but dud theatre. Not *rep*, just dud theatre.

I drove back in the Range Rover with a few oddments from the office and a couple of Euston Road school pictures, including a Graham Bell, that I want to hang at Bratton. Very tired. The garden hasn't really recovered from our three-week absence during the campaign, and I doubt if it will now, this year. We're already halfway through. It was quite a shock when Jane reminded me that on this weekend falls the longest day.

Department of Trade and Industry   *Friday, 26 June*

Rose wanted to go to *Les Misérables*. Naturally there were no tickets. However a quick call to James Osborne and a couple of good stalls were whistled up through the show business underground, and I collected them from the major domo at Aspers' – who wouldn't take a tip.[1] I'm out of touch with these things. I suppose my humble £20 note was beneath him, like Arthur Lee refusing the Star of India for his work on the Civil Service Commission.

I haven't been inside a theatre for ages. How evocative is that smell – greasepaint, dust, scenery – that wafts out across the stalls when the curtain goes up. And how very tiresome and ego and generally oopsy-la are most of the audience (though not as bad, I must admit, at the Palace as at Covent Garden). On the way back, as we walked down Shaftesbury Avenue, everybody seemed to be staring. Women, in particular, were looking at Rose. Did they think they

---

[1] James Osborne, manager of the Curzon Club, at that time in the proprietorship of AC's old friend, John Aspinall.

'recognised' her? Or was it just prurient curiosity? Strange, and unusual.

We had a banquette at the Mirabelle. I kept looking sideways at Rose and thinking how remarkably pretty is her mouth; so cupidic, like those coquettish maidens hidden away in the upper corners of a Tintoretto ceiling. She wanted hock so I ordered a quite decent bottle of Gewürztraiminer. But just after it had been poured she sliced through whatever inanity I was saying and asked the wine waiter to bring some soda water, which she made him pour *on to* the delicious white wine. He was equal to this and didn't bat an eyelid, although I doubt if it happens very often in the Mirabelle.

'Very Byronic,' I said.

Saltwood   *Sunday, 28 June*

The first day of summer (!). We swept the Bailey of grass clippings. Probably the most back-breaking of all gardening jobs is picking them up, moistly resisting and getting into one's nose and ears; throwing them into the back of the Mehari as little puffs of breeze coming from nowhere on a completely still day blow flakes and flickings back in one's face. Then I helped Jane get a buddleia down from where it had been growing in the wall below my father's study window. Then got the pool pump working which, amazingly, it did without too much demur.

We had planned our first outside lunch, M. Goisot and a huge Brie, but forsook it to tend to a baby jackdaw who had got sump oil on his wings and (how, for God's sake?) torn off one of his legs below the knee joint. I thought he was a goner – how *could* he survive? But he had so much fight in him, and his lovely pale blue eyes were so lively that we had to try. Jane washed his wings and tail feathers, rinsing and re-rinsing the Fairy Liquid. He didn't seem to mind; positively enjoyed the warm whirrings of a hair-drier. We stuffed a couple of worms down his throat and left him to gain strength in a basket with a heat bulb glowing over. In no time he appeared to make a full recovery and later that evening, after being returned to the wild, actually *flew* from the sleeper pile to the yew tree by the long garage. Cheered by this, I started the Silver Ghost and went for a drive.

On a fine evening there are very few pleasures comparable to driving a light, open Ghost on country roads. Some will get it from waiting for salmon to take, in dark peat pools, but I am too impatient, and can't stand the midges. In a Ghost you waft along, high enough to look over people's hedges, noiseless enough (as was the original intention) to leave horses unscared. It started at once, of course, although I hadn't been near it since last November. No (*no*) modern car would have done this. Because the Rolls Royce Silver Ghost has – except for the magneto which sparks on a turn – not one single piece of electrical equipment. No battery (flat) or pumps (stuck) or solenoid (up the creek, Squire) or 'black box' (I'm afraid we're talking about a factory replacement unit, Sir, at £873 plus VAT). There are twenty-one separate actions, all of them involving beautifully crafted mechanical linkages, from turning on the gravity petrol feed to actually cranking the starting handle. And after they have been completed in the correct sequence it will – infallibly – fire on the first compression.

My car was built in an epoch when the Grand Fleet dominated the world's oceans. And under the bonnet, in the brass and the copper and the hugely overstrength componentry, there is much trace of marine influence. The factory record shows it going out to India, in Curzon's name (although I doubt he ever sat at the wheel).

Now the Grand Fleet is no more, and Lutyens's beautiful vistas in New Delhi have been overrun by shanty settlements. And yet, even when the Rolls was built brand new, 'there's something wrong with our bloody ships today'.[1]

It is the perennial problem, the need to arrest industrial decadence. At what point does the refusal of innovation overlap with the introduction of the 'black box'? – but not as an enhancement of quality, more a signpost to the soft life and 'shorter working hours'.

I drove for about forty minutes and on my return took a jug of iced lime juice and soda water to the music room where I played the piano, quite competently, until the light faded. A day filled with trivia, but *douceur de vivre* also.

---

[1] Admiral Beatty at Jutland when he lost three battlecruisers, due in part to the inferiority of their armour and the accuracy of the German fire-control systems.

Department of Trade and Industry   *Monday, 29 June*

So hot and thundery. I am feeling exceedingly tired and old. My papers suddenly seem to have got into a total mess. Fatally, I started the practice of having *two* 'In' trays, a priority, or urgent tray and a more dreary waiting-for-attention tray. The dreary one now towers massively, sometimes sliding over on to the 'Out' side which means unsigned papers go back out into Private Office. I just don't have the energy to cope with it. I am flaccid.

An East German trade delegation is in London at present. And it could largely, I suppose, be aversion to this evening's proposed happenings: a meeting with Herr Dr Reichelt, then (monstrously) following sharply on this *another* meeting with Herr Dr Reichelt with a Lancaster House reception ('I think we really must be on time, Minister') as backdrop. Then a massive formal dinner of welcome (for Herr Dr Reichelt). Interpreters. Speeches. Liqueurs? No thanks, etc.

At lunchtime I saw that randy little runt Ian Gladding trying to chat up Rose, and this made me cross.

Later I telephoned Jane and had a talk. She'd bathed.

'I'm so cross,' I said.

'You wouldn't be if you were down here.'

Too true. Ah well, only three weeks to go!

Saltwood   *Sunday, 19 July*

A social weekend at Saltwood. First to arrive (by train, naturally, I met him at Sandling Junction) was Peter Brooke,[1] in a lovely old tweed suit (ambient July temperature 70° plus) stooped and shuffling like a character from LP Hartley. He's so nice, gentle and clever. But almost too Balliol. I know Chesterfield said that one should never allow one's 'innate self' to show, but . . .

Then the Worsthornes.[2] Perry not in an especially good temper;

---

[1] Peter Brooke, MP for City of London and Westminster South since 1977. Paymaster General since the Election.

[2] Peregrine Worsthorne and his first wife Claude. He had become Editor of *Sunday Telegraph* in 1986.

I had forgotten that David Young was originally meant to be coming and that I had mentioned this to Perry and I suppose he was disappointed. Andrew turned up with a couple of brother officers. One of them, surprisingly young-looking, was in fact Tara's[1] father. (She, very splendidly, on first catching sight of Jane had said, 'For God's sake watch out for my father'.) Next was dear Jonathan [Aitken] – *always* a delight in any gathering.

We were changed, drinking champagne in the music room when a commotion was audible from the hall. Dogs barking. The Parkinsons were trying to get in.[2] But William, now more and more a law unto himself, had been disconcerted by Cecil's appearance, his (very loud) change jacket, and slammed the door on him. 'Ooh, you can't come in like that, sir.' I mediated. Cecil's Private Office had failed to tell him, although I had sent many messages, that it was black tie. It's always black tie at Saltwood on Saturday evenings. This is known.

Dinner was longish, before we got the port and the ladies – reluctantly in Ann's case – went away. Then serious conversation began, punctuated at intervals by 'crude' laughs from the other end of the table where Andrew and his Life Guard friends were ensconced with their own decanter.

Perry flew his kite about where is the real opposition coming from, what are the coming ideas, that kind of thing. Cecil responded, but not really very effectively. Jonathan and I were 'ball-boys'. Peter Brooke was completely silent. Perhaps tired, perhaps just faintly disapproving.

Later in the evening I had a chat with Cecil.

She *had* intended to put him in the Foreign Office, and how he had a clear programme to 'sort it out'. He always said he wanted me to go there with him as Min of State, although had it actually came to the point, I'm not so sure. But it was not that that made me feel a great opportunity had been lost. Because all that he said rang so true; all his criticisms of their misplaced – but extravagant – effort are so valid. Cecil also told me that she had clearly planned to groom him as her successor, arranged little private meetings with the Prince of Wales, that kind of thing. Will he ever be able to build it back? I doubt it. She's in love with David Young at the moment. But even

---

[1] A girl friend of Andrew.
[2] Cecil and Ann Parkinson.

there I get the feeling that it could already be waning. *La Donna é mobilè*.

After everyone had gone to bed Jonathan and I talked. I said that I had finally blown it for the Cabinet. He, somewhat tenuously, I thought, advanced the theory that I might be brought in as they were all so *boring*. We both dread the Lady's health cracking up. 'No one can stand this pace,' he said.

Very late that night I tiptoed across the lawn to the Great Library and turned off the tapestry lights. It's spooky over there after midnight, and I was not strong enough to go through to the little lobby where I have positioned that beautiful erotic marble, Boucher's *Captive*, which I bought last week at Sotheby's for double its estimate. (I wonder who the underbidder was?)

On Sunday everyone, thank God, left promptly. Perry had to go to Chequers, and was not sure of the way.[1] We paced on the lawn for a little while. He was disappointed in Cecil, 'He's not a philosopher king. I don't know who could play that role. Perhaps you could?' I'm a sucker for any compliment, and this cheered me up.

There is no doubt that Cecil is better *à deux* than in a general, High Table kind of conversation. He was quite funny about the Lady's health and holidays. 'She *won't* relax, *won't* go to bed.' (I have heard Willie say exactly the same thing.) 'That's why Ian Gow was so bad for her. He *encouraged* her to stay up, later and later. They would sit up in her flat above Number 10, and have just another "last" whisky.' Quite. I can see (but did not say) a number of reasons why Cecil might object to this.

They're expensive, these hospitalities. In drink alone I'm down three bottles of Dom Perignon, three Talbot blanc, four '78 Morgon, one Cockburn '60, and a lot of brandy.

---

[1] In fact the Worsthornes, notwithstanding the clearest instructions from AC, turned right instead of left at the M25, and were nearly two hours late at Chequers.

Charing Cross   *Friday, 24 July*

A muggy, late July Friday, and I am sitting in a first-class compartment of the Sandling train, odorous and untidy, which, for reasons as yet undisclosed, and probably never to *be* disclosed, has not yet left Charing Cross. 'Operating Difficulties', I assume, which is BR-speak for some ASLEF slob, having drunk fourteen pints of beer the previous evening, now gone 'sick' and failed to turn up.

'Term' is over. I will not need to go to the Department more than three days a week – the rest can be done by phone, fax and Dave bringing down boxes. I must now make sure that the hols are not frittered away. Yoga, filing and paperwork backlog, *moderation in all things*.

I am not feeling particularly energetic or constructive. Last night we had the end-of-term binge, organised by Gow, and this year in the Macmillan Room of the Carlton Club. Not a wild success, as poor Ian had a setback at the outset. It came about like this. We had arranged to meet in my room, and go over to the Carlton together. But on the way, I wanted to drop in my little note to Charles about my conversation with the Governor.[1] Half mischievously I showed it to Ian.

He took a long time to read it, although it was only one side of one page. 'But this is addressed to a (sic) Mr Charles Powell.'

'That's right.'

'But he is a civil servant, is he not?'

'Yes.'

'And you are a Minister in the Government, a Minister of State, indeed, the Minister for Trade?'

'Yes.'

'And you, a Minister of State, are communicating directly with a civil servant – and a very junior ranking civil servant – in another Department?'

'Oh come on, Ian, you know Charles's position . . . '

Ian sighed. I mean he Cone Ripman School of Acting sighed, and said no more. But as soon as we got to the Carlton and after

---

[1] The Governor of the Bank of England. On the Monday of that week AC had sat at dinner next to Robin Leigh-Pemberton. The Governor had taken some time to enlarge on his views that the Community would in the end be moving towards a single currency (which was at that time anathema to the Prime Minister).

sinking his first White Lady, he announced that he felt 'ill', and didn't (*most* unlike him) 'want to stay late'.

Poor fellow. He so misses Number 10. I don't really know how much she sees of him now. But those days when he controlled and monitored *everything* are gone — I suppose for ever. He was so good at it. But her problems are no longer (or not at present, anyway) political. Intelligence relating to the parliamentary Party, gentle massaging of their various egos, is less important. Her problems are machinery-of-government problems — both national, and international. And at coping with these Charles is brilliant. Workaholic, but cool.

Star turn at the dinner was (or was meant to be) Nicky Ridley.[1] But he was *désseché* and, as often these days, aggressive even to his friends. He said the 'Old Guard', by which (he made clear) he also included me, were finished. No new ideas. 'Where are the new, young radicals?' The same sort of crap I'd been getting from Perry last weekend.

'We don't want any fucking new ideas,' I said. 'We've got plenty of problems as it is.' I tried to play Baldwin. Consolidate. Stay calm. I told the story of my grandfather advising 'garaging' whenever one starts to get ahead. (Not everybody understood this, but Soames and Hesketh[2] did. Very much a café society litmus test).

Richard Ryder[3] sparkled gravely and intelligently. I used to think he was a bit of a creep, confusing him — because he is of that generation — with the Blue Chip[4] mutual admirationists. But he is far better than any of them. He knows his history, which is important. That's what makes Alastair Goodlad[5] (another example) so much more interesting than he first appears.

---

[1] Nicholas Ridley, Environment Secretary.

[2] Lord Hesketh (3rd Baron). A Government Whip.

[3] Richard Ryder, MP for Mid-Norfolk since 1983. Mrs Thatcher's Political Secretary, 1975–81. At this time an Assistant Government Whip.

[4] Blue Chip: A dining club, self-selected, of ambitious young fellows who entered Parliament in 1979. They met at 13 Catherine Place, the home of Tristan Garel-Jones. Their group portrait, in oils, hangs in the dining room.

[5] Alastair Goodlad, Parliamentary Under-Secretary, Energy.

UK Mission, Geneva   *Wednesday, 29 July*

I am out here for the UNCTAD meeting. Ulterior motives, of course, but they look like being thwarted.

It seemed safe enough, because of all the United Nations quangos this has to be the dreariest and least consequential. Nothing of substance is discussed, no decisions are ever reached, the political impact at home is nil.

My plan, to put in an appearance, shake a few hands, 'Excellency, how very agreeable to see you again; how well you are looking; I would so greatly value your opinion on . . . ; let us get our staff to arrange a short bilateral meeting; such pleasure, such pleasure.' And all that. A set speech to the assembly (not deviating by one iota from the turgid DTI text). And then, hand over to officials, take the train to Visp – one of my three favourite train journeys in the world – and up on the V-Z Bahn to Zermatt in time for a delicious meal in the station restaurant. And the following day a Whymper scramble. I gave them the Chalet phone number. 'I can be back in Geneva at two hours' notice' (lie).

I had reckoned without (how can I still be underestimating this?) the absolute determination of civil servants never to let a Minister out of their sight if they can possibly avoid it, and how they put this objective above all others.

Also, there is a heavy FCO input here, as indeed there is at every international gathering. The Ambassador fusses and clucks; actually offered his own brief of what I should say and do, on a kind of spot-the-difference basis from the DTI brief. He appears to be sending a totally separate set of telegrams to the Foreign Office while at the same time processing our set, which Tony Hutton[1] is writing each evening, to the DTI. And for what? Absolutely nothing.

What a bore for the desk clerk.

Everybody knows the FCO is crazily overstaffed and treasures these sort of conferences as its own private job creation scheme, but there are limits, one would think.

So it was no surprise to be woken by Marjorie this morning at seven fifteen or thereabouts (the taxi to take me to Geneve Gare was ordered for eight thirty) on my jangling bedside telephone and be

---

[1] Anthony Hutton, civil servant in Trade and Industry, then dealing with external European policy.

told, breathlessly – she always gets slight asthma when she knows I'm going to be cross – that things had got rather 'difficult'.

'Meaning?'

'It looks, Minister, as if the UK is going to be *isolated*' (FCO dread-word, she lowered her voice reverently, almost as if she was saying *buggered*) 'on the Common Fund, both in the Community, and in Group "B".'

'So?'

'Well, Minister, I've been talking to Christopher Roberts – '[1]

'Already?'

'Well no, Minister, I spoke to him last night' (once she mentioned Christopher, I knew I'd had it as she's more frightened of him than she is even of me) 'and he feels it would be unwise of you to be away today, Minister.'

I thought it over. It was no good, I couldn't go. There would be too much *angst*, I wouldn't really be able to enjoy the high Alps. And it was the sort of tedious mini-dispute that might just get referred across to Number 10 by the FCO – they certainly would sneak if they could – and then there'd be a 'Where's Alan?' crisis. Blast, though. I was thoroughly dejected.

Sadly I went for an early morning stroll along the corniche. Very very faint evocations did I feel of earlier, unblighted strolls, distant in time. Water slapping against the hulls of launches after a speedboat had gone by. A man slaloming on water skis, and the burble of Riva exhausts; a girl getting out of her red swim suit and laughing. It was not yet eight o'clock and there was already the promise of great heat, with haze over to the Evian side of the lake.

Saltwood   *Sunday, 4 October*

Vilely depressed after a bad night. (Tom kept us awake fidgeting and flapping his ears and when finally I staggered down to the yard with him at two a.m. he disappeared for three-quarters of an hour ratting, and at intervals barking shrilly, behind the log pile.) This morning a

---

[1] Christopher Roberts, civil servant. Deputy Secretary, Trade and Industry, since 1983.

scotch mist, and everything soaked. You can hardly see across the Bailey.

The papers are full of Heseltine, 'to be the star of the Conference', etc. How can he be, if he hasn't got a perch? He'll have to speak from the rostrum, with a time limit – although even as I write I realise there isn't a Chairman of the National Union made who would cut off that man's sound. Four-fifths of Central Office are closet subversives anyway, always have been. He's got a word-of-mouth going, which is why Bruce,[1] who is a terrific Vicar of Bray, was all 'cor' at lunch yesterday. But *what a bore.*

Yesterday evening at dinner I said, 'I'm even tireder at the end of the holiday than I was at the beginning' (little knowing that I was going to suffer a *nuit cassée*), and this morning I'm just sick and fatigued thinking of it all. I've barely got the energy even to be indignant. Why is it always the bad eggs who seem to get to the top in politics? The only other character given heavy billing today is that ambitious creep War(sic)grave.[2]

I went down to the long garage and sheeted the SS 100, some, very little, of whose brightwork I had lethargically and incompetently cleaned in fading light yesterday.

Later that morning I tiptoed across the soaking lawn to the Great Library. Dehumidifier stopped, naturally, full to the brim. I emptied it, collected my notebook, and meandered round the room, drawing all the curtains to prevent fading.[3]

When will I next be over there? To look for a book perhaps, but to work? Not until next May.

---

[1] Bruce Anderson, columnist on the *Sunday Telegraph*.
[2] William Waldegrave, MP for Bristol West since 1979, actually a friend of AC, irritated him by affecting a 'correct' pronunciation of his name that omitted the 'de'.
[3] Centrally heating the Great Library was discontinued by AC when he moved into Saltwood in 1971. It is shut down from November until March.

HS 125, Luxembourg-Northolt   *Monday, 5 October*

A totally wasted day at the Council of Ministers. No conclusions, no nothing. I can't remember what we were discussing although the meeting only broke up an hour ago and the Line to Take from the Foreign Office was 'prepared for any eventuality' and some six pages long. The background brief weighed about four kilos.

Sorghum, I should think. It's always sorghum, sometimes sorghum and maize.

Only mini-recordable event was the appearance of the French Minister,[1] oh-so-fashionably dressed, and wafting a most terribly expensive *parfum*. Wasn't there something that used to be advertised in old copies of the *New Yorker*, 'Tabu' with an illustration of the (implicitly latin) violinist passionately embracing his young singer? This must be it.

I spotted her as soon as I came in, on the opposite side of the table being all lala with her officials. Our eyes met, but my expression was – or was intended to be – *disdainful*. The meeting was late starting, as always. Years, *years*, must have been wasted in aggregate by no Community Ministers' meeting ever starting less than three-quarters of an hour late. I was standing in a little huddle with the UKREP officials just behind my chair, when along came Madame, swinging her hips most outrageously, and all 'get me'. She quite flagrantly (and with great style, I must admit) swept between us, then paused and posed. Poor old David Elliott[2] somewhat gauchely made the introductions.

The whole thing was so outrageous that I had to grin. She immediately froze up, went all don't-think-I'm-that-easy. High horse. Yes, I suppose she is 'attractive' (in quotes), a kind of up-market Irene Worth. But alas (and indeed, as Irene herself found on the *Queen Mary* in 1951) I am not in the slightest degree aroused by 'the older woman'. They are fun to sit next to at dinner, but I don't want to get any closer. For me, girls have to be succulent, and that really means under twenty-five.

As I write these words I look across at dear Rose demurely stuffing

---

[1] Mme Edith Cresson, Internal Market Minister in the French Government (and later Prime Minister).

[2] David Elliott, deputy head of UKREP under Sir David Hannay, Ambassador and UK Permanent Representative to the European Community.

on RAF biscuits. I *insisted* she came, I *challenged* her to come, and dutifully she did. But like all (or many) of my most devious plans, it got snagged. There is an air controllers' strike, so I thought there would be a good chance of being able to show her the old city, etc. But in fact we've got this nice little RAF HS for the whole DTI party and can whizz in and out on our own route. So now we're all heading back to London and it's only five o'clock.

I feel stale and out of condition. All morning I dozed and hallucinated. The Greek soliloquies are particularly good at sending me to sleep as the interpreters alternate, and one of them translates it 'through' French first, which makes it Kafka unintelligible – as it were a foreign female voice reciting a *Private Eye* parody of John Cole.[1]

I revived, briefly, walking across the tarmac to board for the flight home. The dense *Ardennois* woods press almost up to the main runway, and I felt a great urge to plunge in, never mind the Minister's suit and Gucci slippers, walk for four hours, absorb the smells of the wet countryside and watch for the foxtracks.

A few minutes ago there was a break in the clouds, a long sunset strip to the north, reminder of the beckoning wistful call of the Ben Loyal range when we were driving back from Pait Lodge[2] – was it only two weeks ago? Perhaps that was why I dreamed of Pait Lodge last night.

Transit lounge, Bogota Airport   *Wednesday, 28 October*

Totally Kafka at present. An air-conditioning unit *roars* nearby, hatefully lowering an already uncomfortable temperature. It would be intolerably cold were we not at present 'centrally' heated by the bodies and bloodstreams of some three hundred or so fellow passengers. The noise makes conversation, still less comprehension of the gabbled Spanish PA system, impossible.

Outside a motley scrapyard of cannibalised aircraft, mostly DC 3s, lie about forlornly. My first and (so far) only ride in a 707 has consisted

---

[1] John Cole, BBC Political Editor, born and brought up in Belfast.
[2] Pait, the stalking lodge of Colin Stroyan in Argyll, a personal friend of AC, and a family trustee.

in taxiing, trundling rather, to the end of the runway, 'spooling up' unconvincingly, and then returning for *Cosa tecnica*. Now we're two hours late leaving and no one seems to be specially bothered.

Is God trying to do something for me? The programme is that we take off, overloaded – if we're lucky we'll be on maximum load for sea level, and Bogota airport is altitude 6000 ft, more likely they haven't done a weight calculation at all – and then fly over 3000 miles due south with the Pacific Ocean under our starboard wing, and the Andes under our port wing in a very old aeroplane that has done service first with (say) Pan-American, then with a US regional airline, then to Europe – a dodgy carrier – then three or four years doing *cargo* in the Caribbean until finally, thirty years after leaving Seattle, it has ended up here, with Air-Colombia.

But being stuck in Bogota is almost equally dangerous. Haven't I read somewhere that it has the highest homicide rate in the entire world? Nigeria would be nastier I suppose, but at least a British Minister would cut more ice. What about Carlos something-or-other Esteban?[1] Perhaps he could get us out. Where is he?

This morning I rose very early indeed. The call was for 4.45 a.m. As usual I started twitching and turning and putting on and off the light from 1.10. At 4.17 (8.17 in London) I called to Charles,[2] got him out of a meeting with the Foreign Secretary, and told him the 'views' (largely spurious, *my* views would be more like it) of the Venezuelan Oil Industry on the BP share placing,.and how we must not be browbeaten by Salomons,[3] just tell them to say Thank you, ma'am, and sod off. It was an open line, and Charles was discreet: 'I've noted carefully what you have said . . .' etc.

We drove to the Caracas protocol lounge. Empty except for a couple of guards, gun-toting, who chewed. And a big fellow in a rumpled suit who turned out to be a King's Messenger, George Courtauld by name, dozing intermittently on one of the sofas. Had he been there all night?

The Embassy party came to see us off, including that *beauty* whom I spotted going round the Consular section yesterday and to whom

---

[1] The notorious 'Cocaine Baron'.

[2] Powell, at Number 10 Private Office.

[3] Due to the stock market crash BP shares had fallen below the underwritten price, and Salomons, the principal underwriters in the US, were trying to get out of the deal.

nobody would introduce me. A true phew-wotta-scorcher blonde with a lovely figure and lots of sparkle and confidence. Erica. We conversed far too much, I suppose. At intervals other Embassy staff tried to interpose. George Courtauld very splendidly (because he must fly hundreds of thousands of miles a year) said that he never could allow himself to fall asleep on aircraft because he had this private superstition that it was only his will-power that kept them aloft, and if he should doze off they might fall out of the sky.

So now what? I could see this South American trip months away as being potentially odious. But it's still fun staying 'buoyant', and making black jokes while round me the officials become pasty and apprehensive. They, too, are worried about Carlos tarumptico Esteban.

Later

Back in the aircraft. Suspended reality. Jane was the first to spot this; one is halfway to God, or rather, between God and earth. There is a residual fear, and doubtless a great lake of terror to burst its banks if some really nasty symptom should manifest itself ('manifest itself' – what awful solecisms one perpetrates when speed jotting), but I no longer try to hold my breath when flying long distances. Even in this elderly aeroplane I am quite serene. Adrenalin synthesises pleasingly with the detachment that accompanies great distance from home and normality.

Yesterday evening I strolled in Caracas to 'shop'. I bought some shoes, slightly caddish beige brogues, and a couple of nice belts. But I was a zombie, something from *Orphée*.[1] Girls with clean hair in summer frocks, shabby touts, cheeky salesmen, cabdrivers, I am not of your world. I am from the nether regions, and to there, when I am summoned, I will return. I recall this feeling first one fine afternoon of late summer, driving back across Green Park by the back route from Lancaster House. Felt it again very strongly at the Frankfurt Motor Show. Tired, *drained*. A privileged prisoner with officials dogging one's every move, trying constantly to stuff empty corners of one's schedule.

I undress and look at myself in the glass, noting the subtle alterations of shape, the loss of muscle tone first remarked on by Beth[2]

---

[1] The film, scripted 1948 by Jean Cocteau.
[2] Mrs Evans Smith, his physiotherapist, when AC had put out his back in a fall on a difficult ski run in Zermatt.

when she treated me for my second back injury in 1978. Always on such occasions do I remember Moran's[1] words to Churchill, 'Physically, you inherited a fortune, but now you've spent it, nearly all.' We'll see.

The night before I left I had a dream, which only came back to me on waking from a nap in the 747 that afternoon. I dreamed that the old Al, the Al of the sheepskin coat photo and who could swing without stopping twenty-two times from the iron flagstaff bar on the roof at Saltwood, escaped. In the middle of the night he stole away from his bed and went on to the lawn, which was lit by the full moon so brightly that you could almost (although you never really can, in fact) notice the colours of grass and stone – then later, after quite a short while, having to creep back to his enfeebled body, still lying between the sheets, with its many degradations.

I still ponder the significance of this. I had the potential even then. But to release it, get into public life, past all the mistakes and mis(mine)understandings, defeat all those – Ted, Central Office, the Eastons[2] – who were determined to obstruct me, involved an enormous expenditure of the physical capital that I had built up over twenty years, from 1945 to 1965.

I look at my contemporaries. They have sagging waistlines and little broken veins on nose and cheek. The hair on their head is wispy. They drink 'convivially'.

Sometimes I feel certain that I would rather die than become a buffer. But when faced with it, I'm not so sure. I suppose I would settle for becoming a sage, a kind of up-market Anson.[3]

---

[1] Lord Moran, for many years Churchill's doctor.
[2] Rodney and Betty Easton, City Councillors in Plymouth who were opposed to AC's nomination in 1972.
[3] Anson MacKay, ferryman at Eriboll, at that time eighty-nine years old. He died in October 1992.

British Embassy, Santiago   *Friday, 30 October*

And still I expend (physical) capital. It is impossible to get time to relax or reflect. This morning, by gulping my breakfast, I 'made' forty minutes and 'disappeared' upstairs. But no, bloody officials who had (I can only assume) been furtively clustered in the corridor outside my room, promptly alerted by the sploshing sound of a freshly flushed *toilet*, knocked authoritatively on the door before I was even back out of the bathroom and had 'adjusted my clothing'.

'Yes,' I shouted, half snarl, half bellow.

'Minister, we just need to fill in a few details concerning the Miami trip . . . '

'*Miami*? What *are* you talking about? This is Chile, isn't it, I thought we were going back to the Department before we go to Miami, when do we go to Miami, am I wrong, what is this . . . ?' etc., etc.

'Yes, yes Minister, of course but no, but . . . ' (Civil servants are the only human beings beside my mother who can say 'yes' and 'no but' in the same unpunctuated sentence.) 'Post want to get some details settled. You see you're attending the Pan-American Trade Conference, the exhibition *and* the dinner (what a treat), there'll be a bit of a gap in the first afternoon, Post have one or two suggestions for filling it . . . '

I bet they have, I thought. Brusquely I shooed them out of the room. I am so exhausted and resentful that I don't think I will be able to speak to them again on this trip, not socially anyway.

Now I have barely got ten minutes left before the Ambassador[1] will start fussing in the hall and the day – visits to Ministers, a lunch at the Ministry of Foreign Affairs (HE and other officials are for some reason very nervous about this – perhaps they think I will 'come out') then a presentation of the Escondida project (I gather this involves a film show so I might get a nap) and then – Caramba! the centre-piece of the trip (at least in FCO eyes) the dinner for 'leading figures in the Opposition'. Guests 'to start (sic) arriving at 8.30 p.m.', so I suppose we may be sitting down by half eleven.

Actually little White himself isn't so bad. A bit guarded, but that's probably down to the secret FCO biog which precedes me at all destinations. I am not (*not*) getting on with his wife, though. There is

---

[1] Alan White, British Ambassador in Santiago.

this certain type of woman who simultaneously demands that you make a pass (or at least flirt) and then gets show-outraged, demonstratively outraged if you do. I want to say fat chance, dear, calm down. Perhaps this shows. I remember one summer in Florence Dido and Clio[1] used to amuse themselves riding the trams in very tight sawn-off jeans and clingy T-shirts and seeing how many men's faces they could slap – and they slapped really hard – before lunch. But they were aged fifteen and seventeen.

Later (much)

We've finally got rid of the dinner guests. A strange occasion. First a drinks party. As I don't touch the stuff when on duty it meant standing, exhausted, with the same warm glass in my hand for two hours while various locals were produced to say their piece. Only value (in every sense) was a regional director of Rothschilds who spoke interestingly about the world economy. He has his own vineyard, and had the calm, crease-free café-au-lait complexion of the international rich. He asked me to come and stay with him. I must ask Marjorie his name which I, drainedly, have forgotten.

The actual meal was a shambles; Mad Hatter's tea party. The so-called Opposition is variously fragmented and, as is usual in such cases, the various fragments are barely on speaking terms. Those that are in the running to help form a government can hardly believe their luck, and chatter recklessly. One who is tipped as a possibility for President, a chap called Aylwin,[2] got drunk immediately and monologued persistently; although at one point he got into a spat with a couple of others about who 'denounced' whose sister during the period of military rule.

Frankly, I'd have put them all under arrest as they left the building. I might say that to Pinochet, if I get to see him on Friday.

Well, it's nearly one a.m. and I have an early call tomorrow for seven thirty breakfast – or is it seven – to go into the desert and expose myself to sunlight, blinding sunlight, for two days. I haven't packed. I'm cross, fatigue and acids, and I will sleep badly, if at all.

During the 'presentation' of the Escondida Project this afternoon I got a fright. I was thinking – a totally wasted day; then with a start,

---

[1] Daughters of Edward Goldsmith and his first wife Gill (née Pretty).
[2] In fact elected President in 1989.

how many more days have I got left? Two thousand? Three thousand at the most. Each one is more significant, and more important, than its predecessor. Sad, and frightening. I compensated by fantasising on the rumour that George[1] is to be made Chairman of the Party and I could take his place at the MoD.

The VIP lodge, Chuquicamata   *Saturday, 31 October*

Rich, rich experiences today. We had flown up here in a little De Havilland Otter, a high-wing aircraft, with Lycoming propeller engines; quite reassuring, you feel it could put down almost anywhere – unlike a 737 which had overshot the airstrip only a matter of days earlier, broken up in the rock-strewn hinterland and caught fire. Its blackened dinosaur carcase was all too visible.

'Everyone all right, I assume?' lip-lickingly enquired one of the officials.

But no, far from it. They were all dead!

Clean and comfortable, but *icy* cold – though still the air conditioning pours out its refrigerated vapours. We must be at about 7000 feet. The Andes lie to the west, but the belt of foothills and desert plateau is quite wide here. It is unnaturally dry, and the sun shines with an implacable strength that makes Trockener Steg[2] like April in Aldeburgh. Last night a reasonable meal, I stuffed on olives and a coarse brown bread. A grand piano beckoned, and I would happily have strummed from my repertoire. But I have long learned the lesson that it is discreet first to ask if anyone in the party 'plays', because the trained ear is uncomfortable with my renderings of 'Smoke Gets in Your Eyes', or 'Stormy Weather'. And sure enough Kester[3] timidly volunteered. After we had all gone to bed I could hear some quite pretty Chopin for a little while, ending with a sombre passage of Liszt – probably from the 'Années de pèlerinage'.

We left early in two FWDs, a Land-Rover and a (surprisingly nasty) Chevrolet minibus, our destination a village, San Pedro del Acurama, which had prehistoric remains and a folk museum. Hot, glare-dry

---

[1] Younger, Secretary of State for Defence.
[2] A very high ski-run on the glacier behind the Clarks' chalet in Zermatt.
[3] George Kester, Assistant Secretary on the South American desk at DTI.

gravellidos rattled and spat against the bodywork. A 'rest stop' (I am an inveterate pee-er but in this climate the kidneys need every drop, the bladder calls only twice a day) in the Vala da Luna, a terrible place of bleached and twisted rock formations. No vegetation; no soil even, not one scrap of living substance within sight or reach.

San Pedro is an oasis on the banks of a river which spates just often enough to irrigate its immediate environs and even when trickling, as today, offers clean and reliable water from the distant Andean snows. Not unlike Forio[1] in the old days, with a plaza and crumbling shops; house doors opening directly on to the street, bead curtains. Searing mid-day heat and white dust on the trees.

We went round the geological museum. Brand new, the building more interesting than the exhibits. The Curator, prematurely grey, but lean, spoke little English and showed his impatience. That suited me, and so there was time to kill before lunch.

In the 'prehistoric village' (indistinguishable from the *Alt Broch* settlements at Eriboll except that the walls are of mud instead of dry stone) I suggested that we go to the summit on which an ancient lookout tower brooded. HE and the officials were unenthusiastic. Sadismoidly I said, Yes, Yes.

The lean Curator led the way. Within minutes we had outdistanced the main group. It was quite difficult keeping up with him (plainly he was trying to shake me off, or get me to cry 'Pare'). HE, although I suspect younger than I, had, after a perfunctory sprint, settled for 'Guide's Pace'. The official party faded, first from earshot, then sight. I took strength in the last *diréttissima* from Alpine recollections, the Rothorn, the Metalhorn and, of course, that last heart-pounding sprint through the gorse on Gossie Bank.

Incredible view from the tower. I reflected on those ancient civilisations, and the pleasing early maturity of the young in the southern hemisphere. I spoke drawlingly, to show I was not out of breath. The Curator could barely acknowledge. He, too, was controlling his breathing. I've noticed this before with Spaniards. They never salute their adversary. A German, even a Frenchman, would have made a joking aside; some kind of acknowledgment of sporting rivalry that had ended in an honourable draw.

---

[1] Forio d'Ischia, where AC spent many happy summers in the late Fifties.

Westward-bound 747, 2 hrs out of   *Monday, 16 November*
Vancouver

How very *dry* and flushed one becomes on these great long-distance flights. My Harold Acton death spots gleam reproachfully in the lights of the silent, stainless steel lavabos. Round me, my fellow travellers who, some eight hours ago, boarded groomed and confident with their Etienne Aigner luggage, are now pinched and watery-eyed. We have sat through two full-length films, one quite good, watchable, about double and treble agents in the CIA; the other total rubbish. By spastics for spastics. *The Stakeout*, a particular – always embarrassing – Hollywood genre, the 'comedy thriller'. A *Private Eye* parody could not have been more ludicrous or more trite.

Below, the Canadian tundra slips past. Many lakes. Skirting the Northern Ice-cap was deeply frightening – more so even than the Andean Desert. So *utterly* lifeless and bleak. In the desert there would at least be foxes and insects and little roots waiting to be nurtured by the rain. But the Polar route is all ice cliffs, and pale chasms of depth unknown.

Oh, these hateful flights! I look at the map, and there on the UK is marked 'Ben Hope 927m'. And the two stretches of water, Eriboll and Hope, are clearly set out. Within these bounds is my beloved property; the gimmers and the peregrine falcons and the pine martens; the great tawny badgers, the stags, the little musquat deer and the sly peat foxes. I think fondly, sadly, of them all.

If one is nurturing cancer, pre-cancerous, which I often think I am, these hideous great flights must be the very worst thing.

I long, I physically long for a great walk, to breathe deep gulps, and to stretch the spine. We have been in the air eight and a half hours, yet the clock has advanced less than twenty minutes since take-off.

We are almost keeping pace with the sun.

And what am I going to do when I get there? No real objectives – just hang around as a ritual dummy being polite to people, HE's Reception.

San Francisco   *Thursday, 19 November*

I was principal guest at a lunch given by Barclays Bank. Conversation
was lively. More so, at least, than it would have been at an equivalent
function at home. And an absolutely delicious Mondavi white burgundy. The location was a low-ceilinged dining room in the Bohemia
Club. No women present, although there was much talk about their
now having to be admitted.

But I was most alarmed by the appearance of the *waiter*. He was
exceedingly, unnaturally, thin. And his eyes were shiny and overbright.
Why was he perspiring? He had the most dreadful blotchy sores on
his arms which, far from concealing, he *flaunted* by rolling up his
sleeves.

Oh dear. Were we in a district called Haight Ashbury? I read
recently that ninety per cent of the population there is a 'victim'. I
didn't touch the salad.

Afterwards Steve[1] said to me, 'How about that waiter, Minister?'
I groaned. I am trying not to think about it.

Saltwood   *Saturday, 19 December*

On Thursday Ian and I had a very jolly dinner at the Savoy, indulged
ourselves. Also present (at my suggestion) were Francis Maude,[2] and
David Heathcoat-Amory.[3] Both the youngsters were good, and sparkled sensibly. Fine wines were ordered, and consumed. I really think
that the Savoy River Room has the most *reliably* good food in London.
Not the absolute best, perhaps, but I've never been disappointed there.

Ian talked about the next reshuffle, and we pricked up our ears.
(But is he actually as close to things as he used to be? I would say not.)
He started off circumlocutory, became more specific as Puligny-
Montrachet gave way to Beaune. She intends to make Geoffrey
leader in the Lords, and Nigel Foreign Secretary; John MacGregor[4]
Chancellor.

---

[1] Stephen Phillips, Number Two in AC's Private Office.
[2] Francis Maude, now Parliamentary Under-Secretary at the DTI.
[3] David Heathcoat-Amory, MP for Wells since 1983.
[4] John MacGregor, MP for South Norfolk since 1974. Minister of Agriculture.

This seems a pretty tall order to me. Maude, supported by David H-A, said Lawson couldn't be Foreign Sec as a Jew. This made Ian very indignant. 'Do you mean to tell me that today, this very day, in this the Conservative Party – I take it that we are all members of the Conservative Party? – you are seriously suggesting, no asserting...' and so on.

Ian then switched to 'he's not a practising Jew, anyway'. But we couldn't quite swallow it. I said something – something Hurd, and Ian snapped, 'She can't bear him. Can't *bear* him.'

I thought, it's all very well for he and she to swop these sort of ideas over the third or fourth whisky after midnight but come the morning and she's usually more circumspect.

But it's nice to have the Christmas hols, which is always an agreeable time, spiced up by speculation about changes of this weight. I must ring Peter Riddell on Monday, although I expect his scepticism will match my own.

There were three late votes; then Francis and I went to the DTI basement, where the Christmas party was being staged. Matthew was there, having lost so much weight that he is now quite *markedly* handsome. As always full of sense, as well as fun. He told me that Lynda was going to take Arthur Cockfield's place on the Commission – or so the Brussels inner rumour mill claimed. If that happens it could mean Parkinson going to the FCO instead of Lawson (plus A.N. Other!). All greatly preferable to the version we had been getting from Ian at dinner.[1]

As I stood somewhat stiltedly making conversation with Matthew and Marjorie I could see Rose out of the corner of my eye. After a bit she braved their joint presence and came up to me: 'You're terribly late getting here.' I kissed the back of her hand and she stood in *very* close proximity. I could feel my veins raging. She pouted, and nobody pouts like Rose. Nobody has such (I suppose the Barbara Cartland word is *full*) lips. 'It's too hot.'

'Come for a drive,' I said.

Later, when I got home I thought – I've been behaving like this, absolutely unaltered, for forty years. Crazy. Scrawny old time-warp.

---

[1] But equally ill-founded in substance.

Saltwood   *Monday, 21 December*

It's too boring. This lovely holiday break is upon us, James and Sally are coming down, and Jane always does Christmas so well, it's pure pleasure.

But I am now convinced I have got cancer of the jaw. Those symptoms that I have been carefully monitoring ever since that triple-view shaving mirror in my bathroom in the Embassy in Santiago, are gradually amplifying (is that the word?). Will I be able even to 'smile bravely' throughout the festivities?

I am going in shortly to drop in some of the local Christmas cards in Folkestone. Julian[1] is such a dear, I think I'll just ask him for a quick check-up.

Afternoon
Julian was marvellous; saw me immediately; didn't turn a hair when I told him. He said it was 'pretty rare', he'd only seen three cases in the teaching hospital. He made a thorough examination. Glands totally normal. No sign whatever of local swelling or ulceration. 'Pain?'

'Well, er, no.'

'Happy Christmas.'

Phew.

Saltwood   *Thursday, 24 December*

Christmas Eve. I've got £700,000 in my Abbey National Crazy-High-Interest account. But what's the use? Ash, ash, all is ash. Lay not up for thyself treasures on earth. The cars are all getting streaked and rust spotted, the books foxed, the furniture dusty. The window panes, all 52,000 of them are *revolting*, so greasily blotched. Translucent only. And there is moth everywhere. My grandfather's great Roths-child coat, bought in Wien in 1906, is terminally degraded... The whole thing is out of control.

And why? I know why. Because I'm not rich enough to have

---

[1] Julian Smith, FRCDS, the Clark family dentist.

servants. We have to do everything ourselves, and we just haven't got the time, and things get neglected. This morning, rummaging up in the archive room I found the old Wages Book for 1960. That was the year James was born, and we bought our first new car, a dear little red Mini. It was the cheapo model with cloth seats, and we saved a further three pounds and ten shillings by hand painting the registration numbers ourselves. Total cost 'on the road' was £460.

The total wage bill, per week, for the seven servants who worked at the Castle, was thirty-two pounds and five shillings. MacTaggart, a clumsy fellow who had such ugly hands that my mother always made him wear white gloves when he was waiting at table, and who crashed my father's Bentley in circs that will never wholly be explained, in Lee Green, got £12 per week and occupancy of the Lodge.

Everything has decimal points – to the right – or worse. I'm bust, virtually.

Saltwood   *Tuesday, 29 December*

Yesterday we went to lunch at Chequers. I was excited. Some of the lunches over Christmas are very *réclamé*. One is for 'family and close friends'; one is for Cabinet intimates; one is for Court favourites and so on. I hoped, naturally, that it was this third category. But Jane, flier, said no such luck, it'll be Captains of Industry. All too true. They were amiable, quiet-spoken, on good behaviour. Except for her son Mark (is he a 'businessman'?) who kept muscling in on conversations, saying 'something-something *two million* dollars' in Cor! tones. After a bit I got sick of this and said, 'That's not much' (which it isn't) but people affected not to hear.

Sometimes on these occasions she draws me into another room for a little intimate chat. But not this time. Although I must still be in favour as she kept introducing me as 'My wonderful frightfully good Trade Minister', and she had read that book on the Japanese threat which I had sent her via Charles, and had marked passages.

As we left I caught Aunt Ruth's eye,[1] as I always do. 'See you again,' I said. 'Often.'

On the way back, on the last bit of the M25, Dave drove slower and slower, and slower. 'What's up?' He'd forgotten to check the petrol before leaving and was trying to 'conserve' what was left. After we'd filled up he felt 'kind of faint'. Usual story. None of the Government Car Service drivers is capable of driving outside the Metropolitan area. I took over and drove the rest of the way to Saltwood.

---

[1] Viscountess Lee of Fareham, the wife of Arthur Lee, whose papers AC edited. The Lees gave Chequers to the nation in order that the Prime Minister of the day should always have at his disposal a country house for entertaining. One of the provisions of the Chequers Trust is that Lady Lee's portrait by Sargent should always hang in the entrance hall over the visitor's book.

1988

1988

The House has not yet returned but officials, who can't bear it when Ministers are out of the building, they don't quite know where, and they themselves are all in there, shuffling papers around, had arranged for me to meet the '2000 Group', some kind of conclave to assist Japanese 'Inward Investment'. Poor old Patrick Jenkin[1] was 'leading' it. He who had once been Secretary of State, now soft-spokenly hanging about in the waiting area. The democratic cycle. David Young, on the other hand, into whose presence he was finally ushered, was bronzed and silvery-sleek.

Much time is wasted with these sorts of meetings. The delegation believe themselves (I suppose) to be getting 'access'; the 'leader' is earning his fee by 'delivering' access, and the civil servants, who fidget and fuss and make notes, justify themselves and, of course, find such occasions useful in attaining their principal objective, which is always to stuff a Minister's day diary so full that he can't breathe – still less think. I can't think of many occasions when a Minister's mind has actually been altered during a discussion – although it can happen, most notably with the Lynx delegation.[2]

As soon as I got back to my office I asked to see my own 'long term' diary. This threw them, and a long delay ensued. Through the open door I could hear mutterings, heavy rustling of paper, subdued internal phoning. 'Where is it?' I shouted at intervals. When, finally, it was produced I growled at every entry. I must admit, though, it was really quite light. Only two overseas trips, to the Balkans and, possibly, the Maghreb.

This, I suppose, is a bit of a swizz on the outer office. The great perk attaching to the Minister for Trade's staff is the ability to accompany him abroad. As I can buy my own airticket anywhere, compulsory overseas trips aren't so much a privilege, more a bore. Paul went everywhere his officials pointed him at. I know better. '*Les absents ont toujours tort.*'

---

[1] Patrick (now Lord) Jenkin (Life Peer, 1987). Between 1979–85 was successively Secretary of State for Social Services, for Industry and for the Environment.

[2] Lynx was a charity staffed by young volunteers who had visited AC on his appointment as Minister of Trade, and had found in him a kindred spirit. Single-handed, against massive opposition from civil servants in several Departments of State, AC had drawn up an Order which would force fur traders to label garments made of the skins of animals that had been caught in leg-hold traps.

This is the last stretch, isn't it? Or is it? I *should* be made a PC in June, which will allow me to stagger on until the end of the summer hols, 'Government Changes' in September. And then what?

I never want to see Plymouth again. Sometimes I think that all I want is to stay in office here long enough to get my fur legislation on to the statute book. I was looking through some more papers which have come in this morning.

Horrific illustrations. Worst was a great circular crater, some 16-foot in diameter, dug out of the frozen earth (for all around was snow) by a poor badger, just using one hand, as he went round and round and round; caught by a steel jaw on the other leg, chained to a post in the centre, trying (for how long must it have taken him?) to escape, he dug that great pit. Until, finally, he just lay down and died.

There's stacks of stuff about the Inuits, who make their money out of these barbarities and among whom 'the incidence of alcoholism has risen sharply in recent years' (so what?), the likelihood of the fur trade applying for judicial review, the (inevitable) probability of the Foreign Office fussing, Ambassadors (lazy sods, nothing to do) filing whingeing telegrams and so on. Good. Makes me feel I'm doing something really worth while. Fuck them.

Department of Trade and Industry   *Monday, 11 January*

Back fully in harness this morning (fine and crisp – naturally – after a week of wet, moist oozing) and went first to Albany. I turned on fires and radiators, unpacked shirts and meagre provisions. As I rounded the corner into the 'B' staircase I was filled with gloom. Now for months of confinement. The Lent term (as it used to be at Eton) is always the longest of the House sessions. There are no public holidays to break it up; and it gets dark so early that there is no escape home at times of light whipping.

The Christmas break was lovely, but only in the last couple of days did I start to 'feel a little better'. Recovery very limited. I still get tired, overpoweringly tired. I haven't done Gossie at all, it's too muddy and slippery. And twice I've felt rather awful for a little while. It may be psychosomatic, I suppose, it often is. But I've noted myself just sitting glazedly; too short of energy to do a lot of things that need doing, and are quite interesting.

I shouldn't be like this at the end of the hols.

Department of Trade and Industry   *Tuesday, 12 January*

I sit wearily in the office. My 'In' tray is high to twice its own depth. In the mornings, when I am fresh and fast, officials bring me very little paper. But after five p.m. and a day of 'meetings' and outside engagements, the folders flow thick and insistent. I must also finish the *Spectator* review of Terry Coleman's book.[1] Even so, I am sticking to my record of never taking boxes home. I will not leave this desk until the tray is empty; and there is nothing so pleasing as 'I think I'll lock up now, Minister...' and off goes the last one. But it's never Rose. Why? She could easily stay late if she wanted to. Perhaps the others prevent her. Most officials are fearful spoilsports.

On Sunday evening I was prowling about in the Long Garage. I thought I must change the seats round off the Loco[2] and take the Ghost staff car[3] in hand. Great fun, but needs a few days' undivided attention. No chance of that until Easter; and by Easter, God knows, a hundred other pressing tasks will have once again displaced it.

The civil servants have all left. My room is in darkness, save for the desk light, and I am sipping Malvern water. If I was at Saltwood now I would be on my fourth cup of PG Tips, eating hot buttered brown toast and jam.

House of Commons   *Thursday, 14 January*

In and out of the House all day. Now it's back in session I feel better, it's such fun; such a pleasing ambiance. But there are an alarming number of people I simply don't recognise at all. I became irritated with a total stranger who was somehow blockingly, *disrespectfully* reading the ticker-tape in the smoking-room corridor. 'Who's that?' I asked John Taylor, a Whip. Didn't know. Asked a badge messenger,

---

[1] *Thatcher's Britain* by Terry Coleman. In accordance with an understanding between AC and the Cabinet Office the text was shown to Sir Robin Butler, who advised against publication.

[2] A 1908 Locomobile racing car.

[3] A Rolls Royce Silver Ghost.

pointing at the now retreating figure. Didn't know. I pursued him along the corridors. He had a start on me, and a long stride. I had to travel fast, but with dignity. As he turned into the press gallery staircase, 'Excuse me, who are you?' 'John Lloyd, an officer of the House.' What did he think I was? A loony? Or just a busybody? Or was it a case of mistaken identity? Actually he looked not unlike Charles Powell.

I lunched in the Members' dining room with G-J and Rhodes James.[1] RJ relatively amiable; not drunk, though cigaretting mightily. Talk was mainly of Willie.[2] Rhodes James claimed already to have written his obituary, 'not entirely friendly' (I can't imagine Robert writing an *entirely* friendly piece about anyone). We swopped anecdotes. Richard[3] joined us for coffee and told the most pleasing. He had approached Willie, late at night, but early in the Parliament and before it's full horror was apparent, and asked him what he 'thought of' the Poll Tax.

The great man stopped in his tracks, and glared. His shoulders heaved, went into *rigor*; his face became empurpled and sweat poured down his forehead, cheeks and the end of his nose. He wrestled with some deep impediment of speech; finally burst, spluttering out the single word – 'TROUBLE'. Then he turned on his heel.

Department of Trade and Industry   *Friday, 15 January*

I get on well with the Labour Party. The MPs, that is, not the functionaries who hang about in the corridors, still less those crazy hyped-up 'researchers'. There's that dreadful little tick with curly hair and glasses, four foot six or thereabouts, I've never seen him smile.[4]

Frank Dobson[5] and I swop stories. His are *so* filthy that really

---

[1] Robert Rhodes James, historian and biographer. MP for Cambridge since 1976.

[2] Lord Whitelaw had suffered a slight stroke attending the carol service in the Guards Chapel, but was now 'on the mend'.

[3] At this time Ryder was Under-Secretary at the Ministry of Agriculture.

[4] Dave Hill, Director of Communications, Labour Party.

[5] Frank Dobson, MP for Holborn and St Pancras since 1979, and shadow Leader of the House.

they're unusable, even at a Rugger Club dinner. At the moment we're into 'fuck' e.g.s. Question: who said, 'What the fuck was that?' Answer, 'The Mayor of Hiroshima.' Who said, 'Talk about scattered fucking showers'? Answer, Noah, and so on. The fun is to pass notes across the Table during debates. Juvenile. I know who wouldn't like it if he knew – Sir Robert Armstrong.

Last night, while waiting for a division I had a word with Bob Cryer.[1] Speaking as an historian as well as an old mate, I told him Prescott *must* stand.[2] He became very enthused, said Prescott was checking with his Exec Committee, and certainly would. Bob agreed completely with my analogy with the Tory Party in 1976, and how we recovered our confidence when Mrs T. gave us a bit of conviction. The Labour Party is full of 'idealists' (sic.), it depended on ideals. 'That's right,' I said. Stirring.

While we were talking Frank Haynes[3] came over. He and Bob personify the two main strands in the Labour Party. The 'activists' (Bob is really an elected activist), most of whom are subject to a destructive envy; and the Trade Unionists (Frank is old-school NUM), whose convictions are more traditionally rooted. They just want to do as little as possible, and be paid as much as possible for doing it. And who can blame them? Very little different from the standard chinless riff-raff who hang around Smith's Lawn.

Frank said to me, 'You're a very good Minister' and meant it. Like all traditionalist Labour he believes trade policy should be founded on protection. Look after Number One. So he approves of my running battle to keep the MFA in place. But how are these two, and tens of thousands like them, going to tolerate all this natty suiting and buttonholes? Compulsory role fulfilment as local government officials who've taken a correspondence course in glad-handing. They've had it. It won't fool anyone.

---

[1] Bob Cryer, MP for Bradford South since 1987 (Keithley 1974–83).
[2] The Labour Party had changed the terms of its leadership selection, and it was being considered whether Neil Kinnock should be challenged. John Prescott, MP for Hull East since 1970, was eventually a candidate as Labour Leader when Kinnock relinquished the role in 1992.
[3] Frank Haynes, MP for Ashfield since 1979.

Department of Trade and Industry   *Tuesday, 19 January*

Little John Moore is in trouble.[1] It's the NHS debate today and the whole House will turn out, hoping for blood. The poor fellow has been in bad health (Health Secretary, bad health, etc., etc.) and has been 'on the sick list', i.e. not around.

At one of the long tables in the tea room people were gloating, his own colleagues particularly: 'Are you aglow with excitement at the prospect of actually setting eyes on this legendary figure?' said Eric Forth.[2] Titters. Someone else, cruelly, 'You may set eyes on him, but you'll have difficulty hearing him.' The wretched man has had throat trouble for ages, goes terribly hoarse a couple of minutes into his speech.

Why is everyone so beastly? John was literally golden. Although in his forties he has golden kiss-curls like a babyfood ad. He is athletic, and 'trains'. He did time in the States on some election trail or other and has an American wife in PR. What-a-team, etc., etc. Last year, Number 10 were 'letting it be known that' he was the chosen successor, and his speech (not at all bad really) to Conference was billed on that basis. I can see that this can arouse envy and, not that he is scrabbling, *Schadenfreude*. But John has always been perfectly pleasant to me. Shallow, but amiable. Not like some of those wankers who are so ambitious they won't even tell you the time when you ask.

Of course he is mildly of the Right, and has attached himself to Her. I am told that in Cabinet he echoes her views and then later (or even on the same morning) if she alters her view, echoes that too. This irritates. But if I ask myself why Tristan, and Patten, get so cross about him; why it is said that John Major[3] (outwardly the mildest of men) is reputed to have sworn to 'get' him, I must suppose it is because he is the only possible contender for the leadership of the Party who is outside the 'Blue Chip' club.

That tight little masonic group, so ably managed and convened by

---

[1] John Moore, MP for Croydon Central since 1974. Secretary of State for Social Security since 1986, after spells at Transport and Social Services.

[2] Eric Forth, MP for Mid-Worcestershire since 1983. Parliamentary Under-Secretary, Trade and Industry, since 1986.

[3] John Major, MP for Huntingdon since 1979. Chief Secretary to the Treasury since 1987.

Tristan, is determined to monopolise the allocation of higher office, to the exclusion of the Right.

Hounslow Suite, Heathrow   *Friday, 29 January*

I sit here, acid from wine at lunch and weary in my bones and joints. I have been in attendance all day at the French Summit meeting at Lancaster House and then tried, through wet Friday evening traffic, to get to Heathrow in a half hour. I don't think even Joan could have managed it (although I must admit that with her I never actually missed anything). Now I have to wait for nearly two more hours until the next Zurich flight.

These VIP suites are windowless, and heavily sound-insulated, so that nervous travellers are not made anxious by the sound of Boeing turbines on take-off, shrieking at their point of maximum thrust. There is bad coffee, and 'assorted centre' biscuits on offer, and masses of neatly folded newsprint. Gently we are drawn into the nether world of deep jetlag.

I had been looking forward to Davos,[1] and planned that Rose should be 'asked' to accompany me. Predictably, the office thwarted this, although she had coyly agreed. So now I am on my own, flushed and hypochondriacal.

The Summit was interesting, although more for the opportunity that it gave to make personal observations than for any outcome of policy. At the start, the Lady was to greet Mitterrand as he came up the steps into the central hall (*not* at the entrance, I was glad to note), and lesser acolytes hung around in the background. I fell into conversation with Douglas. His is a split personality. *A deux* he is delightful; clever, funny, observant, drily cynical. But get him any-where near 'display mode', particularly if there are officials around, and he might as well have a corncob up his arse. Pompous, trite, high-sounding, cautiously guarded.

Douglas said to me how he used to be so excited before these Summits – history in the making, all that – now no longer. I said it

---

[1] The World Economic Forum, a conference of 'world leaders and opinion formers' convened every year at Davos.

was a bad sign. We were getting jaded. Perhaps we ought to get out? I said that I wanted to get out every Monday morning, as I got dressed and shaved. Rather splendidly, he agreed.

Before the Plenary started I had a few words with Michel Noir. As always, attractive, intelligent. A true Gaullist. I agree with him on practically every issue.

Punctually we were seated. Opposite me, [Jacques] Chirac yawned and cigaretted. He is in his prime. Handsome in a fifty-five-ish sort of way, smelling beautiful, but ill-at-ease with *Le President*. Mitterrand himself is seventy-one, a pale elderly sage, a BB[1] with balls. And plainly determined to hang on. Winston and Anthony must sometimes have seemed like this, although in Chirac's case the succession is far from assured. But at least he looks fit, while poor Anthony was already sickening in 1952. I did notice, too, that whatever he may think of her Mitterrand's manner with the PM was courteous, and grave. Chirac, on the other hand, lounged and fidgeted and doodled and smirked at his own thoughts.

A faintly absurd 'structural' device had been introduced, at the behest of God knows who, whereby Ministers in Attendance (i.e., myself and Noir, Lynda [Chalker] and some little runt from the Sûreté who smelt of garlic and hadn't shaved) should 'present papers' before the summing up.

Naturally, this was a great bore for all concerned. But it did offer scope for the Lady to give one of her little mini-displays of bitchiness and mischief. The order was to be Lynda (as 'Deputy' Foreign Secretary), then the runt from the Sûreté who was going to talk about border control; then Noir, then me. ('I don't think anyone is expecting you to talk for very long, Minister,' i.e., the Foreign Office have asked us to keep it snappy.)

But when the moment came for our contributions the Prime Minister, who was of course in the Chair, said, 'Minister for Trade.'

Buoyantly I sparkled, noticing high indignation among Lynda's officials. Then came the little Sûreté man, then Michel. All the time Lynda rustled with her notes and made kind of 'ahem' noises. Finally, with every indication of reluctance and distaste, the Prime Minister just said, 'Mrs Chalker.'

How I love her for that kind of reason!

---

[1] Bernard Berenson, art historian, connoisseur and sage, lived in Florence until well into his nineties. Always known as BB.

Albany   *Monday, 22 February*

We are just back from a dinner at Number 10 for Cap Weinberger.[1]

Sixty-four guests – but only four Ministers – Howe, Parkinson, Younger and myself. I was high up the table, and this disconcerted a grand lady on my immediate left.

'Why are you here?'

'Because I have been invited.'

'Yes, but why were you invited?'

'That, surely, is a question better addressed to our hostess.'

'Well, I don't see what you are doing here.'

'If you find my presence offensive, then I suggest that you restrict your conversation to the person on your left.'

I turned, ostentatiously, and began to speak to the woman on my right who, fortunately, was 'open'. Nobody pulls rank on me, least of all the dried-up wife of a Permanent Secretary (if that be what she was). We were a mixed bunch. Themes, if one could detect any, were the Falklands, and Anglo-American camaraderie in war. Willie was there, and with him any conversation, however brief, is always a pleasure. I had a word with Charlie Sweeney – now must be the ugliest man in London, bright pink and hairless, though pale eyes still glinting with residual lechery at age seventy-five. I also saw Rowse,[2] A.L., shy and benign but with an *appalling* melanoma on his temple.

The Prince of Wales had (apparently) suffered a *mauvais placement*, being put on Cap's right whereas he should, or so the clucksters maintained, have sat at the right hand of the Prime Minister. Lady de Lisle,[3] who is very splendid in many ways but is not, I suspect, a raging fan of the PM, stirred this incipient row primly but firmly.

Charles [Powell], however, was adamant. Tetchily so.

'Of course we checked with his office. I wasn't born yesterday.'

On Monday Charles had asked me to provide some 'possible headings' for the PM's speech of welcome. In fact I wrote the whole thing, from beginning to end, and was delighted that she used most of it. It was the first time that I have heard my own words and phrases from the mouth of another. Cap responded excellently. Started out

---

[1] Caspar Weinberger, American Secretary for Defense 1981–7.

[2] A.L. Rowse, Shakespearean scholar and Fellow of All Souls.

[3] Lady de Lisle, second wife of the former Conservative Secretary of State for Air and herself the widow of the 3rd Baron Glanusk.

funny, then moving. I recall the first time I heard him, at a Congressional Committee in Washington in April of 1982, just after the Falklands War began. He was flat, and colourless – though he did let go that most excellent remark, deprecatory and engaging, which I have often myself used since, on inviting questions, 'because then there is a reasonable chance that what I have to say should be of interest to at least one person in the room'.

I was pleased to learn afterwards that he had been touched by what the Lady had said 'and the beautiful language', and had asked for a copy of the text.

Sandling - Charing Cross train   *Wednesday, 24 February*

This morning I was out very early with Tom. A completely blue sky without a single trace of cloud and the grass blades all crisp and frosty. We went as far as the lake, which was iced over, but treacherous.

On our return I saw Tom alert and bristling, hackles up, at something in the corner of the 'peppercorn' field where the fence crosses the dyke. Fearing a dead or wounded fox (John often sets a snare at that point, as the fence wire is taut across the water and animals can use the bank to squirm underneath), I walked over with a sinking heart.

It was a badger, still with some life in it. I bellowed at Tom, and he reluctantly followed me, running, back to the house where I telephoned angrily to the farm.

John appeared prompt, but sulky, with one of the Apps boys, and then another. He was carrying a pitchfork with which he tried to pinion the unfortunate creature's neck and head. But the badger was strong still, and dangerous.

'Get some sacks,' I told the boys.

I muffled the badger and he went quiet, knowing I was a friend, while John worked with the wire-cutters.

Once he was released the little Brock squared up to us, bravely and aggressively. Then, when we made no move, bumbled off at a very fair pace toward the old railway line. I hope and believe that he was saved by his rib cage. What is awful is when they worm their way down the noose by exhaling (as foxes, being more intelligent, do) and then tighten it against the lower gut in a final effort to break free.

In spite of my early start this diversion caused me to miss my train, and thus the first of the morning's dreary Meetings with Officials. Good! What are they beside the saving of a beautiful and independent creature of the wild?

Hotel Insulberg, Konstanz   *Saturday, 19 March*

I write this at the conference table – always a good spot for an entry. People think that, assiduously, you are making notes. And the setting is conducive. Universal boredom and a sense of futility make the atmosphere *piano*, sepulchral, almost. This is a *World* (not just EC) Trade Ministers Conference so my next-door neighbour is a little Thai instead of the usual Portuguese mouse. We have been sitting for an hour and a half, and he has smoked seven cigarettes.

Slow and repetitious as are our proceedings in the chamber, they are as nothing to the longeurs of the 'cocktails' and the Reception. I dodged the morning coffee break (far too long) and walked along the Lake front, saying hullo to some feathered friends who quacked and jostled amiably beside the water's edge.

On Thursday evening Bruce [Anderson] told me that he had been in conversations with Wakeham,[1] who had told him, 'She'll have him in the Cabinet if she can.'

And it is true that I am in good favour at the moment. Perhaps because I send her a multitude of little notes and reports, but always through Charles, and I never ask for anything.

But my status is precarious, and I fear that I may be heading for an unwelcome passage of arms, because I have now cleared every single hurdle, even the assent of the Secretary of State himself, for my Fur Order. But the Prime Minister watches everything. She has a lot of furriers in Finchley. And she, herself, has I fear very little empathy indeed with the animal kingdom.

---

[1] John Wakeham, now Lord President of the Council, chairman of many Cabinet committees and believed to be highly influential within Government.

Words of welcome at Brize Norton 1987. (Gorbachev's interpreter is speaking).

Althorp. 'I rallied the Ministers present and, with much chivvying, got them to a room on the first floor where a tame photographer took our picture.'

'Straight in from the hover James stood the little Gazelle on its tail and went into a vertical climbing torque turn directly over the great sycamores.' 21 July 90

Once in each summer by tradition AC braves Weils Disease and swims the length of the moat and back.

'Charlotte wanders dreamily along the battlements to pastiche Brideshead music, murmuring

Spring. The first cut of the lawn.

about "the loveliest place in the whole world".' 10 September 83

'This morning I swam very early, before seven, and the view *from the water* was unbelievable because the eastern light is on the towers – which happens only for a couple of weeks in high summer' 14 July 90

ABOVE CENTRE: Ben Hope (alt 3,080 ft) from the Creaggan Road (eastern side).

Tom guards the game bag.

LEFT: Panorama from the Creaggan Road (western side). Left to right: The small byre; Postie's Cottage; the boathouse; Shore Cottage; LochanDhu; the chapel; Ardneackie peninsula.

DTI ministers at
Saltwood 1988. Back row
(includes) From left:
Francis Maude, John
Butcher, Geoffrey
Sterling, AC, Robert
Atkins, Maxwell
Beaverbrook, John
Taylor, Nick Baker.
Front row: Kenneth
Clarke, Jane, David
Young.

Alfresco lunch at
Saltwood. Jane,
Richard Ryder, Frank
Johnson, Tristan Garel-
Jones, William
Waldegrave.

Ian Gow drinks brandy in
the garden at Saltwood. ...

... and so does Bruce
Anderson.

CARS

The Jaguars: 'SS100',
C-Type, 'XK'.

The 'Ghost'.

The Citroen, always used for
holidays.

The Chalet Caroline in Zermatt, winter and summer. The lower picture also shows the new kiosk (unpainted).

Bratton, Devon.

British Embassy, Sofia *Wednesday, 13 April*

Far too many people seem to know that today is my birthday, which of course I don't like at all as it makes it more difficult for me to ignore the fact that I am sixty. I *refuse* to be sixty. 'Mirror, mirror, on the wall . . .' etc. And the Bulgarians are threatening to sing 'Happy Birthday'.

In point of fact, the mirrors here are kind. And yesterday afternoon on arrival, I seemed glossy and confident. But this morning my face is swollen, and from some angles I could be an *ill* sixty.

I *must* not drink on these tours. Foolishly and youthfully I had two glasses of Fendant and then two of Dole on the Swissair flight from Zurich. I felt cocky at the time, but very tired when I finally got here from the airport, having made smalltalk to HE all the way in the back of the Jaguar. I had to go and lie on my bed and rest the eyeballs before the evening meetings got under way instead of, as I would have preferred, writing up this journal.

At dinner, in the not unacceptable Sheraton Balkan, I drank a glass of vodka with the (vast) shrimp cocktail, and then at least two glasses of Bulgarian white. Christov, my host, three years younger than I but unarguably more crumpled and jowelly, drank copiously as obedient waiters — slow in discharging other functions — refilled his glass.

Conversation did *not* sparkle. Hardly surprising as we had had a meeting at the airport; a formal meeting in his Department; followed by two hours, plus, sitting next to each other at dinner.

Christov asked me what hours I worked.

'Eight thirty in the morning until about seven, seven fifteen. Some days until midnight. Average twelve.'

'I thought it was only Socialist Ministers who had to work that hard.'

'All Ministers,' I said. 'Except perhaps in Italy where, anyway, they don't count.'

HE is quiet, and does not 'keep the ball rolling'. He is hosting a big dinner for me tomorrow, so I hope he perks up. In his last year, so probably free-wheeling a bit. But I have known worse; both more idle, and more beadily intrusive.

Ginev, my other mentor, is heavily built but in good condition the way some overweight men (Strauss another example) can be. He travelled back with me on the Varig flight from Punta del Este, and knows I like girls. So whenever I catch his eye he seems to be twinkling conspiratorially which is, potentially, a bore.

At the end of the meal (which went on *far* too long) Christov walked me over to an adjoining table, and introduced a friend of his, a 'heart surgeon'(!). Also sitting there were a kind of brigand with villainous features, and a very pretty young girl with long red hair below her shoulders.

The Embassy is a fine building. Assertively Edwardian, and with its original nickel-plated plumbing. But HE's wife is *demonstratively* colourless. She seems pleasant and intelligent enough, but apparently has Parkinson's disease. Why is it that only innocent people, never nasty ones, are visited by these disagreeable diseases?

Now I can hear officials padding about in the corridor, preparing for a draining and meaningless day of meetings and protocol. Last night Christov asked me about my hobbies.

'Walking,' I said, and thought of the Creaggan Road.

Velikiye Tournovo   *Thursday, 14 April*

Today should have been quite agreeable – a motor drive across Bulgaria, some pleasantries on arrival with the Mayor, and a more or less private dinner in a tavern with the rest of the party. But nothing (nothing good, anyway) is as we expect it.

I had gone to bed vilely late as the amiable, but useless, buffer of an Ambassador (how freely I now used the word buffer of people who are younger than me) kept us up until gone midnight at a dinner in the Balkan Sheraton, *plying* me with drink, most of which I managed to avoid. Conversation, such as it was, of absolutely minimal value other than a brief passage when, emboldened, HE admitted/boasted that he had twice tried for adoption as a Liberal candidate (not surely the most demanding of ordeals?) and that he was strongly opposed to Trident. I couldn't really be rude, so kept quiet. But long silences, most definitely *not* filled by attentive staff bringing a succession of courses, dragged out the meal interminably.

So I hardly felt a thousand per cent this morning, sinking rather frailly sick into the front seat of the Jaguar and lowering my eyelids. The interpreter, or rather -trix, couldn't quite see, but could sense, that I wasn't paying full attention. Unrelentingly she jarred me. She was of the same school as yesterday, i.e., big greasy gypsy stock. She spoke English well, understood it poorly. 'Freed from the Ottoman yoke' and 'a self-taught master builder' were two phrases which, Kafka-like, recurred a great deal.

Once we were in the countryside I tried feigning sleep, though snapping 'awake' at one point on hearing that 'workers and peasants had united in an anti-fascist uprising in 1923'. Surely fascism hadn't existed in 1923, I growled. It came in with Mussolini. Ah no, though. It was the *concept* of Fascism that they had risen against.

En route, there was the Thracian tomb. (Pillaged in times past, so hardly worth looking at, but I disconcerted one and all by asking for a lavatory – it was nearly three hours since yoghourt and black coffee, four cups; am I the only human being who has to relieve his bladder at these intervals?)

Then, a tour of the Hydraulica factory and a formal lunch. Two set speeches from the Mayor and, obligatorily, two (off-the-cuff) responses from me. The Mayor was beautifully turned out and groomed in the way that only the lower classes manage when they are really trying, bless them. He was not unlike Cradduck[1] (good head of hair, carriage, Pisanello medal, all that balls) and spoke in inflexible paragraphs about the charms of his region. He said that at University he had been President of the Temperance League, and of the anti-tobacco society.

As I could hardly fail to notice that he was 'nipping' freely, and smelt of cigarettes, I asked, 'And then what happened?'

At this he appeared non-plussed, although the company laughed.

In the early part of the afternoon we drove through acres and acres of rose plantations, not yet in bloom, and they told me that it took three tons of rose petals (Heliogabulus)[2] to make a litre of oil. The interpretrix said that 14 February was St Tristan's day, the patron saint of pruners.

In Britain, I said, you send a card, with a message of endearment, to your loved one, but without signing it. And I reflected on how often I have missed this date, with a particular subject in mind. Why,

---

[1] Head gardener at Saltwood for twenty-nine years, from 1951 to 1980.
[2] *The Roses of Heliogabulus* by Alma Tadema, a famous Victorian painting depicting the Roman Emperor being smothered by, and wallowing in, rose petals.

for example, did I not send one to Rose this year – or last, come to that?

British Embassy, Bucharest   *Friday, 15 April*

We changed Jaguars at the Danube bridge and set off through flat, wet country; many horse-drawn vehicles. I saw a sad, friendly dog, like a rather shorter 'Ding'[1] standing with her ears back, lost?, in a truckers' layby. Just before the frontier a wonderfully ramshackle peasant lorry had rendezvoused with us and the occupants had 'shown' the cane garden furniture which, impetuously, I had ordered in Sofia. I issued a cheque for 270 US dollars – a bargain, if I ever see it again.[2]

Bucharest is *incredibly* grotty and rundown. Giant, flooded pot-holes; battered rusty trolley buses looking as if they had done service as roadblocks in the first battle of Rostov, disgorging crowds of sullen, shabby (but overweight) lumpenproletariat. Ceauşescu is bulldozing great swathes of the old town in order to impose a Haussmann-like pattern of squares and boulevards. Partly megalomania but largely, I would suspect, the same motives as Napoleon III's own instructions to Haussmann – in order better to enfilade the mob with cannon.[3]

HE is grey haired and bearded – 'active don', with a U-accent.[4] Slightly *distrait* style, but could be likeable. To my great satisfaction I found that we are in Tilea's[5] old villa. Still with some traces of his decor, or even Syrie Maugham, wrought-iron grilles and open plan in 1930s Florida style. Upstairs, though, the proportions are rather more *Torquay*. The carpets in the living room are exactly the same colour and design as the chaise-longue in the Chalet Caroline, which must have been covered at about the same time.

---

[1] A little mongrel bitch from the farm at Saltwood which AC always coveted as a pet.

[2] The cane furniture was punctiliously delivered in a Bulgarian lorry to the gates of Saltwood and is installed in the Garden House.

[3] Baron Haussmann replanned medieval Paris between 1853 and 1870, replacing narrow streets with wide boulevards to make the constructions of revolutionary barricades more difficult.

[4] Hugh Arbuthnott, British Ambassador to Rumania since 1986.

[5] The Rumanian Ambassador in London in the Thirties. A great socialite and scaremonger, *vide* Cadogan's diaries, etc.

Mrs Arbuthnott is rather attractive, and knows it, with the faintest undertone of mocking curiosity. Reminds me a little of the Dunne girls.

Blast. I've been lying not on but in my bed (the room is freezing) while, as I thought comfortingly, the bath ran. Now I find that the hot tap is lukewarm and the cold has diluted it beyond the acceptance limit. I must make do with a quick Pirbright scrub.[1] Then it's blue suit, white silk shirt, and off. Another formal dinner in prospect.

On the Danube   *Saturday, 16 April*

This is the river trip to Calstock[2] in spades, with diamond and oakleaves cluster. Rule of life, learned far too late, most recently at Konstanz is – never 'put in for' boat trips. The tiny, ill-built, thrumming *Riubeni* is conveying us down the Danube canal to the hotel at Sulina at the mouth of the delta. The return journey, tomorrow, will be against the current and slated (sic) to take over eight hours. It is really quite exceptionally cold – long grey overcast clouds, driving rain and the great river flooding and over its banks everywhere.

A teeny 'sandwich' (cold) has been served, and an 'orange juice' – the thinnest of wartime 'Jacks'[3] orangeade. In an adjoining cabin, the 'lounge', I can hear the Ambassador valiantly holding his own with the heavily made-up *Romantourist* lady who communicates in bad French. So, all in all, it's a dodgy prospect; pyjamas *and* underclothes in bed tonight, I should think, and an early start, curtailing the possibility of a thompson,[4] at 5.45 a.m.

Yesterday evening, however, was more fun. Dinner at the Athenee-Palace in a lovely 1907 dining room with fine-quality Tiffany glass lights set into the ceiling and a (too modest) Orpen maiden in a blue dress and an oval frame over the fireplace. *Musica* interrupted my desultory conversation, in (on his part, at least) poor French, with Mr

---

[1] The Household Division depot, where all recruits are subject to an especially arduous infantry training course.

[2] A habitual Constituency engagement on the River Tamar which AC used to find particularly irksome.

[3] A tuckshop adjoining the fives courts at Eton.

[4] Family slang for defecation.

Vadura, the State Trade Secretary. The violinist and his band played every tune from the big musical box at Saltwood.

Then some 'local' dancers came bouncing on and performed very merrily in national costume. I 'fixed' the best female, a nicely built blonde. Later, in a 'tableau' of four cloggie-type performers, I spotted that the one in a dog's mask was really a girl – from her slightly smaller size and quicker, neater movements. And sure enough, at the end she threw off the mask and a lovely mane of copper red hair fell out. A good round of applause and Mr Vadura said that he had thought she was a man. I said no, and the old interpreter smiled and nodded knowingly.

Later, I may have disconcerted Mr Vadura by trying to explain what I meant when I said Brisbane was the ice-cream capital of the world. He was making Ceauşescu's excuses; the President was 'touring Australia'. But when I talked about young blondes he became uneasy.

Not so the plump and corrupt 'manager' of the hotel who suddenly whipped out a medal and sash, of a *chevalier de fromage* kind, and hung it round my neck. 'Now follow me.' He took me down a narrow spiral staircase directly into the lobby of a *Hullo* nightclub, barking at a couple of (quite good-looking) whores who were sitting on the banquette. HE and the rest of the party were following, I was sorry to see, sheepishly and at a distance.

Live band. Very sympathetic saxophonist in glasses, jacket, open-neck cricket shirt who conscientiously studied his score throughout. And a pleasing floor show. The cuties, sinuous and blonde-skinned, shimmered and bounced with ostrich feathers and other, slender, accoutrements. The vocalists were talented and loud, 'Pasadena', etc. From time to time HE would lean over (he was about four places away at our table). 'You don't really need to stay, Minister'; and 'They won't be at all offended if you leave, you know'; and (desperate now) 'We've got a very early start tomorrow morning . . . '

Unusually for me, I had accepted a huge delicious Cuban cigar from the commercial attaché, and wouldn't move until it was finished. But the night was not so comfortable. Very cold indeed and I had to pee twice, once after a nasty dream about Tom being burned in a train.

Aboard the Riubeni   *Sunday, 17 April*

After breakfast (egg swimming in grease, coarse ham, wet brown rolls, erzatz coffee – which I quite like but HE wouldn't touch – and good natural cherry jam) I found a nice *warm* little cabin which I have designated my own. Outside the rain belts down and the waves (unusual for a river to have waves, surely?) slosh against the side of the hull. The engines throb reassuringly. This is the only heated cabin, but I am not entirely at ease as upright, and waiting for a thompson to announce itself.

The delta is vast. Two hundred thousand square miles or so we are told. Reed and willow trees and huge brackish lakes. Not much bird-life in evidence which is hardly surprising as the boat gives noisy advance warning of our approach. From one island a poor thin dog on a chain barked at us. When was he last fed?

Last night, as I foresaw, it was again '*quarante minutes entre chaque plat*'. And I lost patience at course 4, a nasty-looking steak, and asked for a jug of boiling water. Somewhere in my night case I had a 'portion' package of delicious Swiss *cacao*, pinched from the hotel in Konstanz for just this emergency, and my plan was to retire immediately, drink it, and have a (relatively) good night. But even this took fifteen minutes to arrive and to my – first pleasure, then annoyance – the task of taking it up to my room, with me, was entrusted to the sweeter of the two little waitresses who, in spite of poor complexion – unmade-up, poor little dear – definitely 'had something'; notably a large bust. But she was, we were, escorted most clumpingly up the wooden staircase by the huge and powerful manager and also by the police spy. So she wouldn't even catch my eye when I thanked her and said goodnight.

Later

The Captain, in spite of having four rings on his sleeve, has made a succession of balls-ups, twice ramming the bank, getting entangled with floating tree-trunks, throwing the little craft into 'hard astern', etc. Revving belchingly, he broke off a lot of willow (destroying, incidentally, our aerial so we are now completely incommunicado). I saved two sprigs in case they could be transplanted at Saltwood. I will put them straight into the basin in my bedroom at the Embassy, but I fear they will die before I can get them home.[1] I did manage a 'formal' thompson, one ranking for the *extremis* star along with the all time winner – under the trucks at Ascension Island, Wideawake airport. There was no lock on either outer or inner door, and the 'toilet' itself so narrow that, say, Cyril Smith could not have fitted in, much less on, it.

I caught sight of myself in the shaving mirror. Very heavy and jowelly I look. I must get out soon, and was cheered by the thought of the Privy Council list.[2] But of course there's always 'And yet...' This trip illustrates it in microcosm. *What* a bore it is having to meet the local Party Chairman (the same all over the world), listen to his wooden exposé of the district's 'technical, social and economic achievements in the co-operative sphere'. Yet how agreeable to have instant access and treatment.

And so in my life. Lovely to have the time, now I know what to do with it; sad to discard the trappings.

Department of Trade and Industry   *Wednesday, 27 April*

David Young and I dined together last night at Brooks's. He was very friendly and confiding. 'You're the only person I can talk to...'

I asked about his little grand-daughter, a few pleasantries, then moved in.

'David, it's rather earlier in the meal than I had intended, but I must speak frankly as I have something to say which you may not find welcome.'

'No, no. Far better speak frankly. I'd much prefer it.'

(I suspect David was thinking that some rebuke might be on the way. In yesterday's papers he was criticised for not being in the Lords enough – an obvious plant by Bertie Denham,[3] who does *not* find David congenial.)

---

[1] One survived, and is growing on the south bank of the stream flowing through the arboretum at Saltwood.

[2] A recurrent theme of AC's. In fact he was not appointed to the Privy Council until the 1991 New Year list. See the closing entry in this volume for an account of his induction.

[3] Lord Denham, Government Chief Whip, House of Lords, since 1979.

'Well, the point is approaching when you must start seriously to turn your mind to the question of whether you should enter the Commons.'

I could see at once that he was delighted. 'I'm not talking about the mechanics of it at present. They are not insuperable, if the will is there.'

We discussed the alternatives. His own 'scenario' had him moving in September, to take Health out of DHSS (the present Dept is to be split into two), sort that out, and become Chairman of the Party to win (eh?) the next Election.

His reward – to be Foreign Secretary.

At some point in the *next* Parliament a by-election would be arranged, with the PM's assent. David would then be poised to contest the succession.

I shot this down. Full of flaws. Time-scale too long (at mercy of the unpredictable); uncertainties too prolific – would she consent? Would his 'record' sustain it? Wouldn't it be too obvious that the move was simply in order to pitch at the succession?

I told David that if he was really serious he *had* to have a period in the House of Commons behind him, and experience of one of the great Offices that are open only to Commoners. (Naturally he would like best to be Chancellor.) I said that the very latest he could do it would be at the General Election, swim in on the tide. But he should be prepared to move fast if/when Bufton Tufton keels over in this Parliament.

'How long would a one-clause Bill take?'

'Two hours.'

'Would it have to go to the Lords?' (I didn't know the answer to this, but thought it significant that he should have asked.)

Plainly David is taken by the idea. I know from talking to Robert Atkins that sometimes it is mentioned 'jokingly'. David suggested that I sound out the PM, when next an opportunity offered. And at one point, I seem to remember, there was wild talk of standing at a by-election regardless, like Tony Benn, and daring the Commons to do its worst.[1]

---

[1] Tony Benn, MP for Chesterfield since 1983, who successfully instigated an Act of Parliament that allowed heirs to relinquish hereditary peerages. On the death of his father, the 1st Viscount Stansgate, Benn had been forced to resign his seat (then Bristol South East).

I advised against this. I reminded David that Benn was already in the Commons, having been endorsed by the electorate, when old Stansgate died and the problem arose. David admitted that many – he gave Kenneth Baker as an example – would turn against him once he had discarded the fleece (my analogy) and was running with the pack. I thought of, but didn't mention, Willie.

'That's why it mustn't be too obvious.'

I told David that he must get in, sweat out the initial phase of uncomplimentary profiles, malicious and wounding 'Diary' entries, trials of strength at the Despatch Box – get all this over before the 'Contest' actually starts. The analogy was with Alec [Home], I said. Someone whom nobody saw coming, but once it was settled 'the boys all breathed a sigh of relief'. (But of course Alec *had* done a stint in the Commons, when he was Neville's PPS.)

David began to run through the key personalities. He was voluble, but spoke shrewdly.

John Moore, totally destroyed, finished. Could even be dropped without trace in September. Ken Clarke, lazy, flawed, though 'quite good'. (Irritatingly, when he said 'Ken' I had thought he was referring to Baker, and I rejoined 'very' good.)

I compensated by saying, 'I couldn't work with him.'

'Oh quite. Quite.'

Nigel Lawson and Ridley were both washed out. But I queried this in Lawson's case. I said there was no such condition as 'not wanting' the top job – 'it's like a person's sex drive; there is always *something* there that can be kindled'.

John Wakeham no longer a contender, but wants as always to be the kingmaker. In some situations his conduct will reflect this.

Norman Tebbit was schizophrenic. (I heard various tales of his incompetence at CCO. David said that the book *Campaign*[1] was entirely accurate as regards chit-chat.) Interestingly, David said that Norman was behind all the stories and leaks about Peter Morrison – 'whose career is now at an end'.

David said that Michael [Heseltine] was really dangerous. The front runner. I calmed him. That's what they all say. I made the point that the Leader of the Tory Party has never been seen coming, that the way Michael was going round the place telling everyone he will

---

[1] *Campaign!* – 1987 Election book by Rodney Tyler.

get it, preening himself at Conference and so on, he couldn't keep it up for another two years. I told David that I was the author of those various remarks in Graham Turner's profile, comparing Michael to Lord Stokes, 'what he thinks – if his mental processes can actually be dignified by the word "thought"', etc., and he laughed, spontaneously.

David asked me where I would like to 'go' in September. I emulated Lord Halifax, indicated, but did not say, that I was reluctant to move 'sideways'; Trade was the best of the Min of State jobs, and so on. But equally, of course, I had done it long enough. (Foolishly, as I now realise, I did not say that I had to be made a Privy Councillor in June.) I said that I didn't really care, would just as soon go out.

'Oh no. You mustn't do that.' He asked me about Defence.

'I really feel that unless I were made Secretary of State I would find it so frustrating, I couldn't bear it.'

David made various tangential remarks about George Younger,[1] his father dying, wouldn't be able to hold his seat in Ayr, and so forth.

I didn't get the point until David said that if I was *in situ* when this happened (as Procurement Minister of State) it would be easier for me to slide upwards.

I tried to backtrack. Earlier, when I had said that I would like Paul's job[2] he had nodded, perhaps *over*fast. But he did say, 'She's got to have you in the Cabinet. She *must*. She's so short of supporters.'

Department of Trade and Industry   *Tuesday, 14 June*

We are now poised to put in place my personal *chef d'oeuvre*, the Fur Labelling Order. It has to lie on the table for a month, and then a brief debate in the House, after ten, and if necessary a perfunctory whipped vote on a two-liner. I have devoted enormous energy and time to this measure, and it is a purely personal triumph – over lawyers, Ambassadors, senior civil servants in several Departments including my own; eskimos, furriers, 'small shopkeepers' – they have all been in and alternately (sometime simultaneously) threatened and cajoled.

But yesterday, sinisterly, Charles rang from Number 10 to say that

---

[1] George Younger, MP for Ayr since 1964. Defence Secretary since 1986.
[2] Paul Channon had been Transport Secretary since 1987.

the PM 'would like a word' on the subject, could I come to her room in the House after Questions?

H'm. Could be bad.

Later
House of Commons
Charles was waiting behind the Chair, to catch me before I went in, a bad sign. He tried to soften me up.

'The Prime Minister really wants to drop the whole thing.'

'Not a chance, I'm afraid.'

'She's very worried about the effect on these local native communities of their livelihood being destroyed.'

'That's all balls.'

'Apparently Carol has just come back from there with heartrending stories.'

'She's just been conned.'

'The Prime Minister would like you first to go out to Canada and see for yourself.'

'Sure, I can do that. But it won't make the slightest difference.'

'No, but the Prime Minister's idea is that this would allow you to come back and say that you had seen for yourself and that you were not going to proceed.'

'Forget it.'

'You know that she herself is visiting Canada shortly?'

Of course! She could probably have resisted the Finchley furriers. But that blasted High Commissioner in Ottawa was winding her up with predictions of demos, placards, bad atmosphere, 'attention diverted from principal objectives of the visit', I could see it all.

'Let's go in.'

Hamilton[1] was there, on an upright chair. The PM and I sat opposite each other on those yellow damask sofas in the 'L' of the room.

'Alan, how are you?'

I ignored this. 'I'm so sorry that you should be getting all this trouble from the Canadians.'

'Oh it's not really *trouble*. I think there's more to it.'

This was going to be very difficult. She had a letter from Mulroney;

---

[1] Archie Hamilton succeeded Michael Alison as PPS to the Prime Minister in 1987.

from Resource International (I remember being warned about the clout they carried); she was going to address the Canadian Parliament. As the Prime Minister developed her case she, as it were, auto-fed her own indignation. It was a prototypical example of an argument with a woman – no rational sequence, associative, lateral thinking, jumping rails the whole time.

'Why not labelling of battery hens, of veal who never see daylight, of fish which had a hook in their mouth – what about foxes? Do you hunt?'

'Certainly not. Nor do I allow it on my land. And as for veal, I'm a vegetarian.'

'What about your shoes?'

I ignored this the first time. The second time I said, 'I don't think you would want your Ministers to wear plastic shoes.'

CP and Hamilton smiled. She did *not*.

Too far gone in indignation now, she just said something about the feet breathing better in leather.

'It's not you, Alan. It's so unlike you to respond to pressure.'

'I'm not "responding" to pressure. I'm *generating* it. I believe in it.'

Off we went again. Her sheer energy, and the speed with which she moves around the ring, make her a very difficult opponent. There was talk of wolves around the house.

'How would you like that?'

'I'd love it.'

Her argument, if such a confused, inconsequential but ardent gabbling can be dignified by that Aristotelian term, was 'it's-all-very-well-for-suburban-bourgeoisie-to-inflict-this-legislation-but-what-about-the-noble-savage?' I was prepared to respond on a philosophical plane. I said something-something about it being 'the first step'.

This was a mistake. She gritily repeated the phrase to herself several times, half under her breath, '–the first step?'

'In enlarging man's sense of responsibility towards the animal kingdom.'

She shifted ground again. Didn't like labelling orders, weren't we trying to move away from all that?

After four and a half minutes of this I realised I'd lost.

The meeting, scheduled for fifteen minutes, went on for fifty-five.

About three-quarters of the way through I said, 'Well, if that's what you want, I will obey you.'

Later I said, 'When you go to Canada, don't have anything to do with that "Humane Trapping Committee". It's a put-up job, you'll just make a fool of yourself. They'll think they've conned you.'

She grunted assent.

'I hate quarrelling with you, Alan.'

I snarled, 'I wouldn't do it for anyone else', and went out of the door.

Later
Department of Trade and Industry
A few minutes ago Charles rang. The PM was anxious to try and help me 'out' of this. No note had been taken of the meeting. (All that means, of course, is that the note which *was* taken will not be circulated.)

'I won't land her in it' (thinking of all those nice sincere young people in Lynx whom I was letting down).

No no, of course not, it wasn't that, she just wanted to see if she/we could help at all. Charles suggested that the order did still go on up to OD (E)[1] and that he would put up the Attorney and the Foreign Secretary to co-ordinate a very strong expression of legal opinion that would stop it in its tracks.

I like Charles. But *au fond* he is an apparatchik, although one of superlative quality. But my relations with the Lady are damaged – perhaps beyond repair.

Should I preempt? It would be the first time that a Minister will ever have resigned on an issue concerning the welfare of creatures that don't have a vote.

I rang Jane and she was wise and calming, though sad. Said, don't do anything hasty.

Albany   *Wednesday, 15 June*

I rose at four a.m. and made tea. The House has been sitting all night and, I am assured, will 'lose' today's business. A small stroke of luck

---

[1] OD (E): The Cabinet committee whose responsibility it would be to consider this topic.

as I am First for Questions this afternoon. A delicious sense of benefice – an unused day! I think I will go down to Saltwood, take breakfast there, and tackle estate papers.

But the oppression of yesterday's defeat is unresolved. I woke just after two, lay unhappily thrashing until four. Why had I woken so early? What was that waiting to come through the subconscious? The brain scans for seconds (it seems longer) then all the weight of those as yet unanswered letters, hundreds of them, of praise and encouragement; the thought that at this very moment animals are being caught in the wild; all the pain and despair on which their exploitation depends, I felt utterly dejected. I felt rage, too, at the PM having so totally swallowed the commercial lobby's case. Who has been feeding her all that stuff?

When the cock blackbird started up, on the dot of four, I put my head out of the window, the better to listen to him. So clear and beautiful, as he went through his whole repertoire, he passed to me a lovely message of Nature's strength, her powers of continuity and renewal.

And I drew some small consolation from this.

Nature's timescale is so different from ours.

House of Commons Terrace, evening   *Tuesday, 28 June*

It is humid. Warm but with a very light drizzle. I haven't sat out here to make a diary note for many years. The river boats going back and forth, always with some drunks, who jeer; the smells and breezes still, after forty-three years, evocative of 'Rafts'.[1] It is so hateful being stuck in the House during the summer months. (I must have written this a hundred, two hundred, times.)

As I left Saltwood this morning I said to Jane, the days are getting shorter again. One barely notices it at first but I believe myself at this point to start getting older and stiffer and sleepier, like the peacocks loosing their tail feathers. Whereas in the happy months of April and May, as the light lengthens, I am goat-like, and scrawnily boyish.

---

[1] The rafts and sheds on the Thames at Windsor used by the Eton rowing teams, or 'wet bobs'.

My Private Office are hopelessly incompetent. I had a bad brief for the ECGD[1] meeting. And they themselves are being timid and useless over the text of the press release. This should be hyping the extra billion which I have finally secured for special 'national interest' cover in defence equipment contracts. But there comes a point when officials suddenly lose their balls, become nervous of the Public Accounts Committee, or the National Audit Office.

However dear John Major very nobly allowed me to appeal directly to him, and overruled his own officials who had forbidden me (through *my* officials) to use the word 'extra'. This would of course have robbed the announcement of any impact at all, thus achieving what the civil servants wanted, as they can't bear Ministers making announcements on any topic unless the idea originated with them. I often think that in their ideal world the 'Line to Take' is prepared before the policy concept itself. No programme, but *none* is so true to life as *Yes, Minister.*

At eleven o'clock I left the Department for Aldershot, where the MoD has sponsored an arms sales 'exhibition'. I travelled down by car. Beside me on the back seat (I never like this but could hardly say 'sit in front, please', as I had never set eyes on him before) slumped a totally useless senior official who didn't know the name of any weapon, the calibre of any gun, the size or specification of *anything*, it seemed. Said he'd 'only been in the job six months'. Really! Six *hours* should have been enough for him to answer some of my queries.

I did a tour of the stands with the official following at my heels muttering to himself. I made all the running. Weapons are one of our best exports, and unlike most of the manufacturing sector there are still some bright young people around – though the boffins are better than the 'managers'. If I ever get to the MoD I'd be able to do a lot more. But the whole subject is blighted, in policy terms, by input from three separate Departments, DTI, MoD and Foreign Office. Friction is caused – as much by the *amour propre* of officials whose tenacious defence of their own (frequently illogical and outdated) position generates paper and delay.

At lunch I sat between Prince Michael of Kent and Frank Cooper,[2] the Prince in his ludicrous high collar and 'stock' like a cravat. He

[1] ECGD: Export Credit Guarantee Department.
[2] Sir Frank Cooper, retired civil servant. Permanent Under-Secretary, Ministry of Defence, 1976–82.

warmed to my talking about the Mille Miglia.[1] Anyone who has driven a DBR 1 in that ordeal can't be wholly without interest.

Frank was fascinating. He told me that at some conference in 1977, when she was still only (just) leader of the Opposition, the PM had turned to him and said, 'Must I do all this international stuff?' 'You can't avoid it,' was his reply, and she pulled a face. Frank says she remains a Little Englander through and through. I'm not so sure. I think she now relishes the role of statesman. Who wouldn't, after all, prefer the motorcade to being shouted at twice a week by little Kinnock. Frank said that during that period she and he had met Reagan and Carter, and she was *astonished* at how stupid they were. 'Can they really dispose of all that power?' etc.

Some interesting vignettes about the Falklands. That first Friday evening FC was dining with John Clark and Alistair Frame.[2] The phone rang before they could sit down, and he was called at once to the Prime Minister's room in the Commons. Henry Leach[3] (*not* in uniform, incidentally, that story is a myth) was the only Chief of Staff available.

Leach made a quiet, confident, measured presentation of how he could deploy the fleet. No one, curiously (and in retrospect fortunately) mentioned air cover at that time. Foreign Office officials cowered in a corner, sulky and apprehensive, but quiet. The Army were 'useless, couldn't take it seriously'. The RAF were slow to wake up, then panicked at the idea that the Navy would get all the credit, started moving on flight refuelling, insisted on deploying *their* Harriers for ground attack, etc.

Frank said that at one point there was a school recommending that *all* the Commanders be changed, including Woodward![4]

---

[1] A race over public roads in Italy, restricted since 1958 to 'Classic' cars.
[2] Sir John Clark, Chairman of Plessey, and Sir Alistair Frame, Chairman of RTZ.
[3] Admiral of the Fleet Sir Henry Leach, Chief of the Naval Staff and First Sea Lord.
[4] Admiral Sir John (Sandy) Woodward was Senior Task Group Commander, South Atlantic, during the Falklands Campaign, April-July 1982.

House of Commons   *Monday, 18 July*

The three-quarters of July syndrome. Everything stale and fetid. I walked through the Members' lobby this afternoon, then to the library and down Speaker's corridor. People – many of whom I hardly knew – scuttled and bustled self-importantly. I thought, if and when I 'stand down', not one single person, except possibly Ian and Tristan, will even notice or miss me for thirty seconds. Julian Amery, perhaps.

That fat creep Bruce Anderson[1] again wrote about the reshuffle and *again* left me out (probably prompted by John Whittingdale[2] who has always been doubtful, spelt j.e.a.l.o.u.s.). I have no future. Why should I go on stressing and straining and destroying the substance? 'Go out while they are still calling for more', etc. I suppose there is an off-chance of an upheaval if Walters[3] comes back, Lawson goes completely pouty and things fall apart. But in fact the next major reshuffle 'to take us into the Nineties' (ugh) is scheduled for 1989. And that actually will be the signal for me to be exited. Why hang around until then?

Department of Trade and Industry   *Tuesday, 19 July*

Tedious day. To the Arab-British Chamber of Commerce exhibition. Like an old cavalry horse, I dozed on the hoof as I went round the stands. The Prince of Wales 'opened' it. He has a strong handshake, like all polo players, but is pretty useless, I judge. Trite, tinky sentiments, prissily delivered. During his speech I dropped off into a mildly erotic dream. I am tired and nonno-ish, and my stubble is going grey – *why*?

---

[1] But see other mentions.
[2] A member of the Number 10 Policy group, later head of Mrs Thatcher's Cabinet in exile.
[3] Sir Alan Walters, personal Economics Adviser to the Prime Minister, 1981–4, now back at the World Bank as economics adviser.

Department of Trade and Industry   *Tuesday, 21 July*

I was in today before eight. By six I was completely exhausted, but still thought I might look in on Stephen's goodbye party, on the off-chance of setting eyes on any of the girls I fancy. At the door I ran into dear Judith, sweet and correct as always but looking, I thought, a tiny bit washed out. There was a fattish blonde whose name I don't know but she once said, or sang, 'there's someone following me . . .' when I was behind her, and admiring her dimensions, in the lift lobby – but no favourites.

However S of S was present and in ebullient form. We left together and he asked me back to his room. He said he'd had a 'good talk' with the Lady that very afternoon, and recommended me for Defence (at what rank? I didn't have the courage to ask). He said she had 'not reacted badly'. I was elated. David then said that I should try and get to see her in August 'when there is nothing much going on'. I said, 'But one should never argue one's own case. It's always counter-productive.' Oops! He wanted me to argue *his* case (!). He wants to go to Health, zap it before he becomes Chairman.

So I'm none the wiser. I don't know whether he *really* pushed my case, or whether she *really* reacted favourably, or whether he was saying all this in order to get me to boost *him*. Gossip and tittle-tattle in our game is only very rarely pure invention. The skill lies in objective interpretation.

Back in the House I ran into Chris Patten, told him that things were getting a bit 'closer'. He said that the Defence Dept was totally out of control. 'You'll be the most unpopular man in the Party.' 'I couldn't care. It's got to be faced.' Chris said that 'more and more intelligent people are saying this'.

Only two hours earlier I had been feeling appalling. Now, effervescent with glee and anticipation, I shot round to Brooks's and my dice sparkled. I took £500 off Nick Blackwell and we all crossed the road to dine at Boodles. Delicious claret, and Michael Stoop told several good stories – poignant was his recollection of a beautiful Belgian lady, a Madame Charlier, forty-two years old when as a subaltern in Rhine Army, he loved her after the war. Her body, 'and what we used to do' he recalled perfectly. Forty years later, eighty-two and unrecognisable, she hailed him at a restaurant in Brussels. 'She,' I said, 'who was once the helmet-makers' beautiful wife.'[1]

---

[1] The title of a sculpture of a very old woman by Auguste Rodin.

Department of Trade and Industry   *Monday, 25 July*

This morning I was tranquil. Little work pressing, and my office is full of flowers which Jane has sent up from Saltwood and which, queanly old sommelier, I took time and pleasure arranging.

I thought I might get G-J to dine with me at the Beefsteak (in the summer that long table with the bay window at the end is so much more congenial than Pratts. Pratts is more of a winter burrow.)

'Yes,' he said. 'And we can talk about the reshuffle.'

Got the point a bit too obviously, I thought, but never mind.

Some twenty minutes later I wandered into the outer office – Rose is looking so gorgeous in her yellow dress that, on one excuse or another, I have put my head round the door about six times already – and there on her desk was the early edition of the *Standard* – RESHUFFLE IN PROGRESS. 20 CHANGES.

I knew, of course that I was safe, but I was annoyed at its suddenness and disappointed at being passed over. I sat brooding for a few minutes, and was then interrupted by a summons to go round to the Secretary of State immediately.

David was a *husk*. Hadn't been consulted, hadn't even been warned. Wicks (as always somewhat off-hand) had simply rung to say that 'the name' was Newton.[1] I said that John Nott[2] told me he had absolutely no choice in who his junior Ministers were, and it was very unusual for a Secretary of State to be consulted.

But David was shattered – 'not even the courtesy of . . . ', then stopped himself. His hands shook, his blue eyes were watery. He sees the writing on the wall – a drastic diminution of his own influence.

Clutching at straws I said that 'the big one' (i.e. affecting the Cabinet) could be later. But no, Wicks had squashed that too. Nothing until 1989. Just another year to go through while we all grow older and the young Turks, Patten J., Patten C., Waldegrave, glint and glister.

I tried to extract some comfort from the situation by saying, 'The Nigel thing isn't finished yet . . . '

David agreed. And it is true. But what use will that be? And who

---

[1] Tony Newton, Minister for Health, had been made Chancellor of Duchy of Lancaster and a Minister of State in Trade and Industry.

[2] John Nott, former MP, who as Defence Secretary resigned in 1983, left Parliament and became Chairman of the merchant bankers, Lazard Brothers.

is she talking to? Not Wakeham; not Cecil; not repeat not, DY. Waddington?[1] But that's mechanistic only. Willie? Possibly. He was in London last night.

I drifted over to the House. Francis Maude was already there and we sat at the stationery table in the Aye lobby. Francis was tearful.

'I thought that at least I might have some recognition for all my work in the Financial Services field.'

He looks terrible. Appearance quite altered from the narrow-faced, fresh youngster who used to whip Employment. *So* puffy around the eyes that they are almost closed. His vision must be affected. Francis said that he had a brief meeting with David immediately after me. That he told David to remind Newton that he was only a Minister of State who happened to have a place at the Cabinet table.

DY, apparently, said that he would. But of course he won't, he's too shell-shocked. *Meni Meni Tekel Upharsin.*

Anyway, Newton is quite harmless, not a threat to anybody.

Tristan turned up at the Beefsteak. I thought it more tactful to talk about him – why had he not accepted (sic) a ministerial post? He had to work in Government in order to qualify as Chief Whip in the next Parliament, surely?

Tristan waffled around. Not particularly subtle. I got the impression that he, too, had been somewhat taken by surprise.

He was not optimistic, in the wider sense. Tristan is over-poweringly Europhile, and (as with his opponents in the Party) the subject becomes obsessive, and towers above all others. Great bore. The subject of 'Europe' is almost, though not quite, as bad as Ireland must have been at the turn of the century – and still is for some poor souls, like dear IG. Tristan said that 'confrontation' in Cabinet (what did this mean?) was inevitable 'one way or another'.

But when I ask him what he means he just bites his lip and nods his head, makes elliptic remarks like 'You'll see' and 'Just you wait'. In the end, he said, the Prime Minister will find herself isolated by her three 'heavies' – Howe, Hurd and Lawson – and in a crisis Brittan would go native at once, and add to her troubles.

I changed the subject, and urged that Nick Soames be appointed

---

[1] David Waddington, MP for Ribble Valley since 1983 (Clitheroe 1979–83). Chief Whip.

to one of the vacancies at the Whips' Office.[1] Tristan said that Nicholas didn't want it. His life was very complicated at the moment. Great mistake.

After dinner I told Jane and she said no, no, you must get hold of Nick and tell him not to be an ass.

I had to speak to him that evening, which wasn't easy. He was 'with the Prince of Wales'. But the Downing Street switchboard were magnificent, as always, and located him *via* Clarence House at the US Residence in Regent's Park, and got him away from the Ambassador's dining table.

Nick was sweet, effusive – but adamant. I told him that it's very difficult to make progress as a Minister unless (thinking ruefully of myself) you have done a stint as a Whip. He simply must grit his teeth. But he is worried about looking after his baby son. A good fellow.

Albany   *Monday, 12 September*

I have come from dinner with Richard Ryder[2] at Pratts. He's such fun. So intelligent, and has the right views on practically every topic. But he does repeat himself which, in someone his age, is a bad sign. Or at least it is if he doesn't know he's doing it. Yet some of his stories are so stylised that, Homeric, they depend on and are embellished by repetition. I've lost count of the number of times I've been told the story of Julian Amery on the (recent) parliamentary delegation to Rumania asking about Count Dracula and, after some inter-consultation between the guides, being told that 'Count Dracula is being reassessed'.

But of all Richard's stories I think my favourite, and one he tells with great panache, is a Battle of Britain folk epic which delights me however often I hear it. He and Douglas Bader were debating on opposite sides at a classy girls' school. Somehow, Bader got involved

---

[1] Nicholas Soames, PPS to the Secretary of State of Environment since 1987. He had been equerry to the Prince of Wales, 1970–2.
[2] Richard Ryder, an Assistant Whip since 1986, he was briefly to become Parliamentary Under-Secretary at Agriculture, and in 1989 Economic Secretary to the Treasury.

in telling of one of the occasions when he was shot down over the Channel:

'... And my engine was on fire, I had two of the fuckers on my tail, one fucker was coming up at me from the left, and there were two more fuckers about a hundred feet above me waiting for...' (At this the headmistress panicked and interrupted. 'Girls, as of course you all know, there was a type of German aeroplane called the FOKKER.') But Bader: 'I don't know about that. All I can tell you is these chaps were flying Messerschmitts.'

Department of Trade and Industry   *Wednesday, 14 September*

Last night I walked back from the 'Kundan'.[1] The previous evening I had walked from the Department to Albany. Tiny little saunters – about the same, I suppose, as from Shore Cottage to the Long Byre at Eriboll farm. There was a mass of starlings in St James's Park, chattering and jostling as they turned in for the night. I always like going past Clive Steps, especially in the evening when there are few people around, and I conjure up images from 1938; the great Foreign Office crises, Halifax and Cadogan walking anxiously in the Park. Chamberlain, and Horace Wilson[2] also, used it as an escape route.

As my legs stretched I still had an appetite for more. But how long will this last – five days or so? All too soon one is back in the debilitating routine, slumping on the back seat of the Jaguar even to make the journey from the Department to the House of Commons.

I have a bundle of interesting papers to read this evening. The Lady is going to make a speech at Bruges on the occasion of some Euro-anniversary or other. The Eurocreeps have written for her a really loathsome text, *wallowing* in rejection of our own national identity, which has come up to me for comment in the trade context. They even managed to delete a ritual obeisance to Churchill, his ideals, all that and substituted the name of *Schuman*. Really!

---

[1] Kundan, the curry restaurant in Horseferry Road.
[2] Sir Horace Wilson, chief industrial adviser to the Government, 1930–9, was seconded to the Treasury for service with the Prime Minister, 1935. Permanent Head of the Treasury and Head of the Civil Service, 1939–42.

I hardly know where to start in pulling it to pieces, but Charles, too, is having a go. We must win this one.

Saltwood   *Friday, 16 September*

Yesterday morning I felt vaguely, non-specifically ill; but cheered up when Jane arrived and we went over to Lancaster House for a lunch for the Prime Minister of Malta.

The PM made a *point* of seeking me out in the pre-drinks throng before the meal. She thanked me for my help, said she was going to press ahead with the Bruges notes virtually unchanged, in spite of FCO complaints. (I had earlier seen the revised, third version, and was glad to note that it hadn't altered, at all, from the second). 'You and I agree on this, but Douglas Hurd is completely committed.'

'Bugger Douglas Hurd,' I said. 'He's only the Home Secretary.'

She looked away with that lovely, distant smile she puts on when I 'go too far'.

A pleasing encounter. Fortified, I told a fabulous little blonde waitress, whom I have never seen before at Lancaster House, 'You're incredibly good-looking' as I went into the dining room, and took pleasure from watching to see how long it took for her blush (or flush) to die away.

I sat next to the Maltese High Commissioner, Manduca. A good Anglophile. I hope he's being properly treated. On my right was Carla Powell, and on *her* right sat Rocco Forte. Carla is always so full of life: 'Look at me, what fun to be sitting between two such handsome men, da da da, etc.' But as far as Rocco was concerned she some-what spoilt the effect by pronouncing 'Rrrocco' repeatedly in an accent that my dear Mama would have categorised as *proprio siciliano*. This had the effect of making Rocco *chétif* and ill-at-ease, as clearly he would prefer to be considered, in this setting at any rate, as an English gentleman. He spoke in beautifully clear and modulated tones, rather like the Prince of Wales (on whom, for all I know, he models himself).

Carla told me that Charles was *not* leaving immediately, but they were terribly short of money, having to borrow against the little house in the *Laghi* which had been left to her by her father. He didn't want an Embassy, not unless a real cracker (by which I inferred Paris or

Washington), would really rather go straight into the City. I will try and talk to Hanson, or David Alliance.[1] Some weeks ago, when I mentioned this problem to Jimmy,[2] he said, 'That man is so important he really ought to be paid £200,000 a year just to stay where he is.' Yes, of course. But Jimmy is not always reliable, although his judgments are seldom wrong.

As the lunch broke up I had a quick word with Charles. Practically every suggestion that the Foreign Office have made[3] has been rejected. They were foolish, because by their interference and provocation they have turned a relatively minor ceremonial chore into what could now well be a milestone in redefining our policy toward the Community. Charles is in a difficult position personally, I can see that. But he is resisting his own Mandarinate without flinching.

Department of Trade and Industry   *Monday, 19 September*

An incredible autumn morning, still and hazy. At seven or thereabouts, before going to the station, I walked the dogs over the Seeds.[4] All the fields are yellow with corn stubble, but in the valley the trees are dark, dark green; in that last cycle before they start to shed their leaves.

I am filled with gloom at the thought of having to go through it all again for yet another year. I am often mindful of that passage in the Moran diaries when Churchill is complaining of certain degenerative symptoms – 'Why can't you do something about them?' and Moran tells him, 'You were born with the most wonderful physical endowment. But now you have spent it, every last penny.'

By next autumn I feel that I will be down to my very last reserves of physical, I should say phys*iqu*al, capital. I read a long article in *The Times* on the train, through massive, prolonged, shunting at Tonbridge (even so-called Third World railways can't be this bad, the driver presumably was one of their statutory quota of 'disabled' employees and having an epileptic fit) about *cancer*. I really ought to avoid these blasted A-Doctor-Writes pieces. They're always unsettling. It 'can be

---

[1] Sir David Alliance, Chairman of Coats Patons.
[2] Sir James Goldsmith, founder and proprietor of a number of commercial enterprises.
[3] For the text of the Bruges Speech.
[4] A forty-acre field at Saltwood home farm.

undetected – and undetectable for *a long time* before striking'. Really! I thought the whole point was that it grew at colossal speed and, as poor Annie Fleming told Celly, one had to 'run, not walk, to the nearest doctor'?

I have appointed a new secretary, as Peta is leaving to get married. Tedious. Her name is Alison Young. She was not Peta's preferred candidate, but at the interview she showed spirit. I noted that her hair was wet, for some reason, although it was a fine day.

Saltwood   *Sunday, 2 October*

The place is full of Phillips' employees, doing an inventory. They shuffle about amiably, opening cupboards and chests, peeping and poking. I'm amazed at how ignorant they are. I mean some of them have specialised knowledge, of course, which I can't match on porcelain or silver or 'gems'. But most of them give the impression of learning as they go along. There's that mysterious greenish picture that hangs over the fireplace in the red study; the man from the Getty (I can't remember his name and he's been sacked since coming here) said it was a Bellini; v. unlikely, I feel, but it is important. The 'paintings expert' looked at it for a bit, literally scratching his head, finally said to Jane, 'Did Lord Clark ever meet Bernard Berenson?'[1]

So different from real enthusiasts like Peter Wilson, or Byam Shaw. Something would catch their eye and they would look at it for ages, and really love it. What was it worth? Oh nothing really, two or three hundred pounds, but that didn't matter, the point is they *loved* it. Christie's are the worst. What I really object to is the way that they *sneer* at the stuff as they go round: we don't mind slumming occasionally, but tee-hee, look at this, how quaint, nothing like the one in the Frick, etc, etc. Sothebys are jollier but they charge. And anyway, I don't want them to know what I've got here. No one's got into the keep before, and I'm only doing this at the behest of the Revenue. With a bit of luck some of Phillips's definitions will be sufficiently imprecise as to be untraceable.

---

[1] Lord Clark worked under Berenson in Florence for three years after leaving Oxford. They remained close friends and colleagues for the next fifty years.

Another thing that irritates me is that they are all *men*. Why no birds? I know that the atmosphere at Saltwood, creepy passages and little chambers and casement windows, can have a mildly aphrodisiac effect on female visitors. Once I've separated the girl from her group she gets alarmed, which is fun. They breathe faster, talk nineteen to the dozen, keep changing the subject. (I fear that if I'd come from 'an underprivileged background' I'd probably by now have done time for GBH, or assault, or even what Nanny calls *the other*.)

Damn. Bruce is coming down for a chat over lunch. There are a few dreary papers on my desk relating to the MFA which I haven't looked at yet and if the train was on time he'll already have been waiting, owlishly puzzled, on the platform at Sandling.

Sunday evening

We opened a bottle of Palmer '61. Bruce laid down the law on personalities, and *ratings*. My own shares are badly down after that slip on the Channel Tunnel. She was not going to keep Paul on. Bernard had the briefing to hand. Then at the last minute Paul was reprieved. At the time, and since, I felt that that was my last real chance to get into the Cabinet. And at lunch Bruce made things worse by telling me that the next Transport Minister would be Lynda.[1] How does he know? He can't know. And yet I still believe him.

Bruce was dismissive about Tristan: 'not up to it'; and Gow 'can't get a grip on things'. I don't like this. These are my friends, I mean my close friends. Then he made matters worse by saying that he had had a talk with Michael. 'He is formidable. He' – pause – 'is' – pause – 'formidable.'

I got him back to the station at four thirty, smelling powerfully of brandy. Seeing I was a bit dejected, Bruce said he would plug me with John Major and David Y, with whom he is having lunch at Conference next week. But do I really want it?

These lovely autumn days... Dear God, please spare me for at least one complete season on my own, enjoying freedom, The Philosopher Prince, adding to the store of human knowledge.

---

[1] Chalker. In fact it was to be Cecil Parkinson.

Albany   *Monday, 17 October*

Today the Anglo-Italian Summit, in Maggiore.

I rose early and confident. But Dave *lost the way* in light fog. We had to enter Heathrow by a special security gate on the north side of the perimeter that gave direct access onto the tarmac. Like all the lower classes, he went to pieces quickly and sat rigid at the wheel, slightly leaning forward, squinting into the fog, being overtaken by vans on either side. Too flush-faced to admit that he'd 'done wrong', he would neither turn round, nor even stop to get his bearings.

I was fidgety. I am only too well aware that as a Minister of State I attend these summits only at the Lady's whim. As far as Hurd, Howe, Lawson, *et al* are concerned it's very much on sufferance: 'We seem to be waiting for Alan...' From time to time I uttered peremptory instructions and we would backtrack through sleepy suburban crescents distant, it seemed, from the airport. Paperboys with orange *Guardian* satchels.

Finally, with only seven minutes to spare, we found ourselves at the familiar Spelthorne entrance. I leaped out and asked for directions. Naturally, it was a gate some distance along the perimeter which I had already suggested. It was apparent that we were only milliseconds ahead of the PM. Frantic policemen holding Uzi's[1] waved us on, on... Air Marshals covered in gilt and stripes saluted. Whumpf! I alighted in my seat. Hurd and Younger were opposite in the adjoining foursome bay. Before I could fasten my belt – for the Lady had followed directly on my heels – the engines screamed and we were off. No nonsense about waiting for the tower.

At Malpensa a large, but somewhat scruffy, guard of honour was lined up. Would they play God Save the Queen? Always a source of mischievous pleasure. And yes, they played it. I put on my raybans and walked over to where the helicopters were waiting. Douglas Hurd and I boarded a Bell 212. The Home Secretary, next to me, was nervous and thrummed his fingers. Sadismoidly I drew his attention to an adhesive notice in red just above my window: '*Sling load not to exceed 400 lbs until next* (sic) *overhaul*'. 'It's the word 'next' I don't like,' I said. The Home Secretary licked his lips but didn't answer.

We flew over the lake, and did two circuits of the beautiful Isola

---

[1] The 7.62 mm short-barrelled submachine-gun favoured by 'personal protection squads'.

Bella, home of the Boroneos who had asked the party to call on them and I don't doubt had prepared a wonderful reception. But it had been blocked by the tiresome little HE, officious and bespectacled (who was to materialise later). God, the amount of cumulative damage done to the British image by small-minded gauche and insensitive Ambassadors – *daily* around the globe – must be incalculable.

I remember the Boroneos at Elba[1] in 1966, when they made their entry into the dining room of the Pineti, the Count in a rumpled flannel cricket shirt and tweedy long trousers. At the time we thought they were muddled bourgeoisie out of their depth. Now I know that only the very rich behave like that. I succumbed to a sentimental fantasy of carnal desire for their young daughter. (Shamefully, I can't recall her name.) There was talk of an exchange visit, but it petered out. *Ancora tempo perso.*

Bumboy drivers in nasty little Alfa Romeo sedans took us from the heli-pad to the Villa Taranto. Totally spastic fast-driving with a police escort. So much so that at the villa gates they slid past on locked brakes and had to reverse back over their own skid marks before turning in.

I first had a bilateral meeting with Renato.[2] What a nice, thoughtful, civilised man he is. It's always a pleasure, and I always learn something. But the Italians are useless, the country is a mess – corrupt and unreliable – what earthly point is there in having a 'summit'? The Lady is short of friends in Europe and the Foreign Office have sold her the idea of starting the rapprochement here. But even if we did a deal the Italians wouldn't stick to it. Or the government would change before they had time to deliver.

Anyhow, whatever the Prime Ministers were doing they 'ran over' and the plenary meeting was (thank God) cancelled. We hung about in the garden waiting for the group photo. A policeman tried to keep me out of it – '*Solo Ministri, non funzionari*' – was this a compliment?

At lunch I sat next to Andreotti, old but not gaga. He ate well, though is lean and stooped. He told me the story of the villa's owner, a man named McEachan: before the war McE gave the property to Mussolini in order that the Duce should have a residence by the Lakes. This allowed his janitor to protect it both against the Partisans (it

---

[1] The Albergo Pineti in Elba, where the Clarks took their children for the summer holidays.

[2] Sr Renato Ruggiero the Italian Trade Minister, and AC's opposite number.

belongs to an English milord) and the Germans and Fascisti (it was a gift to the Duce). McEachan married an Italian girl. Having had a premonition, he forbade her ever to take their son in a car. She disobeyed him and the little boy, then aged five, was killed in a crash. McEachan divorced her on the spot. Later he married for a second time, but had no children.

How he recovered the villa after the war I don't know, but he was still comfortably installed there in the Fifties, employing (according to Andreotti), over forty gardeners. He died at the age of ninety and left his furniture and pictures – he had a good collection of Australian art – to the janitor and the house, again, to be a residence for the Prime Minister of Italy. Sadly, but predictably, the Italians have ruined it inside, lowering the ceilings and lining the walls with asbestos panels in order to help the air conditioning in much the same way as the French have wrecked the Chateau de la Muette, by covering part of the boiserie in the dining room.[1]

On the return flight in the VC 10 the PM invited me to sit at her table with Hurd and Geoffrey Howe. She was fussed about Barlow Clowes.[2] Should we bail out the 'investors'? Yes, I said. They were greedy, but small. It's the *big* greedy ones who should be punished, like that slob Clowes himself. I took the opportunity to warn her about Jaguar[3] being in jeopardy, which she didn't like. But what can we do? We just don't have the industrial or financial firepower any longer. But I was interested and gratified to hear her pass a comment showing that she had read *The Audit of War*.[4] She only drank orange juice.

After a bit Geoffrey Howe started getting restive. No one had addressed a word to him. He heaved himself past me, saying that he was going to change into a black tie. 'Good,' I said. 'Then you can serve us all drinks.' He pretended not to have heard, but when he came back, 'Two large gins and tonics, please, and Prime Minister, the maître d'hôtel is here and wants to know what you're going to have?' She didn't say anything, but grinned engagingly.

---

[1] The location of the ministerial lunch on the occasion of the annual OECD meetings.
[2] A financial 'bucket shop' offering very high rates of interest that had just gone bust, stranding hundreds of depositors.
[3] Sir John Egan, Managing Director of Jaguar Cars, had told AC that Ford of America were buying Jaguar shares systematically and threatening a takeover.
[4] *The Audit of War*, by Correlli Barnett.

Luxembourg   *Wednesday, 26 October*

I have been in the Foreign Affairs Council all day. Quite extra-ordinarily draining and repetitious. It is the representatives of the smaller countries (particularly Denmark) who – presumably for their own domestic political reasons – like to 'come in' several times, hashing and rehashing the same subject into finer and finer mince. The European Community must surely be the centre of that great hobby/cult (is it twentieth century, or is it ageless?) which thrives on the creation of problems; the minting of a special language or jargon – itself a *part* of the problem – in which it is expressed, and the long ritual Morris dances by which, very tentatively, a 'solution' is approached.

We rattled – a relative term, mind – through the morning's business, then had a good lunch and prospects seemed bright for the early afternoon plane (the next one doesn't leave until seven p.m.). But over lunch we ran into a Saragossa Sea of indecision on the *form* which the – pretty tenuous – South African sanctions should follow.

Should they take effect by a Community Instrument? Or by individual States' legislation? Or (a real pedant's picnic, this) by a reference to *Vu le Traité*?

Some delegates wished for one, others feared another which might be domestically 'difficult'.

'How do you get observation of a voluntary ban?' Geoffrey was asked. 'What mechanism do you have for enforcing (sic) it?'

'The Honours system,' I said, half under my breath.

This was my sole contribution to the whole morning's discussion. Those who heard it, laughed.

But that was four hours ago. Now we are up in *petit comité*, after two fifteen-minute adjournments, and have got stuck on Syria. The French, shits as always, have gone back on the assurances given before we sat down.

The *huissiers* clear the baize tables, empty the ashtrays, distribute more mineral water. The air-conditioning is turned up. It is remi-niscent of afternoon gambling, and this reinforces the painful sense of waste and unnatural exhaustion.

I used to gamble many years ago. Most notably in the Winter Casino in Cannes, where once I was cleaned out by red coming up nine times in succession. I had to borrow money for the journey home from 'Major Frank', Jimmy Goldsmith's benign old father, who owned a chunk of the Carlton.

Department of Trade and Industry   *Tuesday, 20 December*

Last night I went down to Highgrove.

Late, of course, and the position not helped by Dave getting into one of his M-way trances and slowly, oh-so-slowly (sic), slowing down – from 80 to 75 to 70 to 68 to 62 – then I say, 'Why are we going so slowly? The road's completely clear.' And he lurches forward and attaches himself to the tail (to the *tail*) of whatever is the next vehicle, preferably a TIR lorry, which he catches up.

As we covered the A429 from Malmesbury to Tetbury, past the house where little Sir John Rothenstein[1] took refuge in the early months of the war, and then the corner where I abandoned the Ford V8 drophead, as a child terrified of fire when Newy had left the cigarette lighter stuck in (a good early example of *cigaretters' dyslexia*) and it was smouldering – I thought, that *was* a long time ago, fifty years.[2] And now I'm a Minister of State, going to a private dinner with the Prince of Wales. George VI was on the throne then, and Charles didn't exist. It was 'the little princesses'.

I was the last to arrive, and the Prince had already 'joined the other guests' (in spite of the pretended informality we had all been issued with a meticulously timed programme. Guests were advised to arrive between 7.45 and 8 p.m. From 8 to 8.15 they would talk quietly among themselves; at 8.15 they were to be joined by the Prince, etc., etc., all the way through the evening.)

The sitting room door was shut. Through it I could hear a subdued respectful humming noise. As I entered the 'businessmen' (who else?) stopped talking and looked at me. Some feigned indignation. Most were complacent: 'Hur, hur, he's already blotted his copybook.' The Prince, on the other hand, did not stop talking. The minute and anxious equerry bobbed about trying – in my view gauchely – to interrupt.

---

[1] At that time director of the Tate Gallery.
[2] During the early years of the war the Clarks were living at Upton House, Tetbury.

The Prince – in my view rightly – paid no attention.

I looked about. Chintzes, Edwardian furniture of good quality, masses of photographs of 'The Firm', as they somewhat affectedly style themselves. A few big maritime water colours of a Wyllie-ish kind, and some washier ones that may have been by the Royal hand. No ivories, snuff-boxes, miniatures, objets d'art of any significance. Why not? Royalty have amassed these huge collections, by presentation and acquisitiveness, over the last two hundred years. Where is it all? In vaults, I suppose. Sometimes shown under glass to a dullard public procession. 'The Queen's treasures on view', all that. But this bourgeois unease is only two generations old. Edward VII had a kind of Farouk-like taste, and George V, as I know from my father, had a good knowledge of his drawings, and where they all were.

I had a few words with the Prince. Banal subjects. At one point a pleasing pup materialised, smooth-coated and self-assured, and with a Coster tail[1] and HRH told me that it was a Jack Russell that hadn't been 'docked'.

The purpose of the dinner was to bring together a few favoured 'Captains of Industry', the Secretary of State for Education and Science (Kenneth Baker was in the room, with his Cheshire-cat grin, glinting glossily) and the Minister for Trade, and discuss what could be done to remedy the almost universal inability of British managers effectively to communicate in any language other than English (and not very well even in that).

An important subject. And certainly worth a high-level committee, *provided* it had the power to see its recommendations through. But the trouble that affects all attempts by Royalty to 'inform' themselves is that the other participants are mainly, no, solely interested in scoring goodboy points and ingratiating themselves with the Royal Chair. Whatever for, one is tempted to ask. They certainly wouldn't bother if they knew how the Honours system actually operates.

Prince Charles has a nice voice, as I have often noted in the past. Distinctive, and every word beautifully clear. But he has a certain unhappy searching style of manner and expression, rather like his father, though less aggressive. At one point during the meal he hit the table, not authoritatively, but petulantly, '*Why* can't something be done?... We've got to do something...'

---

[1] The name of a dog belonging to Juliet Frossard, one of AC's personal secretaries, whose tail curled round like a whiting.

I was a long way off. As far, indeed, as I could be. At the opposite end of the table, facing the Prince but heavily covered by a row of cut-glass vases containing (quite prettily arranged) flowers or blooms. Very little drink. Nameless uniformed minions did not refill guests' glasses. Periodically they tried to deflect the Royal Russell and shoo him back through the baize door. But he was equal to this, and weaved his way around under the table. Furtively I fed him titbits.

With the (unbelievably minuscule glasses of) port, the main subject was addressed. Each visitor in turn was invited to make a contribution. In the main, it was auditioning for the All England Local Government Officials' Triteness (Bronze Star) Award. I came late. I tried to sparkle.

'Japan is already the most powerful country in the world. In 1943 she had learned the lesson that military power is a function of industrial power, and vowed to overcome this. Now already she has. Don't be misled by the fact that Japan doesn't make weapons. She could go on to a war footing in six months, produce missiles that would make the US versions look like muzzle-loaders.

'In thirty years' time, although English will be the *lingua franca*, Japan's dominance will mean that English will be no more than the language of the global peasantry. The tongue – *and the calligraphy* – of the Elite will be Japanese.'

The businessmen glowered at me through the cigar smoke. HRH looked uneasy. Only dear Kenneth's smile remained benignly in place.

And the Prince was distant to me when he bade me farewell. But I was glad to see toys and general disorder in the porch.

As we drove off I asked myself why we had all to go down, dressed up, in the middle of the busy week, to Gloucestershire, like unhappy winter Glyndebourners, in black ties in the five thirty rush hour?

On the way back Dave (inevitably) 'came over queer' and I had to take the wheel. When I told Cranley [Onslow], he said next time I should simply accelerate away and leave him on the verge.

All I got out of the whole experience was a pleasing demonstration of what happens when you don't dock a Russell puppy's tail.

1989

1989

Department of Trade and Industry   *Tuesday, 17 January, 1989*

A perfect cold clear winter's day. I have watched the sun move through its parabola, unshielded by cloud, from eight thirty this morning until now, gone two o'clock, when it is sinking. What have I got to show for this? Nothing. Shuffled papers about. I could have been in the Park at Saltwood, or on the Creaggan Road. All that has happened is that I am nine hours older.

I've had it. The Lady no longer knows my name. David pinches all the good 'initiatives' and I'm left with nothing. Who am I?

Other Ministers of State are high-profile. Waldegrave, Patten (both) Mellor (although everyone loathes him), Portillo.[1]

It has been conveyed to me that, after being so prominent a period of obscurity and 'good behaviour' would be prudent and beneficial, show I was 'serious', etc. All that has happened is that I have become obscure and passé. I should have realised that my enemies, who are numerous (why?) will be able, and will do their best, to exploit either condition equally effectively.

Department of Trade and Industry   *Wednesday, 25 January*

I long for July. Today I flagged the last week of that month in my engagement diary with a yellow marker, *Enfin la clef des champs.*[2]

But before I get there I have to traverse hateful deserts, mountain ridges. A trip to Bahrain; night flights to and from Yemen. Austria. The Maghreb. Madrid, Brazil, Mexico. In the very middle of the lovely cherishable Spring Bank Holiday week, when the peat is dry at Eriboll and the bracken starts to uncurl, there is an OECD conference in Paris.

Little MacGregor had a 'collapse' in Brussels. He felt ill, left the

---

[1] William Waldegrave, Minister of State at Foreign Office since 1988. Chris Patten, Minister for Overseas Development since 1986. John Patten, MP for Oxford West since 1983 (City of Oxford, 1979–83). Minister of State, Home Office, since 1987. David Mellor, MP for Putney since 1979. Minister of State, Department of Health since 1988. Michael Portillo, MP for Enfield, Southgate, since 1984. Minister of State, Transport since 1988.

[2] Verlaine.

room, slid to the floor in that long corridor leading from the *salle d'écoute*, and lay there with his mouth open. They took him to hospital for 'tests'.

He had been in continuous session in Council for six hours, and he was due back to lead in the Agriculture debate, with a full day before the Select Committee tomorrow.

The pressures on a Minister. Most of it unnecessary, and all of it gleefully and sadistically co-ordinated by officials with expressionless faces who stand by waiting for the Minister to 'break', and a new one to be delivered.

I am visiting Plymouth a lot at present. Alison comes with me, and we do the constituency correspondence on the train. She is more efficient than Peta, and more fun to be with. Her eyes are blue-grey.

Saltwood   *Saturday, 4 March*

Tristan has been trying to get hold of me.

He told me that Bruce Anderson had come in the previous evening, slumped down in a chair, and said, 'I think Clark is a sell.' Elaborated.

Earlier – not much earlier – BA had in fact telephoned to me, said he was depressed about my prospects but 'the shares are down, but they are undervalued. A buy at this level.'

Politics. How I adore it.

★　★　★

On the early morning of 13 March, AC left for an unofficial visit to the Maghreb. Some of the luggage including the case containing his notebook, was mislaid and his first entry for the period is subsumed in a letter to Jane dated that evening.

Monday, 13 March   *British Embassy (the Villa Dar al*
Ayoum), Tunis

Hello Lovey!

This is the most interesting building, quite grandly laid out – like a Moorish Gloria, with all the walls tiled (as well as the floors) and many old-fashioned fixtures-and-fittings. Given to Queen Victoria by the Bey in 1850, it was Alexander's HQ after the German surrender in 1943 and Macmillan lived, as resident Minister, in the annexe. I am occupying his actual bedroom.

We had tea on the patio where they spread their maps (a little round jug like the one we use[1] squinted at me reproachfully). HE a good man – wrote a thesis praising 'football supporters' for his Foreign Office promotion exam; now that *is* courage!

He told me, prompted by his wife (who is an 'invalid') the story of the resident donkey. This creature was tied to a tree, all the year round, suffering terribly from heat and flies in the summer, for seventeen years. Towards the end of his life he was so downcast that the staff didn't even bother to tie him up. He just stood, cowed and stooping, among the thorns. His plight came to the attention of two maiden ladies who run the Distressed Arab Donkey Society (or whatever it's called) and they reproached HE for setting a bad example. Rightly, in my view. So HE issued directions for its welfare and instructed his staff to get another donkey to keep it company. They, corruptly, bought a broken-down mare actually from *within* the abattoir (and, presumably, kept the change). The mare, covered with sores and her rib-cage showing, nonetheless showed some spirit. She bit the guard at the gate on arrival, lashed out with her hind legs at all and sundry, sank her teeth into the shoulder of the – presumably startled – elderly local resident and chased him round the paddock. In the end the vet had to be called to sedate her (thus, as so often, costing more than the amount 'saved' on the 'bargain'). However (that was a year ago) things settled down. The elderly resident 'picked up'; the mare put on weight and her sores healed; and now, most pleasingly, is pregnant!

She has a beautiful dark coat, like Eva (I insisted on meeting

---

[1] At one point in his career AC most disreputably pouched or pinched from Government hospitality a tiny white milk jug with a crown on it, and the Clarks frequently make use of it on their early morning tea tray.

them); while the buffer though still notably venerable, is handsome and silver. So 'what-do-you-think-of-that, then?'

As you can tell from the length of this letter I have a short period to myself only because, I fear, dinner starts so late. But it was nice to arrive in daylight and get wafts of the hot Pineti smell. Now for a bath (always a risk) and into blue suit for formalities and – inevitably and loathsomely – 'a few words in response' at the end of the meal.

Lots and lots of love

Al

British Embassy, Rabat   *Wednesday, 15 March*

A wonderful long day when refreshing incident balanced, almost, boredom and sense of waste.

We visited a carpet factory. British machinery, and more to come, with a chunk of ATP[1] money. I don't know how defensible it is to subsidise foreigners to buy machines which they will use to put British factories out of work. I suppose that they would get the machines from someone else if we didn't supply them. It is all part of 'restructuring'. But it still makes me uneasy.

Then we drove south, past Enfidaville where the 8th Army linked with the Americans in May of 1943, and Rommel knew the game was up, legging it back to Germany and leaving the scene to von Arnim and Kesselring.

A meeting with the Mayor of Sousse – identical in form and substance with that (almost exactly a year ago) with the Mayor of Velikiye Tournovo in Bulgaria. The district, its charms and attractions, its achievements, ambitions, much statistical jumble. He was a gloomy, though youthful, Levantine with that heavy shading around the circumference of the eye that is a special mark of the Lebanese – the only race that has a completely circular 'ditch'.

In the museum there are marvellous Roman mosaics, particularly those of the sea, and fishes. An elaborate depiction of a courtship/rape in six scenes, including a pleasing one of the girl *viciously* scratching

---

[1] ATP: Aid and Trade Provision, part of aid budget administered by Foreign Office.

the man's face, depicted him – I was surprised to see – detumescent throughout, although naked.

Had they been bowdlerised during 'restoration'? I was also suspicious of the 'Sea-God's' face. Neptune, they said. But it was not Roman at all, or remarkable and unique if really so. I suspect 'forged' in the Renaissance.

Next, I had to take lunch with, and address an assembly of dignitaries at the new, brand-new resort complex of Port El Kantouri. As our cortege, four black Mercedes plus HE's armoured Jaguar, drew up, sirens wailing, a crowd of pink and unshapely tourists gawped. We must, in our suits and dark glasses, have looked like a posse of Mafiosi as we dismounted and strode authoritatively about.

It is an all-white replica of Port Grimaud. The party were conducted into a 'show' apartment, price £80,000 (too much). Directly on the beach, but so what? On the way over I had made a black joke about skin cancer and HE told me, with some gravity, about his sister-in-law who had had to have whole areas of skin 'literally peeled away'. Oh dear, I didn't like the sound of that at *all*.

'It finished her, really.' Worse and worse.

'How old was she?'

'Thirty nine.'

Gah!

Sonorously, I read my speech. My accent, as Glyn[1] told me afterwards, better than that of the (Tunisian) chairman himself. But after a time sheer muscular exhaustion sets in, and one cannot get one's tongue properly around the syllables even though the brain continues to transmit the correct orders. But the audience were pleased by my performance, and flattered.

HE is very good company. On our return we looped inland. The countryside is bleak, but not destitute. And the Ambassador spoke interestingly and informatively. Bedouin tents showed at intervals, like black marquees. The tribesmen are allowed to come in off the desert and graze certain areas, with their goats and camels, at this time of year.

We stopped at a section of the great aqueduct to Carthage. 200 BC. How the Romans did build! Most of the huge sandstone blocks had been removed for local use, but the arches still hung on the rubble and mud-cement that had infilled the pillars.

---

[1] Glyn Williams, head of AC's Private Office.

I detached myself from the party (I expect they thought I was urinating) and found what looked like a route up the vertical face of one pier. I kicked off my shoes – the faithful 'Co-respondents' – and started up, heart in mouth, using even my fingernails. If I got stuck I could hardly call for help.

After about six minutes I was standing in the watercourse itself. A beautiful perspective of the arched duct, lit by inspection holes every thirty metres or so. I hauled myself out through one of these and, standing on the roof, hailed the party (who by now must have thought I was thompsoning, or had suffered a tiny coronary).

They were not pleased, responded with little warmth. Rather as did the 'official' party in San Pedro di Chuquicamata when I had my little duel with the Spanish museum curator.[1]

The flight to Rabat was overlong, and not particularly comfortable. And the drive from the airport was almost entirely occupied with listening to, and reassuring my hosts' complaints about 'Suleiman Rushdi'.

Not difficult for me. Can't we swop him for Terry Waite? I didn't suggest this, however.

Mamounia Hotel, Marrakesh   *Friday, 17 March*

Arrived here 'for a complete rest', *'se reposer'*, entirely at my own (I judge likely to be considerable) expense. I am curious, yellow, as Winston was here before the Casablanca Conference; and down the years other louche figures. It was a *wet* trip – it's still raining now – in M. Benani-Smires' new model Mercedes. His chauffeur seemed uncertain of his metier, hooting at very long range, though somewhat hesitant (due, I assume, to defective vision) about actually overtaking. Except in towns, that is, where he invariably drove too fast, and heedlessly.

Alas, it is my impression that the hotel is now little different from any other heavy clip-joint; i.e., barely civil staff, crowds of objectionable and riff – rather than raff – clients. Much chattering and slummy dress. The assistant manager is pressing me to come to a

---

[1] See entry for 31 October 1987.

'cocktails' this evening, but in truth I feel little more attracted to this than I am by the prospect of the Western Area cocktail party when I am changing in my hotel room at Blackpool.

Have I become unadventurous? Perhaps it is just exhaustion. Monsieur Calouri, who has been deputed to – at long range – exercise custody, titillates me all the time '*vous n'avez que desirer quelque chose . . .* '

Later

After a bath I felt better, went down to the Reception. But it all looked terribly dull, waste of time. I veered off and made for the dining room.

M. Calouri materialised. I not going to the 'party'? Clearly he was disappointed.

I'm pretty sure M. Calouri would procure for me, but I haven't got the nerve to couch (sic) my requirements. And anyway, think of the *boredom* potentially. They'd be bound to take photographs, tape, video everything. For all I know, my bedroom has got a two-way mirror. So embarrassing for the dear PM – 'I'm afraid it, er, looks as if Alan has been behaving, er, badly . . . '

The food was excellent, though 'nouvelle', which means tiny helpings. A number of agreeably low and coarse English blondes tottered past my table as I guzzled. I don't think they were whores – just tight, randy (several of them said 'Good Evening' as they went by) wives. Their husbands were ludicrous. Pink, as-it-were Simpsons dinner jackets and blue bow ties, yet balding and specs. Something of the Midlands fruit Mafia.

The restaurant management had tactfully surrounded their table with portable glass screens, from behind which coach-tour cackling and shrieks could soon be heard.

British Embassy, Warsaw   *Monday, 17 July*

I am now on what must be my very last trip as Minister for Trade. When I get back to London the reshuffle will be in full swing – perhaps over – and I will be at either the Ministry of Defence or the Foreign Office. So what's the point, one might ask. I have some businessmen in tow. But neither I nor any of the Ministers I am going to meet have (it seems in their case, I know in my own) any sort of tenure at all.

I read in the papers that the Defence Secretary after this weekend is going to be Tom *King* (for God's sake). Any idea that I will do Defence Procurement under that man is OUT. And I will give the Lady my reasons.[1] I'd really rather be back on the estate.

Now a boring three days in prospect. Bilateral meetings, prompt cards, interpreters, 'hospitality', *return* hospitality with identical personages. Then, the secret purpose of the visit unfolds — a visit to the Masurian Lakes and on 20 July (anniversary of the *Attentat*) to Rastenburg.

I am tortured by impotence — that utterly negative feeling, a void; zero between the loins. I must look up when I last suffered from it. Also, I am bored blue by the company of businessmen. I have absolutely nothing in common with them. I don't like sitting around with a glass in my hand. I don't understand references to Chelsea FC. I couldn't hit a golf ball to save my life. I like only the heavy movers, people like Arnold[2] or Jimmy [Goldsmith].

I must suspend this entry as it's HE's reception in half an hour and I have neither had a bath nor read the brief.

Masuria   *Wednesday, 19 July*

We drove for some two and a half hours out of Warsaw in a northerly direction, before crossing the old East Prussian border and bearing eastwards into the very heartland of the Masurian Lakes. Mile upon mile of forest — hardly surprising that Samsonov[3] got himself into such a mess — mixed pine and silver birch with a good sprinkling of ash and sycamore. Wooden railed deer fences (so much nicer than the horrid wire and galvanised skimpies in Scotland) and few dwellings. Turning off the 'B' road we went through a No Entry sign and motored for about 150 yards on an unmade surface that lost itself in the trees. The track then smoothed out into newly laid, but little used tarmac that wound and dipped through the woods for some six or

---

[1] But see in fact entry for 24 July, below.
[2] Lord Weinstock, Chairman of GEC.
[3] Commander of the Russian Army at Tannenberg in 1914.

seven miles. I could only judge this by comparing it with the distance from Ardneackie to, say, Foulain[1] (but all the time in dark forest).

We came upon a metal gate, militarily painted in red and white diagonal stripes, guarded by a sentry. He saluted and we passed through. Another mile, another gate, the sentry armed. Some five minutes later we came upon the 'Guest House'. We were greeted, unhappily, by the 'manager'. Like most Poles he is big, but with a tired, ill face. It is a modern two-storey building, right on the water's edge. The only other vehicle in the residents' car park is a khaki coloured police Pobieda.

My room has sliding glass doors opening directly on to a balcony that overlooks the Lake. Below, pleasingly, swallows fly in and out of their nests. Water flat calm, no breeze, great silence. Just a few bird calls. Something, not the smell, evokes Scotland. I suppose we are at the same latitude. Perhaps it is just the enveloping silence. But we are privileged prisoners. Escape from here would be truly impossible.

It is lovely, at my age, still to be experiencing new sensations. Charging the batteries from new terminals. The food isn't bad, and I eat a lot of rye bread and butter. But I am hungry at the moment, and thus irritable.

David Young's message duly arrived, in code (that he 'wanted to meet me on Monday') to say that I was remaining in the Govt. But I have almost decided not to accept anything except S of S Defence. Procurement would be impossible and FCO only acceptable if I was quite clearly Number 2, and *recognised as such*. I will talk it all over with Jane. But it is fun to have the option and to be able to toy, over the weekend at least, with the idea of 'cutting peat'.[2]

Masuria   *Thursday, 20 July*

I woke at four o'clock and the room was quite light. Thinking it was the moon shining, I rose and went on to the balcony to catch the light on the water. But it is already dawn, and the swallows are chirruping excitedly. We are very far north here, deep in the Runic

---

[1] Hirsels on the Eriboll Estate.
[2] A family phrase for escaping to the Highlands.

lands. A long long way from the Judaeo-Christian ethic.

I got dressed and strolled out to the wooden jetty that adjoins the lodge. The forest comes right down to the water's edge, turning immediately into reed-swamp that forms a belt about sixty to a hundred feet deep around the rim of the lake. Here, seventy-five years ago almost to the day, the wretched Russian infantry sought refuge and were cut down, for hour after hour, by the German machine-gun teams, and the waters were stained dark red for a hundred metres out from the shore.

Today we are driving to the *Wolfschanze*.[1] Stauffenberg's bomb exploded, forty-four years ago, just after two o'clock. I hope we get there in time. No one will know what is going through my mind – except possibly Glyn. And he will only know half.

House of Commons   *Monday, 24 July*

I have been hanging around all morning. It is foully hot, and I keep the windows open on to Star Court, which makes the room noisy. There are wild rumours. Maddest of all is that Geoffrey Howe is to be sacked. Apparently he has already been twice to Number 10, and emerged without a statement.[2]

So who would be Foreign Secretary?

I see all this from my own aspect. There are only two jobs that I could be offered (or would consider). One, that Chris Patten mentioned when I made an official call on him a couple of weeks ago, is to be 'Mister Europe', keep an eye on the Commission. Tristan has also hinted at this, and David too – 'as a joke'.

But would it actually be Lynda's job? Could I really work with Geoffrey and, more to the point, could he tolerate it? (Although if rumour is correct this won't actually arise.) It would be lovely to try the FO – but I would have to keep my nerve and insist on the continuity of Lynda's title there, and be *Deputy* Foreign Secretary.

I still think Defence is more likely. So many people have said that

---

[1] Hitler's headquarters at Rastenburg.
[2] Howe, who had been Foreign Secretary since 1983, became Lord President of the Council, Leader of the House of Commons and Deputy Prime Minister. John Major was appointed Foreign Secretary.

I am to go there first as M of S in order to be poised to slither upstairs if George [Younger] inherits, or goes somewhere grander. And it would be bound to be Procurement. Partly because I know all the weapons system specs off the top of my head, partly because the Army brass won't have me in AF because of *The Donkeys*.

Other junior Ministers have been drifting in and out of here all morning. Most are fretful. Peter Morrison doesn't know anything. A couple of years ago he was always first with the news.

Later

The phone rang. It was the harsh-voiced telephone operator from Number 10. I don't know any of their names, but there are two with lovely friendly voices and manners and one, this one, who is like Goneril in *Pinfold*.

'Mr Alan Clark?'

'Yes.'

'Hold the line for the Prime Minister.'

I held on, for an eternity. Then the operator came back, snarled, 'Are you still there?'

'Yes.'

'She [sic] is tied up at the moment. Will you be remaining at this number?'

'Of course.'

Over an hour passed. Nervously I fantasised. Could some miracle be taking place? There was another false start.

Then, finally, it was the Prime Minister.

'Alan, I want you to go to Defence.'

I said nothing.

Her voice flattened in tone. 'As Minister of State.'

'Who is going to be Secretary of State?'

'Well, don't tell anyone, because it hasn't been released yet, but Tom is coming back from Ireland to do it.'

Christ alive! Not only was this an appalling prospect, but it also put paid to my secret scheme/hope of slipping into George's shoes when he moved on.

'I'm sorry, Prime Minister, but I can't work with Tom. I went through all that when I was at DE, I can't do it again. He's too ghastly.'

'I know what you mean, but he is much better now.'

'I just can't do it, I'm afraid.'

'Alan, you've always wanted to go to Defence. I've stood out to get you this job (uh?). You can't let me down by refusing.'

'Oh all right, Prime Minister, thank you very much.'

'Right then, that's settled.'[1]

Oh dear! *What* a feeble resistance. Just a few shots in the air.

It is up to me what I make of this, I suppose. But it will be difficult. In that Department, of all Departments, seniority is everything.

I feel more than a little down. I have always wanted this. But it has not quite come in the form that I would have liked. I see trouble ahead.

And it was all so rushed and terse. Quite different from that lovely private encounter when she made me Minister for Trade.

Garden House   *Saturday, 29 July*

Is it really only five days since the reshuffle? It seems an eternity. I have had tension headache most of the day. There is *so* much to do here – cars, papers and estate. And what should be the very best weekend of the year, the weekend of the *clef* is already warped and occluded by the curtailing, *yet again*, of the holiday summer.

I am having to come to terms with a new set of officials, and they with me. So far I detect two clear divisions. There are polishedly respectful, or rather formally courteous seniors, who probably don't give a toss for a Minister of State *'en passage'*. And an almost openly sceptical Private Office who radiate their unease at my dilettante style. I read Notes for Incoming Ministers in an hour and a half (meekly and subserviently this should have taken me three days or, preferably a weekend).

I had called them in immediately: 'The first thing I want to make clear is that the 'Friday box' comes up on Thursday. Right? I'm not

---

[1] AC's actual title was Minister of State for Defence Procurement.

having everyone clearing their own desks at three p.m. on Friday and sending it up here to sod up my weekends.'

'But Minister, what about the weekend box, Minister?'

'There isn't one.'

They shuffled off into the outer office. I have the communicating door open at all times so that I can bellow and this curtails their own conversation.

After a little while Julian[1] came back in. 'What would you like me to do with Friday's material, Minister?'

'I will read it on the train to Plymouth.'

'But what about material that comes in after you've left?'

'I will see it on Monday.'

'But what about urgent material, Minister, what about weekends when you are Duty Minister?'

'I have a portable telephone and there is a land line to the office in Plymouth.'

'But what if it is too highly classified... ?'

'That is a problem to which, I do not doubt, a solution will be apparent when it arises.'

They load my In-tray with papers of widely varying importance and density, stacked haphazardly – the oldest, corniest trick in the Civil Service. I insisted on colour-coded folders (it is perfectly incredible that in this vast and brontosaurian Department so simple an aid to efficiency should be unheard of). I rang dear Rose at DTI and she sent round immediately a batch – Blue, letters for signing; Yellow, key information; Orange, useless information; Red, action.

It was apparently impossible to get a paginated notebook in which I could make my *own* notes of meetings (another thing civil servants don't like) and ideas. Very difficult even to raise a pencil. When I asked if Ministers could, ever did, circulate each other with notes the concept was greeted with startlement, if not consternation.

I want to send off two notes straight away. One on the importance of retaining the Armilla Patrol;[2] the second on the idiocy of overriding a planning authority refusal to extend the nuclear store at Devonport.

---

[1] Julian Scopes, Private Secretary. Within a few weeks (see later entries) he and AC had become firm friends and confidants, and co-operated closely in the gestation period of 'Options for Change'.

[2] Since the Iraq-Iran conflict at least one destroyer or frigate was permanently on station at Jebel Ali for emergency response.

Both issues show the Admiralty at its worst. They don't like Armilla
because it 'strains resources'. What are 'resources' *for*, for fuck's sake?
And they want to extend a dump for radioactive waste that abuts on
an infants' school at Weston Mill.

I got the little Admiral round. People tried not to tell me his
name, just referred to him as CFS[1] (every one, or thing, here is
denoted by their acronym. All part of a conspiracy to befuddle in-
comers.) I told him that nuclear power was essential to the security of
this country in two fields, and two only: warheads, and maritime
propulsion. If we were to retain public support, or at least assent, for
these we must lean over backwards in assuaging their environmental
concerns. What he was proposing to do wasn't just bad PR, it
amounted to wilful sabotage.

He bounced about in his chair crossly. Conveyed he thought I was
half Red spy, half do-gooder academic. Card marked.[2]

At present my game plan is to stay in for six months, until
Christmas, see my way around the Dept, what's happening exactly,
particularly *where the money is going*, and let the Lady have a considered
three-quarter-page report for reading over the Chequers Christmas
weekend.

But the first thing to do is get Private Office in on Monday and
sort a few things out. They've picked me off with a series of papers
about weapons, and the attendant procurement 'problems'. But how
can I pronounce judgment unless I know the background, the kind
of war we are expecting to fight? Or even against who we are expected
to fight? I see that everyone's career is predicated on the horrendous
Soviet 'threat'. But that's all balls. My problem is that as far as 'top
management' is concerned I appear to be both a Red agent *and* the
man who's going to wreck their careers.

I think I'll also give them a fright about the gauche and spastic
way in which their muttered enquiries and complaints about me are
getting straight back, after hours. Rhodes James tells me what his
secretary, Polly, reports to him. But Julian is married to Polly's daughter
and Polly is the doyenne of the secretarie's room in Deans Yard where

---

[1] Chief of Fleet Support, Admiral (later Sir) Jock Slater.
[2] From the outset of his tenure at the Ministry of Defence AC found that the
Admiralty Press Office in Plymouth was always ready to brief local reporters
about his failings.

everything is repeated. The Westminster hothouse. Doug[1] himself even said to Alison, 'Does he realise how hard he has to work?' which she repeated back to me, at dinner in the Kundan that same evening.

Tom King, meanwhile, is true to the form which I remember so well from DE. Kept me waiting for an hour on Friday afternoon by the phone, then left the building. Much later his office 'stood me down'. Loathsome puffball. Archie Hamilton[2] is something of a *faux bonhomme* and already suspicious of my 'encroachments'. (Just wait until I get started!) Michael Neubert[3] is serious and hardworking but (according to Julian) did not want to be switched across from Armed Forces and be my subordinate instead of the amiable, but somewhat *unversed* Tommy Arran.[4] All rather fun, but draining also.

I must not lose *élan*.

Michael Quinlan[5] is benign. Always hard to tell what he's really thinking. Which is as it should be with Permament Secretaries. The Chesterfieldian masque should be discarded only at times of acute crisis.

Saltwood   *Sunday, 30 July*

Bruce Anderson had asked himself down for a general gossip. I always said I'd open a bottle of 1916 Latour when I got to MoD so we split that as an *apéritif*. He's in my good books as he wrote percipiently about the Government changes, 'Mixing Alan Clark and Tom King could be the only mistake of the reshuffle.' He said he was interviewing David Owen first. 'Why don't you bring him down?' Bruce said he would try. Sure enough, they both turned up.

In strictly social terms David is oddly *unsophisticated*. Almost ill at ease, he said he didn't 'know much' about wine. Gently, I *tâtai le terrain* on the political scene. David said that 'she' had tried really hard

---

[1] Douglas Wiedner, Assistant Private Secretary.
[2] Archie Hamilton had been Minister of State (Armed Forces) since 1988.
[3] Michael Neubert, MP for Romford since 1974. As Parliamentary Under-Secretary newly moved across from Armed Forces to Defence Procurement.
[4] 9th Earl of Arran. Parliamentary Under-Secretary for the Armed Forces, 1989–92.
[5] Sir Michael Quinlan, Permanent Secretary at the Ministry of Defence. Both AC and Tom King had worked as Ministers with him when he was Secretary at the Department of Employment 1983–5.

recently, got hold of Debbie at a Number 10 reception and really turned it on. But he couldn't. How could he switch a third time? 'Winston did,' I said. How could he disappoint yet another group of followers? (What he meant, I suspect, was how could he get re-elected.)

David has this lovely grin – the most engaging grin in politics – and a good sardonic expression at other times. He commented freely and without inhibition. But he is a realist, and he *doesn't see his way.* Ll G, Enoch, now him. Great men, of massive authority and vision, find themselves disqualified by chance of circumstances and their own transient misjudgments. It seems to have nothing to do with quality. But I see no future for him.

While I was out of the room both he and Bruce said to Jane that I could 'quite easily' now get into the Cabinet.

Eriboll   *Thursday, 17 August*

This morning I bathed, before breakfast, in the loch just opposite the targets. I don't know what the temperature is; a tiny trace of Gulf Stream perhaps, but not much. One feels incredible afterwards – like an instant double whisky, but clear-headed. Perhaps a 'line' of coke does this also. Lithe, vigorous, energetic. Anything seems possible.

It was a still, mild day, high cirrus cloud, and I was half minded to attempt the great walk to Loch Stack.[1] But I did not leave enough time, and had to settle for a reconnaissance. I pressed right on beyond the oakwoods at the top of the Stra'beg valley, and started to ascend steeply, past the first of the two big waterfalls there. The second I could only reach by balancing on a succession of huge slippery boulders. Below me the black peat water flowed in that fast and silent manner that denotes great depth. I splashed my face and drank from one of the pools.

Then I left the watercourse and traversed the upper Polla valley – strewn with rowan trees, all carrying their bright orange fruit – and

---

[1] From the shore of Loch Eriboll (north Atlantic) to the shore of Loch Stack (running into the Irish Sea) a distance of some twenty-three miles with the ascent of two ridges over 2,000 feet, eluded AC until May 1991. He and Jane repeated the expedition in July 1992.

began the assault on the An Lean Charn Ridge. This is very steep, both hands are needed. But there is a profusion of heather, and foliage of stunted holm-oak and silver birch – rather like the opening passages of *Erewhon*. Near the col the treeline stops abruptly, and one must negotiate a series of dried peat water-courses, storm channels I suppose they are, which must be terrifying when in spate, with banks six to eight foot high. On the crest of the ridge there is a track (shown on the Ordnance Survey) for the stalkers' ponies and, indeed, hoof marks could be seen. I contemplated following it, but this would have slowly wound me down to Dionard – one of the bleakest and most remote of all the Highland lochs, a kind of landlocked Coruisk – then to God knows where.

I trailed down the hill on the SW side for a little while being unable, for some reason, to bring Foinavon into view, then swung back and down to the Polla valley.

By the time I was back at the Land-Rover I had been on the hill for more than seven hours. The walk *is* feasible, but one would have to allow up to ten, and pray for good visibility.

Yesterday we went to the Lairg Sale.[1] Poor Michael Wigan had the transporter with all his sheep on board in collision (fatally) with the district nurse in her Metro on a corner of the road between Boroboll and Rogart. The great truck turned over and about 100 lambs perished.

In the meantime little Moncreiffe was strutting about in his new plus fours, as pleased as punch with having sold Ribigill for three million or, rumour has it, thereabouts. I couldn't remember his Christian name (he was at Eton with me, but it was thought 'unhealthy' there to know other boys' Christian names) and when I whispered to James 'What's little Moncreiffe's Christian name?' he very splendidly answered, 'Little'.

Moncreiffe made a short, not very good, pompous speech about '. . . the farm will carry on', 'thankyou for buying my sheep', that kind of balls.

He was listened to quite attentively (most unusual in the Ring at Lairg) because everyone wanted to know who had bought Ribigill.

---

[1] A great annual event in north-west Sutherland combining social and economic activity. It is considered obligatory for all the landowners to attend.

Naturally, he didn't say. All it boiled down to was, 'Well, I've trousered a couple of million, and I'm off.'

Royal Navy Equipment Exhibition,   *Tuesday, 26 September*
Portsmouth

Last night I travelled down to Portsmouth for the Royal Navy Equipment Exhibition. I was booked into the Lady Hamilton (sic) suite at the Holiday Inn. A vast room, panoramic windows which, thank God, could be slid open and fresh air sucked in. Far below on the flat roof I could see the air-conditioning plants humming away; puzzled, possibly, by having to cope with this irregularity on the eighth floor. Vast bed, batty bath in the centre of the room, to get into it you had to go up a flight of stairs; sumptuous lounge en suite. But the detail was neglected. The fridge was empty, a bottle of still mineral water on the table had the seal broken and the level was about three inches down, and the telephones were completely congested. It was impossible to get an outside line for thirty minutes, nearly as bad as Warsaw.

Later that evening I hosted a dinner at Admiralty House for the more important foreign delegates. Admiral Jeremy Black[1] received me. Quite impressive (most senior sailors at the present time strike me as hopeless). For some reason – perhaps for that reason he is unpopular with his peers. This may relate to his period in command of *Invincible* during the Falklands. I remember at that time his colleagues were briefing journalists about how bad tempered and obstinate he was. He was not particularly friendly but to my gratification said, 'Didn't you come to the EFA meeting?[2]

'Yes.'

'I thought it strange that the Minister for Trade should be opposing

---

[1] Admiral Sir Jeremy Black, Deputy Chief of the Defence Staff, 1986–9, recently appointed C-in-C, Naval Home Command.

[2] When Minister for Trade, it was arranged by Number 10 that AC should attend a special briefing for Treasury Ministers at the Ministry of Defence where the case for the European Fighter Aircraft was to be argued. At the time Mrs Thatcher was doubtful about the wisdom of so large a programme and hoped that AC's technical expertise would be of use in attenuating the RAF case.

this project. I thought it would have the support of the DTI.'

Maddeningly, I cannot remember who else of the various officials tried to keep me out of that meeting and all of whom spoke at once in order to refute the arguments I was putting, I now see, in the course of my business at the Dept. Of course we could have blocked the whole project if the Lady hadn't changed her mind halfway through. Whether she was right or wrong I simply don't know at present, although I am inclined to think that the best solution is to maintain design and research teams and keep giving them more and more advanced projects to work on. But defer going into production for as long as one can. The moment something goes into production it is obsolescent and all the in-service problems start crowding in.

Surprise of the evening was the US Admiral Peter Hekman. After a slow start he showed himself to be an original thinker, well read in economics and philosophy. We discussed the great formative seminal works. Both agreed that Paul Kennedy demanded a place – to my surprise he had read all Kennedy's learned treatises in historic and foreign affairs. I suggested Keynes's *Economic Consequences of the Peace* but Hekman said although it had had tremendous influence this would be seen as short-lived.

Keynes had formulated the poison but not the antidote.

We touched on the evolution of power, alignments and interests over the next twenty years. Hekman asked which would be least acceptable to European opinion, a standing army of United (i.e., West and East) Germans or a revival of the Japanese carrier fleet. For me, and I suspect for the Anglo-Saxons, it would be the latter. Hekman told me that the Japanese were already 'feeling' for permission to build a carrier, which is presently forbidden under the peace treaty.

Saltwood *Saturday, 30 September*

I have just returned, exhausted but triumphant, from the Chequers CFE Seminar.[1]

Although we left early Dave got in a muddle after leaving the

---

[1] The Conventional Forces (Europe) Treaty, under which mutually agreed Force reductions were to be tied to a timetable. From having been obstructive the 'new' Soviet regime under Glasnost was actually leading the way.

M40, and more time was lost because I, starting nervous, soon developed hyper-anxiety and forced him to stop twice in order that I could relieve myself. Just in time (were we the last? I expect so) we turned down the back drive and into the roadblock of merciless-looking police sharpshooters.

I stayed quiet for most of the first half – although an awful lot of balls was talked, mainly by the heavyweight military men present, and by Michael Alexander, our Ambassador to NATO, whose higher intelligence has made him see that the writing is on the wall.[1] 'The Threat' (that always slightly ludicrous term) has now become a personal one – to their careers.

After an hour or so the discussion moved on to the kind of equipment that was going to be needed in 'the new scenario'. Lawson, who knows that I will be able to save him money, said, 'Prime Minister, could we hear on this subject from the Minister of State?'

I set out my stall, named and costed a number of programmes which could be eliminated without any risk. This induced *show* intakes of breath from the military men, but I could see Lawson and Lamont[2] beaming with approval. Martin Farndale[3] tried to come back at me, but the PM cut him off and she started on a quite well informed (Charles's hand clearly in evidence) summary of the approach to equipment problems, and the need for 'inter-operability' across NATO.

When the Prime Minister said that 'further work was needed' I jumped in. It was now or never.

'Prime Minister, may I have your instructions to draw up a schedule of our equipment requirements over the next five years, in the light of anticipated progress in the CFE negotiations?'

It simply is not allowed to interrupt the Prime Minister when she is summing up at the conclusion of a discussion. Everyone at the table turned and looked at me. I could see TK, some few places away on the other side, jaw dropped open, saucer-eyed. I could guess what *he* was thinking.

'Yes. We must be able to make some savings now. But . . . (going

---

[1] Sir Michael Alexander, diplomat. Former Assistant Private Secretary to Sir Alec Douglas-Home and James Callaghan, and Private Secretary (Overseas Affairs) to Margaret Thatcher, 1979–81. Ambassador, Vienna, 1982–6.

[2] Norman Lamont was at that time Chief Secretary at the Treasury.

[3] General Sir Martin Farndale, outgoing Commander-in-Chief of BAOR.

dreamy-voiced – I know this – it is a defensive tack)... I want particular attention payed to inter-operability.'

What a coup! The meeting ended, and there was no scope for anyone else to get in.

I was ebullient, foolishly so.

'Well done, Alan,' said Lawson, as we drifted down to lunch, but he said it *sotto voce*.

'Do you realise what this means? This is the Defence Review. I've got a free hand to write it.'

'Yes, if you play your cards right. I wouldn't shout it from the rooftops.'

I came up behind Quinlan. 'How about that, then, Michael? This is the Defence Review. We're off.'

'Well, don't call it that, whatever you do.' He didn't seem too happy.

Once in the car I telephoned to Julian at his home.

'We've made it! Single-handed you and I are going to write the Review.'

He couldn't really believe it. I took him through the whole thing stage by stage.

Julian said, 'Minister, you *must* be identified in the Meetings note, otherwise S of S's office, or the Permament Secretary, or both, will take the whole thing over and smother it.'

'Don't you worry. Leave it to me.'

I was exultant, convinced it was the ox's hide.[1]

As soon as I got back here I started trying to reach Charles. I *had* to speak to him before he finalises the note, which he will be doing this very weekend. Finally I got him at Number 10.

He started friendly. 'I think that went rather well.' (All civil servants use this expression unless there has been a complete disaster.) I explained the problem.

'Oh no. I couldn't do that. It would be most unusual. I can really only name the heads of Departments.'

---

[1] From the legend of the Baron who asked his King for 'only so much land as can be encompassed by an ox's hide' and, getting permission, slew the largest ox he could find. He then cut its hide into a long leather lace, within whose circumference the Baron constructed a powerful castle which soon dominated the surrounding country, and from which he came to challenge the King himself.

'If you don't identify me, the whole thing will be stillborn.'

'Oh, surely not. Tom was there. He heard what the Prime Minister said.'

'Come on, Charles, ha bloody ha.'

'Well, I don't really see how I can.'

'Will you please ask the Prime Minister? Will you please tell her of this conversation?'

'If you insist. But I must warn you of my opinion that she will take the same view.'

'Even if she does, I'm no worse off. Please tell her.'

'All right.'

Fingers crossed!

Ministry of Defence   *Wednesday, 4 October*

Yesterday there was still no paper on the 'Conclusions' of the Chequers meeting. Strange. Number 10 are usually so efficient. But I did not dare ring Charles, it would have seemed importunate. There's nothing that I could do now. Every time Julian enquired of S of S's office the answer came that they had not yet been received.

But I was in the cafeteria at lunch, and saw Norman Lamont. He started talking about it. When did he get his copy? Monday. Again I tried Julian, again a blank wall from down the corridor.

In the evening I rang Number 10. Charles was away but his secretary said yes, they had gone over to MoD on Monday. 'Actually, you got the first batch.'

I explained that I hadn't received mine, must be stuck somewhere in the pipeline, could I come over for a copy?

'I don't have any spare copies, they are all restricted circulation.'

But she very sweetly agreed to make a copy of my copy (i.e., of the copy I should have had). I was to collect it first thing this morning.

And, sure enough, at the end of the instruction were the magic words, *Minister, Defence Procurement, to take the Lead* (!)

I showed it to Julian. He could barely believe his eyes. Yet Tom's office will not release our copy, which was sent to them by Number 10 for onward transmission. The most we can get from them, late this afternoon, is that S of S 'is considering how best this can be tackled'.

Ministry of Defence   *Thursday, 5 October*

Ministers was cancelled today, which is highly unusual. At ten o'clock word came for me to go along (subject of discussion not disclosed, again unusual).

Tom was standing behind his desk, motioned to me to sit at a small chair facing him. Simon[1] padded out and shut the door.

'I just want to get one thing straight.'

'Uh?'

'I'm in charge.'

'Well, yes.'

'I've talked to her. I've talked to Charles. I'm handling this.'

'Quite.'

'If we're going to work amicably together, which I'm sure we are, we've got to trust each other.'

'Quite.'

'I cannot have you passing notes to the Prime Minister down the chimney.'

'No.'

When I got back to my office they were all peering at me; what for? Contusions?

'Fear God, and stay calm,' I said. 'No man's way leadeth to harm.'

They don't know that aphorism. Perhaps sometimes they think that I am going off my head.

Plymouth Train   *Friday, 10 November*

I am on my way down to a series of dreary Constituency functions, including a massive surgery list.

I am staying the whole weekend at Bratton, as already (the last one seems only months ago) it is Remembrance Sunday, and the Hoe

---

[1] Simon Webb, head of Tom King's Private Office.

Ceremony. But before I get out there I have to make a speech at Peter Whiteley's house where a rally to raise funds is being held.

In fact I don't mind this part as he is a good chap, a former Commandant of the Royal Marines, and the IRA are always trying to kill him. Pretty wife, too. Peter is of a certain type, whose *heart* (as in 'hearts and minds') is in the right place, but he is undemonstrative. They are valuable, these men.

My days in the Department are very full at present. Because in addition to my routine ministerial duties I am covertly preparing the secret draft of the Defence Review – of *my* Defence Review, I should say.

Alison and I have really done the whole thing together, on the word processor in my Commons Office. The only 'trace elements' have been the periodic requests for facts and figures which Julian has sent down to various desks within the Dept.

Julian is being wonderful. Helpful, tactful, assiduous; he warns me when he thinks that I am going too far. Though sometimes even he can be made to look slightly pop-eyed and startled. We were working late the other evening and when he brought some papers to my desk I smelt whisky.

'Julian, you've been drinking!'

'Yes, Minister, I have had a small whisky, yes Minister.'

I am a spoilsport really. All Ministers have a huge drink allowance, administered by Private Office, and a vast store of bottles for 'entertaining'. It is common practice for Private Office to help themselves in times of need. I never touch it. But many colleagues are convivial, and do a 'sun's-over-the-yardarm' act most evenings.

I am in despair about the Navy or, rather, the sailors. This is the Service which has to be the centre-piece of my plan – swift, flexible, hard-hitting. Yet the only thing they want is to be the forward ASW screen for the United States Navy in northern waters.

That's all over, I say. Forget it. The Soviet 'threat' no longer exists. Raise your eyes. Have not any of them read Mahan? Or Arthur Marder? I suppose the whole thing started to go to pieces when (effectively) we abolished Dartmouth. The soldiers are little better. The careers structure of the British Army is and for the last forty years has been anchored on 'Rhine Army'. They simply cannot come to terms with the change that has occurred. They won't even *train* differently – I suppose because to do so would involve admitting that there may, conceivably, be other enemies, other 'theatres'.

On the whole, though, I am getting on well with the civil servants. They are clever, of high calibre, most of them and not irredeemably set in their ways. And I am lucky that the Permanent Secretary immediately answerable to me, Peter Levene,[1] is thoroughly congenial. A quick mind and – so important – a sense of humour.

Ministry of Defence   *Thursday, 21 December*

It's all a bit awkward. I live dangerously.

But the key thing is, I have finished my paper, boldly entitled it 'The 1990 Defence Review', and lodged it with Charles at Number 10. Afterwards, Alison and I went up to the Pugin Room, split half a bottle of champagne; then another.

My paper is succinct and radical. And I have followed the two guiding principles in such matters – keep it short, (5 pages and an annexe) and get it in first, ahead of any other(s) that may compete for attention. (One thing I have learned in Whitehall is the need to be first 'on the table' and take pole position against which all else is judged.)

I just – *just* – beat the great 'official' departmental paper which Quinlan has been preparing for months, ever since he had that nasty shock at Chequers.

But Quinlan's is a Motherhood paper. All in all, the possibility cannot be excluded, it seems likely that; existing uncertainties, need to consult closely with Allies at every stage, must be careful not to drop or, as important, *seem* (or is it 'seen'?) to be dropping our guard; real savings a considerable distance in the future, need for absolute secrecy, discussion confined to a very small group.

The first meeting, to discuss the Dept's own paper, is scheduled for this evening, at which the Permament Secretary is to distribute draft 'Headings', and explain how he is proposing to 'draw the threads together'.

Julian rightly and shrewdly said that I must get my paper to Tom, and to Quinlan himself, before (but of course only just before) this

---

[1] Sir Peter Levene, Chief of Defence Procurement since 1985.

meeting is convened. Deftly I altered the first page so that of the four copies they appeared to be getting Numbers One and Three.

Unusually, the meeting started in time (Tom is driving down to Wiltshire tonight, immediately the meeting is over, for the Christmas hols). When I got in everyone was reading, avidly and urgently.

Quinlan had his head bent right over my text, lips moving occasionally – like my father's description of Picasso when first confronted with a portfolio of Moore drawings.

No one bothered about the Dept's paper, indeed it was hardly referred to throughout.

Tom waved mine in the air. 'This is pretty drastic stuff.'

He launched into a rambling dissertation on the unwisdom of reducing our strength in Germany, followed by a (clearly) prepared passage on a 'scenario' that involved starving Poles storming a Red Army food train. Bizarre.

'Could put NATO in a very difficult position.'

But he is not a fool, Tom, in matters such as this; and he was eyeing me closely.

'What we have all got to ensure is that this does not get into the hands of the Prime Minister.'

Silence, except for a grunt from Hamilton, who was looking very bad-tempered.

'She'd get hold of completely the wrong end of the stick.'

I said nothing.

'Not straight away, anyway, Alan? Huh?'

'I find myself in a very difficult position.'

'Why?'

'She knows that I am writing it.'

'How does she know that?'

'Because I am doing it at her request. You recall the note of the Chequers meeting?'

'Well, not until we've cleaned it up a bit. It'd be very bad for morale here if this got out in its present form.'

'I don't think it would for a minute.'

'Oh yes, indeed, I'm afraid it would. At least, we must hold on to it until after Christmas.'

Then, poor Tom, he said – was it plucking, or was it sinister? – in front of four other people it was certainly odd: 'You promised that you would not send her any notes without showing them to me at the same time.'

'I am showing it to you.'

'Well, that's agreed, then. We'll all keep tight hold of this until after Christmas.'

'Yeah.'

I was on ultra-thin ice. I could *just* say that, I pretended, because I hadn't handed it to her, but to Charles.

The breathing space didn't last five minutes. Back in my office I used my direct line to dial Charles direct. Engaged. I redialled half a minute later. Still engaged. Then I heard the phone in the outer office.

Julian came in, white-faced.

It was Simon. He had rung Charles to excuse the delay in submitting the departmental paper, which had been promised *for* Christmas, and said that the 'Min DP has also written something to which we are giving consideration'.

'So am I,' Charles had answered. 'It's on my desk now.'

I could feel myself break into an instant sweat. *So* embarrassing.

'Christ. What do I do?'

Julian was thoughtful.

I just wanted to leap into the car, drive down to Saltwood, hide for a week or so. Time, the great healer.

'I wouldn't do that, Minister. I think that you'll have to go round straight away and apologise.'

'Impossible. Anyway, he will have left by now.'

'Just let me see.' He rang Simon again.

'The Secretary of State is still there. He can see you now.'

Tom was seated at his desk in I'm-in-charge mode. And the chair stood directly in front, ready for a pre-caning homily.

'I'm most frightfully sorry. I just couldn't own up in front of all those people.'

He waved my explanation aside, said something about you should always feel free to let me see everything, it makes it so much easier for both of us.

'Anyhow, I've had a word with Charles, whom I know well. He agrees that the Prime Minister should not see this paper before Christmas – otherwise, ha-ha, she'll be making all our lives a misery over the holiday . . . '

'Very good of you to take this line '

'No, no. Yes, yes. It's just one of those things. Anyway, have a good holiday. Going skiing?'

I felt a bit of a shit. But how else could I play it? Good old Tom, though. Magnanimus Sextus.

1990

1990

Here come the Nineties! It's impossible to write anything contemplative without sounding demi-E.J. Thribb.

But am I, for a start, going to achieve my life's ambition? Auguries at the moment – poor.

Total silence from Chequers. Nothing indeed since Charles, rather gruffly, acknowledged in the Cabinet Room at Number 10, the personal delivery, by me, of The Paper before Christmas.

I look back on the start of previous decades.

1970 was miserable. I had been rejected in the selection process for Weston-super-Mare[1] and believed that my last chance to get into the next (or any) House of Commons had gone. We were in Zermatt for Christmas, but James had broken his leg badly, was wan and in plaster.

1980 was little better. The 'new' Conservative Government wasn't getting anywhere. The Lady had surrounded herself with Heathites and was too timid to embrace me. While we were in opposition Humphrey Atkins[2] had been a most objectionable Chief Whip, and had marked my card. Looking at old journals I see it was about now that he gave me a spastic 'dressing down' for smashing one of the House telephones. Just like Jacques at Eton,[3] 'We don't do that sort of thing.' Stupid cunt. Also Peter Thorneycroft, who didn't just censor, he vetoed a complete article that I was commissioned to write for *Conservative Weekly*. I was beyond the pale.

Now, though, my zest for life is stronger than it has ever been. My energy is excellent; the *width* of my appreciation continues to expand, and there is no sign of fading intellectual powers. This is going to be my year. Or...

In fairness, I should say that I really love my job (being racked only by the pains of not being Secretary of State). For the first time in Government I actually look forward to the end of the holiday,

---

[1] For a by-election in 1969 the local constituency selected Jerry Wiggin, who had previously stood as Conservative candidate for Montgomeryshire in 1964 and 1966.

[2] Humphrey Atkins, Northern Ireland Secretary, 1979–81. He was created a life peer in 1987 and took the title Baron Colnbrook.

[3] L. H. Jacques was AC's House Tutor (housemaster) at Eton and they were not in sympathy with each other.

getting back to my desk, where all the papers are so interesting. Before Christmas I was dropping with fatigue and nervous tension, but already I have fully recovered.

First to be decided though, is will I get to the next Chequers meeting? I had hoped, secretly, for a phone call over Christmas. But no contact.

I put my all into that Report. Truly it was the apotheosis of my whole career both as a historian and in public life. But it has turned out, it seems, an embarrassing non-event. Not to be alluded to.

If I am excluded from the meeting TK will be cock-a-hoop. He will no longer be fearful of me, as I will have played my big card, and been ignored. Also I will have lost face with my own Private Office. All Julian's doubts will be confirmed just as, by sheer intellectual vigour, I was converting him. Sad, because he has been splendidly loyal over these last difficult weeks.

Have I overreached? Did I gallop too soon and too recklessly? It's impossibly difficult to set great reforms in train from a middle-ranking position. But I *know* I'm right. Mine is the only way we can keep military clout and not go bust. I couldn't just sit back and duck it in exchange for a comfortable life signing documents and having little exclusives in the HS 125.

This is my last job, isn't it?

Be realistic, Clark. If you're going to make S of S you won't do it just by sitting still and being a goodboy. And we are at one of those critical moments in defence policy that occur only once every fifty years.

Always remember, 'At times of acute crisis in the course of human affairs, a man will emerge. If he does not, it means that the time is not yet ripe' (*Wolf*).[1] A curious inversion of conventional thought. But even if true, not especially comforting.

---

[1] AC sometimes refers to Hitler by this cognomen, which was used only by his 'Bayreuth' circle, Elizabeth Wagner, etc.

Saltwood   *Sunday, 14 January*

I've made it! The Chequers meeting (Mark II) is fixed for 27 Jan – to be *utterly* secret, 'The Prime Minister has asked me to emphasise that if any . . . ,' etc.

I am invited, listed at Number 4, below Hurd, Chancellor and T.K. (How maddening for TK. Hee-hee.)

My paper is, it is clear, *the* lead document. How shrewd and good I was to get it in first! The FCO papers are bulkier, came later, and carry the imprimatur of a committee of officials.

Willie Waldegrave, whose task it is to co-ordinate the material, was not friendly when I saw him in the dining room. Reddish with drink, and small-eyed, he said it was 'very petty' not to circulate the Annexes (which contain the financial provisions).

'Not my idea,' I said.

'Anyway, the Treasury have got hold of a copy.'

Too right they have, I thought, I sent them one.

On the day, everything will depend on (a) her mood, and the level of counter-distraction (b) my own confidence and sparkleability.

Word has spread through the Department, and I am buoyed up by the now open tendency of senior officials to defer to me, quote my views with approval even when (normally unheard of) Tom is present. I retoy with the idea of supplanting him, and promptly.

Of *course* I should be in charge, handling the whole thing at international level also, Washington, Brussels.

My present solution is to move TK to Health, where he could be pinkly affable and repair some of the damage caused by my 'abrasive' namesake. But that could only happen if Clarke has a nervous break-down – unlikely in one so fat – or – perfectly possible at any time, he must make the Norwich Union wince – something 'happens to' him. One mustn't be uncharitable (why not?) but this after all is the roughest game, at the biggest table.

On Thursday afternoon Soames, who was sitting just behind me, occupied a lot of Agriculture Questions (and I don't doubt a lot of TV footage, so it's as well the audience couldn't hear) telling me about an incredibly powerful new aphrodisiac he had discovered.

I liked the sound of this, and after Prime Minister's Questions I drove him back to his flat and he brought down a 'phial'. It has to be kept in the fridge.

Ministry of Defence   *Wednesday, 17 January*

Tom is frantic. He is harrying and pestering officials all over the building to get 'his', i.e., *The Official MOD Position* paper(s), prepared.

He won't let me see it in draft. I doubt if I'll get a sight of it before I walk into the room – if then.

But not only was my paper first in, it was only five pages long. All this stuff they're sending up now is ten, twenty pages per memo. On-the-one-hand, on-the-other-hand balls. No one will bother, and in any case all will be read in the context of my argument.

Julian told me that the Treasury had commented that mine was 'the first decently written paper they had seen for thirty years'.

Ministry of Defence   *Friday, 19 January*

Today I *dominated* the Dept. Repeatedly I sent for Quinlan, Spiers,[1] John Colston.[2] Periodically I talked to Arnold Weinstock. By sheer energy and clarity of thought I put together the deal that saved Ferranti, and its Radar, and thus EFA[3] in time for us to outface Stoltenberg[4] on Monday when the German delegation come over.

John Colston took notes, and tried to keep TK (*baffledly* at the end of a 'bad line' outside his house in Wiltshire) in touch.

I ran the whole thing at a break-neck pace, and afterwards Donald Spiers said, 'It's a wonderful feeling, to get hard decisions and clear instructions.'

But the sweetest moment of all came at the end of the day, after our third meeting, when Quinlan materialised, Jeeves-like, beside me: 'Fingers crossed, but well done!'

---

[1] Donald Spiers, Controller Aircraft, and Head of Profession, Defence Science and Engineering, Ministry of Defence, since 1989.

[2] John Colston, an Assistant Secretary at Defence.

[3] The Germans were already voicing their misgivings about the European Fighter Aircraft (EFA) project. At this time their excuse was that Ferranti (stipulated as the radar contractor) were commercially unviable and this put the project at risk. AC encouraged Lord Weinstock to take Ferranti's radar enterprise into GEC, thus totally altering its commercial status.

[4] Gerhard Stoltenberg, German Defence Minister since 1989.

Ministry of Defence   *Friday, 26 January*

Yesterday a great gale swept through London in the afternoon, tearing at roofs and scaffolding. The police, as usual, overreacted and closed off streets and by-ways at random, blocking motorists and shouting at pedestrians through loud-hailers. The whole of Westminster and the West End went into 'gridlock' from tea-time until about nine p.m., with angry and resentful drivers lurching and clutch-slipping up on to the pavement and abandoning their cars.

I cancelled my trip to Plymouth and, seeing Archie Hamilton in the library corridor, fell into conversation.

I am in the ascendant at the moment, with my place at the Chequers summit assured, and drawing much deference from officials. On Wednesday night there was a big dinner at the RAF College at Bracknell. Moray Stewart,[1] very slightly in his cups it must be admitted, said to me, 'Why don't you take the helm?'

Not bad, from a Deputy Secretary. But I must be careful not to have a tumble. And I wanted to find out a little more about the PM's attitude (her real attitude as distinct from her public posture) to German reunification.

Archie Hamilton and I went into the smoking room – to be alone. Strange, the decline of the smoking room, even in my time. In former days there was spirited discussion, conviviality. Friends and colleagues spoke ill or, very occasionally when they hoped it would get repeated, good, of those who were absent. But now it is frequented only by soaks, traditionalists, and Memory-Lane buffers.

I suppose that the implication was that I would try and conform with whatever her own line was – although this has never been my style.

But Archie was interesting. He claimed not to know what she really thought, just said, 'She's against it, ho-ho.' (You'd think that, having worked as her PPS, he'd know a bit more but I never, I suppose, make enough allowance for the actions of people who want to set me back a few pips.)

Archie said that was the mistake John Moore[2] had made. During

---

[1] Moray Stewart, Deputy Under-Secretary of State, Defence Procurement, since 1988. He would become Second Permanent Under-Secretary, Defence, later in the year.

[2] John Moore had been dropped from the Government in 1989, after three years as Social Security Secretary.

the high months of his status as her chosen successor he framed the Health Service reforms exactly on the basis of what he thought she wanted. But she kept changing her mind. One minute she wanted to go further, the next she got an attack of the doubts, wanted to trim a bit. Each time the unfortunate John agreed, made the adjustments, came back for approval. The result was a total hotchpotch and 'she ended up thinking he was a wanker, and got rid of him'.

Saltwood   *Sunday, 28 January*

I am flat and reactive after Chequers.

Last night on my return I was still on a high ... Percy Cradock[1] had made a point of telling me 'how much the Prime Minister admired your paper', and going into lunch – although we had had quite an argument during the morning – she had said how good it was, 'so full of original thought'. But perhaps I overplayed my hand? Did I trespass too aggressively into the field of Foreign Affairs?

But surely defence policy can only be considered in the context of our foreign commitments?

I suppose, on reflection, that I did not make enough allowance for the fact that every colleague (except the Treasury) and every official (except Charles and Percy) is hostile to me. The Prime Minister herself is friendly, but implacable. I argued cogently for accepting, and exploiting, German reunification while they still needed our support.

No good. She is determined not to.

'You're wrong,' I said. 'You're just wrong.'

Everyone at the table smirked at each other. Now he's really torn it; fucking little show-off, etc.

During the coffee-break I cornered her.

'These are just a re-run of the old Appeasement arguments of 1938.'

'Yes,' she said, eyes flashing (she's in incredible form at the moment), 'and I'm not an appeaser.'

---

[1] Sir Percy Cradock, distinguished diplomat, who had been British Ambassador to Beijing before leading the UK team in negotiations over the future of Hong Kong in 1983. Adviser to the Prime Minister on Foreign Affairs since 1984.

John Major,[1] whom I like more and more, said to me *sotto voce*, 'You're a military strategist. Oughtn't you to be sending your tanks round the flank, rather than attacking head on?'

Saltwood   *Wednesday, 31 January*

I am skiving. Second day of 'flu'. But having been rather awful and restlessly dry-hot yesterday (I took to my bed) I am now over it; and sitting around in the Green Room eating sundry delicacies that Jane sweetly prepares (*not* in *nouvelle cuisine* portion size).

Two 'crises' preoccupy the Department. Neither anything to do with me whatever. Complacently I can spectate. The first is something to do with a 'dirty tricks campaign'. These are always a bore. As far as I'm concerned 'dirty tricks' are part and parcel of effective government. But apparently Number 10 were misinformed by us – or so they claim.

More serious, news is about to break concerning the trouser-leg (sic) fractures in Warspite's cooling system. This could affect every nuclear-powered submarine. The whatever-it-is Authority have already given their advice that we should 'cease to operate' them until the condition is 'rectified'.

The result would be over twenty submarines tied up in UK ports, crews with nothing to do, local papers making inquiries, general trouble.

TK, quite rightly in my view, is continuing to keep the newer ones on station (although whether this is really his decision or was forced on him by the Lady I simply don't know). I suspect the latter because when, sadistically, I rattled him at a meeting, 'If – *if* there is an accident, it's not just you who resigns; the Government falls,' he didn't blench.

In a calm frame of mind I was eating chicken livers on toast when the phone rang. Jane answered. It was Julian.

'Julian at seven p.m.?'

As always looking on the bright side, she suggested, 'Perhaps TK's had an accident?'

---

[1] John Major, briefly Foreign Secretary, 1989, before becoming Chancellor of the Exchequer following the resignation of Nigel Lawson.

'He hasn't. You have,' could well have been Julian's answer.

A leak about the Chequers meeting is to be in tomorrow's *Times*. It is said that it comes from me.

'We *know* it's him,' according to the S of S office, passim 'Number 10' – in other words, Charles himself.

Julian was grave. Very, very grave.

'As you remember, Minister, the PM reminded everyone of the need for total secrecy.'

This has to be a frame-up. It just has to be. Because I know to whom I have spoken, and it's no one. Not just no journalist, no one. Except Julian himself and, very obliquely, Peter Levene.

I padded off, sweating profusely in my dressing-gown and having suffered a total regression, to the tower office, and rang Charles at Number 10. He was bland, diplomatic, but said it was 'regrettable'. Too bloody right. This sort of stain hangs with one a long time. And *completely* without reason.

On reflection, though, as I write this, my suspicions are aroused. Apparently it is to be carried in an article by Michael Evans.[1] Now I've never met Michael Evans. I wouldn't know what he looked like if he came into the room, still less am I on terms to 'leak' him something.

But when I said, both to Julian and to Charles, 'I'm going to find Michael Evans and have it out with him' they both counselled strongly against.[2]

---

[1] Michael Evans, Defence Correspondent on *The Times*.

[2] On Julian's advice AC raised the matter with the Permament Secretary. On 8 February came Michael Quinlan's graceful and elliptic response:

'As promised, I caused Hugh Colver to make some enquiries on Tuesday about the piece in *The Times*. He spoke to Bernard Ingham.

'Bernard said he knew nothing about the idea that Evans had "owned up" to a source, and he found it strange. His assumption was that anything Charles Powell believed about sourcing could only be inference from the piece's contents. Hugh took the opportunity of conveying to Bernard, on my instructions, that I was wholly satisfied that the content did not come from you. Bernard (who is often at odds with Charles) has his own suspicions.

'The only way of taking this any further, it seems to me, would be for you to tax Charles Powell directly. I think it has to be for your judgment whether that would be a useful operation.'

Ministry of Defence   *Thursday, 1 February*

One should not take pleasure from the discomfiture of colleagues, I suppose. But without question it is one of the more agreeable bonuses of the *sport* of politics. So unpredictable, and so random it seems, in those it afflicts.

This morning there is a really *lethal* piece in the *Daily Mail* – a full-scale article on the leader page – about poor old Stradling Thomas, 'Stradders' as he is known; 'Is this the laziest man in the House of Commons?'

It is clear that he took a lot of drinks off the reporter, they were in the Strangers' Bar for hours. But when the unfortunate Stradders came back from voting and the reporter asked him what he had been voting 'on', Stradders didn't know. Great indignation. But we seldom ever know what we are voting 'on'. Apparently the public like to find this shocking.

Anyway, there was poor old Stradders alone at a table in the dining room. Thinking he might be a bit low, nice old stick in the Whips' Office, all that, I joined him.

He was disagreeable. Didn't make sense, started up a totally Kafka-like quarrel (attributing remarks or, at least, thoughts to me and then demolishing them) about pronunciation. 'A Hotel'; '*an* Hotel'; '*an* apple', etc.

Batty. He looked completely degenerate in the way that real alcoholics do; details of personal appearance so neglected as to make a really off-putting, smelly whole. Cardboard City. Serve me right for trying to do a good deed.

During the afternoon Peter Levene came in. He is concerned, like me and practically everyone else in the building, at the pace of progress on the Review. Tom muffles everything, sits on it for weeks. Even his Private Office admit that he is driving them mad. Yet in a way I understand. The buck stops with him. He's racking his brain for catches. He knows there will be a lot of opposition from within the Party.

Let's face it, though. His real problem is he doesn't understand what's going on.

Peter was frustrated and (unusually for him) gloomy. Then *he* said to me, 'Why don't you take the helm?'

That's two Dep Secs in less than a week!

'But how?'

Peter had an ingenious solution. To set up a 'Review Con-
trollerate' with him in charge; three Young Turks from the three
Services; *reporting to me*. Mouth-watering. If the original September
Chequers remit was the ox's hide then this surely (to pursue the
analogy of medieval politics) would be a permit for my own chivalric
Order. But Tom would see it a mile off. The Review is the only real
activity in the Dept at present. If I'm put in charge, effectively I'm
running the whole shoot.

There's only one person who can ordain this. We'll have to see.
At least it wouldn't be so brazen as the time I asked her to take ODA
away from Geoffrey and put it into Trade.[1]

Albany   *Tuesday, 20 February*

I dined at the Cavalry Club with Ian Gow.

He is deeply apprehensive of the future, said that no Government
had ever been consistently (over six months) behind in the polls at
this level, and at this stage – halfway he said – in the electoral cycle,
and gone on to win.

'We aren't halfway, we're three-quarters. The Election would
normally be in '91.'

Ian said that all the indicators were bad for this year, and that
inflation would still be at 8.5 per cent in November. (He's a terrible
old Jeremiah about the inflation rate.)

'Personally I wonder if it matters all that much. It's a million per
cent, or whatever, in Brazil and you can still get taxis and delicious
meals. Sex doesn't stop.'

Usually when I make remarks of this kind, which are Boswellian,
to draw him out, Ian smiles with what is called 'a faraway look'. But
he was serious, earnest.

'Evidently you do not appreciate the significance of the month of
November?'

Of course! The leadership election.

Ian elaborated. There is a real risk of a challenge, and this time a
serious one. He said that even when Meyer was standing last year he
had a hard time persuading many colleagues to vote for the PM –

---

[1] Recorded in July 1986, but not included in this edition.

although then most of them were minded to abstain.[1] He had told
them that if they really were still discontented, felt that there has been
no improvement, 'You will have another chance next year.'

'Are there many?'

'Yes. I am sorry to say there are. Very many.'

I didn't like to ask. Not out of tact but because I didn't want to
hear the answer.

Ian said that Heseltine's disclaimer, 'I can think of no circumstances
in which I would challenge Margaret Thatcher', is susceptible to any
number of let-outs. Acute crisis, Party's fortunes, irresistible pressure,
etc., etc.

'It'd be all or bust for him. I don't think he'll dare,' I tried.

Ian replied, but without much conviction, that Heseltine would
lose anyway.

I'm not so sure. He might win the contest, but lose the General
Election. Then where would we all be?

We are off this afternoon to Scotland. The IEPG conference[2] is
booked at Gleneagles. It's a freebie really, and wives are invited.

But first I must prepare some more notes for the PM on 'Bruges
II'.[3] Am I helping her to dig deeper her own political grave?

Later

A note on the subject came over from Charles, marked SECRET,
PRIVATE and PERSONAL.

'A good way of drawing attention to something,' I said to Private
Office. It enhances my status in the Dept. But it's in total breach of
Civil Service convention, there may even be rules of procedure.

If a civil servant at Number 10 wants to get a message to a Minister
in another Department the correct way to do so is to communicate
with the Private Office of the Secretary of State of that Department –
and if it is a junior Minister (itself an unusual enough contingency)
then it is for the S of S's office to pass it on down to the head of the
office of the junior Minister concerned. Good old Charles.

---

[1] Sir Anthony Meyer, MP for Clwyd North West since 1983 (West Flint, 1970–83)
had challenged Margaret Thatcher as Leader of the Conservative Party. The
result: Thatcher, 314; Meyer, 33; Abstentions, 24.

[2] Annual meeting of European Programme Groups (a euphemism for those senior
civil servants who had oversight of weapons procurement).

[3] At that time the Prime Minister was minded to deliver a sequel to her celebrated
speech at Bruges the previous year.

Gleneagles   *Wednesday, 21 February*

At dinner last night I sat next to the wife of the Turkish Minister. Not one word of English could she speak. She took a chance, said she spoke French '*un petit peu*'. No problem, I gabbled to her in French. Not one word could she understand, or speak. She was fat, and squat. And wore a black dress with very little jewellery.

Earlier, at the reception, I had my first sighting of Chevenement.[1] Odious. Rude, uncouth, objectionable. TK thinks he has established a 'relationship' with Chevenement, and boasts about it.

Dear Tom, sometimes I feel quite protective towards him. How could he possibly think that little Frenchman would do anything but cut his throat if he could get even fifty francs out of it?

This morning, before the session, I went for a constitutional with Peter Levene, and we walked down to the lake, looked at all the manic golfers milling around the club house. Righteous and crazy-faced, they glared back.

Peter is restless. His time at MoD is drawing to an end. He is tempted by Industry, and Arnold Weinstock teases him constantly with chimeric offers.

But Peter fancies also the possibility of remaining, advancing indeed, in the public sector. He would like to be Permanent Secretary at the DTI.

Tricky, I said. The Dept is starved of cash these days and anyway, haven't they just appointed Gregson?[2]

He toyed also with the idea of becoming (sic) a diplomat. Really? Yes, what he'd like best is Washington.

I don't often gulp but, privately, I gulped.

'Well, Peter Jay[3] got it,' I said. 'It's one of the posts that does occasionally go to an outsider.'

I suppose that I am just the same. All vigorous and ambitious men live by considering that anything is within their capability.

---

[1] Jean-Pierre Chevenement, French Defence Minister. Sacked by Mitterand in February 1991.

[2] Sir Peter Gregson had moved from Energy (Permanent Under-Secretary) to Trade and Industry (Permanent Secretary) in 1989.

[3] Peter Jay was Economics Editor of *The Times* when the Prime Minister, James Callaghan (and coincidentally Peter Jay's father-in-law) appointed him British Ambassador to Washington in 1977.

Saltwood   *Sunday, 25 February*

I remain in depression. I might give up drink for Lent. A good start in Arabia next week, as I always enjoy refusing it from an Ambassador – they are so loathsomely *arch* when they produce the whisky bottle, 'I expect you'd welcome some of this, eh? Ho-ho' – and the orange juice at all those meetings is the best in the world.

I thought I would play on the piano. But when I got to the music room there was water pouring in and down the east wall.

Last year I spent £11,000 replacing the lead just on this one roof. What's the point? The Aubusson can really no longer take any more punishment.

Bugger it, I thought, anyway. It can't stop me playing.

Melodiously I strummed. 'Sentimental Journey'; 'Smoke Gets in Your Eyes'; 'My Guy's Come Back'; 'Stormy Weather'.

Always I think of that Pole who played in the NAAFI at the Army Mountain Warfare Training School at Llanberis, in 1945. For hours on end he played – Chopin, Rachmaninov, Liszt, anything from ENSA naturally – preferring when the hall was empty, and it echoed. Was he thinking of home, and his dead children? Of his horse, shot from under him in the last September battles on the Vistula?

I have done, seen and experienced an awful lot of things. And I like in these tall Gothic rooms, with all these beautiful possessions around me, accumulated by my father and by my grandfather, to nostalgicise.

Why am I still, in the main, so zestful?

I know, but I don't like to say.

In case the gods take it away.

Saltwood   *Saturday, 3 March*

Yesterday went on too long.

I left Paddington by the early train to speak at a Party lunch in Truro. Low key, upper-class candidate, a few bright(ish) sparks. I thought these old Etonians were extinct by now – they certainly are in 'safe' seats – Central Office toad/clones have seen to that. Clearly the Association have reverted to the Piers[1] mould.

---

[1] Piers Dixon had been MP for Truro, winning the seat in 1970 and again in February 1974, only to lose to the Liberal David Penhaligon in October 1974. Following

In any case it's ridiculous that Truro should not be a Tory seat. All these rentiers, a few landowners, some contented farmers and a lot of holiday-dependent shopkeepers and boarding house landladies.

The trouble is, once the Libs get stuck in, really stuck in, they are devilish hard to dislodge. Their trick is to *degrade* the whole standard of political debate. The nation, wide policy issues, the sweep of history – forget it. They can't even manage to discuss broad economic questions, as they don't understand the problems – never mind the answers.

The Liberal technique is to force people to lower their sights, teeny little provincial problems about bus timetables, and street lighting and the grant for a new community hall. They compensate by giving the electorate uplift with constant plugging of an identity concept – no matter how minuscule – to which they try to attach a confrontational flavour: 'Newton Ferrers Mums outface Whitehall' and a really bouncy commonplace little turd (or big turd in the case of Penhaligon) as candidate, and they're in.

So I am rather pessimistic concerning the prospects for this pleasant, diffident young man, even though I firmly, and repetitiously, referred to him as the next Member of Parliament for Truro.

I just caught the train back. A long journey.

The box didn't take long and I fidgeted, did a trawl of the seats for discarded reading material, bought and consumed two Mars bars, which gave me a headache.

I couldn't get home as there was a little dinner at Lyall Street.[1] Just Aspers, Jimmy Goldsmith and Charles Powell. The 'guest' was Conrad Black,[2] the purpose to see to what extent he was amenable to being leant on, in the gentlest manner of course, to steer Max[3] away from plugging Heseltine so much. The answer, it soon became clear, was – not at all.

Black is young, quite attractive looking, very clever and widely read. If I look back over the newspaper tycoons I've known it is only Beaverbrook with whom he compares. Some, like Vere, are just thick,

---

Penhaligon's death the resulting by-election in 1987 saw Matthew Taylor retain the seat for the Liberals. In the 1987 General Election he had a majority over the Conservative candidate of 4753; in 1992 this increased to 7570.

[1] Number 1, Lyall Street, town house of John Aspinall.

[2] Conrad Black, Canadian newspaper proprietor, born 1944, who had come to London and bought the *Daily Telegraph* in 1987.

[3] Max Hastings, Editor of the *Daily Telegraph* since 1986.

others like Roy Thomson bluff away and you don't know, but they're boring. Cap'n Bob is the most entertaining, I suppose, but you never quite feel he's giving you his full *attention* — and this for reasons, let's say, unrelated to the setting in which the conversation is taking place.

The subject had to be approached delicately. Charles was diplomatic, Jimmy blunt. But Black simply couldn't care. He made a competent, almost dismissive defence. It's my paper, I do what I think right, anyway he (Heseltine) is an interesting chap, we look like we're in a mess, heading for a bigger one, etc.

Black's preference seemed to be for talking about Washington. He's knowledgeable and interesting here too. But as to its principal objective, the dinner was a failure.

Saltwood   *Sunday, 4 March*

A beautiful day of early spring, quite perfect in light, colour, the shadow and tone of stone and lawn and blossom. We have started to mow with the sit-down mowers that roll and stripe. No more rotaries until September when the plantains grow.

I was resigned to settling back 'with the Heritage' when I had a long call from Tristan which electrified me.[1]

We're 28 points behind in the polls, and the leadership is in a panic. The Lady has rocky moments of self doubt. (This has happened before, I told him, Carol used to tell me how dejected she became in 1985 when all the economic indicators were looking good but people still wouldn't respond.) The Cabinet are all over the place. Most of them are 'pretty doubtful about' (read *loathe*) her but don't know what to do. G. Howe is behaving 'poorly', *chétif* and unsupportive. The Government have got to find a billion, at once, to buy off the Poll Tax complainants.

'That won't be enough,' I sniggered.

No, wait, he said, I told them 'the only person who can give this to you is Alan Clark'.

John Major, somewhat ruefully, agreed.

Exultant, I waxed on how I could square things in Washington,

---

[1] Tristan Garel-Jones had been Deputy Chief Whip since 1989.

fix it with our various collaborative partners that we got out of these fearful projects, kick ass in the Army Council. I ended, for the first time, actually *asking*. I said the only thing for it – and to be done promptly, Whitsun at the latest – was to make TK leader of the House and me S of S Def.

'Thank you very much,' he said. 'This conversation has been very useful.' Then added the usual disclaimer that there was nothing he could do . . . etc. I feel that I am closer to my ambition than I am ever likely to get again.

Saltwood   *Sunday, 25 March*

On Friday I was in Plymouth for the Constituency AGM. The atmosphere was not good. Personally the activists, or 'voluntary workers' as they prefer being called, were friendly. But there was much muttering.

Jane thought it went better than I did, yes, but to balance my own paranoia should be set the fact that everyone likes her. So it's easier for them to respond to her happy personality.

They all (except dear Romaine Palmer) complained, in different ways, sometimes directly, sometimes in code, about Mrs T. But I'm used to that. We had it in 1981, in 1985. It's cyclical. The trough is always two years away from the next Election date.

It's these fucking Councillors, that's what people really like listening to. Their own kind; petty, inarticulate, short-sighted, mildly venal.

Ralph Morrell, who rarely attends the AGM in good times, had got himself (for some technical reason connected with the vote for Treasurer) into the Chair. Ralph is Dean of the Tory local government machine, and 'respected'. He spoke after me. Every time he mentioned the doings of the Councillors he got applause, bigger than anything granted to my own somewhat ritualised performance. A ripple of approval whenever he criticised the Government. This he did mainly on grounds which I simply don't understand, have indeed made no attempt to understand, as the subject bores me.

It's all to do with this spastic concept of 'capping', as it's called. This is itself bound up with the Poll Tax (as one must NOT call it), which has got everyone into a rage. The only objection to the tax, as far as I can see (and as I did in fact point out, to the manifest irritation of the Lady and all eleven other Ministers present[1] except the Chancellor), is that no one will pay. It'll be like jay-walking.

And by 'no one' I mean all the slobs, yobs, drifters, junkies, free-loaders, claimants, and criminals on day-release, who make their living by exploitation of the benefit system and overload local authority expenditure. As usual the burden will fall on the thrifty, the prudent, the responsible, those 'of fixed address', who patiently support society and the follies of the chattering class.

I walked around the town, in very cold winds. I did not want to be recognised, still less accosted, and kept my head down, looking at the pavements.

My surgery was huge, with many time-wasters. Many came in to have a grumble and, in spite of my going into Emergency-Unctuous mode, did not leave satisfied.

Yesterday we lost Mid-Stafford, poor little Heddle's seat, on a swing of 23 per cent.[2] In Plymouth I'd be obliterated. Just as well I'm not standing again.

And yet . . . Jane told me that on the drive down she had been held up by some motor-cycle police for a Jaguar which swept into the Intelligence HQ at Ashford. Suddenly she had a taste of what it was like '*on the outside*'.

I think what saddens me most is the so near and yet so far experience at MoD. I have written the Defence Review. It has, to all intents and purposes, been accepted by Number 10. But no one is getting on with it. It's all being screwed by this absurd 'Options' exercise, which muffles everything.

On Friday I had to circulate a rebuttal of some batty recommendation that we should − effectively − *annexe* East Germany, run exercises there, defend the air space. Simply crazy. A transparent power-play by those in the Dept who are determined to keep the Central Front alive as a magnet/concept for their own careers. But that's all I could do − circulate a paper. It's miles outside the Procurement responsibilities. However taut you stretch the Ox's hide it won't cover straight AF matters, and Hamilton's office (not, to do

---

[1] On the sole occasion which AC attended a meeting of E(LF), the Cabinet Committee which considered the tax.

[2] John Heddle, MP since 1983, had committed suicide in December 1989. At the 1987 General Election he had a majority of 14000.

him justice, Archie himself; or at least he doesn't allow it to show) get
angry, make trouble with Julian.

This happens the whole time. It's not just the slow balls-up of the
'Options' project, it's a hundred examples a week of waste, blinkers,
vested interest, idleness and failure to put the country before narrow
personal, regimental or sectarian considerations. Unless or until I'm
Secretary of State I just have to watch them go rolling past, make a
private note to chase it if I ever get the chance. Julian, though, is
sympathetic, and does what he can.

A long letter today from beloved Tip. He says that the whole of
Rhine Army is completely demoralised. There's a 'freeze' on spares,
so if vehicles break on exercise they're just towed back to Sennelager
and abandoned. The great Panzer workshops that featured in Hitler's
exchange with Jodl after the fall of the Remagen bridge are now a
scrapyard for broken Land-Rovers. The 'chaps' are good, still, and
keen. *They* want to get out into the Empire, sort out the 'trouble
spots'. But he says some of the new recruits are almost illiterate. They
can't even do sports because these are banned at school as being too
competitive.

It's all so depressing. Especially when you think we've had a Tory
Government for the last ten years.

House of Commons   *Wednesday, 28 March*

The Lady is under deep pressure now. It just won't go away. As soon
as one paper goes quiet another one, or two at a time, start up.

As far as I can make out practically every member of the Cabinet
is quietly and unattributably briefing different Editors or members of
the Lobby about how awful she is. This makes it easier for people like
Peter Jenkins[1] to say that 'she has virtually lost all support in Cabinet'.
Malcolm Rifkind[2] is actually quoted today as saying, 'I'll be here after
she's gone.'

There is even talk of a coup in July. Heseltine is quite openly
spoken about as the heir-presumptive, and preens himself in public.

---

[1] Political columnist on *The Independent*.
[2] Malcolm Rifkind, MP for Edinburgh Pentlands since 1974. Secretary of State for
   Scotland since 1986.

How has all this been allowed to come about? The Community Charge has got on everyone's nerves of course, and generated the most oppressive volume of correspondence. Persistent deficits in the polls of a nearly insuperable order rattle people. But I am inclined to think that the Party in the House has just got sick of her. She hasn't promoted her 'own' people much. Her 'constituency' in this place depends solely on her proven ability to win General Elections. But now this is in jeopardy she has no real Praetorian Guard to fall back on. There's been a lot of talk about 'one of us', all that, but most of them are still left to moulder at the '92 dinner table. When's the Revolution? In the meantime, all the wets and Blue Chips and general Heathite wankers, who seem ineradicable in this bloody Party, stew around and pine for her to drop dead.

Most critics move, in the open, under (pretty transparent) camouflage. A number of 'heavy' backbenchers of the 'Centre' (i.e. Left) of the Party have let it be known that her 'Decision-making Circle' should be widened, that they are uneasy about the 'privileged access' enjoyed by 'certain key and unelected advisors'.

This of course is a shot across the bows for Charles and Bernard. But without them she really would be lost, as the Chief Whip, Tim Renton, is Howe's creature; Peter Morrison is of little use as a PPS under these conditions; Gow is neutered and doesn't cut ice any longer and Garel-Jones, who would relish the task of rescuing her as Victor Ludorum in the Whips' Challenge Trophy, is tied up in the Foreign Office, and on overseas visits half the time.

My own position is affected in a number of ways – all unwelcome. My special *access* is less potent because, with the rest of the Cabinet more or less openly plotting their own positions, and jockeying, her disapproval counts for little. We're almost getting to the point where they are no longer afraid of her. And indeed, her sponsorship could actually be damaging. Second, it disturbs my own plans for smooth and easy withdrawal, booking a 'K' at once and a Lords ticket in the next Parliament. Will I even get my PC in May? Finally, I could be faced with the ultimate hideosity of being stuck at MoD during a Heseltine 'reconstruction'. Should I leave immediately, or hang on for certain humiliation forty-eight hours later?

Oh dear. How quickly everything can change.

House of Commons   *Monday, 2 April*

Last night there were riots in Central London – just like 1981. All the anarchist scum, class-war, random drop-outs and trouble-seekers had infiltrated the march and started beating up the police.[1]

There is this strain in most Western countries (except, curiously, the United States) but it is particularly prevalent in Britain, where this rabble have – confirming their middle-class social origins – their own press in *The Grauniad* and *The Independent*. Far from having their capers cut by the revolution in Russia, the removal of a distant but supportive ideological menace, they are flourishing in that very curtailment of discipline and order which the fall of the ancient Soviet autocracy has brought about.

But it is bad. *Civil Disorder.* Could cut either way, but I fear will scare people into wanting a compromise – just as did Saltley Colliery and the three-day week in 1972/3. In the corridors and the tea room people are now talking openly of ditching the Lady to save their skins. This is the first time I've heard it *en clair* since a bad patch (1977?) when we were in opposition. Some of the Lobby, Tony Bevins[2] in particular, hang around outside the Members' post office and fly kites.

There is a wild rumour going round that she may be 'deputised' at the end of July. 'Uh? Deputised?'

'Yes, you know, receive a deputation, the Chief Whip, the '22 Executive, Willie, that kind of thing. Told to throw in the towel.'

Contemptible.

Ministry of Defence   *Tuesday, 3 April*

For months I have been resisting expenditure (some hundreds of millions) on a completely unnecessary new piece of Army Equipment known by its acronym as ACEATM.

It is a 'sideways firing mine' – itself an unlikely, indeed contradictory concept, surely? The idea is that you position one of these incredibly expensive and 'intelligent' devices in the window of a house and when a tank goes past it shoots out at it, 'sideways'.

---

[1] An anti-poll tax demonstration in central London.
[2] Anthony Bevins, Political Editor of *The Independent*. His father, Reginald, had been an MP, and Postmaster-General, 1959–64.

From the first moment I saw the papers it was clear that this was a complete waste of money, conceived at the height of the Cold War, and now totally unnecessary. Trouble is, I'm not really meant to question 'Operational Requirements'. I'm meant to 'seek' and then, by implication, follow advice on anything about which I have doubts. In the nature of things, the advice comes from the same people who drafted the 'Requirement' in the first place.

Finally, after much deferment, a full-scale 'Meeting' was called.

'You leave them behind, you see, to slow up the enemy's advance.'

'What advance?'

'Well, er, his advance, Minister.'

'What enemy?'

'The Warsaw Pact, Minister.'

'The Warsaw Pact no longer exists. It's disintegrated.'

'In villages, in built-up areas,' shouted somebody else, also in uniform. Why the fuck are all these people in uniform? It's not allowed. Just so as to intimidate me, they think.

'I thought the first rule in deploying armour was to avoid built-up areas?'

'Roads, Minister. Choke-points.'

'What happens if a truck goes past? That would be a waste, wouldn't it. How does it know not to shoot?'

'Well it knows, Minister. It's programmed with all the Warsaw Pact silhouettes.'

'Warsaw Pact?'

'There's a lot of Russian stuff Out of Area now, you know.'

'I do know.'

'It's Next Generation, Minister. A very intelligent sensor.'

'Better programme it to recognise all the French stuff, then.'

'Ha-ha, Minister. Oh, ha-ha.'

What can one do? Nothing. I can block this spastic weapon, and make them cross, and complaining. But about *them* I can do nothing.

I want to fire the whole lot. Instantly. Out, out. No 'District' commands, no golden bowlers, nothing. Out. There are so many good, tough keen young officers who aren't full of shit. How can we bring them on, before they get disillusioned, or conventionalised by the system? If I could, I'd do what Stalin did to Tukhachevsky.[1]

---

[1] The purges of the Red Army in 1938–9 when three-quarters of all officers of field rank and above were put to the firing squads.

Ministry of Defence   *Thursday, 5 April*

The Lady scowled startledly at me on Tuesday when she came in for Questions. Although she is completely absorbed in her own brief, hyped to the nines for her ordeal against little Kinnock, and pays no attention to her surroundings whatever, her presence beside one on the bench is always a little constraining.

My own last Question was reached, and my performance was not as relaxed and dominating as it should have been. Is my voice losing timbre?

She spat at me again during a somewhat ponderoso question from Nick Soames about Rhodesia. I reminded her about BMATT and our training detachment out there, but she didn't use it.[1] Pre-programmed.

Somehow this little experience brought home to me how utterly unrealistic is any idea that she might make me S of S. How? Why? Lucky even to get PC next month.[2]

Our position continues to worsen. I urge for blood, and still more blood.

The Last Days[3] and the Whips are divided among themselves. Some want blood. Some, covertly, want 'a change'. G-J's own position is equivocal and he probably thinks, may even have been told, that Heseltine would make him Chief. Renton, the existing Chief, doesn't think strategically – or even tactically. He is amiable, social; but never did his groundwork as a junior in 'the office'. In any case, my suspicion has always been that his loyalties incline towards Geoffrey Howe.

Gow, Ryder, Aitken and I dined at 'Greens' the 'new' restaurant on Locketts' old site, set up under the aegis of Simon Parker Bowles (*relation*, I assume). Confirmed the bad impression when Alison and I tried it out last week. Waiters either *completely* incapable of understanding English – or French, or Italian. Are they Rumanians from an

---

[1] BMATT: British Military Assistant Training Team. AC's younger son, Andrew, had done a year of duty with the unit attached to the Zimbabwean Army.

[2] AC was thinking of the Queen's Birthday Honours when the names of new members of the Privy Council would be announced.

[3] *The Last Days of Hitler* by Hugh Trevor-Roper, AC's tutor at Oxford, now Lord Dacre.

AIDS hostel? – or chinless youths, spaced-outly smiling and chatting to each other in upper-class accents, waiting to get on the waiting list (sic) for Cirencester.

The boys were gloomy. We none of us see our way. Quite difficult to approach the Lady at the moment, as Ian is finding. And what advice do we give her? Shed blood, I said. We are planning to take revenge on Mates. Jonathan undertook to contact Tam and prime him with a question about Singer Link Miles (who pay Mates) who are in contractual relationship with us.

When I fell asleep I had a curious dream; gently ascending the hill behind Sandling station, having resigned, and being at peace with the world. Bernard Braine[1] came into it somehow – perhaps because Jonathan had been telling me that he was determined to stay on, in order to block Ted from becoming 'Father of the House'.

Ministry of Defence   *Wednesday, 11 April*

Last night I won £1,000 off John Sterling at backgammon. This always makes me wake up in a good mood. But today, the last of the 'Lent' term, is just too full. I woke at 5-ish, had made tea and enjoyed Cadogan's memoirs by 7, collected the boxes from the Lodge and read the brief for the DOAE[2] visit by the time the car arrived at 8.15. With luck I will be through in time to catch the 7 p.m. train to Ashford.

I'm looking forward to five lovely days at Saltwood, and mustn't fritter them. Last weekend we drew up a little daily schedule.

As I went along the Rope Walk this morning I worried about the blackbird. No sign this spring. Sometimes, at first light, I can hear one a very long way away. But surely, even if he/she is dead there should be some offspring here? I suppose the *same one* can't still be alive as it has been causing me pleasure since 1975. But to have none is sad.

There is a thrush in Speaker's Court who sings goodnight so

---

[1] Sir Bernard Braine, MP for various Essex constituencies since 1950 and Father of the House since 1983. When he finally retired at the 1992 Election, Edward Heath (also elected in 1950) gained the Father of the House soubriquet.

[2] DOAE – Defence Operational Analysis Establishment.

beautifully each evening. When I can, if I'm in my Commons office,
I come upstairs and listen.

How could anyone shoot a song-bird?

Saltwood   *Friday, 20 April*

A date which usually marks a period of good fortune, and the transition
from spring to early summer. But it is cold and blowy, and there has
been a fall of snow on Hampstead Heath. Only at Eriboll is it
shirtsleeve hot, with the loch like glass. James rang and said that
he had ferried fourteen tups across to their summer quarters on
Eilean Chorain.

Yesterday evening Tristan and I repaired to Wiltons, and took a
pullman.

I told him (uneasily aware that somewhere the cock would be
crowing) that very reluctantly, and with great sadness and not a little
apprehension I had come to a certain conclusion. Tristan said that he
was glad I had admitted to this. Some weeks ago he had written a
paper in his own hand; circulated it to the Chief Whip, Ingham (?!),
Andrew Turnbull,[1] John Major and Mark Lennox-Boyd.[2]

Not, I noted, to Charles. No point, he said, CP 'too fanatically
committed'.

Each of the recipients had 'tried to push him through her door'
(i.e. to say it in person).

'Well, why don't you?'

Yes, he was going to supper at the Number 10 flat on Sunday –
just him and X-B[3] – and told me how he proposed to play it. The
Party was 'lazy, sullen, and frightened'. Unless there was a marked
improvement by early to mid-October *over* 100 votes would be cast
against her at the leadership contest, which was inevitable, in the

---

[1] Andrew Turnbull, Principal Private Secretary to the Prime Minister since 1988.
[2] Mark Lennox-Boyd, MP for Morecambe since 1979. Parliamentary Private Secretary to the Prime Minister since 1988.
[3] X-B: AC here uses the abbreviation employed by Jim Lees-Milne when referring
to Mark's father, Alan (later 1st Viscount Boyd of Merton), Colonial Secretary,
1954–9.

month following. Tristan's view was that over 100 against would mean that she would have to stand down.

I couldn't help grinning. 'Try telling her that.'

Tristan named a number of individuals (ranging from Phil Goodhart[1] to Marlow[2]) who were totally disillusioned, didn't bother to vote any longer. Party discipline was breaking up. All this he would say if necessary.

It is clear, although he didn't say as much, that he has a low opinion of Renton, who has not got a grip on things. In any case, Renton is Geoffrey's nominee, has no feelings towards the Lady.

I said that 'Mid October' was balls. The time scale was far shorter. It had to be settled before the Party Conference and that meant, effectively, in *this* parliamentary term – which in turn means before 15 July, because for those last two weeks of the Summer Term we are all in a limbo of rumour, lassitude and low motivation. Proper consideration cannot be given until after the May local election results have been analysed, so that means that the *band* stretches from mid-May until mid-July, no more.

At this exact point in our conversation I spotted Heseltine coming up the steps from the bar! And with Mates! He was shown, not to a nearby, but to the *adjoining* table. This was ludicrous. He and Mates sat down, got up again immediately, were spirited away.

A nearby group of 'businessmen' were oggly. 'Didn't take long to get rid of *him*,' I said, without reverence.

But I bet Michael was thinking, 'They won't treat me like that when I'm Prime Minister.' One more score to settle with Clark. A little later I signalled to Albert[3] and said would he please give Mr Heseltine my compliments and apologies for spoiling his evening. I would be very glad if he would allow me to settle his bill.

But whether Albert did so or not, I don't know. If he did, the offer was not accepted.

---

[1] Philip Goodhart, MP for Beckenham since 1957.
[2] Tony Marlow, MP for Northampton North since 1979.
[3] Head waiter at Wilton's.

House of Commons   *Tuesday, 1 May*

I had a conversation with IG in the smoking room. Aitken joined us. What could we do to succour the Lady? Do we even want to? We were stuck with the same inflation rate as when we came into power in 1979. Ten, eleven years of endeavour (or however we call all those deprivations to life and family) and nothing to show for it but the passage of time and the intrusion of age.

We had moved into the chess room for privacy, but it was dinner time, and posses of MPs moved past on their way through to the dining room, and made mocking comments. Atkins, in particular, is cocky and hostile now, as he watches the decline of the Praetorians.

We came to no conclusions, but aggravated each other's dejection. After about a half hour I lied about a dinner engagement and made for the Kundan, but it was closed for a reception. I went to Brooks's, lost £150 and my appetite waned. Returned here and ate a toasted bun, first food since a banana at 1.30.

In the tea room I had a chat with Fallon, a nice cool Whip.[1] I complained to him about all this rotten, irrelevant, unnecessary legislation which clogs our time. Firearms; Football Supporters; War Crimes; *Supermarket Trollies (local Authority Recovery Powers) Restricted Amendment* . . . etc., *ad nauseam*. Compounded with the abject failure to sort out the rioters at Strangeways prison it was all accumulating evidence of a government in decline. To my considerable pleasure, he was in complete agreement, citing, additionally, the Iraqi supergun. 'We should be making them, and selling them to everyone.'

'Good God,' he said. 'All this stuff about a decline in our manufacturing capability, but they had to come here to get the barrels made, didn't they? We should put it in a Trade Fair.' Splendid fellow.

Of course, in the nineteenth century this is what *would* have happened. And this morning I was on the roof of the old War Office building, looking around at Whitehall. The Admiralty opposite, the Cabinet office, the Treasury, the Foreign Office. How well it was all planned, how *confident*. We ran the Empire, and the world with the same number of civil servants as presently exist in one Department. Instead of spending no more than ten per cent of our Social Security budget on the Royal Navy, the proportion was exactly reversed.

---

[1] Michael Fallon, MP for Darlington since 1983. Shortly to become Parliamentary Under-Secretary at Education and Science.

I had wandered through the building, empty for years, but destined to be the nerve-centre of the intelligence services. The PSA[1] have a giant job-creation scheme running here. Dust, bare cabling, little transistor radios blare.

Magnificent rooms; heavy Edwardian panelling; oak plank floors one and a half inches thick; all being torn up to take the giant computers and their wiring. I stood in the central hall, grimy but forbidding, still. 'Only Major-Generals and above could use the main door on Whitehall.' (Who thought that one up, I wonder?) I tiptoed into Jack Profumo's private bathroom, still bearing traces of Valerie Hobson's redecoration, and telepathised for him; those moments of anguished realisation, when he must have known the Keeler affair was breaking.

Particularly, too, as I meandered along those gloomy corridors, still untouched, I reflected on past characters, long dead, who had paced excitedly there during those difficult months of the Great War when 'The Big Push' – and then again 'The Big Push' – was being planned. How many hundreds of thousands of Death Warrants were stamped in these rooms?

Albany   *Wednesday, 2 May*

I woke too early for *The Times*, even here, where Herbie delivers it at 6.15, and turned to Chips for solace with my EMT. I became absorbed by some of the very late entries:

Arturo Lopez-Wilshaw at 18, Rue du Centre, and Neuilly. Alexis de Rede, 'the Eugene de Rastignac of modern Paris' (who he?) at the Hotel Lambert. 'Eighteen, semi-gratin and very grand ... Footmen and candelabra on the stairs; gold plate ... the Palazzo Colonna *en petite.*'

'I was particularly glad to see the Etienne de Beaumonts again; They are so intelligent, so *fin*, so decadent, so old, so painted and so civilised.'

This was only forty-five years ago. Now we live in a squalid scrabble. It's nonsense to say we're better off. We're catastrophically

---

[1] Property Services Agency.

poorer due to (a) death duties and (b) 'levelling up' of standards and expectations in the lower classes so that it is completely impossible to find, even if one could afford, domestic servants.

Poor darling Jane drained and cleaned the pool *herself* yesterday. Of course she felt utterly exhausted. Saltwood slowly disintegrates round one, sector by sector (presently the Great Library and my father's study) as poor William – *aet* 70, and *cum* some 370,000 Virginian cigarettes, is terminally ill – gets 'out of reach' and needs a major blitz, up to two full days, to get it back 'up'.

We're too exhausted, and time is too precious, to 'entertain' – although we have the perfect setting. Anyway, it's so expensive, with good claret at £100 – minimum – per bottle.

Albany   *Thursday, 10 May*

Today is the fiftieth anniversary of the German attack in the West. The day that Valentine Lawford, the 'rather second Empire' secretary, omitted to tell Halifax that Rab Butler was waiting in the outer office with a message (that Labour would serve in a coalition under him). Halifax slipped out of the other door – to go to the dentist (!). By the evening it was too late, and Winston was Prime Minister.

I really don't know, I still can't judge, whether that was a good, or a bad, thing for the Britain that I love and cherish, and whose friendly, stubborn, dignified and sensible people have so often been let down by their rulers.

House of Commons   *Monday, 14 May*

The whole Department is in a state of frustration. What *is* happening to the Review?

'Options for Change' – I ask you!

Spastic title. There shouldn't be any fucking 'options'. It should be – 'It's like this. Now get on with it.' As it is, we're just haemor-rhaging away on needless expenditure, and morale is plummeting with the uncertainty.

I have 'leaked' the situation. I chose Andy Marr[1] because he is young and clear-headed, and politically acute. We met, clandestinely, on the terrace, at the far end by the Lords fence. He will run something in the next issue, probably on Monday.

House of Commons   *Tuesday, 15 May*

I am in tremendous form at the moment.

This afternoon I pleased the House at Questions. It is a triumph if you can make *both* sides laugh good-humouredly, as I first discovered, memorably, questioning Merlyn Rees in 1977.[2]

Dale Campbell-Savours[3] came in with an ill-natured supplementary – 'Will the Minister ensure that his Department... does not get into bed with any of the companies from which the Member for Petersfield is drawing a retainer...'

Mates sat staring straight ahead, face as black as thunder.

Much uproar, 'show' indignation, points of order.

When it settled down I was expected to make a pompous rebuttal; at the very least a reference to the Committee on Members' Interests, every confidence, etc., etc.

But I don't like Mates; the House doesn't like Mates.

I said, 'One thing I have learned, Mr Speaker, is that it is never the slightest use telling people who they shouldn't go to bed with.'

Everyone was delighted – except, of course, Mates.

---

[1] Andrew Marr, parliamentary correspondent of *The Economist*.
[2] A smash-and-grab burglar had been given a very light sentence. Many on the Labour side were generating a synthetic row with Merlyn Rees, the Home Secretary, claiming that it was because the miscreant was an Old Etonian (which he was). AC said, 'Perhaps it was because, as an Old Etonian, the Bench took the view that he had already served the equivalent of five years in gaol.' Merlyn Rees, MP for Morley and Leeds South since 1983 (South Leeds, 1963–83), who had not long moved to the Home Office after two years as Northern Ireland Secretary, responded: 'There is one difference – in prison they learn to read and write.' See *Diaries: Into Politics*, 21 June 1977.
[3] Dale Campbell-Savours, MP for Workington since 1979.

House of Commons   *Thursday, 31 May*

I am getting a marvellous press.

The Economist article was just right, all the more so because Andy had sought, and quoted, corroboration from senior officials in the Dept.

Last week I had lunch, privately, at the *FT*, and sparkled. A highly complimentary piece followed on the Saturday – 'one of the most attractive (Hullo!) as well as one of the cleverest of Mrs Thatcher's Ministers'.

'Profiles' everywhere, none of them too embarrassing. I got off the sleeper this morning to find a full leader-page article in the *Mail* by Gordon Greig: 'Could this be the moment when one politician finally gets a grip on the Cold War warriors after 50 years of meekly obeying orders?'

TK is putting a brave face on it. The message from along the corridor is that 'he is keeping his own counsel' (i.e., wondering how the hell he can get even).

Saltwood   *Friday, 8 June*

Yesterday evening I got involved with some kind of 'decision-makers' groupette at the LSE. Brainy people on the up-and-up, with a few heavies to pour cold water.

On my left the scatty (American) boffin in whose honour the meal was being held; on my right, David Sainsbury the (now reluctant) funder of the SDP.[1] Actually, if you didn't know he was so rich you would just think he was just a dreary little Jewish accountant.

The discussion, if that be the term, was quite ably chaired by the School's chairman, but pretty empty for all that. Just another approach to saying if you don't have a strong economy, you're not strong. So? What's new?

I made some provocative remarks about 'The Nation State', and

---

[1] David Sainsbury, Deputy Chairman of the grocers since 1988, had been a Trustee and major contributor to the Social Democratic Party since its inception in 1982.

Sam Brittan,[1] who has disapproved of me for a very long time, shifted uneasily on his (not unmassive) haunches, and mutter-heckled. Finally he came out with it.

'What *is* "The Nation State"?'

'If you don't *know* what The Nation State is,' I said, 'you're decadent.'

John Moore was also there. Oh so golden and youthful looking. But a husk, a husk. Cut down so young.

Albany   *Monday, 11 June*

We went to the Gilmours' garden party, at Syon.[2]

The weather was fearfully cold and, as we wandered the gardens, elderly dowagers were complaining of 'frostbite'. Mollie Buccleuch, with a stick (who was it in the Thirties who referred to her and Mary Roxburghe as being 'randy as schoolgirls'?) One of Ian's sons offered to (re)introduce me, and enjoyed it when I said 'no', she disapproved. I told him the story of the Blenheim raid by Loders, in 1950. He was, of course far too young to remember Miss Ball.[3]

People were keen to talk to me, and admiringly curious. I am still in the backwash of the 'Defence Review' publicity.

Young – *policeman* young – Victor Smart[4] came up, after bobbing round a group, and introduced himself. Light-heartedly I protested about his piece: 'There is now considerable doubt as to whether the two Ministers can continue to exist in the same Department', etc.

Then Adam Raphael[5] came up, all ingratiating: 'We're running a

---

[1] Sam Brittan, principal economics commentator of the *Financial Times* since 1966 and elder brother of Sir Leon Brittan, a Vice President of the Commission of the European Communities.

[2] Sir Ian Gilmour, 3rd Bt. MP for Chesham since 1974 (Norfolk Central, 1962–74). Former owner of *The Spectator*. Married to Lady Caroline Margaret Montagu-Douglas-Scott, younger daughter of the 8th Duke of Buccleuch.

[3] Miss Ball was a fashionable beautician who had a client list of rich ladies of a certain age, including AC's mother, among whom she used with considerable relish to spread gossip.

[4] Victor Smart, political correspondent, *The Observer*.

[5] Adam Raphael, Executive Editor, *The Observer*, since 1988.

Profile of you in the next paper.' After he'd gone Smart said, '*He* was the one who insisted on the 'Two Ministers' bit.'

Willie Whitelaw I also talked to. He was nice, and on the ball and – I was delighted to see – still rheumy-eyed and *repeatedly* calling for his glass to be refilled. He told me I was 'quite right; absolutely right . . . to do what you are doing' at MoD. It had to be done. 'A lot of people will try and block you. But you must press on.'

I was hugely cheered by this. If only Willie were still 'around'.

But Willie was deeply gloomy, in the traditional High Tory way, about electoral prospects. There was a bit of 'does anyone tell her anything?' and 'No good getting mobbed in America, and thinking that's going to work here.'

The fact that Willie no longer has a proper consultative role (in which he was so immensely valuable) is an indictment of our present system of government. He was worked off his feet as Lord President in order, nominally, to 'justify' his position in Cabinet. He chaired a lot of bloody stupid committees that easily could have been steered by any number of different nonentities. In the evenings he had stuffy dinners, on weekends Party functions.

As a result he got a stroke.

Much better to have been four days a week in Penrith, and just coming up for Cabinet, and critical meetings.

We brought Ian and Caroline a tiny present. Their parties are so congenial – pretty girls, children in party clothes excitedly running hither and thither, bishops, Whig heavies, clever journalists, *Refusés* – and I never write a bread-and-butter letter.

It was a bottle of '67 Yquem. I stood it on the dining-room table (we had arrived late and our hosts were already mingling). When we said goodbye it had gone. I hope the staff didn't drink it.

Ministry of Defence   *Thursday, 14 June*

I was host at the NATO Defence College lunch at Lancaster House. Made a routine Darling-you-were-Wonderful speech. The Italian General thought (according to David[1]) that I was Secretary of State and TK was 'just another Minister'.

Kenneth Baker is a clever fellow. When I went to see him at

---

[1] David Hatcher, APS in AC's Private Office.

Central Office[1] – to clear my slate in 'Party' terms – he was effusive. 'You're doing brilliantly well. A textbook. You have my fullest admiration.'

But to TK he had said, 'You must find it very difficult working with Alan.'

I like this. If you are a serious player, it's no good being 'straight'. You just won't last.

Saltwood   *Sunday, 17 June*

This morning I killed the heron.

He has been raiding the moat, starting in the early hours, then getting bolder and bolder, taking eight or nine fish, carp, nishikoi, exotica, every day.

I had risen very early, before five, with the intention of getting a magpie who has been pillaging all the nests along the beech hedge. But returned empty handed. They are clever birds, and sense one's presence.

Suddenly Jane spotted the heron from the casement window in my bathroom.

I ran down and took the 4.10 off the slab, cocked the hammer. He was just opposite the steps, took off clumsily and I fired, being sickened to see him fall back in the water, struggle vainly to get up the bank, one wing useless.

I reloaded, went round to the opposite bank. Tom beat me to it and gamely made at him, but the great bird, head feathers bristling and eyes aglare, made a curious high-pitched menacing sound, his great beak jabbing fiercely at the Jack Russell.

'Get Tom out of the way,' I screamed.

I closed the range to about twenty feet and took aim. I did not want to mutilate that beautiful head, so drew a bead on his shoulder.

The execution. For a split second he seemed simply to have absorbed the shot; then very slowly his head arched round and took refuge inside his wing, half under water. He was motionless, dead.

---

[1] Kenneth Baker, MP for Mole Valley since 1983 (Acton 1968–70, St Marylebone, 1970–83). Chairman of the Conservative Party since 1989 after three years as Education Secretary.

I was already sobbing as I went back up the steps: 'Sodding fish, why should I kill that beautiful creature just for the sodding fish...'

I cursed and blubbed up in my bedroom, as I changed into jeans and a T-shirt. I was near a nervous breakdown. Yet if it had been a burglar or a vandal I wouldn't have given a toss. It's human beings that are the vermin.

At breakfast I had a handsome photograph on the front page of *The Observer*. There was a heavy and tendentious piece about 'Service chiefs have lost confidence in Ministers'. Three columns wide, lead item. 'The Deputy is making all the running'.

Too bloody right he is. But will he bring off the *coup royal*?

Ministry of Defence   *Wednesday, 20 June*

I went to Sothebys to look at some sculpture. There was a pretty alabaster frieze of a hunting scene by William Haydn, which photographed well in the catalogue, shown as 72 inches. But in fact it had been broken, and a piece was missing. The joined-up fragments jarred, and it was in some curious packing-case type frame.

I spotted Nico Henderson, and hailed him. 'My God, Alan!' He turned to an elegant blonde lady *d'une certaine age*. 'You must meet this man. He's the most important man in the Government. He's producing the peace dividend.'

She looked at me through (as it were) her lorgnette. Demi-dreamy, and spaced out. (All these rich old former beauties are *on* something, as Jane said.)

'I knew you as a child.'

It was Marietta, Ronnie Tree's young and (then) nubile second wife. A name to conjure with in NY. Still alive.

---

[1] Sir Nicholas Henderson. Having retired after spells as British Ambassador to Warsaw, Bonn and Paris, was persuaded out of retirement and served as Ambassador to Washington, 1979–82.

Glasgow-Inverness train   *Friday, 22 June*

The closing entry for this volume. The second half of the year will overlap with 1991, in a new notebook which, crisply expectant, sits in the drawer of my desk at MoD. What will it record? A continuing ascendancy — for verily I am in the stratosphere at the moment? Stagnation? Or decline? Or perhaps, most romantic of all, the sudden stop. When the lunatic or the assassin do their work or, simply, the gods lose patience.

How I do enjoy my job! And how full of vitality I feel — mind racing, gifts of expression, spoken and written, better than at any time. My self-confidence is complete. I don't even use the folder at Questions any more, just lounge on the Bench and answer off the top of my head.

'For the second day running,' said the BBC *Yesterday in Parliament*, the star of the Defence debate was Alan Clark, the laid-back but cerebral Minister of State.'

Two more Profiles, both laudatory, are due out on the weekend.

So where do I go from here? The objective must be now — and I mean now, very shortly, July at the latest — to displace the Secretary of State.

Tom remains affable, but wary. He sees Hugh Colver, the Press Officer *for an hour* every day. (I shouldn't think I've had more than five minutes with a press officer since walking into the building last summer.) Tom's office have 'let it be known' that I am 'getting more publicity than is desirable'. 'Desired' by who, pray?

But what can happen to the Secretary of State? Where can he go? Leader of the House is really the only practical possibility now.

But I don't plot. I sleepwalk. My timings are rarely calculated, more often luck and intuition. I cannot predict what will happen, I have no feel for it at all.

Now I am in my beloved Scotland. Past the window glide all those delightful halts, with their tidy white-gabled granite station masters' offices — Dunblane, Gleneagles, Dunkeld, Pitlochry, Blair Atholl, Dalwhinnie, Newtonmore, Kingussie. A list for me as evocative, in its different way, as the route of the Orient Express; which the girl with the golden voice used to recite before the departure from the Gare du Lyon.

I will have a day at Shore, and try walking, The Prince of the

Captivity, in isolation in the hills and coires, and think through my prospect.

Ministry of Defence   *Wednesday, 27 June*

This morning I went out to Greenwich – *what* incredible buildings, better than Versailles, really we ought to be doing something more important with them.

The traffic was heavy, and I had time, on the back seat, to embellish the dreary little text – 'user friendly' – which officials had given me to utter as an 'introduction' to the morning's proceedings.

I am impatient with the sluggish pace, the caution and derivativeness of our warship design. There are many clever and original naval architects, in our ancient tradition, still around – at Vosper, at Swans, at consultants like Yard. But they are feared and disliked by the huge overstaffed troglodyte Admiralty settlement at Bath. Why the fuck isn't *that* place privatised? How can the private sector ever compete with an organisation so closely linked, in terms of career advancement, with its own main customer?

So I added in a good bit about changing needs, different theatres, the need to allow ships the capability to fulfil their new roles. You get pirates in the straits of Malacca, terrorising and robbing civilian traffic. A corvette answers a distress call. Then what? The pirates will have armour piercing 0.5 in Brownings in rubber boats, Republican Guard stuff. What do you use against that, an Exocet?

This was received in pretty piggy silence by my audience, whose 'mix' I couldn't quite, through the footlights, determine. The Admiral, Kenneth Eaton,[1] who was on the platform with me, remained expressionless throughout. But as he neither applauded nor, when others nervously did, laugh, his view was plain enough.

There were high-ranking uniforms scattered about, but the majority were suits, 'industrialists'.

I stayed on for the first 'real' speaker, a Professor of Industrial Trends (I must tell John[2] about this new 'chair'), and he made a few

---

[1] Sir Kenneth Eaton, Controller of the Navy since 1989.
[2] John Sparrow, Warden of All Souls, 1952–77 and a fastidious critic of fashionable trends in higher education.

mildly critical remarks about the government, which were clapped.

I thought if any of those sodding sailors was clapping I'll have him cashiered. As for 'industrialists', they're almost (but nothing, no one, not even 'Claimants' Unions' can be) *as* bad as farmers. If I said to them, 'Look an "exciting" (correct usage at last) new Initiative: In order to cut down on bureaucratic form-filling red tape, etc., I've arranged for you to go next door and my assistant will hand over a cheque on the Bank of England, pre-endorsed. All *you* have to do is fill in the amount'... 'Wha'?'... 'according to your needs' – they'd still grumble.

Directly after lunch I went to E (CP). Chaired as always, soft-spokenly, but firmly, by the Chancellor. Little Gummer[1] made a most halting and turgid presentation of his paper, on *retaining* (for God's sake) the Milk Marketing Board. 'Is he always as bad as this?' I said in a note to John Patten, on my left.

Later we moved on to the de-regulation of motorway restaurants. Roger Freeman,[2] not a man to get into trouble, you'd think, ran into heavy flak, led by Nick Ridley.[3] 'Why can't they be totally free of regulation?' No restriction on hours, area, alcohol. Pure Adam Smith Institute. Then Francis Maude (how does the Foreign Office have an interest in this, pray?) joined in and added to the hard-line free market declamation. Poor Roger tried to remain calm, but was losing. Uncomfortable for him.

I tiptoed out and went to Brooks's, where I had a tryst with Peter Jenkins. He was already there, pouring the tea. He doesn't smile much – at all, you could say. And like many charmless people, he is immune, even when it is being deployed towards him. The only thing he respects is power, or access to power. So I am gratified that he should have invited me. I have come some distance since he used to describe me as a zealot on the far Right, then more recently as a 'loose cannon'.

Now, it's 'the highly intelligent Mr Alan Clark'.

Peter does recognise that I am trying to do something at MoD that it is logical, but difficult. He warned me that the Party would turn against me, if it has not already started to do so. Yes, I said, but not if I was Secretary of State, because I could explain and persuade.

---

[1] John Selwyn Gummer was now Minister of Agriculture.
[2] Roger Freeman, MP for Kettering since 1983. Minister of State, Transport.
[3] Nicholas Ridley, Trade and Industry Secretary since 1989.

As it is, I am tongue-tied, and the vested interests in the Department leak against me.

One of the anomalies is that 'Defence Correspondents' practically never talk to Politicians. They have no sympathy with or understanding of politics. They get all their briefing, and their leaks, from soldiers.

I explained that I was doing my best. But I had to balance Party, Treasury, the PM's own periodic bouts of cold feet and waverings.

Whether any good will come of this meeting time alone will tell. But a certain mending of fences. Of all the Lobby he has the least gossip, and the least small-talk. Admirable, but no fun.

Albany   *Thursday, 28 June*

Last night we spectated at the Queen Mother's special ninetieth birthday parade from the big window at Admiralty House. Chiefs of Staff and their wives, Hamilton, a few minor Royals and the Prince, tetchy and inattentive. TK was beside the QM on her dais for 'taking the salute'. The concept was pleasing. Instead of a lot of bands and soldiers, there was a little detachment, all puffed up and spick and span with pride and pleasure, from each of the organisations of which she was Patron.

Actually, you don't really get a very good view from these windows, especially if you have to be 'polite'. But some participants I did notice, and was cheered by. The pleasing Jack Russell, who confidently led one section; and the jolly beige hens – *Orpington Yellows*, apparently they are called – in their wicker cage. Two fine bulls in trailers also drew applause – was I the only person to reflect on their fate, all too soon? The squalor and terror of the stockyard corridors, the mishandled 'stunning', the mechanical guillotine?

Jane sat in the centre front, with Princess Margaret on her right. The Princess smoked resolutely throughout, at one point reprimanding her nephew who had moved *out* of her line of sight, thus exposing her to a telephoto lens.

Afterwards we repaired to a huge reception at the RUSI. The Queen Mother herself was perfectly incredible. In spite of having stood for at least half the time on the saluting dais, she moved among

the guests for nearly two hours, radiating a deep personal happiness
and concern for all to whom she was introduced.

Somewhat reluctantly TK finally produced us. 'This is Alan Clark,
he must be a neighbour of yours in Scot . . . '

She sliced through the booming and asked me, 'How is the library
at Saltwood?'

We had a nice little chat. She said that Saltwood had one of the
loveliest atmospheres of any place she had ever visited.

TK, out of things, got restive and tried to move her on. She
showed her reluctance.

What a marvellous performance. I could never have managed it,
and I'm thirty years younger.

Albany   *Wednesday, 4 July*

I was reading Cadogan's diaries with EMT. Something made me look
up Oran, and I found that this very day is the anniversary of our
destruction of the French Fleet at Mers-el-Kebir. Winston Churchill's
greatest stroke (not least because it must have been so hurtful for him).
But that action, more than any other, showed that we were going to
fight, and fight rough. From then on we were undefeated – Battle of
Britain, Sidi Barrani, Tobruk, Benghazi. We could have made peace
at the time of the Hess mission and the world would have been
completely different.

Spontaneously, I wrote a note to the PM reminding her, and of
the Foreign Office memo pleading that it would make 'all the difference' (yeah) to our relations with Vichy if we allowed the French
battleships to return to Toulon. Pat dropped it off at Number 10 on
our way to the Dept, and I hope she enjoyed it.

Later, when I was in the Commons, I was caught on the stairs to
the committee room corridor by Don McIntyre[1] thoughtfully, as is
his wont, attentively strained and agonising. He told me that the
Chiefs of Staff, who were seeing the Prime Minister next week,
were going to 'complain' about me. Exceeding my authority, doing
'damage', who's in charge? etc. This is lowering. Of course she'll

---

[1] Don McIntyre, political correspondent of *The Independent on Sunday*.

resist it. But it may shake her faith; make her think it's impossible to promote me there. And this, presumably is what they want, a pre-emptive strike.

Plymouth train   *Friday, 13 July*

My father's birthday. He would be eighty-seven today, if Nolwen hadn't poisoned him, pottering about and probably something of a nuisance. After all, Uncles Colin, Russell and Alan are all in fine health, and in their nineties.

I am in good spirits. Last night at the seven o'clock vote the talk was all of poor Nicky.[1] I said to Iain Lang,[2] so tiredly drawn and handsome, 'There's nothing so improves the mood of the Party as the imminent execution of a senior colleague.'

Robin Maxwell-Hyslop[3] told me that on behalf of the Trade and Industry Committee he had passed a message that I would be their preference as Secretary of State to succeed Nicky (unlikely to swing it, but can't do much harm); and going out through the vote doors Paul Channon[4] fell in beside me, 'Well, I hear you're going to be Secretary of State for Trade and Industry.' Now Paul has very good antennae. Secretly thrilled, I dissimulated.

'Seems obvious to me,' he said. 'Would solve a lot of problems simultaneously.'

Thoroughly delighted with myself I held court in the Lobby. Around me I had John Cole, Colin Brown,[5] a swarthy little fellow from the *FT* and a *very* short cheeky chappie from one of the comics.

---

[1] Nicholas Ridley was under pressure to resign following an interview in *The Spectator*. Ridley claimed that Dominic Lawson, the editor, had kept the tape running after the interview had ended, and then revealed the full text. Certain forthright remarks by Ridley had caused offence in Germany.

[2] Iain Lang, MP for Galloway since 1979. Minister of State, Scottish Office, since 1987.

[3] Robin Maxwell-Hyslop, MP for Tiverton since 1960, had been a member of the Trade and Industry Select Committee since 1971.

[4] Paul Channon had returned to back benches in 1989.

[5] Colin Brown, a political correspondent on *The Independent*.

George Jones[1] hovered; but as he has a low opinion of me – he only talks to Mates and the Left – didn't approach.

I said that Nick's performance was a welcome return to the old doings of the nineteenth century, when major figures in the Govt could digress giftedly and constructively on the issues of the day, without constantly being hauled over the coals by some wanker in the FCO Press Office.

'But in those days it took three weeks for the papers to get to Berlin,' said John Cole, not without reason.

All evening the tide continued to run. Jane and I were at a dinner at the French Embassy – little tables – and as we drifted into the drawing room for coffee the Chief Secretary[2] made a point of coming over: 'By Monday you could well find yourself Secretary of State for Trade and Industry.'

Jane, bless her, is secretly delighted. *Into the big frame at last!* But we dare not say anything, even to each other. And in this morning's papers I am tipped as Number One probability by Gordon Greig in the *Mail*, and as a likely contender in *The Independent*.

At intervals I stop writing, and fantasise. The Prince's Return. To occupy that very office to which formerly I was summoned by Norman, by Paul and by David. To get Matthew to run my Office, with Rose as the Diary queen; sort out a few of those officials who 'took against' me and bring forward the loyal ones.

We'll know soon.

Saltwood   *Saturday, 14 July*
◆

This morning I swam very early, before seven, and the view *from the water* was unbelievable because the sun is on the towers:

> And Lo! The Hunter of the East has caught
> The Sultan's turret in a noose of light.[3]

– which happens only for a couple of weeks in high summer, and

---

[1] George Jones (*Daily Telegraph*).
[2] Norman Lamont.
[3] *The Rubaiyat of Omar Khayyam*, Edward Fitzgerald.

the tobacco plants are in flower. The rays are too flat, still, to touch the poolside and the Morning Glory flares purple. The whole pool area is wonderfully overgrown this year, and enchanted.

I was pleased to find myself tipped this morning in *The Times*, the *Telegraph* and *The Independent*. How fickle and derivative the press are. In many cases these are the same people who regularly predict my dismissal whenever there is talk of a reshuffle.

I spent most of the morning out of doors, though fretting (for the first time in my career) that the phone might be ringing. Why was I so unsettled this time? Realising subconsciously, I suppose, that the chance was good, but it was the last.

I remember saying to Jane, 'Actually none of this really matters compared with whether James will beget a son.'

I took calls from Wastell, B. Anderson, Sherman (time-wasting) and *W. Evening Herald*.

This last, naturally, wanted to talk at length about the Plympton Water Works. Not a word about Ridley or my prospects in Government, although I don't doubt there would have been plenty if I was being criticised, however oblique, remote or irrelevant the source.

(As I write this I am reminded of an exemplary occasion, which I don't think I recorded at the time, when a *Herald* [female] reporter rang me, all of a state, and said, 'You've been black-listed by the Esperanto Society. What have you got to say about that?')

Bruce was his usual slightly dampening self – and nothing from Tristan, a bad sign. Did BA mention Lilley?[1] I think he may have done. He is usually pretty well informed about undercurrents.

By mid-afternoon my private hopes had waned. Then, at tea, the news came through. Nick had resigned, 'and his successor will be announced in about a half hour' – then back to some prat standing outside Number 10.

We sat in silence, rustling stale newsprint, and clinking cups as we poured and repoured.

Some fifteen minutes later the announcement that it was Peter Lilley, 'at forty-six the youngest member of the Cabinet'.

Flatly we sat, reading and grumbling.

Then the phone rang. I made Jane answer, in case it was a reporter or a colleague calling for a concealed gloat. But it was Sally. And I

---

[1] Peter Lilley, MP for St Albans since 1983. Financial Secretary at the Treasury.

could tell from Jane's sudden squeal of pleasure, and the nature of her questions, that she was giving news of a confirmed pregnancy.[1]

How wonderful! And so magically soon after my remark that very morning! With tears in my eyes, I congratulated her. Everything seemed to fall into place now, all the careful structuring of the Trusts, the interlocking provisions and possessions.

I took out the SS 100 and drove down to St Leonard's, prayed and gave thanks in that same pew where I had sat at my father's funeral, immediately behind Nolwen.

I had forgotten his birthday, but now I realise that it must have been confirmed on that day – and is due in February![2]

Ministry of Defence   *Thursday, 19 July*

Still hot, scorching sun. A very end-of-term feeling. The House is tetchy, and mock-playful. Endless votes last night – none of them of the slightest importance, but all subject to 'heavy' two-liners.

Poor old Alan Glyn[3], 'had a turn' in an excessively *ego* location, the library main doorway, at the junction of tea room, smoking room and Speaker's corridors. He was attempting a few shuffling, stompy steps, as very old people do (he's not old at all, but caricatures himself), with Beaumont-Dark[4] and A.N. Other supporting him by holding his elbows. His jaw hung open, slackly. Hours later I saw him sitting, completely glazed over, in the 'porter's chair' by the library entrance.

I catnapped on the sofa in my office, staggering up for the last Division at 1.20 a.m. Seeing Ian Gow I said, 'See you tomorrow.'

'No,' he replied. 'Today.'

Ugh.

---

[1] Sadly the child was later miscarried and Sally divorced James in the following year.
[2] Both AC's own sons were born in February.
[3] Sir Alan Glyn, MP for Windsor since 1970.
[4] Sir Anthony Beaumont-Dark, MP for Birmingham, Selly Oak, since 1979.

The last day of 'term', effectively. There is some patchy business next
week, an Opposition supply day on Tuesday, but nothing to speak
of – ending with the Buck House garden party and a reception at
Number 10.

This morning I woke very early, and with that special late July
tranquillity, before even the buses start in Regent St, and the sky is
still pale grey from heat haze. No shadows as yet, and the promise of
another very hot day.

There are few things more delicious than anticipation of the
imminent long summer holiday – particularly while we still have to
taste the picquancy of the 'Junior Reshuffle'.

Last evening we had the 'End-of-Term Dinner'. Not quite a
dining club, as we only meet on the Thursday before the Long Recess.
There is no actual election process. Membership (and discardment)
are osmotic. Ian 'convenes', though Soames and Ryder are each active
in organisation. Class is undeniably a factor.

The oval room at White's. Boring food – smoked salmon, roast
beef. Who the hell did this, in *July*?

In attendance were Gow, Heathcoat-Amory, Bertie Denham,
Jonathan Aitken, Hamilton, Garel-Jones (a 'first' for him!), Alexander
Hesketh and Cranborne.[1] Fun to see Robert, and a tribute to IG's
discernment as in theory he is out, until 'Harare'[2] dies. But Robert
keeps his finger on the pulse, and is knowledgeable.

An uncomfortable atmosphere. We don't like what we see, and
we don't like admitting, even to each other, that our beloved leader
may be fallible. Not in front of Ian, anyway. But because we don't see
our way, substantial political discussion was at a discount. Gossip was
stale, and people fell back on dirty stories. Pure dirt, I mean, the
Dorm.

I had Soames on my left. 'You'll be in the Cabinet by Monday.
Oh no. This is what I hear . . . ', etc. He is shameless ('Straight to the
Lords.'[3])

---

[1] David Heathcote-Amory, Parliamentary Under-Secretary, Environment, since
    1989; Lord Hesketh, now Minister of State, Trade and Industry. Robert, Viscount
    Cranborne, heir to the Marquess of Salisbury, had stood down as MP for Dorset
    South at the 1987 General Election.
[2] 6th Marquess of Salisbury.
[3] A phrase in the Clark family signifying a glorious finale.

A propos of the Lords, was Bertie Denham sounding me out when he kept asking 'what I wanted'? Was he trying to lead me into hinting at the Lords as a working Min of S? Perhaps I muffed it by saying I wanted to be S of S for Defence. He looked disappointed. He seemed pretty tight, but the Upper Classes *remember* what they (and you) say when they were tight.

At the end of the meal, significantly and in contrast to earlier years, instead of a *tour-de-table* and monologues on the topics of the day, a colleague's failings, or whatever, each person gave a little 'performance'.

Ian, *very* boringly, gave us 'Albert and the Lion'. Waste of time. Bertie was the bluest, Richard the funniest – still – with the Bader at Roedean story. I did 'Frankie and Johnnie'. Most people know the first few verses, but the punch line is in the last:

> Sheriff came over in the mornin',
> said it was all for the best.
> He said her lover Johnnie
> was nothin' but a doggone pest.

We don't *need* to have an Election for two years, we kept telling each other. Technically true, but balls as well.

I thought there would be more talk of a possible 'challenge' in the autumn but, ominously, there was none. The prospect, though, is implacably in the middle distance. A towering thunderhead of Alto-Cumulus, precursor of change not just in the weather, but in the Climate.

That evening, at Saltwood
This must have been the hottest day of the year. Everything is so full, and overripe, and pale yellow.

It is a quarter to nine, and I am sitting out in shirtsleeves by the pool. It is the day of the *Attentat*. A year ago, exactly, I visited the monastery at Rastenburg and strolled around the *Wolfschanze*.

I am worried about growing old. After I had been swimming I went to the top of the towers and hung on the bar. I couldn't do *one* pull-up. In the summer of 1955, my last at Saltwood before I went to Rye, the summer of Marye thirty-five years ago (and yet it seems like six or seven) I could easily do four. And over twenty swings of ankles above my head.

Eight o'clock in the evening, and still overpoweringly hot. I sit out by the pool, which is yellowy-green, and touching eighty degrees.

Today I went to the helicopter show at Middle Wallop. Lunchtime in the VIP tent was a furnace, worse even than the IFA in Madrid,[1] or the BAe tent at the LaserFire demo in Dubai.

Interesting discussions. The two units on which I would most like to spend money freely are the Army Air Corps and (to provide them with a quota of medium-heavy weapons) the Parachute Regt.

But the AAC are guarded in their approach to the 'Air Cavalry' concept. We have a number of good ancient Cavalry regiments which, because of the shrinkage in armoured deployment on the 'Central Front', will have to amalgamate or even disappear altogether. The need to expand the AAC is obvious (or obvious to me, anyhow). These regts have been already – as they saw it – traumatised once when they lost their horses and went into tanks. Would not a reversion to helicopters be symbolic, and welcome? But the officers here (I've noticed this with the SAS at Hereford too) like to keep it small and cliquey, where you know everyone, NCOs and men as well, by their Christian names.

James came and collected me this early morning with a Gazelle. His co-pilot was a Staff Sgt Pengelley, whom I remember for his enthusiasm in the AAC mess at Stanley when I visited the Falklands with the Defence Committee in October of 1982. Like all who have flown in combat conditions he is adamant on the urgent need for *fighter* helicopters, to intercept enemy transport and ground attack, and to defend our own.

As we arrived at Wallop James was at the controls, and too insouciant for Pengelley, who got anxious.

'These lose speed very quickly on approach.'

'That's OK.'

'You can get caught by surprise.'

'I have control.'[2]

I was proud of him. Even more so on the return, when he made a beautiful, totally accurate landing opposite the Garden Entrance

---

[1] IFA: a hotel in Madrid where AC was once marooned with his family after their car broke down.

[2] The phrase indicating – from the captain – that he does not need assistance.

after taking the neater (but more difficult and funked by many visitors) approach from behind Thorpe's Tower.

When they left James was still at the controls and performed a salute on the east side. Going straight in from the hover he stood the little Gazelle on its tail and went straight into a vertical climbing torque turn directly over the great sycamores.

It was spectacular. But in the midst of Life we are in Death. A tiny malfunction of the gearbox, a hesitation in the tail rotor, and the frail little machine would have crashed – before my very gate – and burned to a cinder. I draw strength from reflections such as this. Because if God wants to plunge in the knife, then He can do so – at any time.

The Garden House   *Sunday, 22 July*

I think this is my first entry from over here. It is very warm and silent, well separated from the cares and pressures of the castle. A true *Pavillon* in which to work or contemplate, and extravagantly accoutred to 'self-catering' status. We have cleaned it up, painted the weather-boarding, spent money, 'got it very nice'. Now the easiest part, and the most fun – furnishing and arranging. Few traces of my parents. Of Colette, none whatever. Save for some missing electric light bulbs, she might never have set foot in the place.

I wonder what its fate will be?

This afternoon we went to Bethersden to pick up Jane's Citroën. On the way over we found ourselves drawn to explore the overgrown drive of a concealed manor house.

The façade was dark and had an abandoned air. But the back quarters were a delight. Heavy vegetation had encroached on the yard, and there were saplings everywhere pushing through the brick pave. A half-hearted attempt had been made to cut the very long grass with an Allen which stood, well-maintained looking, but inoperative. Just adjacent was a (still) working oast house.

Formerly there had been HONEY signs fixed to the gate, but not today and Jane needed some persuading to reconnoitre. But our reward was this beautiful friendly home, with low-roofed inter-communicating rooms, comfortable and sheltering. Hens talked inquiringly, and walked in and out of the kitchen. A fine fluffed tawny tabby strolled by assertively with his tail up.

The owner appeared, pleasant, elderly. He could almost have been ex RFC. Most courteously he did produce honey, and passed the time of day.

I felt overcome by a wistful nostalgia for starting again. As Jane said, an utterly perfect place to live as young marrieds, and bring up children.

But you can't put the clock back by two seconds – never mind twenty-five years.

Jane set off alone in the Citroën and I made a detour for Tom Mason's garage, where I got involved in a very long ritualised ceremony to buy a few sidelights, and get some old leather seats 'thrown in' because I had paid him £1000 for a new Silver Ghost hand pressure pump.

On the return journey I cut across to the old A20, passing the sign for Hothfield where in the nurses' quarters on a summer's evening in 1955 I experienced the most perfect physical sensation, never before or since, with Marye. Jealous and inquisitive colleagues tried and rattled her door, departing in the end to get Matron. She, stout woman, portentously interrogated Marye through the keyhole, but the sweet girl (who looked, now I come to think about it, not unlike a bustier version of Jenny on HRT) kept her superior at bay for some precious minutes while I got dressed and climbed out of the window, to stumble across unlit lawns and rose bushes.

Ministry of Defence   *Monday, 30 July*

I must record a curious phenomenon. If something is happening, or has happened, that affects one adversely, is upsetting – 'bad news' – one feels very tired (over that time) even though one still doesn't know. I remember Jane telling me that she had experienced this on the afternoon we were driving back from Hawtreys and Jason was run over.[1] And this morning I felt dreadful in the Sandling train. It's not

---

[1] A sad episode in family history when a favourite labrador puppy was killed.

just feeling a bit sleepy; it's feeling absolutely shattered, as if one was getting polio, only without the fever.

When I got to the barrier Julian was waiting, looking anxious.

'Minister, I have some very, very bad news.'

For a split second I feared it must be Andrew. But something in his eyes was missing (the look of fear, I suppose, and embarrassment that I might actually *break down*). 'Ian Gow has been killed by a car bomb.'

'How spiteful of them', was all I could say. But I thought particularly of the poor Lady. She wept at the first casualties in the Falklands. I wonder if she did today? Because Ian loved her, actually loved, I mean, in every sense but the physical. And then in the end, as lovers do (particularly that kind), he got on her nerves, and she was off-hand with him. He played his last beseeching card: 'I will have to resign.' 'Go ahead, then.' (I foreshorten the exchange, of course) – and that was it.

We talked briefly by the newsagents, and I cautioned Julian to hold his tongue in the car as I did not want Bob 'horning in' and trying to curdle our blood.

Even a silence would have been 'pregnant', so I outmanoeuvred Bob by talking in matter-of-fact tones throughout the journey about the Options Statement, and kindred subjects.

Once ensconced here, I became thoughtful. My old friend. Ian got me into Government, surmounting much opposition and, even from her, misgiving. Very few people had so clear and cogent an understanding of how Whitehall, and the Cabinet Office building worked. Although in recent years Ian had become a little saddened and, indeed, irritated by the way in which the Court had changed and Charles Powell had got the whole thing in his grip. And this, together with his increasing distance from the reality of office, had led him to indulge in *manneristics*. He practised, sometimes beyond the bounds of tolerance, the always tricky *jeu* of self-parody. But Ian remained always witty, clever, industrious, affectionate and almost *painfully* honourable.

My closest friend, by far, in politics.

He was *insouciant* about death. In the garden of his tiny little house, south of the river, he would point up at the tower blocks which loomed to the east.

'The Paddys are up there,' he would say, in good humour, 'with their telescopes.'

Now they've got her two closest confidants, Airey[1] and Ian. I suppose I should be apprehensive that they might come for me. But, strangely (because I am in many circumstances cowardly) I'm not. Just as well, because 'The Police' down here, as in Sussex, are completely useless, if not actually hostile. It was those same Sussex police, wasn't it, who 'cleared' the Grand Hotel in Brighton before the bomb went off?[2] And whose constable didn't like using dogs, 'in case it upset the miners'?

I've only seen the local police twice in the last ten years. Once when a spotty constable threatened to arrest me for using 'insulting language' on the (fat) wife of a parish councillor who had been stealing firewood; once when, very reluctantly, a red-faced coming-up-for-retirement constable 'took particulars' from two youths caught by me red-handed, and detained, while vandalising and trying to steal valuable stained glass from the south guard-room. Naturally, they were never prosecuted. And Jane was once visited by a couple of CID men who wanted to look at some cannabis plants which hippies had planted far over in the woodland, and they suggested (because no one must be beastly to or about hippies) that it was 'probably one of your children'.

I fear that the police have abandoned their old class allegiances. Indeed many of them seem to carry monstrous chips, and actually to enjoy harassing soft targets. And where has it got them? Simply widened the circle of those who resent and mistrust the police. Two or three stabbed every day and the assailants usually discharged by the Magistrates.

There *are* good ones, young, tough and dedicated – just as there are in MoD – but it's the devil's job bringing them forward; because of that customary (and very English) repressive conspiracy of the incompetent.

So, I'm not particularly frightened. I just feel 'What is written, is written'. Although I wish my affairs were in better order, and I could

---

[1] Airey Neave, MP for Abingdon. Opposition spokesman on Northern Ireland after Margaret Thatcher became party leader in 1975, he was murdered when an IRA bomb destroyed his car at Westminster in 1979.

[2] Of course it was in fact the Security Services who had responsibility for checking the hotel. Allowance must be made for the grief and indignation from which AC was suffering at the time of making this entry.

have passed on more to Jane. The tax authorities would love it. A sudden death allows them to really sink their teeth in.

A huge fine, for doing one's duty.

Saltwood   *Sunday, 5 August*

It's crazy hot. The shade temperature today in the yard was 95°. In and out of the pool all day long. But, perhaps because of this, we are listless, and out of condition.

We can neither afford the time nor the money to go to 'Champneys', and detox. But Jane had a brilliant idea – we'll go there 'in all but name'.

As from this evening, no alcohol (naturally); no fats, practically no carbohydrates; no eggs, no nothing. Fruits and astringent. Mineral water. Sluice the kidneys. Torture the body. Lissomly we will emerge, and purified.

Saltwood   *Tuesday, 7 August*

Yesterday I was in MoD all day. The Iraqis are starting to throw their weight around. I wouldn't have believed it possible, not on this scale. For nearly two years the FCO section of Cabinet minutes was a long moan about how the Iraqi Army was on its last legs, and the Iranians were going to break through. Now it turns out there are more Soviet tanks there than in Poland, Hungary and Czechoslovakia combined.

The only consolation is that sooner than expected the Clark *Bahrein* yardstick[1] has its credentials confirmed. But there is no credit in being proved right, here or anywhere else (except, occasionally the Futures market).

I felt ghastly all day long. Persistent headache, stiff joints, 'lassitude', generally out of sorts. Returned by train and cursed and mumbled at

---

[1]In developing his original 'Options' thesis, AC discarded the traditional NATO requirements and asked instead, 'How effective will it (or they) be in holding the end of the Bahrein Causeway?'

all the holiday-makers, so carefree and (some of them) fetching, in their summer frocks.

But at the station Jane admitted that she had been feeling exactly the same. Of course! 'Champneys!'

As fast as we could we prepared, and then stuffed on, an enormous meal; poulet l'estragon with rice and lots of little vegetables cooked in butter and (baby carrots) sugar; fresh home-baked bread and butter (again); six or seven — each — lemon curd tartlets and gobbets of heavy Jersey cream. I drank half a bottle of good Burgundy. We slept like tops and felt incredible this morning.

Saltwood   *Wednesday, 8 August*

We drove over to Ian Gow's funeral service in St Saviours, Eastbourne. An ugly Victorian building selected by Ian — I assume — because of its inordinately *High* practices.

The heat was oppressive and we set off in casual clothes, intending to change *en route*. Some little distance from Pevensey we diverted and found a wooded glade just nearby to the canal, and started to undress. This aroused the disapproval of two people, fat and ugly, who were slumped in deckchairs by the canal bank and who clearly thought we were going to make love. To tell the truth I would have liked that. The proximity of death always makes me feel sexual. But our timing was tight. Guests were enjoined to be in their places at least forty-five minutes before the service started.

I cannot adequately record how ugly those people were. The man squat, paunchy, resentful in his horn rims; the woman *gross*, runkled-up nylon skirt, varicose veins, eating from a paper bag. At intervals each drew on a cigarette. Beside them glistened two luckless baby bream which the man had caught with his line.

Jane had a brilliant idea. That, once impeccably dressed in our funeral weeds, we should reverse back to their site and kill them, leaving the wreath which we were taking over for Ian. And removing instead, a fish, to lay beside the open grave. Lovely and black, that humour. Pure Buñuel.

On and on went the service. The PM read the first lesson beauti-fully. But there was *too much* jingling, and scattering of incense, and High longeurs. Afterwards (about one and three-quarter hours) we gatecrashed the tea party at the Dog House.[1] Uninvited, and thus not on the police list – whether by intention or accident I know not – we were nonetheless hailed at the door by Peter Hordern and our presence accepted as quite natural.

I spoke with the PM at some length, and to Cecil's evident irritation as he had (literally) cornered her against a hedge in the garden. He kept interrupting and trying to edge between us. She was ultra gung-ho on Saddam Hussein, wanted to send a CVS,[2] etc. But I am a little uneasy. Where will it all end?

Jane Gow had quite consciously and admirably left the – very disagreeable – crater in their yard where the bomb had detonated, and there were flowers strewn around. I went through and stood there alone, in meditation, for a while. Jane told us a macabre little tale. After she had returned to the house, following some forty-eight hours of continuous and intensive forensic scrutiny and searches, one of the dogs wandered. When it returned it brought in its mouth a garter of Ian's, blackened by the explosion, though fortunately without any of his body adhering to it, that he had been wearing that morning, retrieved by the wuffler from a nearby paddock or hedge. Further testimony to (let us say) 'overstretch' in the Sussex Constabulary.

Not many members of the Government had bothered to turn up. From the Cabinet only Howe, Brooke, Waddington, Cecil Parkinson. Of junior Ministers just myself, Ryder and, bizarrely, the Bottomleys.[3] She has lost her looks almost as fast as I did when I first went into the House. And her husband is so *odd* that it grates. Even watching him, and that curious little half-giggling smile and 'scamp' haircut, brings out the worst in me.

---

[1] The Gows' house at Hankham.
[2] An 'Invincible' class aircraft-carrier.
[3] Since the 1989 reshuffle Peter Brooke had been made Northern Ireland Secretary; David Waddington Home Secretary, Richard Ryder Economic Secretary at the Treasury, Peter Bottomley, Parliamentary Under-Secretary, Northern Ireland, and Virginia Bottomley Minister of State, Department of Health.

Saltwood   *Thursday, 9 August*

The great heat has subsided. But we still throw ourselves into the pool at 7.15, and take EMT on the heavy oak seat beside the top border.

This morning I was calm, and enlarged on the prospects for an ideal autumn.

Delicious diversions. First Zermatt, the chalet verandah, some nosey-parkering, the climb to Trift, the wild flowers. Then, in late September steal another week before Conference. Eriboll, with the northern light getting thinner and more brittle; and the air colder. The portents of winter and solitude, with the deer beginning to 'come down' and the road traffic non-existent.

But, as I have often found, and endlessly predicted, if you look forward to something keenly it won't happen. The markets are crashing, the price of oil is shooting sky high and the Iraqis are recalcitrant.[1]

In a few minutes I am off up to blitz my desk at MoD, and call on an expensive dentist who has been recommended by John Sterling.

Saltwood   *Monday, 13 August*

It's very late, and Pat has just left, bearing a secret note for Charles at Number 10.

The day started slowly, and tiresomely.

Officials, who relish – and award themselves points for – getting Ministers back from holidays, preferably on a Monday, had insisted I come up in order to approve a response to something that had come over from Number 10.

TK is in Scotland and they couldn't get hold of him. Grimly certain that he would have surfaced by the time I got to the building (I've been caught like this so many times in the past), I set off.

But no, he was still incommunicado – the moors, come on – and I was in charge. Charles's queries were all perfectly valid, points about Rules of Engagement, Command Structures, relation to US Command, Air Traffic Control, etc.

---

[1] Saddam Hussein had shown every indication of resisting by force a UN resolution requiring him to evacuate Kuwait.

Unfortunately Simon is away and those in charge of the office are simply not in the same class. Their limp, partially illiterate (as all too easily happens when fusion is attempted of advice from three separate Desks) response would have irritated Charles and infuriated the PM. I sent for the officials.

Robin Hatfield (not bad, but not used to my 'ways') came up immediately, but there were others whom I found less impressive. They muddled up the various Tornado designations, ADV, GR5, etc., and cross-permed them with Harriers.

I spent some time tautening the response, making sure my name was prominent at the start and at points in the text; made it plain that TK was on holiday and (unlike the PM who is also on holiday in Cornwall but *manically* in touch) ungetattable. While they were working it up I had a good meeting with the US chargé, and his younger, gung-ho aide, who nodded when I was speaking. We *must* get uniformity of ROE. It's humiliating, and dangerous, that the RAF should be subject to a legally binding process of hesitation when the Americans and the Saudis can shoot on assumed hostile intent. But officials, and Peter Harding,[1] were cooperative, and pleased with the result. I dashed for the train, confident that the note would be shortly over with Charles.

Negligent boy. You *can't* be too careful, or too suspicious, in this game. I should have made Pat drive me, so as to be on the phone. But the roads are dreadful with holiday traffic at the moment and the train faster. In fact, I shouldn't have left the building at all until the note had gone over. S of S's office, rightly anticipating his wrath, wouldn't transmit until they had succeeded in contacting him, in spite of frequent promptings at my behest.

At lunchtime TK finally surfaced, on a very bad line (as I have already discovered at Eriboll our special high-power secret-agent type portables are defeated by the Scottish Highlands and don't work north of Inverness).

He took, or rather snatched, the helm. Anything to stop AC getting prominence, currying favour. All references to me were deleted and the text watered back down again to conform with Douglas's (i.e., FCO wankers' line) preference.

Immediately I sat down in the office here and drafted a com-

---

[1] Air Marshal Sir Peter Harding, Chief of the Air Staff.

mentary note, based on my original text, for circulation within the Dept. But the real point, of course, was to get it over to Number 10, show that there is someone here with balls, and it's AC.

Then, an unpredictable stumbling block. Again showing that one should (in Mr Gulbenkian's invaluable – but too often disregarded – phrase) *never leave the Bridge.* Isn't that what had landed TK in it? Instead of indulging myself down here I should be camped in the bloody place, with a sleeping bag, interfering in all and sundry.

David Hatcher said that he 'couldn't' deliver it to Number 10.

'Why not, for God's sake? It's only across the road.'

Well, it wasn't appropriate. He couldn't be party to communication with CP 'behind the back of' the Sec of State's office. Sodbollocks. Am I always to be thwarted? Surrounded by nincompoops and inadequates?

Shortly afterwards TK's 'agreed' draft, characteristically turgid and evasive, came through. Jane fortified me. She said Mrs T. *must* see the stronger version. So out I retyped it, on the old Swedish machine in the summer office here, and gave it to Pat who, very loyally and inscrutably, has guaranteed to put it through the door of Number 10 tonight.

She'll have it when she starts – usually five-ish – tomorrow.

Ministry of Defence   *Tuesday, 14 August*

At twenty past eight this morning the phone rang. It was the Downing Street switchboard. 'Mr Clark? Charles Powell wants a word.'

I assumed that it was about the note, but he brushed that aside, though clearly grateful for it.

'The Prime Minister is anxious that a Minister of State should go out to the Gulf immediately, and the fickle finger of fate seems to be pointing at you.'

I was exultant. 'Bugger the fickle finger. I want to be told that I am the PM's personal choice.'

Ass, Clark. Of course he couldn't possibly say that. Just as at the Chequers seminars, I was being extended over and above my actual rank. Charles was tactful.

'It's probably better to aim (sic) to leave tomorrow.'

I rushed back into the kitchen and hugged Jane; I could feel the adrenalin coursing. Was I to be Resident Minister in the Middle East? Macmillan at the Dar al Ayoun?[1]

I had to have a VC 10, ideally *the* VC 10 which the PM uses. I rang him back. And the press statement had to say that I was the Prime Minister's personal emissary.

Yes, I could have *a* VC 10, but for obvious reasons the wording of the statement would have to be carefully drawn.

'If I'm to have the authority I need it must at least say that I am travelling on her instructions.'

Well, yes, that could probably be included. A 'small pool' of reporters should go along, as well.

I telephoned at once to the Private Office, who were pleased and excited thinking, rightly or wrongly, that it was consequent on yesterday's note about which they are now more than a little shame-faced.

I believed that everything was in hand and, having done a lot of shouting, to staff and to civil servants, I took tranquillising therapy. I polished the top of the tallboy in my bathroom, then tidied and arranged the objects that sit there. When I return, they will greet and smile at me. A last rushed bathe while Jane packed my tropical suits and aertex, then back to the station.

In the meantime, however, a drama had been unfolding. TK, finally contacted on the moors, had taken the idea badly.

'I'm not going to have Charles Powell giving orders to my Department without going through me . . . What? Hullo? This is a very bad line', etc., etc.

Jane Binstead was in a bit of a jam, unfortunate female.

Finally:

'I order you to stop these arrangements. I myself am going out there very shortly. I will bring the dates of my departure forward. This is something *I* handle, it's my area. Nothing to do with Procurement. I order you . . . '

'Wha-?'

'I ORDER you to stop all arrangements concerning this proposal.' Bellowing.

---

[1] See AC's letter, 13 March 1989.

Jane unhappily came along the corridor and gave an account of her predicament. After she had returned David, quite making up for his attack of nerves last evening, adroitly and stealthily rang Charles at Number 10, who at once contacted the PM in Cornwall.

What was then actually said to TK, I don't know. But he climbed down.

A little later another note came over, this time direct (a 'top' at last!) to my office, reaffirming the PM's intention.

And still later TK phoned me, all bland. 'I was a bit doubtful, but I've thought it over... Good luck.'

He went on – inaudibly as well as unintelligibly – to express reservations about the press, and 'Publicity'!

I went over to a meeting at the Foreign Office. Nothing that ever happens anywhere must take place without the Foreign Office claiming (at least) foster-parenthood. Tiny room. Diffident officials. W. Waldegrave chairing. All hunka-munka food. No real info. Dominic Asquith, William's Private Secretary, is irritatingly handsome in a very pale suit, pale tie, etc. But already putting on a little too much around the waist. In five years he'll look like Bruce Anderson.

By the time I got back to the office TK had again 'thought it over' (that's one of the advantages of Scotland, I said, it's a wonderful place to think) and said 'NO PRESS'.

Uh? But CP had said he/she had wanted reporters to go along. Once again we had to refer back, and once again he was overruled.

One might think all this would impair my relations with Tom. But he's so rubbery that it just bounces off. He's a true professional. Whatever our feelings may have been during a duel, we are always genial in each other's company. Or am I being too complacent? Is he harbouring terrible resentments?

Who cares? I am off tomorrow on a wonderful adventure.

VC 10 en route   *Sunday, 15 August*

We are all rather congested in the front portion of a *tanker* VC 10 (storage tanks empty, I trust. I can't believe that we are actually flying fuel out to this so fuel-rich region). Every seat, and they are none too comfortable, is taken and 'facilities' are at a level between 'Business' and 'Standard' classes on a civilian flight.

Alas! All our efforts to get the famous 'White' aircraft with its drawing rooms and beautiful linen were to no avail. But we do have tables, rather like the Plymouth train, on which I am writing this note.

Opposite me is VCDS, Vincent,[1] and his two acolytes. He is a very good man. Clear-headed. I first encountered him at Chequers, where he impressed. Beside me David, and a rather congenial man from the FCO, with hooded lids, who is in charge of subversion and 'dirty tricks'.

On the other side of the bay some pressmen – 'Diplomatic Correspondents' (ludicrous title), of whom the *Times* chap, McEwen, seems amiable; and dear Bruce, beaming benignly. I hope that they don't get disappointed. I have given instructions that they be plied with drink at all times.

When first charged with this I wanted to be more contemplative, solitary, classicist. There may still come an opportunity, although the schedule looks ninny-tight. Maddeningly, I couldn't find my Doughty,[2] and I now feel myself becoming a little rattled. This could be due to loss of sexuality (or could be causing it). Travel jitters can sometimes have exactly the opposite effect, and I need to jump on the nearest WAAF. But in any case all the cabin staff on this trip are male.

Abu Dhabi   *Saturday, 18 August*

The palace of the Amir is surely the most extravagant building in which I have ever trod. The whiteness of the Carrara marble (I was reminded of Jim Lees-Milne's anecdote of the rich American lady who, noticing a mousey governess's necklace and inquiring of what it was made (malachite), said, 'Yeah? At home we've got a staircase made of that stuff') the richness and depth of the Savonnerie, the newness and cleanness of all the silks and stuffs, the glistering of the gold, is dazzling.

In Europe, or in the East, palaces have grown over the centuries,

---

[1] Vice Chief of Defence Staff, General Sir Richard Vincent.
[2] *Arabia Deserta* by C. M. Doughty.

acquired their contents at the behest of many different tastes and proprietors. But in the Gulf the palaces of the Sheikhs are *instant*. One huge cheque was written, wham, and there you are.

The only flaw, but in this instance it is an intrusive one, is the weak and hesitant proportion of the staircase. I see that it is ornamental only, as everyone uses the lifts, but it is central to the hall, and the scale is wrong. Better suited to the 1929 Florida villa from which, I would guess, it was copied.

They are cool, these buildings, and I am comfortable in any one of my identical Lesley and Roberts blue suits. Much more of a uniform, in every way more appropriate than the pale 'summer' fabrics, already at 11 a.m. rumpled and sweat-stained, of my entourage. And I am welcome. The Sheikhs are glad to see an English Minister, especially one who smoothly opens the courtesies by saying, 'The Prime Minister has charged me personally with conveying to you, Your Majesty, her very highest expressions of personal regard.'

These old Sheikhs are very wise. And of them all my own preference is, I think, for Sheikh Isa of Bahrain. Such beautiful manners. Such cool and practical judgment. Only very occasionally does he become agitated, shifts in his robes and worry beads appear in his hand. He has a little of Woodie[1] about him (come to think about it, they must be around the same age).

They have come from the desert, these old men, and their fathers fought with Lawrence, with their rag-tag cavalry and camels, against the Turks. I quite see that their new wealth is so abundant, so vastly prolific that they cannot keep a really close eye. What is wealth for, but to improve the quality of life? If hours every day are to be consumed with checking 'books', complaints, rival claims of scheming accountants, then what's the point?

But one or two tiers down lies a whole stratum of parasites, competing, dealing, cutting each other's throats. Everywhere a pudgy 'Crown Prince', café-au-lait smooth, will sit in on conferences, puzzled and fidgety, sometimes in military uniform. He will be his father's favourite. But lurking, too, and occasionally glimpsed, are the lean and hawk-eyed 'nephews'. Expressions burning with ambition and lust.

When we get down to business, it is soon plain that these 'Ruling

---

[1] Ian Woodner: see entry for 12 November, 1990.

Families' are more than a little apprehensive. Iraq, more than any other, is the country of the mob. And was not Baghdad the city where the mob, it seems like yesterday, burst into the Royal Palace and dragged the regent Nuri es Said into the street, cutting out his entrails and pulling him along the gutter, still alive, behind the royal limousine?

So the assistance they hope for is of a specialist kind. Each, in their different way, has asked for a strong detachment, preferably with light armour as well, to protect *them*, personally. Because of course if things really start to disintegrate they couldn't trust even their own bodyguard.

The request is never put so crudely as this. The danger of 'raids' by Iraqi 'Special Forces' is usually the closest they approach to an admission of their real fears. But I understood immediately, and as soon as I did and began to expound on the kind of mix needed they would become excited and pleased.

Free water, of course, open facilities of every kind, special provision for RAF aircrew – and much else. There is no problem with any of these. But it is their own skins that concern them most.

Nor is this a request that should be treated lightly. If the ruling families start to pack up, emigrate to their lodges at Newmarket or Longchamps or, worse, patch up some 'Arab Solution' deal individually with Saddam, as that oily little runt Hussein, the King of Jordan, is openly recommending, then we've had it.

Midnight:
We have landed at Riyadh to take on fuel.

Tom has specifically 'barred' me from going to Saudi, claiming it as 'his' area. But the Ambassador, Alan Monro, a very good man indeed, keen and clever, came out to meet me.

The airfield is half blacked out and we walked, he and I, in the heavy night heat – it must still have been over 85°. I could sense, and occasionally hear, junior officials searching for us. Periodically we stopped, tacit co-conspirators, in the deep dark shadow of a C 140 wing, or took cover behind an undercarriage leg. We were joined by Sandy Wilson,[1] another very good man. Both of them told me that the Americans were going to attack, no doubt about it – but when?

There are F 16s here wingtip to wingtip, and more transport

---

[1] Sandy Wilson: Air Vice-Marshal Sir Andrew Wilson, at that time Commander, British Forces, Arabian Peninsula.

aircraft than I have seen since Wideawake on Ascension Island in 1982. Once a military build-up passes a certain stage battle becomes almost inevitable.

It is the railway timetables of 1914, and the Guns of August.

Albany   *Sunday, 19 August*

I got in to Brize at 3.40 this morning, and drove directly to Saltwood, alternating between Red Boxes (three) and all the Sunday papers. After two hours the back of the Jaguar was a giant rat's-nest of mussed-up newsprint, 'supplements', and official folders.

Home at last! And, again, unscathed.

I changed into softies, ate a big scrambled egg breakfast, lots of coffee, bread and honey; and wandered over to the Garden House to look at the new 'summer' furniture which had been delivered while I was away.

After a very long flight I like always to *oxygenate* by taking a really strenuous walk, expelling the toxins of recycled air and 'petit fours'. But something (thank God) made me first ring the Duty Clerk at Number 10, to check in.

The clerk was crisp, unready to be generous. Sunday was no different from any other day. Worse, in this particular instance, because Mrs Thatcher was due to return from her 'holiday' this evening. He left me in little doubt that she would be expecting my report at the top of her first box.

'But I haven't even typed it out, my handwriting is illegible, there's no secretarial staff at MoD . . . '

'The office facilities here are at your disposal' (*not* calling me 'Minister').

Groan! I thought I'd gorge some of the caviar, take the 2.40. Then realised – providentially, as it turned out – that this would be too tight, so skipped lunch entirely and just made the 1.40. No driver, so walked in warm humid rain from Waterloo to the House where confused and faltering 'Security' men reluctantly emerged to fumble and mutter with bunches of keys. (The police all seem to take Sunday off.) It took me about fifteen minutes actually to get installed in my room.

David had kept the folder, and all my 'green' notes.[1] The whole report had to be written, from scratch, in my hand. *Then* -- but was there time? – transposed into a clear typed text. I was much interrupted by reporters and radio who jangled me at the desk.

Round, finally, at 5.35 in the faithful little Porsche, to Number 10. There I dictated solidly, for over two hours to Sally, leading Garden Girl and brilliant typist and screen operator.

By that time the PM was almost due back from Cornwall. I did *not* want to be caught by her in 'half-change', with the Porsche lending a somewhat frivolous tone to the Downing St car rank, so accelerated away straight after signing the fair copy – except having first rather cruelly but deliberately booked a call to TK through the Downing St switchboard, though not staying to take it. ('What the hell's Alan doing at Number 10 on a Sunday evening?')

Now it is late, and I have been 'on the go' for nineteen hours, or longer if you include the flight. Tomorrow I am to attend a meeting at Number 10 at 9.30; just Hurd and TK besides the PM. The inner, inner group. Anything could happen. But I must thank God. He could have lifted his protection a hundred times in the last eight days.

Ministry of Defence   *Monday, 20 August*

My report was 'On the table'. Both the Lady and Charles congratulated me. But Hurd put in the standard courtesy put-down, 'looking forward to reading it'.

Unless a document has been written by a FCO Minister or, better, filed by one of those useless resident 'diplomats' it's not a real 'report'.

Tipped off that I was attending by, I would guess, Len Appleyard, a former ambassador and now No. Two in the Cabinet Office, Douglas had insisted that Waldegrave also came along. If Tom has a Minister of State with him then the Foreign Office should also field two Ministers. When William appeared there was a certain amount of agitation of a 'the Prime Minister wants to keep this to a very small group' kind. And, at intervals during the meeting, she snarled and spat at him

---

[1] When writing in his own hand on Government papers AC always affected a green pen.

which, in his rather splendid nonchalant way (Etonian education, of course, because I happen to know he actually feels quite rattled), he took in his stride.

At lunchtime I was on the news both going into, and emerging from, Number 10! I do hope Jane saw it at Saltwood.

Ministry of Defence   *Tuesday, 21 August*

I was caught today, had to say 'No, Prime Minister' at the morning's meeting.

The whole thing was a complete set-up. The Foreign Office control the telegram traffic. There was an important telegram referring to a new Resolution of the United Nations, governing our powers of interception on the high seas. Hurd's office kept it until the very last minute, then sent it over to Simon just as (it transpired) we were on the verge of setting out. Naturally nothing came near me.

Consequently when the Lady said, to me, 'Have you seen it?' and I said, 'No', she will have assumed that it was just idleness on my part. Al not doing his homework properly.

One of the oldest tricks in the Civil Service.

Ministry of Defence   *Thursday, 23 August*

Early this morning Tom sent for me. He was bumbustious. Archie should go to these meetings. Of course quite often there was no need for a Minister of State, but if there should be, then obviously it ought to be Archie.

'Quite.'

Tom then, shamelessly, picked my brains for three-quarters of an hour. He's going through one of his terrifically good-form phases, which usually coincide with his having got the better of me.

As soon as I got back to my room I rang Charles. But he had a lot on his mind. 'It's a bit hard to justify giving the Procurement Minister a higher access rating than the Armed Forces Minister at a meeting of this kind.'

Shafted.

Saltwood   *Wednesday, 29 August*

I have been in a vile mood all day, and beastly to Jane.

This fucking Saddam thing has given the AF side of the Dept a renewed *raison d'être*. A war to fight! Whee-ee. As a result everything has gone on hold, the Consolidated Fund 'tap' is unlocked – buy anything, order anything. All great fun, but I sense that those who are opposed to me and what I am trying to do are in the ascendant.

I am 'back in my kennel'. I have a lot of extra approving to do, of emergency procurement. But I am completely excluded from policy meetings (although TK often picks my brains ahead of them). The irony lies in the fact that this is exactly the kind of conflict which my Chequers paper anticipated – but before we are ready for it.

Even my weapons effectiveness test, 'how quickly can it get to, and how able will it be to protect, The Bahrain Causeway?' is eerily prescient.

Saltwood   *Friday, 31 August*

A long day yesterday. I was up at six, took an early train to Cannon St, then drove to Plymouth via Bristol. The picture restorer in Bristol is helping with the huge Duncan [Grant] centrepiece; the enormous canvas of the youth (Present it to the Terence Higgins Trust, Jane said) and the two only slightly less big ones of the ladies playing their lutes. They are good craftsmen but the whole operation now looks like costing more than £20,000 – good money after bad?

I got to Addison Road about three-quarters of an hour late for my surgery and gaga-ly went into the wrong house via the back door, interrupting a solicitor's conference.

'Can I help you?' said a lady, pretty icily.

'No thanks,' I said. 'Oh well, yes. You could move that white BMW that's stopping me putting my car there.'

At the Conservative offices Roy Williams was in charge as Anne is taking her holiday.

'How are you then, Alan, all right?' He always says that, like that. Quite a few times. Is it paranoia, or do I detect a hint of (non-specific) reproach? How very *black* his hair is, and how yellowish-ill his skin seems through the cigarette smoke.

A journalist took a picture of me behind my desk with Roy sitting in as a 'patient', and I thought ruefully of that photo, posed with Veronica (a more fetching 'patient' than dear Roy) that I used in my 1979 Election Address. My hair was glossy brown and I was still wearing those giant halter collars now only sported by Prince Michael of Kent, and Algy Cluff.

'Alan Clark takes a few hours off from the Crisis to deal with constituents' problems . . . '

'Each person has their own crisis with their own problem – it's important for them,' I fed in.

That should be OK.

Then I went down to the Council Chamber to a specially convened 'Policy' committee, where I was somewhat startled at being suddenly told to 'stand' for Ron King who had, it seemed, died in the night.

I recall him as comparing favourably with his Tory counterparts. Genial and shrewd – though always with that somewhat *tight*, suffused bodily appearance that predicates the sudden X.

The meeting was wholly pointless, as far as I could see. Simply an ego trip for the deputy leader while Tom Savery, the titular Tory boss, was away. Mike Lees (how muddlingly ludicrous, infuriating and utterly Plymouthian that the Association Treasurer and active wheel, a very *short* man, should be called Mike *Leaves*, and the chairman of Plymouth's largest private employer, another very short man, should be called Mike *Lees*) read out the text of an internal letter which had already been leaked. Neither of the two committee members, who are also Tory councillors in Sutton, made any attempt to speak to, or to acknowledge me. They get cross when I turn up at these sort of events as it interferes with their dossier of malfeasance.

Their problem is, they don't see how they can quite get rid of me while I'm still a Minister. Their immediate concern is of course the local elections next year when, if they are trounced, they will blame the Government; if they are returned they will delight in recounting how 'on the doorstep' people are saying we'll vote for you, but we're not going to vote Conservative in a General Election.

It was gone six o'clock when I got away. Ravenous, I turned off the motorway, to stop in the Johnnie Crow lay-by[1] where, exhausted, we sometimes took a snack during the campaigns. As I wolfed my Marmite sandwiches I thought, Well, I *am* glad not to be going through all that again.

I know, and they *don't* know. As I think about it I realise I could have only a year left. Relief at last! But I fear that I will be sad to leave the 'tawny male paradise'.

The House is being recalled next week, which will be fun. An occasion. But unlikely, I feel, to compare with 2 April 1982 – the most electric moment that I have ever experienced in that place; or it for many years I suspect, perhaps since 8 May 1940. There is something about the atmosphere, the clarity of purpose, that will be absent.

Because the whole Gulf affair has sunk back into a kind of stalemate, with the wily Saddam paying out the hostages like a salmon line and – God knows how he fixed it – the ghastly Branson 'standing by' with an airliner for his 'mercy mission'. It's been a bad day for those who wish ill of slobs because Ronson and Parnes have *already* (twenty-four hours) been moved to Ford Open where they can loll about making phone calls, playing the market, and sending out to Fortnums for food and drink.

Saltwood   *Saturday, 8 September*

I've done, it seems, what I have managed to bring about in quite a few years since entering politics: just *lose* my summer holiday.

Exceptional circs, of course. But when it happens it's always exceptional circs, of some dimension.

Trouble is, I always fall for the beguiling notion that if you let everyone else go in August you have an easy time while they're away, and are then due a pleasing free period when they all start work.

But it never goes like this, although admittedly I stole a march on

---

[1] Johnnie Crow lay-by: so called after a large and benevolent crow who would perch on driving mirrors and ask for sandwich crusts.

TK with the Gulf trip. The departmental diary is filling up – and with things which I miss at my peril. I am tired, with that late August staleness that only the Alps can remedy. Even as I write this, I am determined to get to the Chalet – if only for forty-eight hrs.

The martins have gathered, chattering urgently, and gone. The swallows are diminishing in number – just a few fussed parents and their second broods. It is grey and breezy. Dead hollyhock leaves lie on the surface of the pool, and the water temperature is below 70°. It won't go back through that band until next May.

Ministry of Defence   *Thursday, 13 September*

There were two boxes in the car, lots of interesting stuff. Pat drove me directly to the Dept and I had to go straight in to a meeting which TK had convened to discuss publicity – his favourite subject – for tomorrow's announcement.[1]

It went on for one and three-quarter hours. I was dry and sardonic. A palpable chill of embarrassment spread across the room when Tom said that he would like a huge montage of a tank behind him, a photo blow-up. The soldiers weren't too keen. But 'I suppose you could wear a flak jacket,' I said.

Laughter, in which, good naturedly, he joined.

I recommended against having an FCO presence. Waldegrave wants to sit on the platform.

'At least make sure he doesn't bring a child.'

Smirks only. Officials aren't meant to laugh (except in Private Office) when one Minister makes a joke about another one.

I am scratchy and ill-tempered. TK consults and asks my advice the *entire* time. On technical questions. And also on strategic and political ones. Before meetings with Generals, before going to Number 10. But in truth, deftly and effectively, he's sidelined me.

If I was really a clever politician I'd lay a trap for him, suddenly and critically give him *bad* advice, watch him get in a twist. But I just can't. It would offend against the Socratic concept.

---

[1] Conveying our participation in the Gulf Force.

Saltwood   *Wednesday, 19 September*

A good example today of how mulishly vindictive is the Tory Party.

David Young's book is out. A kind of memoir, not very well written, which he has called, innocently, *The Enterprise Years*. His publishers staged a party, and took the ballroom at the Savile. But no one – *no one* of his former colleagues turned up except Patrick McLoughlin, who is a nice man but not a card of very high value, having served only a short time under David and in a very junior position.[1]

What are they all so cross about? The book doesn't seem to me to be so very indiscreet, save only for that enjoyable and all too obviously true account of the great panic at Number 10 on 'Wobbly Thursday' when David gripped Norman Tebbit by the lapels and said, 'We're going to lose this fucking Election.'

That, and the attendant whisperings and scamperings on the staircase at Number 10, was all a very good read. This extract was serialised in the *Sunday Times*. But after, I would assume, the guest acceptance list had been published, because they all stayed away.

Of course they were jealous of David, and frightened also, because of his special powers of access to the Prime Minister. Unlike most Peers in the Cabinet, he had never served an apprenticeship in the Commons, with all the hateful and long drawn-out initiation rituals of late votes and constituency pressures. David had not even served as a *junior* Minister. And so once he was down, they kicked him.

But David was very pleasant to work with; clever, and possessing of a quick mind. He had fresh ideas, though was a little too ready to 'devolve' to the private sector; not seeing that this can cheapen the responsibilities of Government in more than one sense.

If David had a fault, a weakness rather, it was that he could become a little nervous when in the company of his superiors in a small room. He would become *over* affable, crack too many jokes, and laugh at them himself, when it would have been better to be icy, and ruthless.

David had set his heart on becoming Chairman of the Party, and indeed when his bandwagon was really rolling anything seemed possible.

---

[1] Patrick McLoughlin, MP for West Derbyshire since 1986 who had been Lord Young's PPS, Trade and Industry, 1988–9. Now Parliamentary Under-Secretary, Transport.

Willie, though, was always doubtful, and stories were spread of 'poor attendance' and 'disrespect' in the Lords. Bertie Denham would brief shamelessly to the Lobby.

What finally brought David down was his picking a quarrel with the Brewers. I had no idea how many Tory MPs are on that payroll until I saw how widespread was the opposition within our own Party. Even big Jim Couchman,[1] a PPS in the DTI, would raise his voice at closed ministerial meetings. It coincided of course, with falling out of favour with her. She was already beginning to transfer her affections (*La Donna é mobilè*) to John Major.

But if you were a sociologist you could say that David was brought down by two traditional strains in the Conservative Party: anti-semitism, and the brewers' lobby.

Saltwood   *Sunday, 21 October*

Bloomsbury evening at Saltwood. We entertained the 'Friends of Charleston'.[2] I don't know what they charged for tickets, but I hope they made money.

I had the brilliant idea of stuffing the Garden House, which has been standing more or less empty since Colette moved out, with all our Bloomsbury 'items'. We hung and distributed everything, thirty-seven in all, plus a good few ceramics, save only the giant Queen Mary Duncans. The whole made a pleasing, and entirely private exhibition.

I made a little speech of welcome, fraudulently and bogusly referring to my father's death 'from a falling tree'. What mischievous impulse made me do this?

Pure Roger Irrelevant. I did just manage to keep a straight face,

---

[1] James Couchman, MP for Gillingham since 1983. His entry in the 1990 Register of Members' Interests included under 'Employment or Office' – Chiswick Caterers Ltd, Adviser to the Gin Rectifiers and Distillers Association. The post of PPS is unsalaried and does not require Members of Parliament to relinquish their outside interests.

[2] A charitable body dedicated to the maintenance of the farmhouse where Duncan Grant and Vanessa Bell had their studio, where Keynes wrote *The Economic Consequences of the Peace*, and Lytton Strachey and others were habitués.

although William, from the far end of the room, gave me an odd look.

We then processed over to the Great Library, rich and enclosing as always on such an occasion, for the performance by Eileen Atkins of Virginia Woolf's essay, 'A Room of One's Own'. How well she did it! And what a beautiful, moving and dignified text it is. The audience listened in a rapt silence and at the end I had tears in my eyes.

Olivier Popham materialised; benign and knowledgeable. I remember her, just, at Portland Place. Very sleek and dark like a young seal. She asked to see Graham's pictures, and chided me gently for selling her portrait which he had painted in 1939, in the great Death Duties sale.[1] I could hardly say, 'I thought you were dead.'

Her big, deliberately common-voiced daughter Cressida, who is famous for 'fabrics', accompanied her. Both showed a true Bloomsbury mocking spirit when confronted by the great Nurnburg 1490 iron safe in the lower hall.

'Is it a Coca-Cola machine? Or a coffee dispenser?'

Another character, gently on the way down, was a blonde, attractively composed, and underdressed, who was in tow behind Professor Skidelsky. She was Victoria Heber-Percy, Robert's daughter and in her day (would it have been the late Sixties?) a great society beauty. She got married to batty, cross, erratic Peter Zinoviev but later, I suppose, got rid of him. The League of Helmet-Makers, Beautiful Wives.

Saltwood   *Sunday, 4 November*

The papers are all very bad. Tory Party falling apart, the death blow,[2] that kind of thing. Something in it, I fear, unless we can get a grip on events. The only person who can restore order in the parliamentary ranks is Tristan. He can do it short-term (like many intelligent people

---

[1] Olivier Popham was the mistress of Graham Bell, who was killed in the RAF in 1943.

[2] Sir Geoffrey Howe had resigned from the Government the previous Thursday, and his resignation speech was awaited with some trepidation.

T. can only see things very long or very short) but that's enough. Get
us past November.[1]

After breakfast I telephoned Chequers.

'The Prime Minister is speechwriting.'

'Who with?'

'Charles Powell.'

'When will she be free?'

'There might be a minute before lunch.'

'When's that?'

'One o'clock sharp.'

I was being kept at bay. Unusual. The Number 10 switchboard
girls are always helpful. With Chequers I've had this problem before.

'Oh well, please pass her my name, in case she wants to take a call
then.'

It was a lovely crisp day of late autumn. I had said I'd join Jane in
the garden. Now I was going to be stuck indoors waiting for a call.
But I had barely got to the doorway to give her a shout when the
phone started ringing.

'Alan . . . '

I tried to cheer her up: 'There's an awful lot of wind about',
'Hold tight and it'll all blow away', 'Geoffrey was past it by now,
anyway.'

I said, with suitable preface, that I would never seek to tell her
who she should employ or why; but that if she could find something
for 'Tim' to do . . .

'Tim who?' (thinking, I suppose, that I wanted her to bring
someone called Tim into the Cabinet. Blast, blast. Too oblique. Never
works with her.)

'Renton. You really ought to make Tristan your Chief Whip.'

A very long silence. I almost said 'hullo', but didn't.

'Oh but he's enjoying his present job so much . . . '

I don't think she realises what a jam she's in. It's the Bunker
syndrome. Everyone round you is clicking their heels. The saluting
sentries have highly polished boots and beautifully creased uniforms.
But out there at the Front it's all disintegrating. The soldiers are

---

[1] November was the month when under the Leadership Rules, a challenger was
permitted to offer himself. Once the month has passed there would be no further
opportunity until the new parliamentary session.

starving in tatters and makeshift bandages. Whole units are mutinous and in flight.

Saltwood   *Sunday, 11 November*

Back from Plymouth with what is, by tradition, the nastiest weekend of the year behind me. The Constituency engagements are dense and unyielding. The surgery is always particularly crowded and irksome. I invariably have a cold, often flu, and the Remembrance ceremonies on the Hoe drag and chill. New, and unwelcome, ecumenical balls caused the service to grate. Some nameless mystic read out words, unintelligible, from an unknown text. Drenching rain.

But at the civilian Memorial a magnificent Grenadier in a bearskin handed me my wreath, and (as I always do) I *hammed* the role, stiffly bowing and clicking. From a corner of the crowd I could see Vera and Tom oggling crazily, but I acknowledged them only with my eyelids.

At last I was free. I climbed into the valiant Little Silver, and drove exhilaratingly fast. A lot of the time I was running up to 120 mph, and the very last home straight on the M20 at a continuous 140. Average speed for the whole journey from the Hoe car park to Saltwood Lodge gates, including fuel stops, contraflow, caravans in Langport, roadwork lights, was 77.8 mph. One of the best ever.

I had no time even to open a newspaper. But now I see that they are all packed with Heseltinia. Plugs of one kind or another. Some, like the *Mail on Sunday* (who had a heavy flirtation with David Owen at one point, I seem to recall), have quite openly changed sides. Every editor is uneasy. In the woodwork stir all those who have lived for the day when they could emerge and have a gloat without fear of retribution.

It looks to me as if Michael is going to get forced into a position, whether he likes it or not, when he'll have to stand. He's cunning and single-minded, yes. But he's also a bit, well, *dyslexic*. Galvanised, jerky movements. On the only two occasions when I have had anything to do with him on matters of policy, I recollect him getting into a great state.

When I was at Employment the question arose of whether a second frigate should be built at Cammell Laird, or at Swan Hunter.

Michael has this infatuation with Liverpool, Merseyside, and it was all bound up with him showing his mettle to the crowd. He gabbled over the phone, was wild-eyed in the lobbies. Apparently threatened to resign. Why not? Get lost, she should have said, *then* give the contract to Cammells.

The second time was, of course, Westlands. I only spoke to him twice, something to do with Bristow's new fleet, quite marginal really, and found him almost off his head with rage and – to my mind – persecution mania.

Ministry of Defence   *Monday, 12 November*

I lunched today with Charlie Allsopp[1] at Christies. He's unsquashable really. 'Sharp' but engaging. He told me that Ian Woodner had died.

Good old Woodie, the auctioneer's friend. He will have been sad not to have outlasted Armand Hammer who was (a lot) richer and (only a little) older.

He loved drawings, and he bought and bought in the closing years of his life, almost as if to prolong his expectancy. He went to prison for a while, as rich people in America sometimes do but, like Eddie Gilbert, was revered by the convicts, whom he helped in those tiny ways which make uneducated people grateful.

I have two clear memories of him. Bidding, implacably, at the Chatsworth sale in the summer of 1984. Some of the stuff was wonderful, worth every penny. Not all, though.

Once Col brought him down to Saltwood and made me set out a lot of drawings, normally kept in the safe, for his edification. Woodie was silent in the main, and stroked his moustaches. He made a half-hearted show of interest in the Renoir Circus girls; but the only piece that really excited him was the Quail and Lute. In the Catalogue Raisonée[2] I showed him the entry *Locativa Incognita*, and he became agitated.

Not only did Woodie have taste, but he was an accomplished artist in his own right, modelling himself on, and being obsessed by, Odilon

---

[1] Charles Allsopp, Chairman of Christie's since 1986.
[2] Of the work of Giovanni da Udine.

Redon. He once threw a huge dinner party at Claridges, taking the entire dining room and, at the end of the meal, he delivered one of the most moving personal testaments of the meaning of art, and draughtsmanship, to which I have ever listened.

On the way out Charlie showed me into the room where the English furniture for the next 'important' sale was accumulating. A *quite* nice cabinet, bow-fronted, was offered up, faded walnut and marquetry.

'Did you know Billy Wallace? It came from his widow.'

Poor Liz! So pretty and bejewelled as a smart-set groupie when we were all at Oxford. She must be in her mid-fifties, and childless. And Billy, too. Whom I remember meeting and half hero-worshipping at Lavington in 1945 when he had an old SS 1 with a blown exhaust, and drove about at night. Two years ago he died from cancer of the mouth. What a lot of people I've seen 'out'. And still I prance.

I came back here, but couldn't concentrate, and strolled over to the House. We are on the verge of great events. Wild rumours are circulating about the leadership 'contest' for which nominations close on Thursday. Today's favourite is that there just won't *be* a contest this year.

'Too close to the Election, old boy. Frozen.'

This has to be balls.

The Whips have totally clammed up. A bad sign. Already they have gone into 'neutral' mode. Secret policemen burning the old files, ready to serve.

The ballot would, should, be on Tuesday of next week. Only eight days to go and I have a dreadful feeling – not all the time, but in waves – that Heseltine will stand, and that he will win. I haven't communicated this to anyone. No one at all. But I wish Ian was alive.

House of Commons   *Tuesday, 13 November*

The Party is virtually out of control. Mutinous. People are not turning up for divisions. Dissidents get bolder and bolder with their little off-the-cuff TV slotettes. Code is abandoned. Discipline is breaking up. Geoffrey will make his resignation speech this afternoon, and apparently the entire text is the work of Elspeth. Received wisdom is that this will finally tear the whole thing wide open.

But why should it? Who gives a toss for the old dormouse? Yet I suppose on the Berkeleian principle, if everyone thinks something is important, then it is important.

After Ministers this morning I signalled Andrew MacKay[1] to come into my room. He is so shrewd, he really knows the Party as well as any Whip. Why has he twice refused an invitation to join the Office?

We agreed that the situation is serious, very serious. It's the arithmetic that looks so nasty. There is this *bolus* of wankers, mainly in the North, who are fearful of losing their seats, and will try anything. Elizabeth Peacock:[2] 'We can't be any worse off than what (sic) we are.' Add this to Michael's own claque, itself at least fifty because adhering to it is the whole *Salon des Refusés*, plus all those like Charlie Morrison who have always loathed her, and before you know where you are you're dam' close to 150. Then, there is the considerable body of the soft optioneers, the abstentions. 'An honourable protest.' Crap on every side.

What a lot of people don't realise is that if we get a bad result, closeish figures, she will be hamstrung.

One can write Hugo Young, Peter Jenkins, Robin Oakley,[3] all those who've been waiting for this moment, off the top of one's head. Broaden the Government; must think very long and hard about policy; Heseltine must enter the Cabinet; 'effectively Number Two'; the death-knell of Thatcherism – the clichés, leavened by spite, will roll.

At mid-day I had a meeting with Peter Levene. He told me that at the Lord Mayor's banquet last night she was greeted with virtually complete silence. She started punchily, then got flatter and flatter. I've seen her do this in the past. If the punchy bits don't get them going she reverts to text, and only rarely (Conference being one of the exceptions) are her texts any good.

We are at present in a state where any news, however slight and tenuous, spreads like wildfire if it is damaging. The effect is cumulative, and reinforces doubters, sceptics who need an excuse for transferring loyalties. 'She's virtually lost all support outside, you know . . . '

I change my own mind by the hour. In some ways it would be better for her to go completely than to hang on mutilated, forced to

---

[1] Andrew MacKay, MP for Berkshire East since 1983. PPS to Tom King.
[2] Elizabeth Peacock, MP for Batley and Spen since 1983.
[3] Columnists Hugo Young (*Guardian*) and Peter Jenkins (*Independent*); Robin Oakley (Political Editor, *The Times*).

take in a Trojan Horse. But she has not got the nature to make a withdrawal to Colombey, and for that course it is now really too late. We're down to ensuring that Heseltine doesn't win in a stampede. And Douglas, who could play a role here, is deeply reluctant.

Later

I forced my way along the Minister of State's bench, stopping two places short of Janet [Fookes], who always sits, massively, in the camera-hogging spot just behind the PM. The House was very full indeed, with much chattering and giggling from recusants. The loyalists are glum, and apprehensive.

From the moment he rose to his feet Geoffrey got into it. He was personally wounding – to a far greater extent than mere policy differences would justify. Elspeth's hand in every line.

All those Cabinets (seven *hundred* he said) when the Lady had lashed and basted him (there too, it must be admitted, more savagely than could be explained by nuances of attitude. But it was to a smaller audience and did not, I think, start until about three years ago). In his mind he will also have been carrying the brutal briefing on the 'non-existent' role of Deputy Prime Minister, the messing-around over the houses. It all seethed and bubbled in the cauldron.

The Labour benches loved it. Grinning from ear to ear they 'Oooh'd' and 'Aaah'd' dead on cue. At one point he illustrated his sense of betrayal with some cricketing analogy, being 'sent in to bat for Britain . . . only to find that before the game the bats have been broken by the team captain'. Everyone gasped and I looked round to catch Jonathan's eye. He had that special incredulous look he occasionally gets, mouth open.

Geoffrey ended his speech with an ominous, and strange, sentence: 'I have done what I believe to be right for my Party and for my Country.' (They all say that.) 'The time has come for others to consider *their own response* to the tragic conflict of loyalties with which I myself have wrestled for perhaps too long.'

Afterwards a lot of people, semi-traumatised, didn't want to talk about it. The atmosphere was light-headed, almost.

I spoke with Norman Lamont. He very naively ('I can see *you* weren't at Eton,' I said) questioned whether any member of the Government – not Cabinet, *Government* – could vote against her on the first ballot. 'Quite monstrously disloyal,' etc.

Afterwards I thought maybe it was a plant. You can't trust anyone at present.

We were joined by Tebbit. Wildish and gaunt he seemed. He mouthed a bit about a special role he was going to play; he had been in close touch with Peter M., and so on. Interestingly, he said we must *not* go for a compromise candidate. We must fight all the way, to the death.

This appeals to me. Leonidas at Thermopylae. But we don't win. It's the end of me. I came in with her. I go out with her.

House of Commons   *Wednesday, 14 November*

A curious state of limbo. Briefly, and unaccountably, the House has gone quiet. Many are leaving early for their constituencies to take the temperature.

The papers are terrible. The Lady is said to be 'foundering'; 'holed below the waterline'; 'stabbed'; 'bowled middle stump', and similar far from original metaphors. Much worse than Westland. There are even rumours (in the press, I can find no trace of them in the corridors so it may be a plant by Mates or Hampson[1]) that Cranley Onslow is going to advise her not even to *contest* the election.

Perfectly ridiculous. No one seems to have given a thought to the constitutional implications, still less the international. How can a narrow caucus in a singular political party unseat a Prime Minister just because it calculates that it may improve its election prospects thereby?

Tristan rang from his car. He's driving in from Heathrow, just back from some pointless and diverting voyage when he should be tirelessly cigaretting at the very centre of things here. Counting and calculating and ordering our deployment. Naturally he was *very* against NT's idea of a 'last stand'. He thinks he can fudge up a solution that will keep H out.

'Of course,' I said. 'If it works.'

'It's got to fucking work,' he answered.

Exciting, but unnerving, times.

---

[1] Dr Keith Hampson, MP for Leeds North-West since 1983 (Ripon 1974–83). PPS to Michael Heseltine, 1979–84. Before becoming an MP he was a personal assistant to Edward Heath in the 1966 and 1970 General Elections.

Saltwood   *Saturday, 17 November*

I have been listless and depressed most of the day, with ill-at-ease tummy. Perhaps I drank too much in Denmark.[1] But it was mainly Schnapps. Poisoned on the aircraft, more likely. The papers are terrible. Only exceptions being the leader of the *Daily Telegraph*, and Paul Johnson.

Everything else is tipping Heseltine. Bandwagon. And the five o'clock news was even worse. Heseltine doing this, doing that; going down (or up) escalators; leaving (or arriving at) his house. And all the time with that uneasy, almost Wilsonian smirk. But among Conservatives *in the country* she still has majority support. Alison, who is sensible, remains a fervent fan. 'What *are* you all doing?'

The Lady herself is away, out of the country. It's absolute madness. There is no Party mileage whatever in being at the Paris summit. It just makes her seem snooty and remote. And who's running the campaign? Who's doing the canvassing? Who's putting the pressure on?

I became more and more dejected, decided to telephone Tristan. He attempted to calm me, said that Peter Morrison was in charge of collating the votes, that he was calmly confident. But when pressed Tristan shared my scepticism as to whether this was really the true picture.

He launched into some dissertation as to how Douglas (who will be in Paris with the PM, about to go into a Banquet – shades of Potsdam) and John Major (who will – for God's sake – be in *hospital*, having just had four teeth taken out) will speak to each other in that first critical hour between 6 and 7 p.m. on Tuesday and, it is to be hoped, settle what should happen next.

I don't like the sound of this. It will be Halifax, Churchill and George VI, and they may decide who runs. In which case, *passim* Halifax, Douglas will probably stand aside. We're then left with John Major who, being calm and sensible, is infinitely preferable to that dreadful charlatan, H. But John is virtually unknown, too vulnerable to the subtle charge of 'not yet ready for it'.

He has personal handicaps, not of his own making. The product, indeed of his virtues. He's not at all *flash*, and a lot of colleagues think

---

[1] AC had been in Copenhagen for an IEPG meeting.

it's flash that we need at the moment. And he's not classy, which doesn't worry me in the slightest, but worse, he doesn't (like Mrs T.) even *aspire* to be classy.

Pinkish toffs like Ian [Gilmour] and Charlie [Morrison], having suffered, for ten years, submission to their social inferior see in Michael an arriviste, certainly, who can't shoot straight and in Jopling's damning phrase 'bought all his own furniture', but one who at any rate seeks the cachet. While all the nouves in the Party think he (Michael) is the real thing.

'Look,' I said. 'All these arguments are being tossed around on the assumption that we have to go to a second ballot.'

'That's right, Baby.' (A strange affectation of Tristan's, calling me 'Baby'. I don't mind, but I do know from experience that it usually presages some piece of news which I am not going to like.)

An appalling thought struck me. Michael couldn't actually *win* first time round, could he? I put the question convolutedly. 'Do you think it more likely than not that he won't get a majority in the first ballot?'

'Yes.'

'Do you put the odds on this happening at worse than (longish pause) sixty per cent?'

'No.'

This is terrible. He's barely worse than evens.

Did I start gabbling? I don't remember. Tristan cut through it saying if there was any 'uncertainty' (good neutral word for the tapes) a group of us are to meet at Catherine Place after the 10 p.m. vote that evening.

I remain deeply anxious that The Establishment simply hasn't got the machinery, or the people, in place to operate effectively in that very narrow timescale.

I went down to the Winter Office, and drew up a little table showing the three alternatives. There are only three, none of them other than bad, though in varying degree, for me.

1) The PM survives, but maimed. The wind-down period, perhaps to a Gentlemen's Coup in the spring. This is the best one can hope for, and would at least give me time to make some plans. I suppose it is just possible, by a combination of luck and circumstance such as she has enjoyed in the past, for her to make a gargantuan effort of 'projection', dump the Poll Tax, win the war, call a khaki election at once (it'd be nearly four years, after all) and once again be mother of

her people. Certainly that is what I would advise. But good though she is, she's not in the shape of 1983, or even 1986 when she routed them over Westland.

2) It's A.N. Other, after a messy second ballot. Either Douglas or John Major would keep me, I'm pretty sure. Fun to watch a new administration getting the feel of things, but I would no longer be on the inner loop.

3) MH wins. Sudden Death. He might even have time to strike me off the PC list. Would anyone else refuse to serve? Cecil, I would think. Micky Forsyth[1] and Eric Forth[2] certainly ought to. Peter Lilley and the rest would just cower until he sacked them.

That's Politics (Baby).

House of Commons   *Monday, 19 November*

The whole house is in ferment. Little groups, conclaves everywhere. Only in the dining room does some convention seem to have grown up (I presume because no one trusts their dining companions) that we don't talk 'shop'.

'Made your Christmas plans yet?' All that balls. God, the dining room is boring these days, even worse than Pratts'. Big, slow, buffers 'measuring their words' oh-so-firmly; or creepy little narks talking straight out of *Conservative News*.

But in the corridors it is all furtive whispering and glancing over shoulders. The institutional confidence (seen at its most obvious in those who have served a prison term, and which I first noticed in my early days on Warren Street[3]), that special grimacing style of speech out of the corner of the mouth, eyes focusing in another direction, is now it seems the only way of communicating.

Most people are interested – not so much in the result, as in knowing what the result will be in advance, in order to make their

---

[1] Michael Forsyth, MP for Stirling since 1983. Minister of State, Scottish Office, since 1990.

[2] Eric Forth, MP for Mid-Worcestershire since 1983. Parliamentary Under-Secretary, Employment.

[3] AC worked as a dealer's runner in Warren Street (at that time the focus of the trade market in used cars) for several months after coming down from Oxford.

own 'dispositions'. To ingratiate oneself with the new regime – *a* new regime, I should say, because the outcome is by no means certain – even as little as a week before it is installed, looks better than joining the stampede afterwards. The issue, which can be discussed semi-respectably, is who is most likely to deliver victory at the General Election? But it is packaging, conceals a great basket of bitterness, thwarted personal ambition, and vindictive glee. Talk of country, or loyalty, is dismissed as 'histrionics'.

And there is a strange feeling abroad. Even if the Lady wins – and here I am writing 'even if', pull yourself together Clark, say 'even after she's won' – there will be no escaping the fact that at least one hundred and fifty of her parliamentary colleagues will have rejected her leadership. That's a big chunk. Some people, particularly those who pose as Party Elders, like Tony Grant,[1] are intimating that it might be 'better' if, faced with so blatant a show of No Confidence, she decided to 'heal' the Party by announcing her intention to stand down at a given date (i.e., become a lame duck which the Labour Party could taunt and torment on every occasion, and a busted flush internationally).

And as the savour of a Heseltine victory starts to pervade the crannies and cupboards and committee rooms, so more and more people are 'coming out'. 'Oh, I don't think he'd be so bad, really...' 'He's got such a wide *appeal*.' 'My people just love him, I must say...' 'I know what you mean, but he'd be so good at dealing with...' (fill in particular problem as appropriate).

Most conspicuous in canvassing are Hampson (loonily) Mates (gruffly) and Bill Powell[2] (persuasively). Michael himself is quite shameless in offering all and sundry what they have always wanted. For example, he would probably have got Paul's support anyway, but 'sealed' it with an assurance that Paul would be Speaker in the next House; Soames fell straight away for the 'your talents are long overdue for recognition' line, as did little Nelson[3] and Rhodes James ('you've been treated abominably').

Michael stands in the centre of the Members' lobby, virtually challenging people to wish him good luck. He gives snap 'updates' to

---

[1] Sir Anthony Grant, MP for Cambridgeshire South-West since 1983 (Harrow Central, 1964–83).
[2] William Powell, MP for Corby since 1983.
[3] Anthony Nelson, MP for Chichester since 1974.

journalists, and greets suppliants who are brought along for a short audience by his team. The heavier targets he sees in his room. The Cabinet play their cards close to the chest, although Mellor,[1] apparently, speaks to Michael twice a day on the telephone. Some, like Kenneth Clarke, want her out so badly that they don't need even to blink. And I would guess that there are a fair coterie of Ministers of State and Parly Secs like Sainsbury[2] and Trippier[3] who feel uneasy with the Lady and like the idea of a change.

At the top of the ministerial staircase I ran into G-J. He was bubbling with suppressed excitement. I don't think he actually wants 'Hezzy' as he (spastically) calls him, to win. It would be disruptive of the Blue Chip long-term plan. But he's high on the whole thing.

Tristan said, 'Of course every member of the Cabinet will vote for the Prime Minister in the first round.' Like hell they will.

I said to him, hoping he'd deny it, 'One cannot actually exclude the possibility that Heseltine will score more votes than her on the first ballot.'

'No, I'm afraid one can't.'

'Can one, even, be completely sure that he will not get both the largest total and the necessary margin to win without a second ballot?'

'No, I'm afraid one can't.'

This was really chilling. Apocalypse. Because time is horrendously tight if we have to organise an alternative candidate. Four working days and a weekend. But if Michael scoops it in one gulp then that is the end of everything.

Maddeningly, I had to return to the Department. Meetings, and an official lunch. Scandinavians.

'I assume that there is no likelihood of Mrs Thatcher being defeated for the position of Prime Minister?'

'Oh no. None whatever. It's just one of these quaint traditions we have in the Conservative Party.'

But the encounter made me realise the enormity of what we're doing – *changing the Prime Minister* – but without any electoral

---

[1] David Mellor, Minister of State, Home Office, since 1989.
[2] Tim Sainsbury, MP for Hove since 1973, at that time a Parliamentary Secretary at the Foreign Office.
[3] David Trippier, MP for Rossendale since 1979. Minister of State, Department of Environment, since 1989.

authority so to do. I thought I'd have a talk to Peter,[1] although he
doesn't encourage it, and I cancelled my early afternoon engagements
and went back over to the House.

I listened outside the door. Silence. I knocked softly, then tried
the handle. He was asleep, snoring lightly, in the leather armchair,
with his feet resting on the desk.

Drake playing bowls before the Armada and all that, but I didn't
like it. This was ten minutes past three in the afternoon of the most
critical day of the whole election. I spoke sharply to him. 'Peter.'

He was bleary.

'I'm sorry to butt in, but I'm really getting a bit worried about
the way things are going.'

'Quite all right, old boy, relax.'

'I'm just hearing bad reactions around the place from people
where I wouldn't expect it.'

'Look, do you think I'd be like this if I wasn't entirely confident?'

'What's the arithmetic look like?'

'Tight-ish, but OK.'

'Well, what?'

'I've got Michael on 115. It could be 124, at the worst.'

'Look, Peter, I don't think people are being straight with you.'

'I have my ways of checking.'

'Paul?'

'I know about Paul.'

'The Wintertons?'[2]

'The Wintertons, funnily enough, I've got down as "Don't
Know's".'

'What the fuck do you mean, "*Don't Know*"? This isn't a fucking
street canvas. It's a two-horse race, and each vote affects the relative
score by two, unless it's an abstention.'

'Actually, I think there could be quite a few abstentions.'

'Don't you think we should be out there twisting arms?'

'No point. In fact it could be counter-productive. I've got a theory
about this. I think some people may abstain on the first ballot in order
to give Margaret a fright, then rally to her on the second.' (Balls, I
thought, but didn't say.)

---

[1] Peter Morrison was in charge of Mrs Thatcher's campaign.
[2] Nick Winterton, MP for Macclesfield since 1971, and his wife Ann, MP for
   Congleton since 1983.

'What about the '92? They're completely rotten. They've got a meeting at six. Are you going?'

'No point. But I think *you* should.'

In deep gloom I walked back down Speaker's corridor. It can't really be as bad as this can it? I mean there is absolutely no oomph in her campaign *whatsoever*. Peter is useless, far worse than I thought. When he was pairing Whip he was unpopular, but at least he was crisp. Now he's sozzled. There isn't a single person working for her who cuts any ice at all. I know it's better to be feared than loved. But these people aren't either. And she's in Paris. '*Où est la masse de manoeuvre? -Aucune.*'

I went into the members' tea room. The long table was crowded with Margaret supporters, all nonentities except for Tebbit who was cheering people up. Much shouting and laughter. Blustering reassurance. Norman was saying how unthinkable it was to consider dismissing a Prime Minister during a critical international conference. 'Like Potsdam in 1945,' I said. No one paid any attention. If they heard they didn't, or affected not to, understand the allusion.

The crowd thinned out a little and when he got up Norman said that he wanted a word. We went into the Aye lobby and sat at that round table in the centre with all the stationery on it.

'Well ... ?'

'It's filthy,' I said.

'It could be close. Very close.'

I agreed, '*Fucking* close.'

'If it's like that do you think she should stand in the second ballot?'

I simply don't know the answer to this. Governing would be very difficult with half the Party against her. She might have to make 'concessions' to the left. I asked Norman if he thought she would have to bring Heseltine into the Cabinet?

'She'd certainly be under a lot of pressure to do so.'

'Renton.'

'Yeah.'

I said that the key tactic was to get Chris Patten to stand, and draw off the left vote. At least the hard left vote, Charlie Morrison, Bob Hicks,[1] all the wankers. Norman said, 'And Ken Clarke.' I told him no, if you have too many candidates people just get in a muddle and

---

[1] Robert Hicks, MP for Cornwall South-East since 1983 (Bodmin, 1970–March 1974; October 1974–83).

Heseltine walks through them, just as she did in 1975. Norman said that a lot of people now regarded Michael as a *right*-wing candidate anyway.

'Well, we know different.'

'Too true.'

Norman said, 'If it's open season, I'm dam' well going to put my name in. The right must have a candidate they can vote for.'

'You'd lose.'

'It's likely I would, but at least we'd know our strength. That could be useful in a changed situation.'

'Look, Norman, we want to put additional names in to reduce *his* total, not ours. I don't think Heseltine has that big a personal vote. It's just an anti-Margaret coalition.'

I could see he was thoughtful. But he didn't want to prolong the conversation, which we were conducting in tones just above a whisper, though still arousing the curious attention of passers-by.

Raising his voice Norman said, 'Well, this time tomorrow everything will be settled,' and gave one of his graveyard cackles.

The '92 meeting was in one of those low-ceilinged rooms on the upper committee room corridor. The mood was tetchy, and apprehensive. There was a kind of fiction running from several (Jill Knight, for example, shockingly), just as Norman had foreseen, that 'Michael' – as defectors call him (supporters of the Prime Minister always refer to him as 'Heseltine'; and this is quite a useful subliminal indicator of how the speaker is going to vote when he or she is being deliberately or defensively opaque) – was 'really' on the right.

The trouble with this club, to which I was elected almost as soon as I arrived here, but with which I have never really felt comfortable, is that it personifies in extreme form two characteristics found in the majority of MPs – stupidity and egomania. It is only the shrewd and subtle guidance of George Gardiner[1] that has prevented them becoming a laughing stock in recent years. But such integrity as they might originally have possessed has been eroded by the inclusion of many from marginal seats. None are quite as awful as Elizabeth

---

[1] Sir George Gardiner, MP for Reigate since 1974. Secretary of '92.

Peacock, who spoke squatly and fatly against Margaret – why bother, she won't be here in the next Parliament anyway[1] – but most are concerned solely with saving their own skins. I spoke loyally and, should have been movingly, of our debt of loyalty to the PM. But there was a hint of what's-she-ever-done-for-us from the audience and with some justification, so few ministerial appointments having come out of the '92. I tried to make their flesh creep with what Michael would do, got only a subdued ritual cheer when I said Margaret is undefeated, and never will be defeated either in the Country or in this House of Commons. I'm not particularly popular with that lot. They think I'm 'snooty'. Perhaps my boredom threshold shows. But in the ballot tomorrow I'd say they will divide no better than 60/40.

After dinner I had a word with Norman Lamont. He'd just come back from somewhere-or-other. 'I don't like the smell,' he kept saying. 'There's a bad smell to the whole place.' He's right, of course. It's the smell of decay. It's affecting everything, the badge messengers, the police, the drivers. Something nasty is going to happen.

I write this very late, and I am very tired. Perhaps I'm just needlessly depressed. I'd ring the Lady if I could, but she's at a banquet. She's not even coming back for the ballot. Lovely and haughty.

Albany   *Tuesday, 20 November*

I was at my desk in MoD early, but spent most of the first hour scanning the newspapers. At nine o'clock Carla Powell rang. 'We must do something about poor Bruce.[2] Couldn't you ring Conrad Black, and get him to give Bruce back his job?'

I told her that we were all in limbo. No one, not even Mrs T. herself could today cut any ice at all with anyone.

'Poor Bruce. It's so unfair.'

Yes, yes. I quite agree, it's awful. Everything's awful. It was a little

---

[1] In fact the prediction by AC was in the result shown to be defective. In the 1992 General Election she retained her seat by a margin of 1408.

[2] Bruce Anderson, columnist on the *Sunday Telegraph*, had been fired following an alleged breach of confidential information.

foretaste, the first one, of how diminished how deprived of influence and access we are all soon to become.

Of course I write this very late on the night, in the full knowledge and shock of what has happened. But I think that even this morning we, those of us who can *feel* these things, were despondent, fatalistic.

I worked for most of the morning and had lunch, a long-standing engagement with Robert Campling.[1] Hard to get further away from politics than that. Alison brought him down to the Strangers' tearoom, and the three of us talked about his ideas for Bratton, about Charleston, and Bloomsbury matters in general.

The afternoon hung interminably. Labour MPs were everywhere, ghoulish and heavy-handed with their jokes. Our fellows seemed all to be in hiding.

As is my style at all 'counts' I went up to the committee floor very late. A huge crowd in the corridor. The entire lobby, TV teams from all over the world. (How did they get in, pray – all part of the general breakdown of order and discipline which is licking, like stubble fire, at everything in the Palace these last two days.)

There was, inevitably, a balls-up over the figures. We, the Tory MPs, packed tight and hot and jumpily joking to each other in the committee room, did not (a monstrous error by Cranley Onslow, for which he will pay at the next election[2]) get the figures first. We heard a loud noise, something between a gasp and a cheer, from outside the door, as the journalists digested first the closeness of the result, then the killer element – that there had under the rules to be a second ballot.

Four votes, that was all there was in it. I get so cross when I remember Peter Morrison asleep in his office. For want of a nail a kingdom was lost.

I dined with Jonathan Aitken and Nick Budgen. Bruce was at the table. To my amazement they were all confident. 'She'll wipe the floor with him next time round.' 'The abstainers will all come in.' 'You don't understand, Alan, all those people who wanted to give her a fright, they'll support her now she's up against it.'

---

[1] Robert Campling, a young artist who paints in the Bloomsbury style and whom AC had commissioned to redecorate certain rooms at Bratton.

[2] The error was to give the voting figures to the press first. At the next election for the chairmanship of the 1922 Committee Onslow was defeated by Sir Marcus Fox.

How can people get things so wrong?

Perhaps there was a lot of this kind of muddled thinking around before the ballot. But that's historic. She's a loser, now. Doomed.

I hardly bothered to argue with them. I suppose my dejection was infectious because, by the coffee, we were all silent. Save Bruce who, although jobless, is going to shut himself away and do a Randolph,[1] an instant book on the leadership campaign.

At the ten o'clock vote Tristan found me in the lobby, pulled me into the window bay by the writing table. 'We're meeting at my house, straight after this.'

'Who's "we"?'

'Oh just a few mates; *Chris* and people. We need to talk through the next steps.'

'How do you mean?'

'Ways of supporting the Prime Minister.'

But he wouldn't accede to any of my suggestions; Aitken, Maude, David Davis[2] or Lilley, in that order. Even Andrew MacKay (not obviously of the right, as were the others) caused Tristan to pull a long face.

'We're all friends. It's a very small gathering, we all know each other and can speak freely . . . '

As soon as I walked into the room it was apparent why no one else from the right had been allowed in. 'Blue-Chips' wall-to-wall. Five Cabinet Ministers. Rifkind, who was the most dominant, and effective; C. Patten, also good but (relatively) taciturn; Newton, and Waldegrave.

Waldegrave was sympathetic, in a relaxed, jokey way. The only person to say what a personal tragedy it was for her, how she was still of a different dimension to all the others. Lamont was there, stood throughout, Mephistophelean in his black tie. He shocked me by saying at the outset that he could conceive of Michael as being quite an 'effective', *tolerable* (sic) Prime Minister.

Patten said, 'Well, he's not mad, is he? I mean after you've had a

---

[1] In 1963 Randolph Churchill wrote *The Fight for the Tory Leadership: A Contemporary Chronicle* (Heinemann) an account of the way in which the Conservative Party selected Lord Home as leader following the resignation of Harold Macmillan.

[2] David Davis, MP for Boothferry since 1987. PPS to Eric Forth, Parliamentary Under-Secretary, DTI.

meal with him you don't get up from the table and think, that fellow was mad, do you?'

There were three Ministers of State in the room, besides myself, Hogg and John Patten. Tim Yeo[1] was there 'representing' Hurd, whose PPS he is, but stayed silent.

Douglas Hogg piped up, 'I think any one of us could serve under him [Michael].' And there was a sort of cautious mumble of assent. What I assume he meant, of course, was, 'I don't think any one in this room is likely to be sacked – so we can all enjoy ourselves.' Mutual preening took place.

I said it wasn't quite as easy as that. What we had to ensure was that the person who replaces her is the one most likely to win the Election.

'All right, then, Al; what do you think?'

Michael was unreliable, I argued. Any electoral capital he brought would soon be expended. What we needed now was a Baldwin, someone to reassure rather than stimulate. I expanded, people were nodding. But when I said Tom King, Chris Patten laughed aloud. And John P., taking his cue, said, 'I presume you're joking.'

Tristan said, 'Come on, Al, you'll have to do better than that.'

Only Douglas Hogg, surprisingly, admitted that he saw the point.

I had one more go. I did *not* say that Tom was Willie's choice as well as mine. That might have generated a class backlash. But I dwelt on his overall departmental experience in Northern Ireland, how good he was on the stump, as I had often seen.

Yet as I was speaking it dawned on me that winning the Election was not uppermost in all their minds. They were, most of them, twenty years younger than me, carving out their own career prospects and wanting to identify with the new winner.

Not only was there no one of my generation, there was no one (although Richard, who is a Norfolk Squire, came in very much later) of my background. There was no one, except possibly Tris, who understands and loves the Tory Party for all its faults, knows it as an old whore that has been around for 400 years.

Young Turks. And Young Turks are bad news, unless there is some dilution. They all poke fun at Tom now. But if he became Prime Minister, assumed the authority, he could metamorphose and

---

[1] Tim Yeo, MP for Suffolk South since 1983. He had been PPS to the Foreign Secretary since 1989.

put them all in irons. The old Postman in Remarque's *All Quiet*...

Although I had been expecting Tristan to try and rig it for John Major, the concensus did in fact build up quite rapidly for Douglas. I remained doubtful. He is *too* much of an Establishment candidate.

Of course, this is a crisis for the Establishment, and they have left it horrendously late to organise. But DH looks, speaks, moves, articulates as prototypical Establishment. I'm not sure the Party wants that. It's very risky, unless there is another candidate from the left who will peel off a tranche of Heseltine's total.

It is difficult. If we confine the contest to two candidates, the issues are starker. If there are more than two there will be some cross-transferring, but there remains a danger that Michael's core vote will be strong enough – just as she herself (opposed by the Establishment) was in 1975. Never mind the abstruse calculations according to the 'Rules', the third ballot is a foregone conclusion. Whoever gets the highest total next time, wins.

It was only when I got back here, at ten minutes to one a.m. that it dawned on me: at least five of the people in that room fancied themselves as 'New Generation' candidates, in the nearish future. They want Douglas, but *as a caretaker.* They're not quite ready, themselves. As we were breaking up one – it could have been William – actually said, 'If we put John in, he'll be there for twenty-five years.'

The really sickening thing, though, was the urgent and unanimous abandonment of the Lady. Except for William's little opening tribute, she was never mentioned again.

Albany   *Wednesday, 21 November*

This is going to be – politically – The Longest Day. I woke very early, in spite of having gone to bed at twenty past one, and with a restless energy matched only by that on the February morning in 1986 when I knew that at last I had escaped from the DE and was to be appointed Minister for Trade. Yet today it is the exact reverse. Not only my own prospects, but the whole edifice which we have constructed around the Lady, are in ruins.

It's quite extraordinary. Fifteen years have gone by and yet those very same people – Dykes, Charlie Morrison, Tony Grant, Barney Hayhoe[1] – who have always hated her and the values she stood for, are still around in the lobbies, barely looking any different, grinning all over their faces – 'At last we've got her.'

I can't think of a single anti-Thatcherite who has died or receded throughout that entire period.

By 6.30 my tea was cold and I had read the papers. Still an assumption, in some columns, that Michael will be defeated in the second ballot – but by whom?

Always remember what she did in '75; all that shit about now its 'really' going to be Willie, or Jim Prior,[2] or you name it. The Party may be just entering on one of its periodic bouts of epilepsy.

I put a call through to Paris. They're one hour ahead, and I wanted to interrupt the pre-breakfast conference. Peter came on the line. I said I must have two minutes with her. Charles would have always put me through. So would Bernard. He gave me the usual runaround. Frightfully tied up just at this minute, try and fit it in before we go down to breakfast . . .

'Go *down* to? Don't you have it in the room?'

'There's a Working Breakfast.'

'With a lot of fucking foreigners, I suppose. I want to talk to her about last night.' I gave him a (selective) résumé of events at Catherine Place.

'I'll try and call you back.'

'When?'

'Well, within half an hour.'

'Peter, you will tell her I rang, won't you?'

'Yes, yes. Yes.'

'Because if you tell her, she will call me. And if she doesn't call me, I'll know it's because you haven't told her.'

High-pitched giggle. 'Don't worry. I'll tell her.' He won't though. Cunt.

---

[1] Sir Barney Hayhoe, MP for Brentford since 1970.
[2] Jim Prior (Life Peer 1987). MP for Lowestoft, 1959–83 (Waveney 1983–7). A former Leader of the Commons, Secretary of State for Employment and Northern Ireland Secretary.

Later
Ministry of Defence
No work is being done in Whitehall today, whatsoever. My 'In'-tray
is about an inch deep. I don't think a single Minister in the Govt will
be at his desk; or if he is, it will be only so as to telephone to a
colleague or to a journalist. The civil servants (all of whom, down to
Principal level, I suspect, were terrified of the Lady) just can not
believe their eyes.

Yet still she won't return. There is talk of a 'fighting statement'
later. But this wastage of time in Paris is sheer lunacy. Harold at
Stamford Bridge.

It is the general sense of disintegration now affecting everything,
that is so damaging to her. Unless MH is slaughtered in the final
ballot – impossibly unlikely – she herself is going to find it highly
difficult to reassert her authority, even if eventually she emerges as the
victor. Short, that is, of giving them the full coup-loser's treatment –
arrest, manacles, beaten up in the interrogation room, shot while
trying to escape. Real blood, in other words. Fun, but a bit *Angolan*.

Before walking over to the House I called Andrew MacKay into
my room and we had a long talk about Tom. Earlier, we had both
lingered after Ministers and sounded him.

Tom likes the idea, preened himself, straightened his jacket; but
he is cautious. He would need to be sure of at least thirty votes to
even 'put down a marker'. And in any case, convention obliges that
no member of the Cabinet puts his name forward while she is still
standing. (I hear rumours that that pudgy puff-ball Kenneth Clarke is
considering breaching this, but am keeping that in reserve.)

'Look,' I told him. 'If the Lady is doomed, our Number One
priority is to find, and instal a leader who will win the next General Election. And we haven't got long. Who is best suited to do this?'

I told him that Heseltine would burn out very quickly. His rhetoric
pleased Party Conference, but was less reliable in the national context.
Anyway people are sick of passion, they want reassurance.

The only two figures who can do this are Tom and John Major.
Douglas is now past it; is thought rightly or wrongly to be a buffer
and a bureaucrat. John is more engaging than Tom in some ways,
with a lovely grin, but seems really too youthful. There is no time to
project him. Even in the House he is barely known, has never been
seen under fire. Tom, on the other hand, does have gravitas. Also he's
good on the stump, in small groups, canteens and so on.

Andrew was in broad agreement. But:

'Tom won't make a move while she's still in the field.'

'So what do we do?'

'I tell you what I'm doing, if she stands second time round – voting for Michael.'

I was appalled. Here was this good, intelligent man, tough and (in so far as it still means anything) right wing... More than any other experience this conversation has made me realise that she will lose, finally, head-to-head against Heseltine. But if she does stand again we are in a log-jam; the only people who will join in the contest are wankers like Clarke who are not worth twenty-five votes.

Andrew said that he would, very quietly, take soundings for Tom. The immediate priority is to find a way, tactfully and skilfully, to talk her out of standing a second time.

Now I must close this entry and walk over to the House.

House of Commons

I was greeted with the news that there had been an announcement. 'I fight, and I fight to win.' God alive!

Tebbit is holding an impromptu press conference in the Members' lobby.

Fifty feet away, down the tea-room corridor that mad ninny Hampson is dancing around on his tippy-toes calling out to passers-by, 'Tee-hee, she's standing. We've made it. We can't lose now, etc.'

I came back here, to my room. I kept the door open and an endless succession of visitors trooped in and out. No one seems to have any idea of what we should do. Her 'Campaign' is a shambles now. John Moore (who he?) is running around with bits of paper – 'draft statements' – asking people what they think. He seems to have a temporary HQ in Portillo's room, which is next door to mine. First I heard that Norman Fowler was going to take charge; then John Wakeham. Or was it the other way round? Gamelin's been sacked, Weygand is on the way out; Pétain's in the wings. '*Où est la masse de manoeuvre? – Aucune.*'

Every time I trawl the corridors I run into another batch of chaps who say they're going to switch, or abstain, or when-are-there-going-to-be-some-more-candidates-to-choose-from? The only visitor who has made any real sense is Francis Maude. He claims, forcefully, that John Major has a better chance than we all realise. But John won't make a move while the Lady remains in the field. 'I must get to see her. Can you help?' Apparently Peter stands sentinel, and is outside her door the whole time.

I have closed the door. These random conversations are too discursive. Tomorrow is the last day for nominations. I must clear my head.

1) If she fights head on, she loses.

2) Therefore, the opposition vote has got to be diluted by a candidate from the left – preferably Patten, making it triangular. Besides dilution, this has the advantage that it will crack Cabinet 'solidarity' open and others may lose their scruples. Therefore:

3) Try and talk Patten into standing. QED.

Archie Hamilton's just been in. Didn't make any sense. One minute he says she 'could still' win; the next that we've all 'had it'. I'm off now, upstairs.

Later
Kundan Restaurant
It is very late, and finally I have withdrawn here for a vegetable curry, and to write up the traumatic happenings of this evening.

I made first for Chris's room. On the way I passed her outer door and said to Peter that I must have a minute or so. He looked anxious, almost rattled, which he never does normally. 'I'll do my best. She's seeing every member of the Cabinet in turn ... '

'Francis wants to see her too.'

'I'm doing my best.'

Chris wasn't in his room. The Secretary of State's corridor was deserted. Hushed, but you could feel the static.

The policeman by the lift said he was 'in with Mr Rifkind'.

I knocked and went in without waiting for an answer. Also in there, loathesomely conspiring, was little Kenneth Clarke. Her three great ill-wishers! Clarke wasn't friendly at all. If he'd said anything to me, I'd have answered 'Fuck you', so just as well.

Chris was quite amiable.

'How many votes she got at the moment?'

'It's a rout. She's down to ninety.'

'*Ninety?*'

'You've got to stand. You can't let Michael corner the left.'

He was diplomatic. A discussion was impossible. God knows what they were talking about, but it stank. Never mind, I have sowed the seed; or watered what was already there.

I went down the stairs and rejoined the group outside her door. After a bit Peter said, 'I can just fit you in now – but only for a split second, mind.'

She looked calm, almost beautiful. 'Ah, Alan . . . '

'You're in a jam.'

'I know that.'

'They're all telling you not to stand, aren't they?'

'I'm going to stand. I have issued a statement.'

'That's wonderful. That's heroic. But the Party will let you down.'

'I am a fighter.'

'Fight, then. Fight right to the end, a third ballot if you need to. But you lose.'

There was quite a little pause.

'It'd be so terrible if Michael won. He would undo everything I have fought for.'

'But what a way to go! Unbeaten in three elections, never rejected by the people. Brought down by nonentities!'

'But Michael . . . as *Prime Minister*.'

'Who the fuck's Michael? No one. Nothing. He won't last six months. I doubt if he'd even win the Election. Your place in history is towering . . . '

Outside, people were doing that maddening trick of opening and shutting the door, at shorter and shorter intervals.

'Alan, it's been so good of you to come in and see me . . . '

Afterwards I felt empty. And cross. I had failed, but I didn't really know what I wanted, except for her still to be Prime Minister, and it wasn't going to work out.

I sat on the bench immediately behind the Speaker's chair, watching the coming and going. After a bit Tristan came and sat beside me. But he had little to say. What is there to say? She's still seeing visitors. Then, along came Edwina.

'Hullo, aren't you Edwina Currie?'[1]

'Now then, Alan, there's no need to be objectionable.'

'If that is who you are, I must congratulate you on the combination

---

[1] Edwina Currie, MP for Derbyshire South since 1983.

of loyalty and restraint that you have shown in going on television to announce your intention to vote against the Prime Minister in the Leadership Election.'

'Alan, I'm perfectly prepared to argue this through with you, if you'll listen.'

'Piss off.'

Which she did.

Tristan said, 'She's not a bad girl really.'

At half past eight I left to come over here. The archway exit from Speaker's Court was blocked by the PM's Jaguar. She had just taken her seat, and as the detective's door slammed the interior light went out and the car slid away. I realised with a shock that this was in all probability her last night as Prime Minister. I came in with her. I go out with her, and a terrible sadness envelops me – of unfinished duties and preoccupations; of dangers and injustices remaining, of the greed, timidity and short-sightedness of so many in public life.

Albany   *Thursday, 22 November*

Very early this morning the phone rang. It was Tristan.

'She's going.'

There will be an official announcement immediately after a short Cabinet, first thing. Then the race will be on. Apparently Douglas *and* John Major are going to stand. I said I thought it was crazy, Heseltine will go through between them. I could sense him shrugging. 'There you go.'

Anyway, would I come over to his room at the Foreign Office and watch it from there?

Afterwards, very *triste* and silent, I walked back to the MoD and sat in on a late (and unnecessary) Ministers' meeting. Tom told us that it had been 'awful'. She started to read a prepared statement to them, then broke down, and the text had to be finished by the Lord Chancellor.

Listless, I drifted over to the House. I had a word with Charles, drafted a couple of valedictory passages for her speech[1] this afternoon, did I don't know how many impromptu TV bites.

---

[1] Not in fact used. Mrs Thatcher told AC that if she had, she would have broken down again.

Heseltine is meant to be coming to Plymouth tomorrow, for a fundraising dinner. I rang Judith,[1] told her we couldn't possibly allow him to use us as a platform to plug his own candidature. She only half agreed, so I immediately telephoned to the *Western Morning News* and told them that I had 'instructed' that the invitation be withdrawn. (Not unrich, considering I was not the host, and had long ago told everyone that I wanted nothing to do with it.)

I didn't think I could bear it, but curiosity drew me into the Chamber for the Lady's last performance. It would have been too macabre to have sat in my habitual place, next to her PPS, so I watched and listened first from behind the Chair, then from the Bar of the House. She was brilliant. Humorous, self-deprecating, swift and deadly in her argument and in her riposte. Even Dennis Skinner, her oldest adversary was feeding her lines; and at one point Michael Carttiss[2] shouted, 'You could wipe the floor with the lot of 'em.'

Too bloody true. What is to become of her? Aclimatisation will be agony, because she is not of that philosophic turn of mind that would welcome a spell at Colombey. Can she just remain on the back benches? It will be hard. What happens when she starts to be 'missed', and the rose-tinted spectacles are found in everyone's breast pocket?

This evening I had a strange, possibly a significant experience. There is a semi permanent prefab studio on College Green, where endless conclaves of MPs record their comments on the respective vices and virtues of the second-round candidates. Around it are many secondary groupings, each with a shoulder-held video and a very bright light, recording any, yes any, it seems, comment by any, yes, any one who is going past.

Emerging from this brilliantly lit pool into the darkness at its edge, I was accosted by a familiar figure who, being dazzled, I did not at first recognise.

'Hey, Alan, take a look at this.'

It was Bob Worcester.[3] He showed me a poll, the first to be run, asking how respondents would vote if (names) were leading the Tory Party. One of Michael's great hidden strengths has always been the huge margin which he had over Mrs Thatcher in this very context.

---

[1] Judith Roberts, Chairman of the Sutton Division.
[2] Michael Carttiss, MP for Great Yarmouth since 1983.
[3] Robert Worcester. Head of MORI, the opinion polls organisation.

To my amazement, I saw that John Major had already drawn level! And in one case was actually ahead, actually preferred – notwithstanding the *continuous* exposure which Michael has had these last two weeks.

'Christ, Bob, these have to be rogue figures.'

Bob took umbrage. 'Look, Alan, we're MORI. We don't have "rogue" figures.'

This could be critically important. If John can break through here, he's won.

Not so many in the Party really want to vote Heseltine, for himself. Some do, and will, just to spite her. But the bulk of Michael's support comes from his so-called Election winning powers. People have guilt about condoning what he did to Her. Once they have a real reason to do so, they'll abandon him.

Tomorrow's papers will tell us more. I am taking an early train to Plymouth to 'sound out' feeling (i.e., get cover for the way I cast my vote). But even if I can't get a single person in the town to tell me to vote for John Major, that's what I'm going to do.

In the Ruler of Oman's DC9   *Wednesday, 28 November*

I am winging my way out to the Gulf.[1] I am *not* a Minister, as Private Office were (unhealthily) eager to explain to me. So there will be no HE to greet me with his Union Jack bedecked Jaguar. I will have no status with dignitaries or administrators (like hell, I thought, just watch me). This is because, with a new PM, all ministerial appointments lapse, revert to his gift, and have to be 'confirmed'.

Immediately in front of me is the bald pate, surrounded tonsure-like by a wreath of wispy white hair, of my old friend the distinguished historian Alistair Horne. He wrote *The Price of Glory*, that brilliant and harrowing study of the battle of Verdun; still, I believe, the best of non-contemporary accounts of the Great War. But after that he went a bit soft, and got heavily involved with Macmillan who I still think would have been better done by Robert Rhodes J. I remember once in the Fifties when Alistair and his wife at the time, Renira,

---

[1] The *Cercle*, an Atlanticist Society of right-wing dignitaries, largely compered by Julian Amery and Herr Franz-Joseph Bach, staged one or two conferences a year and this one was travelling to Oman at the hospitality of the Ruler.

came to stay at the Chalet, a very handsome couple, tall and athletic, and skied with us. Why do I make these little obituary-like notes when I run into friends from former times? They always look older than me, sometimes at death's door. But there is a *Recherche du Temps Perdu* aspect as well. My other life.

Now we are all on our way to Muscat, as guests of the Ruler, the whole thing most ably arranged by dear Julian Amery, so that one can be confident that it will be smooth, interesting, and subject to much deference. There is a distinguished attendance list, and Jonathan Aitken, who knows absolutely everybody in the world has, amusingly and indiscreetly, guided me through it.

It is pleasing to be at 35,000 feet, carving our route to the warm waters of the Arabian Gulf, while behind in Britain colleagues lick their wounds, or feel stale with anti-climax. Was it only last night that Jane and I watched Cranley, on the TV screen in Needham's office,[1] bellowing the figures, and then very shortly after, Michael conceded?

There was one strange, unscripted episode. Very late in the evening, after I had seen Jane off in the car, I was coming up that back staircase which leads from the transport office and comes out in the Members' lobby. At the last turn in the landing I heard the top door open in a rush and there, quite alone, wild-eyed and head to head stood Heseltine.

'Hullo Michael,' I said.

He made no answer, rushed past. He could say he had 'cut' me. But he was a zombie, shattered.

It was Mates who brought him the numbers. Must it not at that moment have been:

> A Great Hope fell.
> You heard no noise
> The Ruin was Within.[2]

Later
Eighth floor at the Al Bustan
I have a vast suite here. Bedroom, master bedroom, bodyguard's bedroom. Sitting room, dining room, conference room, ante-room (for the bodyguard).

---

[1] Richard Needham (Earl of Kilmorey, but does not use the title). MP for Wiltshire North since 1983 (Chippenham, 1979–83).
[2] Emily Dickinson.

With all my traveller's experience, I still think this is the best hotel in the world, with its incredible hall, like the new Mosque in Islamabad, and a thousand minions to bring room service at any time of the day or night. There is a French restaurant, an Italian restaurant, and an Arabic restaurant, and always the sound of wavelets caressing the soft sand of the beach.

Andrew[1] appeared, tall and beautiful as ever. He moves among the delegates with a very faint smile on his face, but his eyes are always watching. What experience in childhood, what gene, makes him instinctively so observant, and from which side of the family does this gene come?

There was the sound of water sloshing, and the head of the Dutch Secret Service emerged through a swing door, looking haggard, but relieved.

'Greywater after the flight,' said Andrew. 'Airline food.'

I detached myself from the group and we had supper together. Andrew told me of his tales, and of the mood among the Military. Oman is a long way from Iraq, and their traditional apprehension is of Iranian muscle, their principal irritant is South Yemen. But the men, many of them, think privately of Saddam as a hero, who is leading the West a dance.

A certain undercurrent against the 'white-eyes'.

Can it have felt like this in Cawnpore, in 1857?

Al Bustan, Muscat   *Friday, 30 November*

I sit at my balcony. It is not yet 6 a.m. and all is still, save for the soft-soled attendants who are cleaning, bleaching, arranging the towels, chairs and surroundings of the vast swimming pool, a hundred feet below.

Last night our delegation had dinner with the Ruler, Sheikh Qaboos, at the Barakha Palace. The drive was nearly a mile long, and every palm tree was floodlit. On either side of the entrance there were great braziers of smouldering frankincense, and the odour was all pervading.

---

[1] AC's younger son Andrew, a Major in the Life Guards, was serving as 2 i/c of the Sultan's Armoured Force.

It was a buffet, but one a very long way, in every sense, from the second floor of the Guildhall in Plymouth. The boards groaned; superlative and exotic dishes that one could eat with confidence. I could have stuffed for hours, and become bloated. But there appeared to be some convention governing the courses (was my gluttony leading me into solecisms?), because at intervals the whole dining tent went still, and the Ruler would suddenly click his fingers, rise and sweep over to lead a new assault on the tables.

Qaboos had put me on his left, with Julian in the place of honour on the Ruler's right hand. He is intelligent, quick, almost feline in his responses, and commands the most perfect English – a mixture of Sandringham and Miss Newman.

In contrast to the other Ruling Families on whom I had called in August, he is not frightened of Saddam. And his contempt for the oily little King of Jordan, who is, was palpable. Qaboos said that Saddam was, at this moment, scared, but that he was a 'slippery fellow' and had a reputation in the bazaars, which he cultivates, for getting out of scrapes.

'He's going to need an awful lot of MiG's to get out of this one,' I said.

But Qaboos was thoughtful. Arab coalitions are fragile creatures, he told me. If it should be thought that Saddam may survive there are many who would like to 'take insurance'.

Qaboos is delightful company. Wholly royal in manner and deportment, but never *remote*. He engages with you. Detached yes, but so different from the Windsors (except the dear QM) who are all of them remote – and obtuse.

At lunch I had sat next to General Schwarzkopf,[1] and formed a high opinion of him. At West Point he was an amateur wrestler, and looks it. But he has a keen brain and an infectious humour. Earlier he had given us a most competent and interesting 'presentation'.

Schwarzkopf was in Vietnam, first as an Adviser, then in command of a battalion, and has no illusions as to the military prowess of Third World countries. He told me his one dread was to find his spearhead still stuck in the 'berms' and wadis of the enemy line at first light after a night attack, and then to be drenched with chemicals. Gas is of little

---

[1] General Norman Schwarzkopf, Commander of the US forces in the Gulf, who would gain celebrity during the Gulf War.

value in the mobile battle, but can be seriously nasty against fixed positions.

Already this morning I have swum. The sea temperature must be about 85°. I walked the length of the beach, barefooted on the volcanic sand, in a state of reflective melancholy, brooding on the sadness of affairs of the heart, and unrequited prospects.

'Behold a gift, designed to kill.'[1] Whenever I am in the desert I think always of that brilliant, worrying poem and its strange imagery.

My own career is now on a descending parabola. The events of last week have inserted a new generation and, episode by episode, the effects will make themselves felt.

Both Jonathan [Aitken] and Paul [Channon] are teasing me mercilessly, and with not a little secret spite, about how probable it is that ('sadly') I will be left out of John Major's new administration.

'You've lost your protector,' Paul kept saying.

Rude, because it implies that I have no individual merit, just held the job(s) down for seven years because I was a favourite. There are no true friends in politics.

We are all sharks circling, and waiting, for traces of blood to appear in the water.

Now I am going to start work on the script of my lecture. I am lying low this morning, in order to get it polished, although I fear it will not be widely welcomed. This entire outing is a right-wing think (or rather thought) tank, funded by the CIA, which churns Cold War concepts around. I am going to tell them that the Cold War is over and NATO is washed up, unnecessary, a waste of time and money and (as is the 'streetwise' expression) space.

Al Bustan   *Saturday, 1 December*

I had a good meeting with Erik Bennett.[2] He is a courtier of the very highest class. What are the characteristics? The voice, the intonation, the clarity of diction. The superficial speaking well of all and everyone.

---

[1] Keith Douglas.
[2] Air Marshal Sir Erik Bennett, Commander, Sultan of Oman's Air Force since 1974.

The way all communication occurs by the lightest of implied comment. Smooth, unwrinkled skin, and limitless endurance through ceremonial tedium. Also, in Erik's case, intelligence and wit.

He has set up a draft letter 'from' HM inquiring about surplus military equipment sales after (EB said) 'rapprochement with Iraq'. I substituted 'a clearer determination of unpredictability in the region', which he admitted was preferable.

Last night another huge dinner, given by the distinguished Doctor Omar. In contrast to the previous evening the pleasures of the flesh were much in evidence. Lashings of alcohol – the claret was all '85, and there were some wonderful white Burgundies. Sinuous and scented lovelies shimmered about.

At the end of the meal a belly dancer performed. On and on she went with graceful, but ever more suggestive, rhythms. Her stamina was unbelievable and never once did she repeat herself. From time to time she 'fixed' particular guests in their places, a special treat.

But she was defeated by Anthony Cavendish, who had early on become tired and was fast asleep, head on his chest.

There was a French Admiral sitting next to me, his face expressionless. I said, it helps one to understand how women can experience ten or eleven orgasms in one night. Myself, three render me *complètement, totalement épuisé*. Ruefully, he agreed.

Albany   *Thursday, 6 December*

There was a rumour running round the Lobby that Tom, who had gone to Brussels to attend some idiotic NATO meeting, had been taken ill with 'flu' (covers everything) and come back prone, on a stretcher.

I kept my ears pricked, and at the ten o'clock vote Andrew MacKay *pulled* me from the chamber and recounted that Tom had been 'taken straight to' St Thomas's and operated on immediately for a quite minor 'blockage' (uh?) in his 'back passage'.

'Quite,' I said, and, 'What bad luck', thinking I hope that never happens to me.

I went back to Brooks's, where I was playing in the backgammon tournament, in high spirits. Room here for some fantasising.

When finally I left the Club Bruce Anderson was standing on the pavement with a pretty willowy blonde in a black coat. 'What's happened? What's the matter? What's he got?'

I was in good form and treated it lightly. 'I don't know, I wasn't in the theatre.'

She giggled. Are, suddenly, the stars running?

Albany   *Monday, 10 December*

This evening I gave the Liddell Hart Memorial lecture at King's. My text was a cleaned up version of the 'NATO today – a bureaucracy in search of a pension' theme, with which I had teased the Cercle at the Muscat seminar.

It went well, and afterwards Laurie Freedman[1] and Frank Cooper (both good judges) were appreciative.

But for me, it was symbolic. Basil was my tutor in Military History, and in much about life, as well. He was godfather to James, and nurtured me when I was young and obstreperous and made mistakes. But he always had faith in me, told people like Michael Howard[2] who (quite understandably) disapproved, that I would go far.

Many of Basil's aphorisms are essential in politics. 'When questioning the validity of a piece of information ask always who was the original source', and, 'On every occasion that a particular recommendation is made, ask yourself first in what way the author's career may be affected.'

I stood at the rostrum, and I knew that he would be beaming.

It was a close-run thing, though. I had to get *some* cover because what I was saying was very contentious. Shamelessly I 'bounced' dear Peter and an unfortunate junior in 'Policy' who, unable to master – or perhaps to believe – the subversive conclusions that were implied,

---

[1] Professor Laurence Freedman, Professor of War Studies, King's College, since 1982.
[2] Sir Michael Howard, former Regius Professor of Modern History at Oxford and a noted military historian.

reluctantly 'passed' it. I was meant to be at King's for tea and small talk at 4.15. Like the Review, it had to be done 'privately', and it was not until 4.30 that Alison took the last sheet out of the printer. We got there, helter skelter at 4.58 to deliver a lecture billed for 5 p.m.

Thirty years ago, when I was writing *The Donkeys* at Bratton, I would have thought this evening the very pinnacle of attainment and recognition.

But now, alas, having 'arrived' I know that soon I am about to depart.

Ministry of Defence   *Tuesday, 11 December*

Tom occupied most of Ministers this morning telling everyone how his 'complaint' was very common, happens to practically everyone at some time, and so on.

As we dispersed he indicated that he wanted me to stay behind. The 'pupil's chair' was drawn up facing his desk, and he told Simon to leave – always a bad sign.

'How are you?' I drawled.

'I'm perfectly all right. It's you I want to talk about.'

He gave me a heavy basting. 'If you want to criticise Government policy, then you must do it from outside the Government.'

'I wasn't criticising Government policy.'

'Well, that certainly isn't the impression held by the Prime Minister. Or Douglas. Or the Chief Whip.'

Suspected balls, I thought.

'I can't go on defending you, you know. I think you'll have to look on this as your last chance.'

Back here I thought about it. If I am sacked (which I don't think I will be) then it is for saying what I believe, and what is manifestly true. How much consolation is that? Some, I suppose. But there's poor old Keith Speed, sacked for 'speaking out' nearly ten years ago, and still no 'K'.[1]

---

[1] Keith Speed, MP for Ashford since 1974. Parliamentary Under-Secretary (Navy) who resigned in protest at the reduction of frigate numbers set out in the 1981 Defence White Paper (Cmnd. 8288).

Ministry of Defence   *Wednesday, 12 December*

Last night I dined with Franko and Perry at Wiltons.[1] We had a
'pullman', but I noticed Paul and Ingrid Channon at that dud little
on-the-edge table on the right, at the junction of the L.

Perry, *vu grand, comme toujours*. He spoke of the sweep of the
Thatcherite legend, how we all had a duty to propagate it. Both were
plainly getting ready to be 'disillusioned' with the unfortunate John –
whom I personally believe to be tougher and more clear-headed than
they realise.

I took the whole thing as a bit much coming from Perry who, in
his day, has written the most flesh-crawling stuff about the dear Lady
not having the 'class' that you need in adversity, deploring the absence
of Gentlemen, all that sort of demi-balls. Frank, at least, has shown
real affection and loyalty, only pulled her leg from time to time.

There was some talk about who would do *The Book*, how important it was. I must say my spirits fell when they said John O'Sullivan
was going to 'ghost' it.

Ghost! Good God! The greatest political story of the century,
and they're looking for a 'ghost'.

During the night I thought, why shouldn't I write it? She would
trust me, I'm sure, with the papers. As a Privy Councillor I can get
access to Cabinet Office records. I am trained as a historian, and she
has often said (in public) how much she admires *Barbarossa*.

Early this morning I caught Peter on the ministerial floor, and
expounded. He was enthusiastic. Said the present situation was 'a
mess', 'too many cooks'. He promised to speak with her, and this
time I think he is going to.

Ministry of Defence   *Thursday, 20 December*

Tom is looking strained and lined, still. He cut his leg on the weekend
with a sickle and now, being full of every kind of antibiotic, finds it
going 'septic', and has to keep it propped up on a chair.

---

[1] Frank Johnson (political columnist on *Daily Telegraph*) and Peregrine Worsthorne
(Editor and columnist of the *Sunday Telegraph*).

All due to Al, Jane said, who is harrying him while he is run down. An article by Peter McKay, always fresh and amusing, in yesterday's *Evening Standard* – 'Top Dogs, Wrong Collars' – suggested that we should simply change places. Harmful to me, but fun nonetheless.

I was having a chat with David Davis, and he told me an interesting footnote to the leadership affair.

After they received the figures of the second ballot Heseltine's claque – notably Mates, Hampson and Macfarlane – were frantic that he should hang in there, contest the third 'in order to strengthen his position'. H. ignored this, immediately conceding. (Presumably calculating that his total could well go down, and reduce still further his bargaining strength.)

However, when he met with John Major Heseltine made no attempt whatever to get places for his acolytes, being concerned only for himself, and cut the painter immediately. Later Mates threw a tantrum, and has apparently been promised something (unspecified) 'in the next Government'.

Saltwood   *Friday, 21 December*

The shortest day. Darkness and depression.

Bruce Anderson came to lunch, arriving terribly late. We didn't sit down until 3 p.m. Although he had asked to come and talk about his book on the leadership he hardly mentioned the subject. A general and rather repetitious gossip about where we're at, who's in, who's out.

He left me in little doubt that my shares are a listless market. I am the oldest member of the administration. My chances of getting into the Cabinet are nil. There was some (I thought slightly bizarre) talk of my being John's PPS in the next Parliament. I'd have done it straight away, but I won't do anything in the next Parliament unless it's from the Lords.

I have OD'd this last month, on politics. I have a huge backlog – for the first time – of work in the Dept, most of it turgid. But after I had seen Bruce on to a train I felt limp, and sated. Even my PC, to which I am greatly looking forward, is somewhat blighted by having acquired, it seems, the status of the *Medaille militaire* in the Charennes hospital at Verdun.[1] (The Lady's list, out today, contains little of interest or importance, although a K for poor Peter M, and a KCMG for Charles Powell – the latter most signally deserved.) Bruce told me of a comment on Derek Lord, the gay, intelligent, ludicrously self-assured black companion to Michael Brown, who was active in the Gayfrere Street bunker. From a rough Derbyshire farmer, a constituent of Michael's; 'Eee that twat's dad moost've eaten a posh missionary.'

Saltwood   *Christmas Day, 1990*

A lovely blustery day, cold driving rain and the glass falling fast.

We went to Communion. Not many people, but immediately behind us an *incredibly* tiresome woman, whom I've never seen in the village before, who thought she had a classy voice. She RADA'd up the responses – though at all times with a hint of reproach in her tone that, I came rapidly to believe, was directed at me personally.

Her buffer of a husband – pink face, watery eyes – blundered in occasionally, nicotine tones, and always out of time, so that momentarily he came to be 'leading' some of the prayers.

Now it's lovely to be here on our own. Snug, pressure-free, with presents to open, a huge meal, and a bottle of Giscours '61.

Leafing through a bound copy of *The Car* of 1906 I came across a delicious piece of useless information. Byron (no less) once rhymed 'intellectual' – troublesome, admittedly – with 'hen-pecked you all'.

I must contrive an opportunity to use this, 'spontaneously', in the House.

---

[1] Awarded to those dying of their wounds.

1991

1991

Just as obituary pages nearly always cause satisfaction – if not *Schadenfreude* – so do Honours Lists invariably irritate. Like Parliamentary Selection, they seem always to be bestowed on the wrong people.

I have tried very seldom to secure 'recognition' for anyone – although I did get an OBE for Betty.[1] So by now my two particular nominations – Phil Drabble for all he has done to enlarge our knowledge and enjoyment of nature and the countryside and the relations between man and beast; and Alex Moulton, for being a brilliant inventor, who has always risked his own money in putting his ideas into practical effect – are overdue to come up. But no. Who got the 'Industry' K's? A couple who personify all that is wrong with British 'businessmen'. Morton[2] – aggressive, nasty and stupid. And Sheehy[3] – self-indulgent, nasty and stupid. It's a practically infallible rule (though, most fortunately, vitiated in our recent leadership election), that the bad guy always wins. I can barely think of a single 'businessman' who has ever deserved a K except Ian MacLaurin[4] and Colin Chandler.[5]

I was with the Lady today. A strange menage. The tiny little house, lent her by Alistair McAlpine,[6] on College Green, still carries the faintest whiff of Number 10. Sloaneish secretaries bustle about on the ground floor, where telephones ring; handsome, though slightly effete young men slide in and out of her sitting room, bend over her ear, carrying sheaves of papers.

'I detect a distinct aura of Elba,' I said.

'Elba? Elba?'

'Where Napoleon was exiled before his return.'

'Yes yes I know *that*, I mean – how interesting.'

We talked for a little about the events of last November, and Peter Morrison sat in, lobbing her the occasional softball. Her sense of

---

[1] Cllr Mrs Betty Easton, OBE, Chairman of the Sutton Division for many years.

[2] Sir Alastair Morton, British Chairman of Eurotunnel since 1987.

[3] Sir Patrick Sheehy, Chairman, BAT (formerly British American Tobacco) Industries since 1982.

[4] Sir Ian MacLaurin, Chairman of Tesco, knighted in 1989.

[5] Sir Colin Chandler, Managing Director, Vickers plc, since 1990.

[6] Lord McAlpine of West Green (Life Peer, 1984). Honorary Treasurer, the Conservative Party, 1975–90.

betrayal is absolute, overrides everything. Lamont had been scheming; Patten plotted the whole thing; Kenneth Clarke had led the rout from the Cabinet Room. Rifkind was a weasel. Even John Major (who announced yesterday that some benefit was to be uprated, depicted in this morning's press, gleefully, as a 'Reversal of Thatcherite Policies') is by no means cloudfree.

I remembered a remark I had once heard Norman Tebbit address to her in private. 'Prime Minister, it is you who chooses your Cabinet', but said nothing. What was the point?

Gently, I brought the subject round to the book.

'I want *you* to do it, Alan, because you are a believer.'

'It shouldn't be "a believer's" book. It doesn't need to be.'

'How can you say that?'

'The facts speak for themselves. They illustrate the scale of your achievement.'

'But look how it ended. The treachery...'

'Margaret, these aren't Memoirs. You don't want to get into that game. This is your *Biography*. Where you came from, how you got there, what you did for the Conservative Party, and for Britain. A major work of political history. It will go into every university library in the World.'

As our conversation developed I could see she was having second thoughts. I told her that I would pay proper attention to the strange and disreputable circumstances of her ousting. That I could see the symmetry between what happened to her, and the way Grantham Council treated Alderman Roberts (being a subject to which she adverted several times).

But the standpoint *had* to be objective. A tract, even a great big thick tract, would be a wasted opportunity.

She didn't much like all this. I changed the subject to that of money. Michael Sissons[1] had told me that he could envisage a total take of about eight million (sterling). I said I didn't want any royalty. I would write it for a fee, but it would take me three years...

'Three *years*?'

'Minimum. This is a major book, six hundred pages. It has got to be impeccable. I'll have to pay an assistant.'

I have often found that once sums of money under discussion pass

[1] Michael Sissons, Chairman and Managing Director of the literary agency, Peters, Fraser and Dunlop.

beyond a certain level – no more than a couple of million usually – reality tends to be discarded, 'quotes' get wilder and wilder. It's all Monopoly.

Apparently Mark had been winding her up: '... Could be as much as twenty.'

Who's going to 'handle' it, anyway? There was talk of a hot lawyer in New York. Mark's favourite was apparently someone called McCormack, who plugs Sports 'Personalities', where the sums are enormous.[1]

I'm doubtful about all this. It's tempting, I can see, to allow yourself to be regarded as a 'property'. But slightly demeaning for the premier politician of the Western world. Better by far to keep the whole thing on an astringent, almost academic level. In the long run the yield will probably be little different.

Feeling the whole thing to be slipping away, I thought I ought to make one point absolutely clear. 'I am the author, not the Ghost. It's the Official Biography *by* Alan Clark. Not "as told to", or anything of that kind.'

I think that tore it. Perhaps just as well. I don't want another round of 'negotiation' in which she makes some concessions, and is then taken aback by my request – and I appear 'unreasonable'. But what she wants, I fear, is *Margaret Thatcher. My Story.*

It's all rather sad, particularly for future generations. Dilks[2] could do it. But he'd take an eternity. Possibly John Charmley.[3] But a 'ghost' hack will spoil the tale. Hard to say of course, as it depends who they choose, but could be even worse than if she tries to write it herself.

Winston did, why shouldn't she? she may be thinking. But consider for example that wonderful passage in Moran when Churchill explains the difference between scansion and resonance in a text.[4] I don't think she would be aware of that, bless her.

---

[1] Mark McCormack, chairman of International Management Group.

[2] David Dilks, Professor of International History, University of Leeds, since 1970. Edited *The Diaries of Alexander Cadogan.*

[3] John Charmley, historian, lecturer in English History at University of East Anglia. Author of *Duff Cooper, Chamberlain and the Lost Peace* and *Churchill: The End of Glory.*

[4] After his death Lord Moran, for many years Churchill's doctor, published *Winston Churchill: the Struggle for Survival.*

Saltwood   *Sunday, 6 January*

First dinner of the year. David Davis and his wife (good strong chap, very much our sense of humour. Did the 'black' route without turning a hair, then retraced his footsteps, hands in pockets – first time *that's* ever been done!). Richard Ryder and Caroline,[1] the Deedes,[2] the Michael Howards. We were eleven and the table and the food were terrific. But the meal somehow lacked *Stimmung*.

Tristan, a last-minute addition, performed sparklingly. But Bill Deedes, though splendid, and still a minter of delicious unfinished sentences is going deaf and 'misses' things. Even so, he remains one of the great ingredients in any grouping. He is wise, politically shrewd, still; and has a vast, archival fund of historic experience. Bill told Jane that he used to play golf with Philip Sassoon[3] before the war and Philip was so impatient that he employed two extra caddies who were sent ahead to see where the balls landed, so that Philip and his partner wouldn't waste time looking for them. (I know nothing about golf, but thought that 'looking for the ball' was one of the secondary ritualised pleasures?)

Lady Deedes, whom I called 'Evelyn' but Michael Howard (I don't doubt correctly) addressed as 'Hilary', was a pool of tranquil, though amiable *longueurs*.

When the ladies exited, I started the conversation on the lines of what are we to do about Margaret?

Following my meeting with her on Thursday, and the very bitter feelings of betrayal which she so evidently holds, my feeling is that she, her behaviour, could present the Party with one of its most vexatious problems over the coming months. There was some desultory talk about 'the book' (I gave nothing away. Only Richard knows that she and I are talking). Agreement on the general 'problem' of Mark. We couldn't really get into a good gossip, as Tristan would have done, left to himself.

---

[1] Caroline Ryder, MBE, the daughter of a former Clerk to the House of Commons, was a secretary to Margaret Thatcher.
[2] Lord Deedes (Life Peer, 1986). Journalist (Editor of the *Daily Telegraph*, 1974–86), who was MP for Ashford, 1950–74 and Minister without Portfolio, 1962–4. Allegedly the 'Dear Bill' to whom *Private Eye*'s Denis Thatcher letters have continued to be addressed (Thatcher and Deedes have long been golfing partners).
[3] Sir Philip Sassoon, 3rd Bt. Unionist MP. Private Secretary to Sir Douglas Haig, 1915–18. Under-Secretary for Air in the National Government in the 1930s.

Bill to some extent inhibits this – the Old School. And Richard was totally, *owlishly* silent. So much so that I thought he must be terribly tired, half asleep (he had been shooting in Norfolk all day). But on the few occasions that he uttered, monosyllabically, it was slicingly to correct errors of fact made by the participants. As a personality he is deeply pleasing – intelligent and '*aimable*' in the French sense.

DD also impressed. The concept of having clever, tough, *congenial* people in the Whips' Office is relatively new. In former times they were just fieldsport enthusiasts whose last and only fulfilment-period had been bullying (and in some cases buggering) Lower Boys at Eton. Now it is recognised as a nursery for junior Ministers. (I remember Nigel,[1] when I reproached him for going there, saying that the experience was essential – how Parlt works, how 'Business' is arranged, if one is to do a ministerial job properly.) As for myself, although I like to boast of having been blackballed – 'both to have been proposed, and to have been blackballed is equally complimentary' – I am sad not to have done a stint there.

At present we are all a little constrained. I first noticed this at the End of Term dinner last July.[2] The polls are implacable. The date of the Election approaches. I think we will win, but I can't tell how. And behind everything lurks this tedious, unnecessary but debilitating 'question' of Europe. We are all (except for dear Tristan) true Tories. But we cannot give expression to our true feelings.

Ministry of Defence   *Monday, 7 January*

I have been 'on call' all day, i.e., can't leave the building, because TK 'may' want to see me urgently.

The UN deadline[3] expires in a week's time and the place hums. But it has been conveyed to me, *via* the Private Office network, that I am not to take any part in the TV coverage of the war. The Press Office have been instructed to refuse all 'bids', and I am to refer those that are made to me personally. Where? Back to the Press Office.

---

[1] Nigel Lawson had been an Opposition Whip, 1976–7.
[2] End of Term dinner: see 20 July 1990.
[3] The ultimatum requiring Saddam Hussein to withdraw his forces from Kuwait.

Catch 22. 'Must make sure we all speak with the same tongue.' But of course it's not that at all. They recognise that I am more glamorous, and have a quicker mind, than the other Ministers, who mustn't be 'outshone'. It's like a trendy Local Authority banning competitive sports.

Ah! Peter has just come in; it's coming up to 7 p.m. and S of S office have rung to say I can 'stand down'. I assume that he was intending to huff-locute this instruction to me personally, then either lost his nerve or got involved with some other topic.

I have been whiling away the time reading through a bundle of congratulatory letters.[1] Those from officials please me most, and of them Charles wrote much the nicest. A document to be treasured. But do officials write in much the same way to every Minister who gets a PC? Perhaps. With very slight variations.

It is an important, but highly specialised form of recognition. The *Herald* came on, but couldn't understand it at all. 'Does this mean you'll be able to do more for Plymouth?'

Plymouth train   *Friday, 11 January*

I have already finished the box. Very little for me these days. The whole Dept is concentrating on the war and, at all costs, Archie and TK have to keep me away from that.

Reading through *Classic Car* I saw a photograph of Jack Fairman. I suppose he must be about seventy now, but he looked at death's door. He was the first of what we now call 'The Mews'[2] whom I ever met, when I went over to Horley (while still at Eton, and risking the sack) to look at the cars in 'Speedsters' garage.

Fairman was clipped and authoritative, with a black moustache and experience (he implied) of war in the desert. He took care to distance himself from E.W. Gillette, who was the proprietor of 'Speedsters', claimed (as far as I can recall) to be his landlord, the proprietor of the huge bus garage in Redhill where the stock of cars,

---

[1] On the announcement of AC being appointed a Privy Councillor.

[2] A family expression for the Classic Car 'movement', the majority of whose emporia are located in South Kensington Mews.

even then very glorious and glamorous – 'the cream of pre-war sporting machinery' – and today, I should think, worth getting on for £100 million, was housed.

No. Fairman was 'not in the dealing line'. But I do remember him on several occasions in the Fifties and Sixties as an indifferent competitive driver with a curiously inflated reputation. Did he ever win a race? Even I have won a race, after all. But he was a player on the scene, memorable for the defiant 'I spun the car' quote during the Nurburgring 1000 km race in 1959, to which Jane and I went with Desmond O'Brien and Noel Cunningham Reid. Stirling Moss[1] won, against very strong opposition, in a DB 3S, in one of the most epic drives I have ever witnessed.

Anyway, there he is now, gaunt and old. And further on, pictures of Fangio[2] (now eighty) *crashing* a Mercedes 'W' Grand Prix car on a 'demonstration lap' in Australia. The great man then took Sir Jack Brabham[3] (another golden oldie) round in a Princess-Diana-model 500 SL to 'open' the track, and crashed *that* too.

It's age, I fear, pure age. When's going to be the first time I do it? I haven't had a crash for twenty-five years, since silly little Juliet led me into an ambush in the $3\frac{1}{2}$-litre Bentley, in Wiltshire, and old Lord Margadale suddenly turned up on the Bench as visiting Lord bloody Lieutenant and, odiously, fined me £450.

James is already making mischief by saying he has followed me in the Porsche in Scotland and that I drive dangerously. And Alison flinches whenever we drive in traffic.

Yesterday in Brooks's I heard that Julian Earle (age sixty-two) had died 'suddenly' of a heart attack. Bland, keen golfer, not many grey hairs. What's going on?

Coming out of the gents I ran into Jim Slater,[4] who repeated the news.

'You're next,' I said, then realised that the humour may have been a bit *too* black as he looked alarmingly blotchy, and his suit hung loosely. Cancer, I suppose.

---

[1] Stirling Moss, racing motorist, 1947–62. Competed in 494 races, rallies, sprints, land speed records and endurance runs and won 222, including 33 Formula One Grand Prix.

[2] Juan Fangio, Argentinian racing driver. Five times Formula One World Champion.

[3] Sir Jack Brabham, racing driver. Three times Formula One World Champion, retired 1970.

[4] Jim Slater, former Chairman, Slater Walker Securities.

Ministry of Defence   *Tuesday, 15 January*

The UN deadline runs out today, and the air attacks could start any time. TK is relatively benign, now he's fixed my PR for me, very kindly. And he goes through the *motions* of being hyperactive. But he hasn't really got control over the place, or what's going on. Increasingly the Military are taking first slight, then medium, soon major decisions and then 'advising' Ministers afterwards. I sense it is with relief that TK settles back into more mundane, but congenial topics like photocalls and the briefing of foreign correspondents.

Yes, I am bitching. But I have been completely sidelined. Nothing of any interest comes into my box, nor is my opinion sought on any issue. I am being treated like a middle-rank executive in a large corporation who is going to be forced out by having his desk moved around the whole time.

It makes me cross and frustrated; but it's also bad luck on Private Office who are supportive and loyal and can remember the days when Charles used to phone and send stuff over from Number 10 all the time, for info or 'suggestions'.

1990 was such a wonderful year, almost until the end. I have a terrible feeling that 1991 is not going to be happy.

Ministry of Defence   *Tuesday, 22 January*

TK is bumbustious this morning. His press conferences are being carried live in the US! Heaven help us.

Ministerial meetings are a complete waste of time now. Jokes and small talk. They were all in good form, though keeping straight faces, this morning.

There had been a heavy headline in the *Sunday Express*: REVENGE IS SWEET AT THE MoD.

A biggish picture of me, entitled – *Disliked*: Alan Clark. If I'd been in stronger form I might have enjoyed it. 'Deeply disliked by both Civil Servants and Ministers . . . ', went on to talk of one of the most prestigious posts in the Government in coming weeks, 'the front men will be King and Hamilton. Clark will be kept entirely [sic] out of the limelight.'

Buttocks. The whole piece is long, and prominent. I know how the press works. This isn't just a sliver of overheard gossip. It has to be a specific plant from the Press Office, with the tacit concurrence of Tom or Archie. Quite unnecessary, as I had already agreed to this arrangement. No one at all mentioned it at Ministers, which is a clear (though gauche) indicator of a guilty conscience.

Ministry of Defence   *Wednesday, 23 January*

We're five days into the air war, but I am unhappy about the strategy. Attacking missile sites is always wasteful, has very little tactical effect and occurs mainly in response (as most obviously now) to political demands.

We lost another Tornado last night. That's now *five*. I can't help noticing that traditions (ancient and revered) of Bomber Command are reasserting themselves. From the Tabuk mission last night, out of ten sorties six either aborted for technical reasons, or 'jettisoned ordnance while manoeuvering to avoid (sic) SAMs', or took targets of opportunity. (Uh? At night?)

The sad thing is that it's always the brave ones, the true grit, who press on regardless (the contravening tradition) and get killed. Of the Italian flight of six *five* turned back and only one brave boy went ahead. They got him. It's the difference between James and Andrew. But I want James to survive, don't I?

MGO[1] has been here for an hour and a half. There's a potential ammunition crisis in some calibres. Unbelievably our NATO 'partners' are being most reluctant to pool their stockpiles, even though we're paying cash. The smelly little Belgians, who would never fire a shot at anyone and never have, and who did their best to shaft the BEF in 1940, have actually refused to let us have anything, except 'humanitarian supplies' − bandages and general past-its-sell-by-date detritus we don't need.

We talked about the Battle Plan. It's good news, at least, that we have been moved out now to the 'left hook', on the desert flank. But

---

[1] Master-General of the Ordnance. Sir John Stibbon, the senior General under AC.

I was apprehensive that our Sappers, 'because they are so good', were going to have to lead the breaching operation. There shouldn't *be* a breaching operation at all. We should go to the Euphrates, Basra if necessary, and draw the Republican Guard out in the open to attack us. Alam Halfa.[1] Not bother to go near Kuwait until it just falls off the tree.

Time lies on my hands. I spend much of it with Alison, and we do the *Guardian* crossword in the cafetaria. I am glum, and must be poor company.

Saltwood   *Saturday, 26 January*

It's a Saturday, but I've got a splitting tension headache.

I was doing a regional broadcast from Bristol on Thursday night, fairly routine stuff, when the commentator suddenly asked me how well our NATO allies were helping.

Just as one can sometimes be less on one's guard abroad, or in a foreign studio (foolishly and recklessly ignoring the fact that news can be flash-faxed to Whitehall before one has even got out of the door) so one can easily think that regional radio is a bit *hick* – particularly in the W. Country.

Hick! They had a teeny television camera concealed in the sound room and gleefully sold the whole interview as a TV performance (which of course I have been 'banned' from doing). I was cross, and feckless. I made some rude remarks, 'more concerned with heading for their cellars', totally unreliable in a real crisis, etc.

Afterwards, as always, a certain remorse. There was a lull. Was it all a strange dream?

But after a day's lull it has exploded, first in the *FT*, quite small, then everywhere.

I am under siege, refusing all requests for comment or interviews. Could still go either way. It had to be said. People *in the street* are very supportive.

---

[1] The classic 'drawing on' armoured battle fought by Montgomery before Alamein.

Ministry of Defence *Monday, 28 January*

I loathe being in London on Sunday evenings, and last night I had to come up so as to be in time this morning for another of these useless ministerial conferences, scheduled for 8.30, never start until after 9.

The flat is bleak and shabby, and takes a couple of hours to heat up. There is dust and grime, and crumbs in – not on, *in* – the carpet. The great damask curtains, that originally hung between the Partridge pagodas at Upper Terrace, are torn and fragile, so that the soft white felt lining bulges through the fabric. I hear of 'Sets' no different from mine changing hands for seven, eight hundred thousand. But B5 is squalid – almost, the straitened quarters of an Edwardian bachelor on his uppers.

The 'Conference' follows its usual pattern. Beforehand, at about 8 a.m., one is shown, with much flaring of feathers, a folder marked SECRET, an 'Operational Sitrep' consisting mainly of items little different, it seems, from those to be found on page 2 of that morning's *Daily Telegraph*. Then (always late, although TK has only to walk across the street from Admiralty HO) we sit round for a monologue. On and on goes the droning, round and round come the (same) subjects. As we dispersed this morning Tom indicated that he wanted me to stay behind.

'Well, you're not exactly flavour of the month, again.'

'Oh really?'

'John isn't at all pleased.'

'Oh dear.'

'You go and do this just at the moment Douglas is trying to get Kohl to stump up some cash towards our costs in the war.'

'I'd have thought it might help. Shame them.'

'The fact that you can say something like that, shows, *if I may say so*, that you're really not quite *au fait* with things. It's all a bit tricky.'

Actually, the old thing wasn't unamiable. He knows I'm not a threat to him any more and he can draw mild satisfaction from my digging deeper into my own hole.

I'm dreadfully tired. I hardly slept last night and the adrenalin that would pump if I had any role whatever in this place at present just isn't flowing. I'm indifferent about resignation – were it not for the fact that I want to put certain *concepts* in place before I go. And particularly to order the new tank. There's a lot of pressure building up there – in the wrong direction.

CSA[1] came in to see me. A routine call, but our conversation took flight of fancy. He is a nice man, and clever also. Furthermore, he always searches for the best solution *for Britain*; none of your fucking 'in the interests of reaching an acceptable compromise' balls.

The need for an intermediate nuclear weapon. The danger implicit in the American development of G-PALS[2] (a good litmus test of the Nationalist, this. I see it as most unwelcome that the US should have implied power of veto over our ballistic systems, still further concentration of power in the Washington dung-heap). The advisability of getting back into the (satellite) launch business. (*I* had to suggest using up the old Polaris rockets, constructing a makeshift base area at Ascension.) We agreed on the need for extending the range of EFA. Adapting Tomahawk to SSN 20 tubes. The total untrustworthiness of the French, in any co-operative context whatever. All in all, the US our only reliable friends – and even there the limits may start to encroach as the Pentagon-Congressional Committee axis loses weight.

All rather depressing, and the only effect to make me wish, or re-wish, that I was Secretary of State.

A little later came a message via Private Office that Quinlan had been 'very impressed' with my contributions at the Steering Group meetings. Butter. I expect he wants to restrain me from being too radical. You never know with Clark. He's underemployed at the moment. He may be writing some tiresome paper.

To cap it all, I believe myself to be 'fighting' flu. In my experience, 'fighting' flu is like 'fighting' cancer. You always lose.

And I have run out of fizzy Redoxon.

Albany, 11.40 p.m.
Just got in from the House. At the ten o'clock vote I was 'lionised'. Colleagues from all sides coming up and saying how they agreed, endless 'well-done's from people I hardly knew. The press has been kind, and I hear that even *Time* magazine is going to run a favourable para.

My cup runneth over; with a typical performance by that creep Hugh Dykes who told the TV cameras I should be sacked at once.

---

[1] Professor Ronald Oxburgh, Chief Scientific Adviser, Ministry of Defence, since 1988.
[2] The US developed anti-ballistic missile system, Global Protection Against Limited Strike.

Albany   *Wednesday, 30 January*

Today I visited Shorts in Belfast. Interesting weapons, the 'Streak' family. Very much the next generation, light, accurate, crazy-fast. And conforming with my long-held view, which I expressed in the Sopwith Memorial Lecture last year, that missiles should be *multi-elemental*. One close-range type should be adaptable to sea, infantry and helicopter use. It's always the Navy who resist this, isn't it? They love to spend millions and millions on 'systems' that only sailors can use.

Northern Ireland is unbelievably nasty. Grey, damp, cold. Big puddles just lying; blackthorn hedges; low standard of life. I saw one pretty girl, in a crowd that had been evacuated from a building on account of a '200 lb bomb scare'. They were all standing, patient but dejected, on the pavement. White police tape everywhere. On her own, she was jumping about excitedly, *very* nice legs.

But the general atmosphere is bleak; overlaid with the oppression of terror; deep and perpetual feuds, suspicion and callousness.

I am confirmed in my opinion that it is hopeless here. All we can do is arm the Orangemen – to the teeth – and get out. This would give also the not slight advantage that, at a stroke, Infantry 'overstretch' is eliminated.

Constituency Office, Plymouth   *Friday, 1 February*

I got off the sleeper this morning and picked my way along deserted streets to the Duke of Cornwall, which opens for breakfast ahead of the other hotels in the City. 'Picked' I say, because it was *black ice*, and I was carrying a heavy box and an overnight bag and wearing *tutti* town slippers. If one had been on form, showing off and laughing, the gradient outside Sainsburys was schussable.

I ate my international traveller's breakfast – a double cornflakes and natural yoghourt – which I have consumed all around the world from Sydney to Bogota to Anchorage, often the only swallowable food offered all day, and read the local paper. It must be over a year since I called here, and I doubt if I will ever do so again, as I have no intention of getting into that sleeper train any more if I can possibly avoid it.

The place is redolent of memories, particularly of the early days.

The downstairs 'Conveniences' were always unpleasant, wiped rather than cleaned, and smelling of beer and ablutions. But I could find, still intact and unchanged, now nearly twenty years and no one has yet thought to put a hook on the back of the door for your coat, the little private thompson loo on the first floor, and used it well.

To get there I had to traverse the corridor – not just looking but smelling – identical to that climacteric evening when Norman Fowler and I were waiting, on two separate settees, for the outcome of the parliamentary selection.

Fowler, the Central Office choice, shovee you could say, had by now got an uneasy impression that things were 'going wrong'. And sure enough when finally Tom Bridges[1] emerged he walked past the unhappy MP (as he then already was, but for a seat that was going to be Labour next time), did no more than grunt at him, and came over to me, hand outstretched.

Now all I have left, at the very most, is a year. I am trying to steel myself to the great transition. What are my objectives? Limited, I suppose, by comparison. Full and proper attention to my papers and to the Heritage. A dilettante man of letters? A (old Etonian) Guru? A more attentive husband? Freedom to travel at will, and EARLY NIGHTS. The deferral of old age, I suppose. But this is in itself rather wet and feeble, and invites Nemesis.

The sheer scale of the enforced change, the fact that I will be *excluded* from the Commons, from the beloved, magical electric aura of the Chamber, and by my own hand, has yet to sink in. Although periodically, as now, I try and face it. But I would not wish to grow old in the House. Rumpled. Dandruff. The young ones pushing past.

Will I get a peerage? Claimants always say they want it for their wife, but I would so like to present it to Jane while she is still young and pretty. Sometimes I have been foul to her. Why? Hormones, I suppose.

But they'll do their best to stop me. I have lots of enemies at middle rank, perhaps even in the Cabinet Office – although not, I hope, Robin whom personally I like (although it is easy to make the mistake of thinking that those one likes reciprocate the feeling). I doubt if I have a single friend in the whole Foreign Office, not a male one anyway.

---

[1] Chairman of the Sutton Division, 1972–5.

Then there are the two heavies. Hurd has always been against me, told the Lady not to make me Minister for Trade – which she very splendidly repeated to me on the evening of my appointment. Arsehole. He's looking more and more like Aldridge Prior.[1]

And of course Michael. Michael *knows* – just as when one has had some frightful bout of food-poisoning one always by instinct knows which particular dish caused it – he knows that it was me who tipped the scales in the two days immediately after the coup, by winding up the Constituency Associations. And my podgy namesake.[2] He's always been suspicious of me, and actually *sued* the manufacturers of Trivial Pursuits because they had muddled us up.

None of these people can face the idea of me in the Lords because instead of treating it as a Garden of Remembrance I might actually say something. *Unpredictable.*

Only dear Richard [Ryder], who is intelligent and sweet, would be my advocate, though not, I fear, as resolutely as Ian did in finally persuading the Lady to 'try' me in Government some eight years gone by. And Chris (Patten), I don't think would mind. I hope not, at least, as he is a good guy.

If they could, my enemies would block a 'K' as well, although this is more difficult unless the subject has actually been corrupt (practically the only failing, I suppose, that I never have had).

But in any case, I wouldn't want to rank myself with Buck and Emery.[3] Perhaps better to compose myself always to being 'Mister'. Like John Wilkes.

House of Commons   *Tuesday, 5 February*

Today I was inducted into the Privy Council. A rehearsal of the ceremony had been fixed twenty minutes before at the PC office in Whitehall. I changed – in the dark little lobby outside the bathroom which I share with the Chief of the General Staff – into my new navy

---

[1] Aldridge Prior – The Hopeless Liar, a character in a strip in *Viz*.

[2] Kenneth Clarke, the Health Minister.

[3] Sir Antony Buck (Kt, 1983), MP for Colchester since 1961, and Sir Peter Emery (Kt, 1982), MP for Honiton since 1967 (Reading, 1959–66).

suit, which still carries O'Brien's[1] 'delivery' creases and which I don only very sparingly. I thought my shoes looked scruffy. No one in the outer office (why not? Julian always had a pack) had any shoe polish. So I had to go via the Commons. I bickered briefly with Alison, got my fingers black-streaked with the Kiwi. Had to go into the drivers' loo and continuously scrub under the (boiling) tap. All water, everywhere, in the House of Commons is *always* screeching hot, especially in July. I was now late.

Just as we drew up outside the Cabinet Office the carphone rang. Private Office. Where was I? etc., etc. All right, all right, I'm at the door. I could feel my bladder contracting and remembered I'd forgotten to pee. Blast.

A discreet attendant in spectacles was waiting for me. He conducted me into the presence of the Privy Council Secretary, a dear old thing not unlike Farky[2] at Kings in 1943. He and, more particularly, *his* secretary sized me up at once as being 'difficult', i.e., not sufficiently overawed and softspoken. 'We've just got time, I think,' he quavered.

'*Just*,' snarl/sneered the assistant secretary.

They 'took me through' the ceremony. Quite long drawn-out and, because of its repetitious quality, easy (as I was to discover) to skip a stage.

'I think we'd better go to the Palace now.'

'I'll follow you.'

'I'm afraid we may get separated. I've got a special ivory pass that lets me through Horse Guards Arch.'

'So've I.'

Taken aback somewhat he told me a put-down story about when he was a Dep Sec at the Home Office he had tried very hard to limit the issue of the ivory passes. I retaliated with the tale of the occasion when Andrew refused to let Geoffrey Howe through. Deuce.

At Buck House I was indeed the last to arrive (I should nervously and respectfully, have been the first). MacGregor,[3] the Lord President, Bertie Denham, Paddy Mayhew,[4] Nick Scott, Wakeham. We hung

---

[1] Mr O'Brien, head cutter of Lesley and Roberts in Savile Row.
[2] Warden of the college, 1929–43. AC was taken over to visit him by John Sparrow from Eton in 1943.
[3] John MacGregor, Education Secretary since 1989.
[4] Sir Patrick Mayhew, Attorney General since 1987.

about in the hall through which one processes on Garden Party days. Small, very small, talk.

We were joined by two Palace functionaries – handsome, nicely dressed, middle-aged; both of them with that shallow courtesy, smooth complexion and careful coiffure of the Establishment homosexual.

Tactlessly, I interrupted a lot of cant about cold-weather allowances for the aged – poor people, what a good idea, etc., etc. – with a crack about the opening that very day at the QE II Centre of a World Conference on Global Warming.

Conversation petered out.

Then, jarringly, a 'household' electric bell rang and little MacGregor sloped off for a preliminary audience. About eight minutes later it rang again. The Councillors trooped in, me last. Stop at the door. Bow. Approach the Monarch, bow again. Take the Hand, *ultra* lightly. Walk backwards or rather crabwise, into the line-up.

A smallish room, much Savonnerie, indifferent pictures. The Queen sat at, or rather adjacent to, a *secretaire* copiously encrustulated with boule. A vase of blueish flowers, conventionally arranged. Moyses Stevens.

The business of the Council was announced. First item 'to receive into the Council', etc. (they gave me my courtesy title). I stepped forward, knelt awkwardly on the stool (bloody difficult), held up the Testament in my right hand and the dear old boy read out the oath. 'I do,' I said, firmly. I rose, advanced about ten feet diagonally to *another* stool, bowed, knelt, took the Monarch's hand and 'brushed it with my lips'; rose, bowed, back into line.

A pause ensued. Why? I made to go forward, down the line, shake hands with the Lord President as forewarned and instructed. No. Blast, fuck, etc. There was *another* oath. The old Clerk, secretly delighted, rolled his eyes in mock resignation and signalled me to raise, again, the Testament in my right hand. He then read out a very long passage the substance of which, as far as I could make out, was that I undertook to maintain total secrecy even, particularly indeed, about colleagues concerning whom I might hear unsatisfactory things. (The more I think about this the odder it seems.)

This time, when I said 'I do' I looked directly at the Queen. I bet many don't. But I was glad to see that she was looking directly at me. I then did the handshaking act, Lord President, Attorney General, the rest, and returned to my place at the end of the line. At which the Queen got up from her chair and moved over, *regally*, to initiate a painfully, grotesquely, banal conversation, loosely devoted to the various other Orders in Council that were on the business list. Inevitably, these were all concerned with Euro-legislation. Most of them, today, seemed to be concerned with lifts, or *ascenseurs*. Some light banter was attempted, notably by Paddy Mayhew. Splendid fellow, totally unsquashable. And when there were a couple of hesitant jokes about continental lifts 'that don't have sides' I nearly told one about the Ganymede lift at St Thomas's that goes round and round and can invert the passengers. But I was just too far down the line to guarantee getting it across.

This last phase was somewhat drawn out. Not for the first time I wondered about the Queen. Is she really rather dull and stupid? Or is she thinking, 'How do people as dull and stupid as this ever get to be Ministers?' Or is, for her, the whole thing so stale and *déjà vu* after forty years that she'd really rather be going round the stables at Highclere, patting racehorses on the nose? I suppose it might feel different if she had real power. And yet she *does* have the power. It's all there in the Constitution, all she has to do is renounce the Civil List for her ill-favoured siblings, pay taxes on her private wealth, and get on with it.

I drove back to the House, and had a boring, overcooked lunch in the Members' dining room.

Episodes 5 and 6 of the BBC television adaptation of The Alan Clark Diaries *are based on* The Last Diaries 1992–1999.

When this, the third volume of The Alan Clark Diaries, *opens, Clark is Minister of State, Ministry of Defence, where Tom King is Secretary of State. With the first Gulf War under way, Clark travels to Reading University to address a meeting of undergraduates. With him is his mistress, 'x'.*

Ministry of Defence   Thursday, 7 February 1992

Despite my resolve to keep 'x' out of this volume I find it practically impossible to concentrate effectively on anything else. She is in my thoughts the entire time, sometimes exclusively, some of the time in parallel, as it were, with whatever else one is meant to be doing.

The journey down to Reading University in the snow. I was so dejected. She was quite perky. Very cold on arrival; no one to meet us. We sat at 'the bar', drank half a pint, G&T. I said 'all I really want to do is to kiss you . . .' She bridled. Enjoys it, but doesn't want to seem timid. After meeting up we were guided to the Common Room, then the Hall. They had totally balls'd it up, turned it into a *public* meeting packed with SWP [Socialist Worker Party] and anti-war groupies. I acquitted myself well and she was 'encouraged', and alone among the audience asked a helpful question. In the train back I felt immensely weary. When I leaned forward and put my elbows on the table she leaned back; but when I slumped back – and stayed back for the whole journey – she leant forward to counter this.

She looked incredible in her Russian hat, totally Zhivago. I hold this image in my mind at the moment; it gives me a nodule headache on the left side now, and a sort of despair really. How *is* this going to end? It's such agony. I haven't the nerve to cut it off.

It's preposterous. I'm actually *ill*, have been for a month, lovesick it's called. A long and nasty course of chemotherapy – but with periodic bouts of addiction therapy when I delude myself that I may be cured without 'damage'.

MoD   *Monday, 4 March 1992*

Darling Jane is looking a wee bit strained. She knows something is up, and is quiet a lot of the time. But she doesn't question me at all – just makes the occasional scathing reference. I do want to make her happy – she's such a *good* person.[1]

And what of my medium-term plans? I must get rid now of 'x'. What then? I *very* much wish an early Election. I popped over and spoke to Richard Ryder [Chief Whip] this morning. He was in agony from a recently (18 hours) ricked back – playing tennis. But benign and delightful as always, said wait until 20 April – but of course it doesn't matter giving late notice to the constituency. Registered my bid for a 'working peerage' with a smile, but indicated approval. Also nodded sagely when I said what a fool and how objectionable, was Tom King.

★   ★   ★

After five years 'in the wilderness' having stood down from the Commons at the 1992 General Election, Alan Clark returned to Westminster as MP for Kensington and Chelsea, being elected at the 1997 election, which saw Labour gain a landslide majority.

EMT   *Friday, 25 July 1997*

Yesterday we went to the end-of-term party at Buck House. One had been 'placed' (I suspect by a resentful Lord Chancellor) on the duds day. Not a single member of the governing classes up at the top corner of the tea-tent, where, naturally, one gathers; just as the domestics separate themselves at a grand wedding and congregate around the great circular tree seat by the lavatories. I drank four of the delicious iced coffees. The iced coffee at Buck House is the most delicious in the world.

---

[1] A few days later AC confesses: 'I fear I am as bad as I have ever been. No progress at all. And darling Jane somehow knows. She was cross, just a little sad and puzzled and listless. I would love to do something to really make her happy.'

Saturday, 4 October 1997

Today our 'last' bathe at Hythe beach.

Each afternoon we have been going down there; Jane always 'mock' reluctantly, but with her bathing dress under. It is quite delicious, the water now clean and the great long arc of the shingle like the Chesil Bank – or even Biarritz. The pleasure of swimming 'overarm' with lots of space (too frightening, as well as too chilly, to 'let oneself go' at Eriboll) make them real bathes and put me in mind of 42 years ago.

Now I am somewhat debilitated, but still happy and well, and my shape not unrecognisable, and I thank God.

Saltwood, EMT   *Friday, 7 May 1999*

We buried TC [tame jackdaw] today at noon, in the *Pavillon*.

He was laid in the little portable hamper, with a host of personal 'belongings' selected from his diverse and conscientious 'nest' assembled over so long and with such Herculean effort. That special silk scarf (which he used to keep purloining even after it was 'reclaimed'; also his/her tiny, miraculous eggs; her 'tin'; a biro, a clothes-peg, a silver spoon and the little horse-brass of Jane's which she had carried (although heavy) all the way along the passage from the back stairs windowsill. 'Money-for-the-journey', an 1868 Victorian sovereign which had for several years been lost on the floor of the Winter Office and which I knew his magic would lead me to immediately, and I put my hand straight on it, beneath the desk. Brilliantly, Jane made me snip off with the kitchen scissors a ¾ length of the grey marker ribbon from the orange PDF day diary, which he would always try and remove at EMT, and this was about his person.

It was a sad, a very sad, little ceremony. Last night in bed a sad couplet from the childhood nursery rhyme kept going through my head:

> 'All the birds of the air fell a sighing and a sobbing . . .
> – as they learned of the death of poor cock Robin.'

We are very very low, at losing someone who had so much magic. Did

I betray his trust? Accidentally – yes. But perhaps it is this which makes me so dejected (and Jane, also, I suspect). I did say, aloud, a short prayer for him/her. 'I don't want to say it aloud,' I said. (Jane and Lynn were both in the Pavillon.) 'It'll make me cry.' 'Cry, then,' Jane said. And quite right too.

For the rest of the day I was completely dejected. I had no energy at all. And a recurrence of toothache in the right lower wisdom (which is, of course, 'false', i.e. made by Bertie Arbeid, or whatever that root specialist was called). This must be sinister. I was also made lower by inner lippen which seemed to be expanding.

I feel now as if I may be about to die, possibly quite soon, 'nearing the end of my life'. A huge sadness, as if I am/may be looking at so many things for the last time. Somehow I am going to be cheated of my chance to get hold of the Tory Party, and this realisation, coming on top of the accumulated stress, will do me in.

After lunch dozed off in the Pavillon, deeply. Then wrestled with fruiting bodies [blackberries] on the GH bank. In its own way even this was depressing because of the sense of neglect, and the way they have been killing the azaleas. Tea, and we decided to go for a walk, along the front. Almost empty, mild, and tried to take in lungfuls. Some nostalgia for the great days. We returned along the shingle, and could almost have plunged in the sea, which felt inviting. A clinical regime, as in 'Depressed Prince Enters Clinic'. Then a nice bath, and into pidgys. Trying to calm down and de-stress. Now going in to dinner, but afflicted by a particularly unwelcome symptom – the absolute non-effect of alcohol. Normally this is a time when wine inspires the mind. Not at the moment. There has been (on our TV screen) little Hague, in his 'Bruce Willis' haircut (whatever that is) and his dreadful flat northern voice. I find it just awful, skin-curdling, that the Party – our great Party – formerly led by Disraeli, Balfour, Churchill, Macmillan, Thatcher (even) could be in the hands of this dreadful little man who has absolutely no sense whatever of history, or pageantry or *noblesse oblige*. The whole enterprise to be conducted on the basis of a Management Consultancy exam tick-box, and the 'findings' of a 'focus group'. 'Is not the 1922 Committee a valid "focus group"?' as Eric Forth, justifiably, complained.

Saltwood   *Sunday, 1 August 1999*

Fact is, I've got brain cancer. And it is fairly disagreeable.

My body realises that there is no hope. I mean what is the next stage? The next (local) demon with which to wrestle?

My wrist shakes – why? I could not eat, even put into my mouth, any of the delicacies prepared at lunch time today. Or even the 'accompanying medication' which hourly makes Jane very depressed.

I am afflicted by a kind of despair, also.

The Amazings [Clark's younger son Andrew and his wife] coming in tomorrow. What can I say to them?

The house is like an oven now, excepting the rooms on the north side.

Although this was Alan Clark's last diary entry, Jane started to write a journal, in which she recorded the final five weeks of his life. Extracts appear in The Last Diaries.

EPILOGUE

And all my endeavours are unlucky explorers
come back, abandoning the expedition;
the specimens, the lilies of ambition
still spring in their climate, still unpicked;
to find them, as the great collectors before me.[1]

[1] Keith Douglas, 1944.

INDEX